Overcoming Onto-theology

ACKNOWLEDGMENTS

Permission to use the following previously published materials is gratefully acknowledged.

Part of the Introduction appeared as "Onto-theology, Meta-narrative, Perspectivism and the Gospel," *Perspectives*, April 2000, pp. 6–10.

Chapter 1 appeared as "Overcoming Onto-theology," in *God, the Gift, and Postmodernism*, ed. John D. Caputo and Michael J. Scanlon (Bloomington: Indiana University Press, 1999), pp. 146–69.

Chapter 2 appeared as "Heidegger's 'Theologische' Jugend-schriften," *Research in Phenomenology* 27 (1997), pp. 247–61.

Chapter 3 appeared as "Hermeneutics as Epistemology," in *The Blackwell Guide to Epistemology*, ed. John Greco and Ernest Sosa (Oxford: Blackwell, 1999), pp. 415–35.

Chapter 4 appeared as "Appropriating Postmodernism," *ARC, The Journal of the Faculty of Religious Studies, McGill University* 25 (1997), pp. 73–84.

Chapter 5 appeared as "Christian Philosophers and the Copernican Revolution," in *Christian Perspectives on Religious Knowledge*, ed. C. Stephen Evans and Merold Westphal (Grand Rapids, Mich.: Eerdmans, 1993), pp. 161–79.

Chapter 6 has not previously appeared in print.

Chapter 7 appeared as "Positive Postmodernism as Radical Hermeneutics," in *The Very Idea of Radical Hermeneutics*, ed. Roy Martinez (Atlantic Highlands, N.J.: Humanities, 1997), pp. 48–63.

Chapter 8 has not previously appeared in print.

Chapter 9 appeared as "Deconstruction and Christian Cultural Theory: An Essay on Appropriation," in *Pledges of Jubilee*, ed. Lambert Zuidervaart and Henry Luttikhuizen (Grand Rapids, Mich.: Eerdmans, 1995), pp. 107–25.

Chapter 10 appeared as "Laughing at Hegel," *The Owl of Minerva* 28, no. 1 (fall 1996), pp. 39–58.

Chapter 11 appeared as "Derrida as Natural Law Theorist," *International Philosophical Quarterly* 34, no. 2 (June 1994), pp. 247–52.

Chapter 12 appeared as "Faith as the Overcoming of Ontological Xenophobia," in *The Otherness of God,* ed. Orrin Summerell (Charlottesville: University of Virginia Press, 1998), pp. 149–72.

Chapter 13 appeared as "Divine Excess: The God Who Comes After" in *Blackwell Readings in Continental Philosophy: The Religious,* ed. John D. Caputo (Oxford: Blackwell, 2001).

Chapter 14 appeared as "Nietzsche as a Theological Resource," *Modern Theology* 13, no. 2 (April 1997), pp. 213–26.

INTRODUCTION

SOME OF THE BEST PHILOSOPHERS whom I count among my friends are postmodernists. But they do not share my faith. Others of the best philosophers whom I count among my friends share my faith. But they are not postmodernists. Decidedly not. At varying degrees along a spectrum that runs from mildly allergic to wildly apoplectic, they are inclined to see postmodernism as nothing but warmed-over Nietzschean atheism, frequently on the short list of the most dangerous anti-Christian currents of thought as an epistemological relativism that leads ineluctably to moral nihilism. Anything goes. When it comes to postmodern philosophy and Christian faith there seems to be an agreement that

> East is East, and West is West
> and never the twain shall meet . . .

I am not so sure.

I often find myself *philosophically* closer to my postmodern friends who do not share my faith than to the Christian philosophers who do; and it is postmodern *philosophy* that concerns me here. Some refer to a very broad cultural change when they speak of a "postmodern world." They often focus on the transition from a modern world in which science was king to a postmodern world in which science has lost its hegemony; and they often suggest that this change is not limited to intellectual elites but is a broad-based, popular trend attested by a variety of phenomena lumped together under the heading New Age and by what we might call the new supernaturalism in storytelling, narratives filled with angels and vampires taking their place alongside of *science* fiction.

Without denying the reality and importance of either of these phenomena or the postpositivistic philosophies of science that challenge the simplistic concepts of scientific objectivity that were part of the Enlightenment project, I have reservations about this analysis of the "postmodern world." From the seventeenth century on, as Bacon, Hobbes, Descartes, and now Heidegger have made especially clear, the Enlightenment project was one of science in the service of technology. And the human race has never lived more completely under the hegemony of its scientifically grounded technologies than at present. Quibbles about the nature of scientific rationality and fascination with angels and vampires are like a little Zen meditation in the midst of a multinational corporation, purely epiphenomenal. The computer at which I write about postmodernism declares the glory of modernity, and its modem, which gives me instant communication with my Christian friend in Moscow and my postmodern friend in Melbourne, shows its handiwork.

In an earlier book entitled *Suspicion and Faith: The Religious Uses of Modern Atheism*, I argued something like this: Marx, Nietzsche, and Freud are among the most widely influential atheists of the last couple centuries. But looked at closely, their arguments about the various ways in which religious beliefs and practices can be put, with the help of systematic self-deception, in the service of quite irreligious interests, both personal and social, have two striking characteristics: they are all too true all too much of the time (even if they are not the whole story about religion, as this trio is all too eager to assume), and they have striking similarities, in spite of diametrically different motives, to the critiques of the piety of the covenant people of God to be found on the lips and in the writings of the Old Testament prophets and of Jesus, Paul, and James.

So I found myself accusing Marx and Freud of shameless plagiarism (Nietzsche acknowledges the link between his critique and Jesus' critique of the Pharisees) and proposing that instead of denouncing this trio, religious thinkers acknowledge the painful truths to which they point and use them for personal and corporate self-examination. The opening chapter is entitled "Atheism for Lent," and at least a couple of churches developed Lenten studies around this suggestion.

Looking back I am reminded of Balaam's ass. Better known for his braying than for his praying, this humble servant of the Lord (by no design of his own) nevertheless spoke God's word of rebuke to another (this time self-professed) servant of the Lord, who needed to hear it just as badly as he wished not to hear it.

Turning to the major postmodern philosophers, I adopt the same strategy. Such thinkers as Nietzsche, Heidegger, Derrida, Foucault, Lyotard, and Rorty are no friends of historic Christianity. Most are overtly atheistic, and even when this is not the case, God is conspicuously absent from the world as they present it to us. The atheistic or at least nontheistic character of their thought is not modified by the religious motifs that emerge in the later thought of Nietzsche, Heidegger, and Derrida. It is widely assumed, by friend and foe alike, that the central themes of the postmodern philosophers and the central loci of orthodox Christian theology are mutually exclusive. While this is true of the (anti)religious postures of the philosophers named above, I am not so sure it is true of their central themes, the arguments and analyses developed in the context of their (anti)religious assumptions. So I have argued for the possibility of a Christian (or, more broadly, theistic) appropriation of certain postmodern themes.

This appropriation is a recontextualization in which the themes in question are removed from the anti-Christian or a-theistic settings that are the horizons of the postmodern philosophers and articulated within the framework of Christian/theistic assumptions that are, I claim, their proper home. Thus, for example, the hermeneutics of suspicion developed by Marx, Nietzsche, and Freud finds (in *Suspicion and Faith*) its true home in the Pauline teaching about the noetic effects of sin, the idea that in wickedness we "suppress the truth" (Romans 1:18).

As an example of a distinctly postmodern theme, consider Lyotard's account of the postmodern condition as "incredulity toward metanarratives." Like 'onto-theology' (of which more in due course), 'metanarrative' is often used by assistant professors who have appointed themselves campus terrorists and, alas, by senior scholars who should be more careful, as a kind of sci-fi conceptual zapper. You aim it at any theology archaic enough to affirm a divine providence in history and vaporize it by intoning the magic word 'metanarrative'. In my experience no other post-modern theme, not even Derrida's (in)famous "There is nothing outside the text," generates as much apoplexy among Christian scholars or as high a degree of certainty that Christianity and postmodernism represent a dyad like truth and error, light and darkness, good and evil, and so forth.

There aren't many senior Christian scholars as knowledgeable about Derrida as one I recently heard give a paper exploring possible points of convergence between his own Christian thinking and deconstruction. Ignoring the fact that the paper was about Derrida and not Lyotard, another senior Christian scholar of considerable repute (like the original speaker from my own Reformed tradition) irately insisted that never the twain could meet since Christianity is a metanarrative and postmodernism is defined as "incredulity toward metanarratives." A graduate student in the audience gave a succinct and accurate account of what Lyotard actually says about metanarratives and then suggested that Christians have good reason to share his skittishness about them. The objector acknowledged the latter point, explaining that he had never read Lyotard and had no idea who Lyotard's targets were, how he defined 'metanarrative', and what his objections to it were.

Even more recently I heard another senior Christian scholar, once again of considerable repute and once again from my own Reformed tradition, taking the metanarrative issue as the non-negotiable point of irreconcilable opposition between Christian faith and postmodern philosophy. Christianity is a metanarrative, she insisted. "We know how the story ends." I immediately found myself singing (silently, to be sure) a song I had learned in childhood:

> I know not what the future holds,
> but I know who holds the future—
> It's a secret known only to Him

and saying to myself, "Yes, in a certain sense Christians know how the story ends. But in an equally important sense we do not. And it's important to keep clear about what we know and what we don't."

So what does Lyotard mean by metanarrative? In the first place, a philosophy of history, a big story in which we place the little stories of our lives as individuals and communities. In this sense Christianity is undeniably a metanarrative, a *Heilsge-schichte* that runs from Creation and the Fall through the life, death, and resurrection of Jesus to the Second Coming, the resurrection of the dead, and the life everlasting. Amen.

But in philosophical discourse, 'meta' signifies a difference of level and not primarily of size. A metanarrative is a metadiscourse in the sense of being a second-level discourse not directly about the world but about a first-level discourse. Now, undeniably Christianity is a *mega*narrative, a big story. But the story that begins with "Let there be light" and ends with the "Hallelujah Chorus" under the baton of the angel Gabriel is not a *meta*narrative. The recital of the *Heilsgeschichte* in creeds and in sermons, in lessons and in songs, as well as its enactment in sacraments, belongs to first-order Christian discourse. It is kerygma, not apologetics.

There are two other ways in which the Christian *mega*narrative is not a *meta*narrative in Lyotard's sense. One concerns legitimation, the other origination. The issue of legitimation is absolutely central for Lyotard, the tight link between modernity and metanarrative in his mind. Having overthrown various ancient regimes both of knowledge and of social practice, modernity finds itself needing to legitimize its "new authorities," and it resorts to narrative to do so.

There is an irony in this. Modernity has hitched its wagon to science, a form of discourse that challenges and undermines traditional narratives. But in order to legitimize itself, science needs a story of progress from opinion and superstition to scientific truth and on to universal peace and happiness. The Enlightenment project is inseparable from its self-legitimizing metanarratives.

Modernity's "new authorities" are socio-political as well as well as intellectual, and modernity's big stories concern themselves not only with legitimizing the truth of its knowledge (science) but also the justice of its practices (the state or the revolution). Lyotard takes the production of such legitimizing metanarratives *by philosophy* to be the quintessence of modernity. The Enlightenment of the seventeenth and eighteenth centuries told a variety of such stories, and he mentions, for example, the story of the emancipation of the rational subject

(Descartes, Locke) and the story of the creation of wealth (Adam Smith). But he focuses analysis on two nineteenth-century versions, Hegel's and Marx's.

Lyotard calls Hegel's story the speculative narrative, the one concerned with the "dialectics of Spirit" and the "realization of the Idea." It primarily concerns itself with the truth of our knowledge and seeks to legitimize modern, western humanity as the absolute subject whose knowledge of itself as such is absolute knowing. (As a kind of fringe benefit, we might observe, the Hegelian story also seeks to legitimize the modern, capitalist state.) Marx's story is the emancipation narrative. It concerns itself with the justice of our practices and seeks to legitimize the proletarian revolution that will abolish private property and usher in the classless society.

At the descriptive level, Lyotard merely observes a widespread skepticism toward these stories and the self-legitimizing project that gives rise to them, defining the postmodern condition in terms of this incredulity. At the critical level, he sides with the unbelievers who remain outside the temples of Spirit and the Revolution, and not just by describing them as the shrines of unkept promises. The Enlightenment project has not just been unsuccessful; as a totalizing project it is inherently illegitimate.

'Totalizing' is another po-mo shibboleth often bandied about as an undefined hi-tech zapper with which to deep-six anything that is not PC this week. Aim. Click. Vaporize. But here it has a rather precise and plausible meaning. In its quest for universal peace and happiness, modernity has conceived its goal as an essentially homogenized humanity. As science it has sought to suppress conceptual difference; and as either capitalism or communism, it has sought to suppress social difference. Wittgenstein, Lyotard's clear hero, was closer to the truth in recognizing the plurality of language games humanity plays and in refusing to award hegemony to any one of them (or even to the class to which science belongs, those that concern themselves with correctly describing the world).

The third and final difference between the Christian story and modernity's metanarratives concerns origins. The former has its origin in revelation, not in philosophy, and most especially not phers and the Copernican Revolution" develops the argument of the previous essay by arguing that Christian thinkers ought to be, precisely by virtue of their theism, Kantian anti-realists. It is but a short step from Kant to the hermeneutical turn. All that is necessary is to recognize the historical contingency and plurality of the presuppositions (a priori elements) that make our construals of the world possible.

It was in an essentially Kantian context that Schleiermacher developed a hermeneutical holism that, over against both Spinoza and Hegel, defined the finitude of human thought in terms of the impossibility of all totalizing strategies for attaining Truth as final adequation between mind and world. "Totality and Finitude in Schleiermacher's Hermeneutics" shows how "postmodern" Schleiermacher is by giving a detailed analysis of his construal of construal and then comparing it briefly with Derrida.

Mention of Derrida brings us to Heidegger's successors, in particular Gadamer and Derrida, who are mentioned briefly at the conclusion of "Hermeneutics as Epistemology." For me there are two important points. First, Gadamer is not on the list of usual suspects when postmodernism is under discussion, but he is an important chapter in the story of the hermeneutics of finitude. In other words, the critique of such totalizing knowledge claims as metanarratives and onto-theologies is implicit in other philosophical traditions and is not the unique property of those who get labeled postmodernists. If one is sufficiently multilingual, philosophically speaking, one can find the hermeneutical turn in Dewey and Quine, Sellars and Wittgenstein, Hanson and Kuhn, and, of course, Gadamer and Ricoeur, all of whom are perspectivists at least to the degree to denying to human knowledge the "view from nowhere" as anything but at the very most a regulative ideal.

Second, against the claim that Gadamer is the reactionary and Derrida the radical son of Heidegger, I argue that they are equally radical and that appearances to the contrary stem from the fact that while Gadamer emphasizes what we can have, Derrida stresses what we cannot. But the one who says the glass is half full and the one who finds it half empty are pretty much in agreement about how much water there is in the glass. Behind objections are. It argues (1) that Christian theism is not ir ently onto-theological, (2) that at its best it is as "postmoderi Heidegger in resisting onto-theological tendencies, but (3) tl can all too easily lapse into the conceptual idolatry that is c theology.

The explicit critique of metaphysics as onto-theology com the forties and fifties; in other words it belongs to Heidegg. But its seeds can be found in *Being and Time* and even ear "Heidegger's *'Theologische' Jugendschriften*" is a review of ume 60 of the *Gesamtausgabe*, which appeared in 1995 under title *Phänomenologie des religiösen Lebens*, and traces the origi the critique in some of Heidegger's earliest lecture courses.

In *Being and Time* itself the crucial move is what we now the hermeneutical turn. Against the claims that human un standing can be pure reason, the mirror of nature, the voic being itself, the hermeneutical turn is a radical analysis of finitude of human thought. "Hermeneutics as Epistemology devoted primarily to expounding what can be called the her neutics of finitude in *Being and Time*.

The next six essays explore this turn in greater detail. "App priating Postmodernism" addresses another way in which p modernism is often seen to be wholly antithetical to Christ theism. The finitude of human thought is sometimes express in the slogan: The truth is that there is no Truth. I argue that t claim stems not from analyzing the interpretative character human thought but from placing that analysis in an atheis context. If our thinking never merits the triumphalist title Truth *and* there is no other knower whose knowledge is t Truth, then the truth is that there is no Truth. But if the fi premise is combined with a theistic premise, the result will I The truth is that there is Truth, but not for us, only for God. Tl is the appropriation or recontextualizing of the hermeneutics finitude I propose.

The following essays explore that hermeneutics in terms important predecessors (Kant and Schleiermacher) and succe sors (Gadamer and Derrida) to Heidegger, always with the que tion in view: Is not this analysis of the finitude of huma knowledge entirely compatible with and even required by a th istic understanding of our created finitude? "Christian Philos.

the differences of rhetoric and vocabulary there is deeper agreement between Gadamer and Derrida than is usually supposed; or so I argue in "Positive Postmodernism as Radical Hermeneutics" and "Father Adam and His Feuding Sons: An Interpretation of the Hermeneutical Turn in Continental Philosophy."

It is often claimed that postmodern philosophies either are or lead directly to moral nihilism. This is the aforementioned "anything goes" objection. There may be forms of postmodernism in which ethical categories are displaced by aesthetic categories, but Derridean deconstruction, perhaps the most widely discussed form of postmodern philosophy in North America, is not one of them. In three essays I look more closely at the Derridean text in order to show this.

"Deconstruction and Christian Cultural Theory: An Essay on Appropriation" shows that the play theme in Derrida does not mean, as is often alleged, that we are the players and can play by any rules we please. Play is rather something that happens beyond our control (though we desperately try to control it). "Laughing at Hegel" shows us a Derrida sympathetic with Bataille's laughter at Hegel's hubris (just as Kierkegaard's Climacus thought laughter was the best refutation of the System's silliness). But what is the point of the suggestion that the ultimate horizon of human meanings is unmeaning? Does it mean that there are no constraints, that we can do as we please? Or does it mean that no human meanings are ultimate and there is a certain (unavoidable) hermeneutical violence involved in imposing any system of construals, factual and normative? In "Derrida as Natural Law Theorist" we find Derrida decisively opting for the second alternative.

Is there a link between the postmodern and the premodern? Does the contemporary critique of modernity undermine to any significant degree the latter's repudiation of historic Christianity? Does the unmasking of pure reason as the offspring of hubris and illusion discredit the project of religion within the limits of reason alone? Or, to ask the question differently, does postmodernity reopen the door to premodernity? "Faith as the Overcoming of Ontological Xenophobia" continues the exploration of Derrida's thought. In the context of his attempt to distinguish deconstruction from negative theology, I argue, Derrida opens the door (without entering it) for an Augustinian understanding of divine alterity in terms of the combined motifs of creation and fall, as developed by, well, Augustine, as well as Aquinas and Bonaventure.

In "Divine Excess: The God Who Comes After" I pursue this theme in greater detail. After summarizing three forms of the postmodern critique, those of Heidegger, Levinas, and Marion, I suggest that the God who comes after postmodernism is the God of Augustine, especially as presented in the *Confessions*.

I conclude with "Nietzsche as a Theological Resource," a nice title for reflecting about the possibility of a Christian appropriation of postmodern insights. This essay plays two roles. First, the essays in this volume have been concerned with the hermeneutics of finitude, that is, the understanding of human understanding as interpretation rather than intuition and, moreover, interpretation from the perspective of historically contingent and particular presuppositions (Kant's a priori, Heidegger's pre-understandings, Gadamer's pre-judices). The discussion of Nietzsche's perspectivism and the discussion of objections that can be raised to it are as relevant to Heidegger and Derrida as they are to Nietzsche.

Second, hermeneutical philosophy, as I understand it, consists of two major branches, the hermeneutics of finitude and the hermeneutics of suspicion. My argument for a Christian appropriation of these, even when developed by postmodern philosophers with no love for Christianity, is theological. The hermeneutics of finitude is a meditation on the meaning of human createdness, and the hermeneutics of suspicion is a meditation on the meaning of human fallenness. Because I have discussed the latter extensively in *Suspicion and Faith,* as mentioned above, I have not included it in this volume. But the discussion of Nietzsche's hermeneutics of suspicion in the latter half of this last essay is a reminder of another whole region of possible appropriation, this time with Foucault rather than Derrida as the primary French postmodernist.

It is perhaps worth mentioning that, as in Augustine, there is an extensive hermeneutics of finitude and of suspicion in Kierkegaard as well as in Nietzsche—which is perhaps another way to see that there can be a postmodern Christianity as well as a postmodern atheism.

Some of the essays gathered here were originally presented to quite specific audiences. No effort has been made to eliminate the occasional character they reflect. In all of these essays, however, I ultimately have two audiences in mind: my postmodern friends who do not share my faith and my Christian friends who are allergic or even a bit apoplectic when it comes to postmodern philosophy.

Overcoming Onto-theology

Works of Heidegger will be cited in the text and notes by means of the following abbreviations:

AWP — "The Age of the World Picture," in *The Question Concerning Technology and Other Essays,* trans. William Lovitt (New York: Harper & Row, 1977).

BT — *Being and Time,* trans. John Macquarrie & Edward Robinson (New York: Harper & Row, 1962).

CT — *The Concept of Time,* trans. William McNeill (Oxford: Blackwell, 1992).

DT — *Discourse on Thinking,* trans. John M. Anderson and E. Hans Freund (New York: Harper & Row, 1966).

EPTT — "The End of Philosophy and the Task of Thinking," in *Basic Writings,* ed. David Farrell Krell (New York: Harper & Row, 1977).

ER — *The Essence of Reasons,* trans. Terrence Malick (Evanston: Northwestern University Press, 1969).

GA — *Gesamtausgabe,* followed by volume number.

GA 15 — *Seminare* (Frankfurt: Klostermann, 1986).

GA 60 — *Phänomenologie des religiösen Lebens* (Frankfurt: Klostermann, 1995).

GA 61 — *Phänomenologische Interpretationen zu Aristotles: Einführung in die phänomenologische Forschung* (Frankfurt: Klostermann, 1985).

GA 63 — *Ontologie: Hermeneutics der Faktizität* (Frankfurt: Klostermann, 1988).

HCT — *History of the Concept of Time: Prolegomena,* trans. Theodore Kisiel (Bloomington: Indiana University Press, 1985).

ID — *Identity and Difference,* trans. Joan Stambaugh (New York: Harper & Row, 1969).

IM — *Introduction to Metaphysics,* trans. Ralph Manheim (Garden City, N.Y.: Doubleday, 1961).

LH — "Letter on Humanism," in *Basic Writings.*

MFL — *The Metaphysical Foundations of Logic,* trans. Michael Heim (Bloomington: Indiana University Press, 1984).

OM — "Overcoming Metaphysics," in *The End of Philosophy,* trans. Joan Stambaugh (New York: Harper & Row, 1973).

PIRA — "Phenomenological Interpretations with Respect to Aristotle: Indication of the Hermeneutical Situation," trans. Michael Baur, *Man and World* 25 (1992), pp. 355–93.

PR — *The Principle of Reason,* trans. Reginald Lilly (Bloomington: Indiana University Press, 1991).

PT — "Phenomenology and Theology," in *The Piety of Thinking,* trans. James G. Hart and John C. Maraldo (Bloomington: Indiana University Press, 1976).

QT — The Question Concerning Technology," in *The Question Concerning Technology.*

WM/1929 — "What Is Metaphysics?" in *Existentialism from Dostoevsky to Sartre,* ed. Walter Kaufmann 2nd expanded ed. (New York: New American Library, 1975).

WM/1943 — Untitled postscript to WM/1929 in Kaufmann, *Existentialism.*

WM/1949 — "The Way Back into the Ground of Metaphysics," Introduction to WM/1929 in Kaufmann, *Existentialism.*

WNGD — "The Word of Nietzsche: 'God Is Dead,' " in *The Question Concerning Technology.*

1

Overcoming Onto-theology

> We go to church in order to sing, and theology is secondary.
>
> Kathleen Norris[1]

NOT LONG AGO I participated in a conference on biblical hermeneutics. It asked about the relation between trust and suspicion for Christians reading the Bible. The keynote addresses by Walter Brueggemann and Phyllis Trible were brilliant. But for me the highlight of the conference was the workshop led by Ched Myers, whose radical reading of the gospel of Mark is one of the finest pieces of biblical interpretation I have ever read.[2] To be more precise, the highlight was the moment in the middle of the workshop when he had us sing.

He was developing the claim that biblical interpretation in the service of some relatively closed theological system (there are many) and biblical interpretation in the service of some species of historical criticism (there are many) are not as different as either side would like to think. Both are best understood in terms of the Marxian analysis of the fetishism of commodities, for they turn the text into an object to be mastered by the interpreter for the advantage of the interpreter, a source of theoretical treasure to be accumulated and owned. (Elsewhere I have described this as the King Midas theory of truth.)

In the middle of the argument, Myers stopped and said it was time to sing. But first we would have to clap, and soon all forty of us were clapping rhythmically. (If you know anything about Christians in the Reformed tradition, you know that we were

---

[1] *Dakota: A Spiritual Geography* (New York: Ticknor & Fields, 1993), p. 91.

[2] *Binding the Strong Man: A Political Reading of Mark's Story of Jesus* (Maryknoll: Orbis, 1988).

participating in a performative refutation of Hume on miracles!)
Then he began to sing:

> O Mary, don't you weep, don't you mourn.
> O Mary, don't you weep, don't you mourn.
> Pharaoh's army got drownded.
> O Mary, don't you weep.

The second time through we all joined in; then he would sing
the verses, and each time we would join in again on the refrain.

I didn't want the singing ever to end. But when it did, Myers
invited us to reflect on the phenomenon of American slaves singing about the liberation of Jewish slaves three thousand years
earlier, a story they had made their story, and he asked us who
Mary might be. We realized right away that first and foremost
she was the mother of Jesus at the foot of the cross. Blissfully
ignoring the realities of time's arrow, the American slaves were
seeking to comfort Mary with the song of the Exodus, reminding
her, as it were, of her own song, the Magnificat. Our leader did
not have to point out that by singing the old spiritual and reflecting on it we were making the story of Miriam and Moses
our story too, opening ourselves to be seized once again by its
message of hope (insofar as we are oppressed) and judgment
(insofar as we are oppressors).

Almost immediately I thought of Heidegger's critique of onto-
theology. He thinks it is bad theology because we "can neither
pray nor sacrifice to this god [of philosophy]. Before the *causa
sui*, man can neither fall to his knees in awe nor can he play
music and dance before this god" (ID p. 72). It seemed that as we
joined the slaves in their song we had overcome onto-theology
without even trying. For while we were not singing and dancing—that would be too much of a miracle to expect of Christians
from the Reformed tradition—we were singing and clapping before the God who drownded Pharaoh's army.

The onto-theological God enters the scene "only insofar as
philosophy, of its own accord and by its own nature, requires
and determines how the deity enters into it" (ID p. 56). The God
to whom we were singing had entered the scene without the
imprimatur of the learned, saying, "I have observed the misery
of my people who are in Egypt; I have heard their cry on account

of their taskmasters. Indeed, I know their sufferings, and I have come down to deliver them" (Exodus 3:7–8). We should not be surprised to read that Miriam sang and danced with tambourines before this God who threw horse and rider into the sea without consulting *ta meta ta physica* or the *Wissenschaft der Logik* (Exodus 15:20–21).

Miriam and the American slaves did not need to overcome onto-theology. They were never tempted by it. The situation is more complex for us, even if (heaven help us) we are ready to sing and clap, if not quite to sing and dance, with them. We have immersed ourselves in traditions where onto-theology is at work, and we have listened as Heidegger has thematized and named a practice whose purest but by no means only forms are those of Aristotle and Hegel.[3] Perhaps, however, we have not listened carefully enough. For Heidegger's term is often bandied about in a manner not supported by the text.

It will be useful to recall how in the fifties, here in the United States, the term 'communist' came to mean "anything to the left of my right-wing position." Then, in the sixties, and no doubt inevitably, 'fascist' came to mean "anything to the right of my left-wing position." The United States Congress, it turned out, was made up wholly of communists who called themselves Democrats and of fascists who called themselves Republicans. The terms 'communist' and 'fascist' were not used to inform but to inflame, not to assist sober analysis but to avoid the hard work of analysis by resorting to name-calling.

The term 'onto-theology' is all too often used in this way. Without too close a look either at how Heidegger uses the term or at the specifics of the discourse to be discredited, 'onto-theology' becomes the abracadabra by which a triumphalist secularism makes the world immune to any God who resembles the personal Creator, Lawgiver, and Merciful Savior of Jewish, or Christian, or Muslim monotheism. The only religion that escapes the Lord High Executioners who speak as Heidegger's

---

[3] Kant uses the term 'onto-theology' to describe the attempt to prove the existence of God "through mere concepts, without the help of any experience whatsoever." *Critique of Pure Reason*, A632 = B660. Heidegger's usage is quite different.

prophets is religion that is pagan/polytheistic, pantheistic, or a/ theistic (with or without the slash).

When this happens, the Pascalian character of Heidegger's critique is overlooked. It is not directed toward the God of the Bible or the Koran, before whom people do fall on their knees in awe, pray, sacrifice, sing, and dance. It is a critique of a metaphysical tradition that extends from Anaximander to Nietzsche and includes Aristotle and Hegel as high points (WM/1949).[4] It is also a critique, by extension, not of theistic discourses as such, but of those that have sold their soul to philosophy's project of rendering the whole of reality intelligible to human understanding. Their fault does not consist in affirming that there is a Highest Being who is the clue to the meaning of the whole of being. It consists in the chutzpa of permitting this God to enter the scene only in the service of their project, human mastery of the real.

As a restatement of the ancient question What has Athens to do with Jerusalem? Heidegger's critique is a reminder of how hard it is to sing "the Lord's song in a foreign land" (Psalms 137:4), in this case that Greco-Germanic land to which Heidegger himself was to become so fatally enamored.[5] As such it is an invitation and challenge to theology to be itself, to refuse to sell its birthright for a mess of philosophical pottage. Reminding the theologians of the Pauline question—"Has not God let the wisdom of this world become foolishness?"—Heidegger asks, "Will Christian theology make up its mind one day to take seriously the word of the apostle and thus also the conception of philosophy as foolishness?" (WM/1949, p. 276; cf. IM p. 6, "From the standpoint of faith our question [of being] is 'foolishness'."). Perhaps this is why a couple years later Heidegger would write, "If I were yet to write a theology—to which I sometimes feel inclined—then the word *Being* would not occur in it. Faith does not need the thought of Being. When faith has recourse to this thought, it is no longer faith. This is what Luther understood."

---

[4] Aristotle is the paradigm of onto-theology in WM/1949, just as Hegel is in ID.

[5] For a critique of this infatuation in Heidegger's work, see John D. Caputo, *Demythologizing Heidegger* (Bloomington: Indiana University Press, 1993).

And perhaps this is why Jean-Luc Marion has tried to think God without Being.[6]

It is thus a mistake, I believe, to identify the God of onto-theology simply as "the omnipotent, omniscient, and benevolent God" or as "the God who divinely, eternally precontains all things in a mind so immense that all creation is but a supplemental *imago dei*, a simulacrum of the Infinite and Eternal, which means Infinitely and Eternally the Same," even with the further claim that this is an "excessively Eleatic idea of God which has overrun the biblical traditions ever since Philo Judaeus decided that Yahweh needed to square accounts with Greek Ontology, the result being that Greek ontology settled the hash of Yahweh and Elohim."[7]

There is a lively and legitimate debate as to whether we should speak of God in this way. But, at least in the Christian traditions (I cannot speak for the Jewish and Muslim), the primary motivations for attributing omniscience, including foreknowledge, to God are biblical rather than philosophical, even if the vocabulary in which the matter gets discussed is, for better or worse, often Hellenic. Further, Kierkegaard is surely, with

---

[6] Marion cites the Heidegger passage from GA 15, pp. 436–37, in *God without Being*, trans. Thomas A. Carlson (Chicago: University of Chicago Press, 1991), p. 61. Conversely, Heidegger writes, "Someone who has experienced theology in his own roots, both the theology of Christian faith and that of philosophy, would today rather remain silent about God when he is speaking in the realm of thinking" (ID pp. 54–55). For Marion's suspicion that this silence is itself, ironically, metaphysical and an expression of the will to power, see *God without Being*, pp. 54–55, 60.

[7] The first quotation is from Hent de Vries, "Adieu, à dieu, a-Dieu," in *Ethics as First Philosophy*, ed. Adriaan T. Peperzak (New York: Routledge, 1995), p. 218. The second and third are from John D. Caputo, *The Prayers and Tears of Jacques Derrida: Religion without Religion* (Bloomington: Indiana University Press, 1997), p. 113. Caputo is speaking here in a Derridean perspective, which is not the problem; for Derrida's critique of the metaphysics of presence and Heidegger's critique of onto-theology are deeply akin. Another example: when Levinas expresses his reservations about "the factitious transcendence of worlds behind the scenes," in *Otherwise than Being or Beyond Essence*, trans. Alphonso Lingis (Dordrecht: Kluwer, 1991), pp. 4–5, John Llewelyn says he is "endorsing Nietzsche's proclamation of the death of the God of onto-theology"; *Emmanuel Levinas: The Genealogy of Ethics* (New York: Routledge, 1995), p. 150. On p. 156 he identifies "onto-theological transcendence" with "a God of the *Jenseits*, the Beyond." As if theism were automatically onto-theological.

Heidegger, one of those who calls Jerusalem back to itself from Athens by contrasting the God of the philosophers with the God of living faith. But his Climacus presupposes the God just described as onto-theological when he says that reality is a system for God, though not for us human observers.[8] In a similar manner, Climacus insists that God is capable of the philosophy of world history to which Hegel aspires, though we, including Hegel (as long as the latter has not become God), are not. There is a metanarrative; it's just that we aren't in on it.[9] We may have access to aspects of it on a need to know basis, but that gives us far less than philosophy requires for its purposes; for its need to know is the absolute need posited by objectivity, while the believer's need to know is the limited need posited by subjectivity.

Kierkegaard helps us to see that the onto-theological gesture consists not in positing a God who differs radically from us by satisfying the requirements of Hegel's Logic and Philosophy of World History, who sees the world synchronically as system and diachronically in terms of a grand metanarrative. It consists in positing such a God as an excuse for making the claim that we can occupy the divine perspective on the world, or at least peek over God's shoulder. Spinoza let the cat out of the bag when he acknowledged that philosophy needs to see the world *sub specie aeternitatis.* There is all the difference in the world, the difference, say, between Kierkegaard and Hegel, or Pascal and Spinoza, between affirming that there is such a point of view and claiming that we (the intellectual elite, whether we call ourselves philosophers or theologians) can embody it. With Kierkegaard and Pas-

---

[8] *Concluding Unscientific Postscript to* Philosophical Fragments, trans. Howard V. Hong and Edna H. Hong (Princeton: Princeton University Press, 1992), vol. I, p. 118.

[9] *Postscript,* vol. I, pp. 141, 158. While Climacus finds it necessary to emphasize the difference between the human and divine perspectives, he finds no need to deny the reality of the latter. So, when Caputo writes, "Cast in a deconstructive slant, God is . . . not the eternal but the futural" (*Prayers and Tears,* p. 113), Climacus responds, "For an existing person, is not eternity not eternity but the future, whereas eternity is eternity only for the Eternal, who is not in a process of becoming? . . . the *eternal* relates itself as the *future* to the *person in a process of becoming*" (*Postscript,* vol. I, pp. 306–7). The implication is that the phrase "not the eternal but the futural" projects onto God the limitations of the human condition.

cal one could fall on one's knees in awe before such a God, but only so long as there is an infinite, qualitative difference between that God and ourselves. Perhaps onto-theology consists in the pride that refuses to accept the limits of human knowledge.

The debates over whether there is indeed such a divine knower and whether such ideas are appropriate to a particular religious tradition can continue unabated. (They are likely to do so with or without our permission.) The critique of onto-theology has little if anything to contribute to them. For it is directed not at *what* we say about God but at *how* we say it, to what purpose, in the service of what project. It might seem as if any affirmation of God as Creator, a necessary condition, I should think, of any authentic Jewish, Christian, or Muslim faith, is an onto-theological gesture; for it implies that the whole of being is ultimately to be understood, insofar as we can understand it, with reference to the Highest Being. But the believer might speak as follows:

> In affirming God as Creator I am affirming that there is an explanation of the whole of being and I am pointing in the direction of that explanation; but I am not giving it, for I do not possess it. To do that I would have to know just *who* God is, and just *how* and *why* God brings beings into being out of nothing. But both God's being and God's creative action remain deeply mysterious to me. They are answers that come loaded with new questions, reminding me in Heideggerian language that unconcealment is always shadowed by concealment, or in Pauline language that I only see "through a glass, darkly" (or "in a mirror, dimly," 1 Cor. 13:12). My affirmation of God as Creator is not onto-theological because it is not in the service of the philosophical project of rendering the whole of being intelligible to human understanding, a project I have ample religious reasons to repudiate.[10]

---

[10] For a sophisticated version of such an argument in the context of natural theology, see Brian Leftow, "Can Philosophy Argue God's Existence?" in *The Rationality of Belief and the Plurality of Faiths*, ed. Thomas Senor (Ithaca: Cornell University Press, 1995). In conversation, Leftow has put it this way: "When I offer a version of the cosmological argument I find to be sound, I am trying to prove the existence of God, not to explain the world." On the inextricability of unconcealment and concealment, Heidegger quotes Hamaan as saying, "Lucidity [*Deutlichkeit*] is a suitable apportionment of light and shadow"; *The Principle of Reason*, trans. Reginald Lilly (Bloomington: Indiana University Press, 1991), p. 9.

Not only might the believer speak this way. With or without help from Pseudo-Dionysius, theologians such as Augustine, Aquinas, Luther, Calvin, and Barth have spoken this way. All of them have insisted, with or without help from Rudolf Otto, that the God of the Bible and of their theologies is Wholly Other in an epistemic sense as being the *mysterium*. I must confess, with all the contrition I can muster up (which, I confess, is not much), that I get too much fun out of reminding my Thomist and Calvinist friends of these themes in their masters and suggesting that the latter are Kantian anti-realists, insisting that our knowledge of God is not an instance of the *adequatio rei et intellectus*. For they strongly insist that as human our knowledge of God suffers from qualitative and not merely quantitative limitations and that we do not know God as God knows God, as God most truly is, as unmediated presence to the intellect. But if they are Kantian anti-realists, they are not onto-theologians. They are trying to make the best sense they can of their faith, but they have not bought into the project of making the whole of reality intelligible to human understanding with help from the Highest Being. Far from grudgingly conceding the epistemic transcendence of God to Dionysius and Otto, they go out of their way to insist upon it as being of the highest religious significance. They agree with the twentieth-century psalmist who sings, "I cannot worship what I comprehend."[11]

In developing this argument I have appealed to the distinction Climacus makes in *Concluding Unscientific Postscript* between the *what* and the *how* of our theological affirmations.[12] Does this work for Heidegger as well? I will try to show that it does, that when he protests against letting God enter the scene only on philosophy's terms, it is the *how* rather than the *what* of theological assertion that is his target.

For Jewish, Christian, and Muslim monotheism, God is the

---

[11] Leslie F. Brandt, *Psalms/Now* (St. Louis: Concordia Publishing House, 1973), p. 175.

[12] This distinction is crucial to Climacus's notion of truth as subjectivity. For my analysis in the context of this larger theme, see *Becoming a Self: A Reading of Kierkegaard's* Concluding Unscientific Postscript (West Lafayette, Ind.: Purdue University Press, 1996), ch. 8.

Creator. This means that God is not created. The devout child, brought up in one of these traditions, knows how not to look for an answer to the question And who created God? The child will not say that God is an uncaused cause or is *causa sui,* though after a couple of courses in philosophy she might come to think that such language expresses quite nicely what she has believed from childhood. When Heidegger praises "the godless thinking which must abandon the god of philosophy, god as *causa sui"* by suggesting that it is "thus perhaps closer to the divine God . . . more open to Him that onto-theo-logic would like to admit" (ID p. 72), is he telling our young believer that she must give up her faith in God as Creator? I think not. I think he is warning her that the language she is about to adopt for expressing that faith is dangerous, that it comes from a land foreign to that faith, and that in its native habitat it is part of a project antithetical to that faith. Appropriation of some sort may be unavoidable, but it is always dangerous.

We could begin to make this point by noting that Heidegger has no special resources for showing that there is no loving, personal Creator, and that he does not appeal to such traditional attempts to show this as the argument from evil in the world or a positivistic interpretation of the natural sciences. But it is not necessary to do this because Heidegger is quite emphatic that this is not what he is up to: "For the onto-theological character of metaphysics has become questionable for thinking, not because of any kind of atheism, but from the experience of a thinking which has discerned in onto-theo-logy the still *unthought* unity of the essential nature of metaphysics" (ID p. 55). While insisting that the biblical words "In the beginning God created heaven and earth" are not an answer to the philosophical question of being, Heidegger notes that this does not settle the ontic question of their truth or falsity (IM p. 6).

Further, in the *Letter on Humanism,* he writes, "With the existential determination of the essence of man, therefore, nothing is decided about the 'existence of God' or his 'non-being'. . . . Thus it is not only rash but also an error in procedure to maintain that the interpretation of the essence of man from the relation of his essence to the truth of Being is atheism." He then quotes a passage from *Vom Wesen des Grundes:* "Through the

ontological interpretation of Dasein as being-in-the-world no decision, whether positive or negative, is made concerning a possible being toward God." After rejecting the hasty conclusion that
philosophy doesn't decide for or against the existence of God
because it is "stalled in indifference," he insists that he is only
trying "to think into the dimension in which alone that question
can be asked. . . . Only from the truth of Being can the essence
of the holy be thought. Only from the essence of the holy is the
essence of divinity to be thought. Only in the light of the essence
of divinity can it be thought or said what the word 'God' is to
signify" (LH pp. 229–30; see ER p. 91, n. 56.)

Attributing to Nietzsche Kierkegaard's distinction between
New Testament Christianity and Christendom, and recognizing
that his own critique is a confrontation with Christendom as a
cultural phenomenon, Heidegger insists that such a confrontation "is absolutely not in any way an attack against what is
Christian, any more than a critique of theology is necessarily a
critique of faith" (WNGD pp. 63–64).

It is in the light of statements like these, I believe, that we must
understand Heidegger's repeated insistence on the atheistic
character of philosophy.[13] I have argued elsewhere that this atheism is methodological rather than substantive,[14] but perhaps
'methodological' is not the best term in relation to Heidegger. It
would be better to say that philosophy is atheistic on his view,
not because it takes an ontically negative stand on the question
of God's reality but because it asks ontological questions that
are prior to all ontic questions and neutral with respect to all
ontic answers. Even if we suspect that this notion of philosophy's neutrality is an ironical relic of modernity's Enlightenment notion of reason as pure, uncontaminated by the particular
commitments that give to traditions their positivity, we can recognize that Heidegger's critique of onto-theological thinking
neither presupposes nor argues for the unreality of an uncreated
Creator.

Why then does he get so apoplectic at the notion of God as

---

[13] See the Aristotle lectures of GA 61, pp. 196–97; PIRA p. 367; CT p. 1; HCT
pp. 79–80; MFL 140.

[14] See "Heidegger's 'Theologische' Jugendschriften," Research in Phenomenology
XXVII (1997), pp. 247–61. See ch. 2 below.

causa sui? Negatively speaking, it is because God as *causa sui* and *causa prima in a certain context* "corresponds to the reason-giving path back to the *ultima ratio*" (ID p. 60). To put it more briefly, the *how* of onto-theology is calculative-representational thinking. Because it is "the onto-theo-logical constitution of metaphysics" (ID p. 42) with which we are dealing, the critique of onto-theology is one way to talk about the task of overcoming metaphysics. But metaphysics is both calculative and representational thinking. Sometimes Heidegger lumps them together to make it clear that they are two sides of the same coin (EPTT p. 377; cf. OM p. 100). Elsewhere he discusses them separately, speaking of calculative thinking to emphasize the project of modern technology (the will to power become the will to will) and speaking of representational thinking to emphasize the theoretical foundations of modern technology, not just in modern science but in classical metaphysics going all the way back to Plato and Aristotle.

The goal is to have the world at our disposal (*verfügbar, zur Verfügung stehen,* etc.), in the one case practically, in the other theoretically. It is the latter need that makes philosophy, long before modern philosophy, "a technique for explaining from highest causes" (LH p. 197). Heidegger's fullest account of representational thinking as placing the world at our cognitive disposal is *The Principle of Reason*. It is Leibniz who hatches this egg, but it has been incubating since Plato and Aristotle (PR pp. 4, 53, 118, 121). It begins as the demand for reasons (PR pp. 22–30). But as the demand for completeness (PR pp. 32–33), since an unexplained explainer leaves things ultimately unexplained, the principle of reason becomes an appeal to God as *ultima ratio* (PR pp. 26, 101, 117, 125).

One can even say that for metaphysics, constituted in this way as onto-theology, "God exists only insofar as the principle of reason holds" (PR p. 28). This goes beyond the evidentialist posture that will believe in God only if pure reason can prove God's existence. God's raison d'être has become to make it possible for human reason to give ultimate explanations. This is what Heidegger means when he says that "the deity can come into philosophy only insofar as philosophy, of its own accord and by its own nature, requires and determines that and how the deity enters into it" (ID p. 56). God is at the beck and call of human understanding, a means to its end of making the whole of being intelligible in keeping with the principle of reason. In order to place the world at the disposal of human theory (and practice), it becomes necessary to place God at our disposal as well. But there is no awe, or singing, or dancing before such a factotum. And if there is any clapping, it will have the form of polite applause. "Please join me in welcoming the Ultima Ratio."

Heidegger's objections to the calculative-representational thinking that places not only the world but God as well at our disposal are more Kierkegaardian than Kantian. What we lack is not so much the power to pull off this project (though, of course, we do) as the right to attempt it. The "swaggering comportment" (DT p. 81) of this "unconditional self-assertion" (LH p. 221; cf. WNGD pp. 68, 101) issues in an "insurrection" and "assault" (WNGD p. 100), a "monstrousness" (QT p. 16) that makes us into the "tyrant of Being" rather than the "shepherd of Being" (LH p. 210). We become "that which places everything in relation to *itself*" (OM p. 87). "Man becomes that being upon which all that is, is grounded as regards the manner of its Being and its truth. Man becomes the relational center of that which is as such . . . man contends for the position in which he can be that particular being who gives the measure and draws up the guidelines for everything that is" (AWP pp. 128, 134). In short, calculative-representational thinking is hubris on a world historical scale.

We have already seen that God is part of this world that revolves around "man." (Heidegger does not note the gendered character of the humanism he criticizes.) This is where the specifically religious character of Heidegger's critique comes to the fore, for "even God can, for representational thinking, lose all that is exalted and holy, the mysteriousness of his distance" (QT p. 26). For Heidegger, philosophy not only begins in wonder but must never lose touch with the awe, wonder, and even dread we experience before the mystery that metaphysics as onto-theology seeks to demystify.[15] This is every bit as crucial for any theology that would remain religiously significant.

---

[15] See, for example, WM/1929, pp. 251, 256; WM/1943, pp. 260–64; DT pp. 55, 63–68, LH p. 199; PR pp. 54–55, 61–62, 68.

In postmodern contexts, onto-theology is one of the seven deadly sins. But one is not necessarily committing onto-theology when affirming God as *causa sui*. It is not as if after Heidegger philosophy somehow knows better than to affirm the reality of an uncreated Creator. But it is dangerous to do so in the language of *causa sui*, for this language has its provenance in a project that can be traced from Anaxagoras to Nietzsche (for the project survives the death of God) and that is deeply antithetical both to authentic philosophy and to authentic theology. This project is the *how* that turns the *what* of Jewish, Christian, and Muslim monotheism into onto-theology, leaving us with the God of the philosophers instead of the God of Abraham, Isaac, and Jacob.

The critique of onto-theology by name belongs to Heidegger II.[16] But at least implicitly it can be found in Heidegger I and even earlier. There is, of course, that passage early in *Being and Time* where Heidegger reminds us that Being is not a being and that thinking Being consists "in not 'telling a story'—that is to say, in not defining beings as beings by tracing them back in their origin to some other beings, as if Being had the character of some possible entity" (BT p. 26, translation modified). Early and late, metaphysics is the forgetfulness of Being, and that theme is part of the critique of onto-theology. But not the best part, nor the part that has a bearing on how theology can avoid lapsing into onto-theology (for theology does not come home to its proper task by making the question of being prior to the question of God). The most compelling themes in that critique can be, and in Heidegger often are, developed independently from the ontological difference.

Accordingly, it is to a different text from Heidegger I that I turn, namely, the 1927–28 lecture "Phenomenology and Theology." Heidegger tells us that it is guided by the notion of phenomenology given in ¶7 of *Being and Time*. But even more important for understanding the lecture are the notion of knowl-

---

[16] Of, if you like, to Heidegger II and III. See Reiner Schürmann, *Heidegger on Being and Acting: From Principles to Anarchy* (Bloomington: Indiana University Press, 1987), introduction.

edge as a founded mode of being-in-the-world (BT ¶13), the notion of assertion as a derivative mode of interpretation (BT ¶33),
and the distinction between *Zuhandenheit*, the ready-to-hand,
and *Vorhandenheit*, the present-at-hand or objectively present (BT
¶¶15–16, 33).[17] In other words, we are dealing with a critique of
the primacy of the theoretical. As a project of rendering the
whole of being intelligible in accordance with the principle of
reason, onto-theology presupposes and practices the primacy of
theoretical reason.

Heidegger quotes Luther's definition of faith as "letting ourselves be seized by the things we do not see" and adds his own
negative and positive account: "faith is not something which
merely reveals that the occurring of revelation is something happening; it is not some more or less modified type of knowing.
Rather, faith is an appropriation of revelation. . . . *Faith is the
believing-understanding mode of existing in the history revealed, i.e.,
occurring, with the Crucified*" (PT p. 10). But this means that since
"theology is constituted by thematizing faith" (PT p. 11), it "is
not speculative knowledge of God" (PT p. 15).

This does not mean that faith and theology should be given
the noncognitivist interpretations familiar from positivist or
Wittgensteinian contexts. Faith is a *"believing-understanding mode
of existing,"* and it stands in relation to something actual. Heidegger's believer surely believes that "in Christ God was reconciling the world to himself" (2 Cor. 5:19). But with Luther,
Heidegger refuses to allow faith to be understood as the *pistis*
that Plato puts on the lower half of the divided line. We misun-
derstand faith terribly if we assume that the believer really
wants to be an onto-theologically constituted metaphysician,
but, failing to be part of the intellectual elite, settles for a second
class, "more or less modified type, of knowing."[18]

Every positive science concerns a domain that is "already dis-

---

[17] Marion will suggest an even stronger dependence of the lecture on *Being
and Time*; see *God without Being*, pp. 66–69.

[18] When Levinas distinguishes his own critique of onto-theology from Pascal's, it is because he surprisingly assumes that Pascal assimilates faith to opinion on Plato's divided line. See "God and Philosophy," in *Collected
Philosophical Papers*, trans. Alphonso Lingis (Dordrecht: Martinus Nijhoff,
1987), p. 155. But cf. the reference to "reasons that 'reason' does not know" on
p. 172.

closed," prior to any "theoretical consideration," in a "prescientific manner of approaching and proceeding with that which is." Science always presupposes this "prescientific *behavior* [*Verhalten*]" (PT p. 7, emphasis added). For theology as a positive science, faith is the "prescientific *behavior*" in which the *Sache* that concerns it is "already disclosed." In the case of Christian theology, what is disclosed is above all "Christ, the crucified God" (PT p. 9). Of course, faith is dependent on revelation for its *positum*, but that does not mean that faith is simply the assent to new information. Rather, "existence struck by this revelation becomes aware of its forgetfulness of God. . . . [B]eing placed before God means that existence is reoriented in and through the mercy of God grasped in faith. . . . [The believer] can only 'believe' his existential possibility as one which human existence itself is not master over, in which it becomes a slave, is brought before God, and is reborn. . . . *Faith* = *Rebirth*" (PT p. 10). It is immediately after this account of faith as an existential paradigm shift that Heidegger identifies with Luther's understanding of faith as opposed to the Platonic reading whose *Wirkungsgeschichte* has distorted so many discussions of faith and reason.

Faith is the "appropriation" of revelation, and theology is the "thematizing" of faith (PT pp. 10–11). Hegel thinks the task of thematizing faith belongs ultimately to philosophy and that it consists in transforming faith into absolute knowledge by translating *Vorstellungen* into *Begriffe*. But this is just Plato's divided line translated into German. Heidegger is too Lutheran to buy into this project (from one who professed to be a Lutheran!). He has learned from another Lutheran (Kierkegaard) that it trivializes the appropriation of revelation in which existence is reoriented and the believer reborn by replacing this task with a speculative task that is at once too easy and too elitist to be anything but an enemy of faith.

So when he tells us "Theology is not speculative knowledge of God" (PT p. 15), he has two things in mind. First, the task of theology is not to "found and secure faith in its legitimacy, nor can it in any way make it easier to accept faith and remain constant in faith. Theology can only render faith more difficult" (PT p. 12).

Second, this is because the goal of theology "is never a valid system of theological propositions" but rather "concrete Christian existence itself." Because faith is both the motivation and justification of theology, "this objectification of faith itself properly has no other purpose than to help cultivate faithfulness itself. . . . Every theological statement and concept addresses itself *in its very content* to the faith-full existence of the individual in the community; it does *not* do so subsequently, for the sake of some practical *'application'"* (PT p. 12). In other words, because its goal is the *praxis* of the believer as a distinctive mode of existence, *"theology in its essence is a practical science."* Unlike onto-theology, theology properly understood is " 'innately homiletical," but not "due to any accidental requirements which demand, say, that it apply its theoretical propositions to a practical sphere" (PT pp. 14–15). The apostolic kerygma that "in Christ God was reconciling the world to himself" is already the entreaty, "be reconciled to God" (2 Cor. 5:19–20).

Theology arises out of a "prescientific behavior" and has as its goal what we might call postscientific behavior. It is as if Heidegger is saying, I have found it necessary to deny theory in order to make room for practice. Of course, as we have seen, the denial of theory is not its abolition but its *Aufhebung,* its teleological suspension, its reinscription in a context where it is neither the *arche* nor the *telos,* neither the *terminus a quo* nor the *terminus ad quem.*

This polemic against the primacy of the theoretical is found as early as the 1920–21 lectures *Einleitung in die Phänomenologie der Religion.* By contrast with the 1927–28 lecture, Heidegger even denies that philosophy (in this case as a phenomenology of religion) should think of itself as a science (GA 60 pp. 3, 8–10, 15, 17, 27, 29, 35). This is because it seeks to be faithful to experience, which relates to the world in its *Bedeutsamkeit* rather than to "objects" (GA 60 pp. 8–16). We have here a clear anticipation of the distinction between *Zuhandenheit* and *Vorhandenheit,* whose importance for the later lecture has already been suggested.

It might be objected that in the later, explicit critique of onto-theology, Heidegger links it to calculative-representational thinking, the essence of modern technology. Thought is too closely linked to a certain practice. With Heidegger I, by contrast, it seems that the linkage of knowledge to action is an important desideratum. So how can the earlier emphasis on the embeddedness of knowing in doing, both in general and specifically in the life of faith, be an anticipation of the later critique of instrumental reason?

But we must not interpret the distinction between *Bedeutsamkeit* and objects, or between *Zuhandenheit* and *Vorhandenheit* only in utilitarian terms, nor allow the famous hammer of *Being and Time* to turn Heidegger into a crude pragmatist. We radically misconstrue our being-in-the-world when we portray it as an objective pole made up of facts whose only job is to obtain and a subjective pole whose only job is to mirror these facts.[19] Attention to the use of a tool helps us see this; but we need something like the Aristotelian distinction between *praxis* and *poiesis* to indicate that our concernful dealings with beings that are positively or negatively meaningful in relation to our projects are not necessarily instrumental. A theoretical or representational interpretation of our being-in-the-world is as inadequate to the "Hammerklavier" Sonata as it is to the hammer, to say nothing of the word of the Lord which is "like a hammer that breaks a rock in pieces" (Jer. 23:29). Or, to put it a bit differently, God is not a tool; but both as *fascinans* and as *tremendum*, the *mysterium* is *Bedeutsamkeit* and not mere object, is *zuhanden* and not merely *vorhanden*. Before such a God one can fall on one's knees in awe.[20]

But the onto-theological project commits the fallacy of misplaced concreteness. It abstracts the cognitive dimension of the religious life and gives it essential primacy. In each of the three dimensions of its relation to human action it is a danger to faith. (1) For the sake of absolute conceptual mastery, it seeks to free

---

[19] Nietzsche writes, "We are not thinking frogs, *nor objectifying and registering mechanisms with their innards removed*"; *The Gay Science*, trans. Walter Kaufman (New York: Random House, 1974), 2nd ed. preface, section 3. Emphasis added.

[20] Reference to awe suggests that our concrete being-in-the-world has an affective side that must not be overlooked. In "Hermeneutics as Epistemology" (see ch. 3 below), I trace the double reduction in *Being and Time* from the merely theoretical to both the practical and the affective, a "reduction"that, unlike Husserl's, seeks to recapture the natural standpoint. The account of *Befindlichkeit* in ¶¶29–30 belongs to the early, implicit critique of onto-theology. "The fear of the Lord is the beginning of knowledge" (Prov. 1:7).

knowledge from its rootedness in pretheoretical practice so that it can become self-grounding. In this way it gets itself stuck to the epistemological tar baby that has paralyzed so much of modernity. (2) When mathematical physics replaces theology as the queen of the sciences, pure theory discovers that it has wonderful technological applications.[21] Heidegger's critique of God as the highest value is a reminder that the technological attitude can rub off onto faith, that piety can degenerate into an instrumental religion in which God becomes a means to our ends (WNGD p. 105). (3) In its more overtly theological modes, ontotheology finds that it has cut itself off from the modes of appropriation, singing and dancing, for example, that constitute living faith.

In relation to *Phenomenology and Theology*, however, there is a more serious objection. Theology becomes onto-theology when Jerusalem sells its soul to Athens by buying in on the latter's project. Within Christian history, the critique of onto-theology belongs to a tradition of dehellenizing repristination. Heidegger explicitly links his critique with Luther, and thus, by implication, with a tradition that looks back to Augustine and ahead to Pascal, Kierkegaard, and Barth.[22] He seems to confirm Jerusalem's declaration of independence from Athens when he writes, "On the grounds of its specific positive character and the form of knowing which this determines, we can now say that theology is a fully autonomous ontic science" (PT p. 16)—not, of course, in relation to the revelation upon which it depends, but in relation to the other sciences.

But a problem arises when he immediately asks specifically about the relation of this science to philosophy as the ontological science. Theology needs philosophy, he says, but neither for its *positum*, revelational content, nor for some rational legitimation.

---

[21] We have just seen Heidegger explicitly deny that "application" is the right way to think the relation of theory to practice in theology.

[22] On the importance of Luther, Pascal, Kierkegaard, and, in this connection, both Paul and Augustine, see John van Buren, *The Young Heidegger: Rumor of the Hidden King* (Bloomington: Indiana University Press, 1994); Theodore Kisiel, *The Genesis of Heidegger's* Being and Time (Berkeley: University of California Press, 1993); and the essays by Van Buren and Kisiel in their jointly edited volume *Reading Heidegger from the Start: Essays in His Earliest Thought* (Albany: SUNY Press, 1994).

Rather, "all basic theological concepts . . . have as their *ontological* determinants meanings which are pre-Christian and which can thus be grasped purely rationally." Thus, for example, the theological concept of sin must be understood in terms of the ontological interpretation of guilt," presumably as found in *Being and Time* (PT pp. 17–18; cf. LH pp. 229–30). At first Heidegger calls this relation one of guidance, but then he describes it no fewer than nine times as "correction" (*Korrektion, Korrektiv,* PT pp. 19–20). In this connection he reminds us that faith is "the mortal enemy of the *form of existence* which is an essential part of *philosophy*" by virtue of an "*existentiell opposition*" between faithfulness and a human's free appropriation of his whole existence" (PT p. 20).

As a Christian thinker, Marion is more than a little nervous at this suggestion that theology must be corrected by philosophy. The idea that Heidegger might help free our thinking of God from the question of being and its close link with the onto-theological project turns out to be illusory.[23] Under Heidegger's tutelage "every theology remains subject to the question of Being." By virtue of his own attempts at overcoming metaphysics, he seems to side with Luther, Pascal, and Barth in their attempt to overcome the Babylonian captivity of faith to philosophy, but this is only to substitute a new philosophical master for the old ones. When Marion looks the (Trojan) gift horse in the mouth, what he sees is an "ontic independence, which implies an irreducible ontological dependence. . . . It seems that the question of 'God' never suffered as radical a reduction to the first question of Being as in the phenomenological enterprise of Heidegger."[24] Heidegger makes theology autonomous vis-à-vis chemistry, but not vis-à-vis Heidegger!

Why shouldn't Marion be offended? Why should Christian theology submit itself to correction from a life form that is its "mortal enemy" and that employs "pre-Christian" and "purely rational" concepts as its tools?

---

[23] It is worth noting in this connection that Pseudo-Dionysius points to a God beyond being because he is a proto-Kantian who sees 'being' as a category of human understanding that is inadequate to the divine reality. See *Pseudo-Dionysius: The Complete Works*, trans. Colm Luibheid (New York: Paulist Press, 1987), pp. 49–50, 53, 63, 135, 138, 263.

[24] *God without Being*, pp. 68–69.

But perhaps the matter isn't quite that simple. Let us take a closer look at the role Heidegger assigns philosophy vis-à-vis theology to see whether there remains a possibility of theological appropriation rather than the either/or of capitulation/repudiation. First, Heidegger says that the ontological meanings philosophy furnishes are "pre-Christian" and can be grasped "purely rationally." As already indicated, it is surprising to hear Heidegger appeal to pure reason. The repudiation of the view that philosophy can embody the view from nowhere is central to his critique of Husserl and Dilthey, and, indeed, to his whole corpus. So we can turn our attention to the notion that Heidegger's ontology is "pre-Christian."

At this stage of the game (the twenties) it is not so much the pre-Socratics that concern us as Aristotle, who plays a significant role in the development of the hermeneutics of facticity that becomes ontology in *Being and Time* (see GA 61, GA 63, and PIRA). But, as Van Buren, Kisiel, and others have shown, Heidegger draws very heavily on a variety of Christian sources, including the Pauline epistles, in trying to break the stranglehold of pure theory on the life of faith. So perhaps the correction to which Heidegger subjects theology is in significant measure self-correction rather than imperialistic hubris. My account of the critique of onto-theology, both early and late, has focused on just those features for which this is most arguably the case, features that are separable both de jure and often de facto from the project of thinking being.

Second, Heidegger claims that the corrective guidance philosophy offers to theology is purely formal, and he invokes the notion of formal indication (*formale Anzeige*) that plays such an important part in his earlier work (PT pp. 19–20).[25] Hegel once told a similar story. The contents of theology and philosophy, he solemnly intoned, are the same. The only "corrective" philosophy supplies concerns its form—and this from a philosopher whose Logic insists on the inextricability of form and content. Kierkegaard has taught us to laugh loudly (so as to keep from crying) at this pretense under which Hegel seeks to subject

---

[25] For the meaning and importance of this concept, see all three of the works cited in n. 22.

Christian faith to the canons of autonomous human reason. A similar laugh should greet Heidegger's "Who me? I'm only concerned with questions of form. All the content comes from the Christian *positum*."

Except . . . Heidegger derives his formal indications, not from pure reason but hermeneutically; and, as we have just been reminded, the texts he reads are very largely Christian texts. So once again, we are free to look for those elements that are authentically theological; and once again these may not revolve around the ontological difference. Further, just to the degree that the heart of onto-theology concerns the *how* rather than the *what* of discourse about God, there is something formal about what is at issue.

Finally, we are told that the "demand" for philosophy to play a corrective role in relation to theology "is not made by philosophy as such but rather by theology" (PT p. 20). There may be a touch of megalomania here. Just as Heidegger later would think that the National Socialist movement desperately needed him to clarify its identity and would freely turn to him if it understood both its own and his greatness, so here he thinks that (Christian) theology needs him and is most fully itself when it turns to him for correction.[26] Still, just to the degree that Heidegger's critique has genuinely theological origins, as we have been noting, it makes sense to see "correction" as self-correction and the demand for a critique of onto-theology as arising from a theology that recognizes its own onto-theological tendencies and sees these as temptations to be resisted.

My project is to appropriate Heidegger's critique of onto-theology for theistic theology, for religiously significant discourse about the personal Creator, Lawgiver, and Merciful Savior of Jewish, or Christian, or Muslim monotheism. Because appropriation is always recontextualizing, it is always both affirmation and negation; it is a little bit like an Hegelian *Aufhebung*, though without the implication of logical or conceptual necessity. That

---

[26] It would seem that Heidegger had more luck with the theologians than with the Nazis on this score, as is seen in the work of Bultmann and in volumes such as *The Later Heidegger and Theology*, ed. James M. Robinson and John B. Cobb, Jr. (Westport, Conn.: Greenwood Press, 1979).

is why for each of the three themes just discussed in relation to philosophy's "correction" of theology, I found something to reject (à la Marion), and something to preserve from Heidegger. This has led to the notion that theology must submit itself to the discipline of Heidegger's critique, now understood as prophetic self-criticism. And this may seem to run counter to the argument that the critique of onto-theology concerns its *how* and not its *what*, an argument apparently directed toward getting theology off the hook of Heidegger's critique. So let me try to clarify.

When I address an issue like this I always have two audiences in mind, one quite secular (or at least anti-theistic), the other rather traditionally theological, often in a Thomistic or Calvinist way.[27] To the first I say, "The critique in question is very powerful, but closely examined it does not do the work you would like it to do. It does not discredit theistic discourse as such, does not make the world safe from the God of Abraham, Isaac, and Jacob (and Moses, and Jesus, and Mohammed). It only discredits certain forms that discourse can/has/does take(n)." To my Thomist and Calvinist friends I say, "Don't get too comfortable. While the critique in question does not do the work its anti-theist enthusiasts would like it to do, it has a lot of legitimate bite. Moreover, there are good theological reasons to take it seriously, for it identifies and critiques ways in which the most orthodox God-talk becomes idolatrous."

The main argument of this essay has been addressed to the first audience. I have argued that both the explicit critique of onto-theology in the forties and fifties and important anticipations of it from the twenties are directed toward the *how* rather than the *what* of our God-talk and that they have more the spirit of Pascal than that of positivism. That is to say, they do not provide or seek to provide a philosophical case against belief in a personal Creator (as is all too often implied); they rather seek to keep open the space for religiously meaningful God-talk by resisting the "metaphysical" tendency, whether found among

---

[27] This is true, for example, in my treatment of the religion critique of Marx, Nietzsche, and Freud in *Suspicion and Faith* (New York: Fordham University Press, 1998). I adopt a similar posture in relation to Derrida's critique of the metaphysics of presence, which I take to be very closely related to Heidegger's critique of onto-theology.

philosophers or theologians, to imprison theological discourse within a primacy of theoretical reason under the rule of the principle of sufficient reason. What is necessary to overcome onto-theology is not the abandonment of theistic belief but the avoidance of this temptation to have God at our disposal, conceptually speaking.

This reading weakens Heidegger's critique, I think, only for those who have hoped it would do for continental philosophy what positivism once did for analytic philosophy. It still retains plenty of force not only against such paradigmatically onto-theological systems as those of Spinoza and Hegel but also against what we might call onto-theologies of the right, more popularly known as fundamentalisms. While the latter may not speak the language of sufficient reason and *causa sui*, they do treat God as being at their disposal conceptually (it's scary how much they know about what God is up to) and convert this quite quickly into the project of having the world at their disposal practically as well. Theocracy legitimizes itself onto-theologically.

Between these extremes we can locate two other sites where Heidegger's critique has force against onto-theological tendencies that may not have prevailed so completely but that are nevertheless very real. Closer to the fundamentalist end of the spectrum are those theologies, Protestant and Catholic, that are sometimes designated 'scholasticism'. This term has negative connotations precisely when its use points to onto-theological tendencies to which theistic discourse can but need not succumb. Closer to the other end of the spectrum, ironically to be sure, are certain invocations of negative theology. Marion speaks of the discourse "that disqualifies or deconstructs the very notion of God; this discourse consists in speaking of God in order to silence him, in not keeping silent in order to silence him. . . . [I]t does not see the difference between silencing and keeping silent."[28] But silencing God is one way of having God at our

---

[28] *God without Being*, p. 55. Cf. Feuerbach's analysis of those who declare God unknowable so that God's existence "does not affect or incommode [them]. . . . The alleged religious horror of limiting God by positive predicates is only the irreligious wish to know nothing more of God, to banish God from the mind"; Ludwig Feuerbach, *The Essence of Christianity*, trans. George Eliot (New York: Harper & Brothers, 1957), p. 15.

disposal and protecting ourselves against being seized by what we do not see. The act of protesting against onto-theology can become an onto-theological gesture.

As we move away from the extremes toward cases like these last two, we move into situations that are at once ambiguous and closer to home. Because of their ambiguity we need to look closely to determine just where and to what degree God-talk becomes the arrogant humanism that puts God at our disposal; and in light of the distinction between the *how* and the *what*, we should not expect to be able to answer these questions simply in terms of propositional content. Because these sites are closer to home, we need to look closely to see to what degree our carefully crafted critique is directed at ourselves.

So far I have spoken as if overcoming onto-theology means both learning correctly to identify it and learning to avoid it. But, at least for the theistic discourses that primarily concern me, learning to avoid means learning to speak of God otherwise than onto-theologically. Something must be said, however briefly, about the positive meaning of this overcoming. We can take Heidegger's implicit slogan "I have found it necessary to deny theory in order to make room for practice" as our key.

For a gloss on the positive meaning of denying theory, I turn to Wagner's *Lohengrin*. It can be read as a tenth-century *Shane*. The hero rides into town, takes care of the bad guys, and then rides off into the sunset, alone. But I propose reading it as a retelling of the story of Cupid and Psyche. Motivated by the desire to rule, Ortrud turns Gottfried, rightful heir to power in Brabant, into a swan by means of sorcery. She then persuades her husband, Telramund, to accuse Elsa, the young boy's sister, of being his murderer. (This will clear the path to power for Ortrud and Telramund.) The matter is to be settled by combat. When no local knight is willing to defend Elsa's honor, the magnificent Lohengrin arrives in a boat pulled by a swan. Needless to say, it is love at first sight between Elsa and Lohengrin, but to her he is more than her hero and husband to be. In language heavy with theological overtones, she calls him her *Retter* and her *Erlöser*. She gives herself to him totally.

Mein Held, mein Retter! Nimm mich hin,
Dir geb' ich Alles, was ich bin!

Lohengrin, whose name is not yet revealed within the drama,
asks Elsa to promise never to ask his name or country.

Nie sollst du mich befragen
Noch Wissen's Sorge tragen,
Woher ich kam der Fahrt,
Noch wie mein Nam' und Art!

Elsa promises solemnly to honor this request and, at Lohengrin's request, repeats her promise to obey his command (*Gebot*).
He vindicates her by defeating Telramund, and in ecstasy she
repeats "Nimm alles was ich bin!"[29]

But now Ortrud's shame adds desire for vengeance to her lust
for the throne. Standing between Satan and Iago, she plants the
seeds of doubt in Elsa. Her lover came by magic. How does she
know he won't leave her and disappear just as quickly? (Doesn't
every Shane leave a woman behind, weeping?) Shouldn't she
know his name? At the end of the second act, Telramund, once
again Ortrud's dupe, accuses Lohengrin of sorcery and publicly
challenges him to reveal his name. Lohengrin says that he will
do so only in response to a demand from Elsa, but she renews
her pledge:

Mein Retter, der mir Heil gebracht!
Mein Held, in dem ich muss vergeh'n!
Hoch über alles Zweifels Macht
Soll meine Liebe stehn!

For a third time she insists that trusting love shall triumph over
the doubt born of *Wissen's Sorge*.

At the beginning of the final act we hear the familiar wedding
march, and then the lovers are alone in the bridal chamber. Al-

---

[29] I am assimilating *Lohengrin* to a long tradition of allegorical readings of
the Song of Solomon, according to which the relation of beloved to lover no
longer concerns the relation of woman to man but the believing soul (male or
female) to God. Thus Mary's "Here am I [*me voici*], the servant of the Lord; let
it be with me according to your word" (Luke 1:38) makes her a model, not of
ideal womanhood, but of devout humanity. This is perhaps most easily seen
by hearing her words echoed in those of her son, "not my will but yours be
done" (Luke 22:42).

most immediately their ecstatic joy is disturbed by Elsa's request to know her lover's name. At first she says it was so wonderful to hear him say her name and she wants to return the favor. You can tell me, she says, I won't tell anyone else. He warns her that she is on the verge of ruining everything and pleads with her to let love prevail over doubt as she has promised.

Then we learn how effective Ortrud's intimations have been and what really motivates Elsa's doubt. She is afraid that some day Lohengrin will tire of her and leave her. He came by magic, and she seeks some magic to bind him to her. The ancient linkage between knowing the name and the ability to conjure, only hinted at earlier, now becomes explicit.[30] Elsa's *Wissen's Sorge* is not born of self-giving love but of the desire to be in control, to have Lohengrin at her disposal.

He tells her that he is Lohengrin, son of Parsifal and a knight of the Grail. The magic that brought him to her would have left them together forever if she had trusted him. But it requires all knights to return to the temple of the Grail once their identity is known. The swan returns and is restored to Elsa as Gottfried. But Lohengrin sails away, leaving Elsa to cry out in anguish and pass out in her brother's arms.

In C. S. Lewis's retelling of the Cupid and Psyche story, the demands of walking by faith and not by sight are even stronger. As Psyche tells her sister about the god to whom she has been married and with whom she lives in a magnificent palace, she explains, "Oh, Orual . . . not even I have seen him—yet. He comes to me only in the holy darkness. He says I mustn't—not yet—see his face or know his name. I'm forbidden to bring any light into his—our—chamber."[31] To make matters worse, although they are standing right in front of the palace, Orual can-

---

[30] Martin Buber interprets Israel's request (anticipated by Moses) to know the name of their deliverer as a desire for magical power. Accordingly, he interprets the famous answer of Exodus 3:14 not as "I am who I am" but as the promise "I shall be there" with the meaning "you do not need to conjure Me, but you cannot conjure Me either." *Kingship of God*, trans. Richard Scheimann (New York: Harper & Row, 1967), pp. 104–7. Cf. *The Prophetic Faith* (New York: Harper & Row, 1960), pp. 27–29, and Gerhard von Rad, *Old Testament Theology*, trans. D. M. G. Stalker (New York: Harper & Row, 1962), vol. I, pp. 179–84.

[31] C. S. Lewis, *Till We Have Faces* (Grand Rapids: Eerdmans, 1966), p. 123.

not see it. It is hard to know whether to say that Psyche's God-relation takes place in hidden inwardness or in hidden outwardness. But even the site of their communion is invisible and inaccessible to her unbelieving sister.

Whether it is just the name that is forbidden, or in addition to that the beloved is not allowed to see her lover's face, the challenge of faith is the same: the believer is called upon to sustain a beautiful and loving relationship through trust in a lover about whom she remains significantly (though not totally) in the dark and who, though he gives himself to her freely, is not at her disposal. The relationship is destroyed when the beloved succumbs to *Wissen's Sorge* and insists on Enlightenment, on dissipating the darkness of mystery with the light of human knowledge, on walking by sight and not by faith.

To be able to resist this temptation, faith must deny theory, or, to be more precise, the primacy of insight. For such faith, Plato's divided line and Hegel's modern version thereof as the movement "beyond faith" to knowledge are not the ascent from that which is inferior (body, senses, epistemic risk, opinions available to the many) to that which is superior (soul, intellect, the certainty of sheer presence, insights available to the culturally elite); they are rather the withdrawal from the site at which alone is possible a loving, trusting relation with a God before whom one might sing and dance (or at least clap).

This love, this trust, this relationship—these are the practice for the sake of which it was necessary to deny theory. This is not to abolish theology. It is to see that theology's task is to serve this life of faith, not the ideals of knowledge as defined by the philosophical traditions Heidegger variously calls calculative-representational thinking, metaphysics, and onto-theology.

Who knows better than Pseudo-Dionysius the importance of silence before the mystery of God? Yet he also knows that the life of faith is very vocal, and he spends much of his time, especially in *The Divine Names*, telling us, not how not to speak about God, but how to speak about God. It is as if he can hear his audience asking again and again, But if the point of our discourse about God is not to pull (or push) God out of the cloud of unknowing into the light of sheer presence, what is the point of it? To which he replies, again and again, In a word: praise.

For praise is an essential component in the practice of faith. We accompany our "wise silence" with "songs of praise."[32] For Marion it is because God is *agape* and gift that "predication must yield to praise." We receive the gift of love in silence. "Only then can discourse be reborn, but as an enjoyment, a jubilation, a praise."[33]

"We go to church in order to sing, and theology is secondary." One way to see how far we have overcome onto-theology is to ask how strongly we are inspired by our theology to sing songs of praise to the God who triumphed over political, economic, and cultural oppression when "Pharaoh's army got drownded."[34]

---

[32] *Pseudo-Dionysius: The Complete Works,* pp. 50–51. Dionysius echoes an older tradition. For example, Cyril of Jerusalem writes in the fourth century, "But some one will ask, If the divine Being is incomprehensible, what is the good of the things you have seen saying? Come now, am I not to take a reasonable drink because I cannot drink the river dry? Of course I cannot bear to fix my gaze upon the sun in its strength. But is that any reason for not glancing up at him if I need? . . . I praise and glorify our Maker, seeing that 'Let everything that hath breath praise the Lord' is a divine command. I am now trying to glorify the master, not to expound his nature, for I know quite well that I shall fall far short even of glorifying him as he deserves. . . . For the Lord Jesus comforts me for my insufficiency by saying, 'No man hath seen God at any time' "; *The Catechetical Lectures,* vol. VI, p. 5 in *Cyril of Jerusalem and Nemesius of Emesa,* Library of Christian Classics, vol. IV, ed. William Telfer (London: SCM Press, 1955), pp. 128–29.

[33] *God without Being,* pp. 106–7. Cf. Krzysztof Ziarek, "The Language of Praise: Levinas and Marion" *Religion and Literature,* 22, nos. 2–3 (autumn 1990), pp. 93–107.

[34] This essay was supported by a grant from the Pew Evangelical Scholars Program, which I am pleased to acknowledge with gratitude.

2

Heidegger's *"Theologische"* *Jugendschriften*

EARLY HEIDEGGER is proving to be every bit as interesting as early Hegel. In both cases the posthumously published *Jugendschriften* are of intrinsic interest as well as providing invaluable keys to the subsequent writings. Heidegger's postwar lectures as Privatdocent in Freiburg (KNS 1919 to SS 1923) have already appeared in volumes 56–59, 61, and 63 of the *Gesamtausgabe*. Now volume 60 appears under the title *Phänomenologie des religiösen Lebens*. It consists of (1) "Introduction to the Phenomenology of Religion," a lecture course from WS 1920–21 based on five *Nachschriften* (IPR); (2) "Augustine and Neoplatonism," a lecture course from SS 1921 based on Heidegger's manuscript and three *Nachschriften* (AN); and (3) notes and sketches prepared by Heidegger for a course entitled "Philosophical Foundations of Medieval Mysticism" (MM). The mysticism course was scheduled for WS 1919–20 but canceled so that Heidegger could expand his first "Basic Problems of Phenomenology" course.[1]

Based on various degrees of access to the manuscripts, these texts have received considerable recent attention prior to their publication.[2] They can fruitfully be read as belonging to the *Ent-*

---

[1] Published as GA 58. The volume translated into English under that title by Albert Hofstadter (Bloomington: Indiana University Press, 1982) is from SS 1927 and is GA 24.

[2] See Theodore Kisiel, *The Genesis of Heidegger's* Being and Time (Berkeley: University of California Press, 1993); John D. Caputo, *Demythologizing Heidegger* (Bloomington: Indiana University Press, 1993); John van Buren, *The Young Heidegger: Rumor of the Hidden King* (Bloomington: Indiana University Press, 1994); and Theodore Kisiel and John van Buren, eds., *Reading Heidegger from the Start: Essays in His Earliest Thought* (Albany: SUNY Press, 1994). Earlier there was the brief discussion in Otto Pöggeler, *Martin Heidegger's Path of Thinking* (New York: Humanities, 1987; German original, 1963), and Thomas Sheehan, "Heidegger's 'Introduction to the Phenomenology of Religion,' 1920–21," *The Personalist* (July 1979), pp. 312–24.

stehungsgeschichte of *Being and Time*.[3] Equally important, in relation to the later Heidegger, is John Caputo's story of how Heidegger, before the "myth of the single origin" of thinking in pre-Socratic Greece, finds a dual impetus to thought in early Christianity and Aristotle. I want to suggest a third context for reading what Theodore Kisiel calls "the religion courses," not in the least mutually exclusive with the other two, namely, Heidegger's later critique of metaphysics as onto-theology.

In *Identity and Difference,* Heidegger notes that God enters into philosophy, when it is onto-theologically constituted, "only insofar as philosophy, of its own accord and by its own nature, requires and determines that and how the deity enters into it." The mainstream of the philosophical tradition that Heidegger has in mind has as its task to render the whole of reality intelligible, to render everything present to the light of reason; and it makes God into the Highest Being as a means to this its own end. This imperialism puts us in touch with a construct, not with genuine religious experience: "Man can neither pray nor sacrifice to this god. Before the *causa sui,* man can neither fall to his knees in awe nor can he play music and dance before this god."[4] This complaint (1957) echoes the earlier warning (1949) that Christian theology should not buy into the onto-theological project but should remember the Pauline reminder that the wisdom of the (Greek) world is foolishness before God.[5] Far from being a Nietzschean assumption that theology is by its servile nature willing and eager to be colonized by philosophy, Heidegger's critique is an open invitation to theology to find a way to be true to itself.

The 1949 appeal to Paul echoes in turn the religion courses before us, especially IPR. The connecting link is the 1927 lecture "Phenomenology and Theology," where Heidegger distinguishes theology as an ontic science from philosophy as an onto-

---

[3] For reservations on this approach, see van Buren's review of Kisiel, "Is It an Objective or Subjective Genitive?" *International Philosophical Quarterly* XXXV, no. 4 (December 1995), pp. 483–89.

[4] *Identity and Difference,* trans. Joan Stambaugh (New York: Harper & Row, 1969), pp. 56 and 72.

[5] In the 1949 Introduction to *What Is Metaphysics?,* "The Way Back into the Ground of Metaphysics," in *Existentialism from Dostoevsky to Sartre,* ed. Walter Kaufmann, 2nd ed. (New York: New American Library, 1975), pp. 275–76.

logical science. Theology has faith as its Alpha and Omega and "can find sufficient motivation for itself only through faith." Faith is, as Luther says, "permitting ourselves to be seized by the things we do not see," but this does not mean that faith is "some more or less modified [inferior] type of knowing." It has a different motivation. But if faith is not primarily a kind of knowing, "Theology is not speculative knowledge of God."[6] At about the same time, Heidegger writes in *Being and Time* that theology is "seeking a more primordial interpretation of man's Being towards God, prescribed by the meaning of faith itself and remaining within it. It is slowly beginning to understand once more Luther's insight that the 'foundation' on which its system of dogma rests has not arisen from an inquiry in which faith is primary, and that conceptually this 'foundation' not only is inadequate for the problematic of theology, but conceals and distorts it."[7]

Reading backward to the postwar Freiburg lectures, we might expect to find in the religion courses a theological discourse on the nature of faith and of theology as its expression—all the more so when we find Heidegger describing himself to Löwith right after the second religion course as a "Christian theologian."[8] But this claim is highly dubious, as three considerations will indicate. First, just two months later he writes to Löwith that *in the eyes of Husserl,* "I myself am no longer even regarded as a 'philosopher', I am 'still really a theologian.' "[9] Second, as he turns in his first religion course from methodological considerations to an intensive engagement with the Pauline epistles, he warns his students not to mistake his phenomenological enterprise with either dogmatic (that is, systematic) or exegetical theology (p. 67).[10] Finally, when we read the lectures, we discover

---

[6] *The Piety of Thinking,* trans. James G. Hart and John C. Maraldo (Bloomington: Indiana University Press, 1976), pp. 10–11, 15.

[7] *Being and Time,* trans. John Macquarrie and Edward Robinson (New York: Harper & Row, 1962), p. 30.

[8] The letter, dated August 19, 1921, is found in Karl Löwith, *Martin Heidegger and European Nihilism,* trans. Gary Steiner (New York: Columbia University Press, 1995), p. 235–39.

[9] Quoted by Kisiel in *Genesis,* p. 150.

[10] Otherwise unidentified page references in parentheses are to volume 60 of the *Gesamtausgabe* (GA).

an overwhelming preoccupation, not with the proper nature of theology, but rather, in keeping with GA 56/57, *Zur Bestimmung der Philosophie*, GA 58, *Grundprobleme der Phänomenologie*, and GA 59, *Phänomenologie der Anschauung und des Ausdrucks: Theorie der philosophischen Begriffsbildung*, with the true meaning of philosophy. The theme that thunders through the opening lectures of IPR like the timpani strokes at the opening of Brahms's first symphony is not "Theology is not speculative knowledge of God," but "Philosophy is not a science" (pp. 8–10, 15, 27, 29, 35). It is philosophy that Heidegger wants to rescue from onto-theology, not because philosophy has a place for God but because it approaches God—and everything else, for that matter—in the wrong way. His concern is to discover what it means for philosophy to be phenomenology *rather than science*.

The result is a sustained and massive assault on the stranglehold of the theoretical posture on philosophy. Stated in its simplest form the argument is this: Religious life is typical of life in general, and, since neither is in the first instance a theoretical posture, neither can be adequately grasped as the object of a theorizing subject. This means a decisive break with two of the deepest sources of Heidegger's philosophical inspiration, Husserl and Dilthey. If philosophy is not a science, then surely it is not *strenge Wissenschaft*. The primacy of the theoretical, of objectifying acts (judgments), which Husserl posits in his *Logical Investigations*, the text with which Heidegger was most concerned, and reaffirms in *Ideas*, is the very opposite of a phenomenological insight.[11] No part of *Being and Time* is adumbrated more strongly in the religion courses than ¶33, "Assertion [Judgment] as a Derivative Mode of Interpretation."

At the same time, while life replaces consciousness as the central theme of phenomenology, there is a decisive break with both the positivistic and the Hegelian Dilthey. In the former mode,

---

[11] See Husserl's approval of Brentano's claim that all mental phenomena "are either presentations [*Vorstellungen*] or founded upon presentations"; *Logical Investigations*, trans. J. N. Findlay (New York: Humanities, 1970), p. 556. Cf. pp. 636–40 and 648–51, and *Ideas Pertaining to a Pure Phenomenology and to a Phenomenological Philosophy, First Book*, trans. F. Kersten (The Hague: Martinus Nijhoff, 1983), ¶¶116–21. In his Jaspers review Heidegger calls *Logical Investigations* "a phenomenology of the theoretical logos" (GA 9, p. 35 = *Wegmarken*).

philosophy is a *Methodenlehre* for the *Geisteswissenschaften,* which are to attain objective knowledge by means of *Verstehen.* In the Hegelian mode, philosophy itself is the objective understanding of various historically distinct forms of life and the queen of the *Geisteswissenschaften.* But both versions of Dilthey are preoccupied with the attainment of scientific objectivity in the face of historical relativism. The religion courses will lay the foundation for the rejection (≠ refutation) of this kind of skepticism in WS 1921–22. Philosophy is indeed a radical questioning, but "theoretical skepticism within the theoretical domain as a skeptical assertion about the theoretical domain from within that domain" is "not suited for authentic questioning" (GA 61, p. 197; cf. GA 60, p. 165).[12]

Of Heidegger's primary philosophical mentors during this time, it is Kierkegaard who comes to the fore. Philosophy is indeed reflection and not the immediacy of life, which Heidegger now calls factical life experience or, simply, factical life. But the goal is not to reflect oneself out of the subjectivity of one's embedded involvement in the world (as *Umwelt, Mitwelt,* and *Selbstwelt*) so as to become objective, but by means of reflection to awaken oneself from the everyday complacency of worldly life to a full realization of its difficulty and challenge. Philosophy could be science only if it became a worldless ego in possession of eternal (*überzeitlich*) truths (pp. 15, 35). But factical life experience, as a worldly temporality that is not to be construed fundamentally as knowing (p. 9), is both its point of departure and its goal (p. 15). If phenomenology is to be the hermeneutics of facticity in general, the genitive is subjective and not just objective, for "hermeneutics is factical life caught in the act, vigilantly caught in the act of interpreting itself. . . . [F]actical life does the interpreting as well as the living."[13] Thus, to take the case of religious life, theology has the life of faith as both its presupposition and its purpose.

The impetus toward scientific objectivity is just one of the ways factical life seeks to secure itself against the uneasiness

---

[12] Cf. Heidegger's rejection of the debate over the reality of the external world in *Being and Time,* ¶43.

[13] David Farrell Krell in *Reading Heidegger from the Start,* pp. 364–65.

(*Beunruhigung*) of historical existence (pp. 45–65; cf. pp. 9, 17–18). Far from having a special privilege, as Platonists like Husserl and Dilthey assume, this posture fails to open access to the things themselves. In objectifying history it negates history, and in finding historical context for troubled life (*das bekümmerte Leben*) it manages to overlook its significance (p. 51). As Heidegger had already made clear in his Jaspers review,[14] psychologism and historicism are dangerous, not as relativism but as objectivism.

Accordingly, it is the task of phenomenology to free philosophy from both the metaphysical and the epistemological concerns that are driven by the assumption that objectivity is our highest calling. The debates over realism and idealism (p. 13) fade away when we realize that prior to a motivated but misleading abstraction, we do not experience ourselves as subjects making 'S is P' judgments about objects, but as factical, that is, historical life in a threefold world that can be summarized, not as a manifold of objects, but as *Bedeutsamkeit* (pp. 11–16). One would be tempted to say that the world is in the first instance not fact but value, if the concept of value had not already been distorted into the object of theory from Plato to neo-Kantianism (p. 16).

Against the background of this assault on the primacy of theory, judgment, and objectification, methodological considerations about formal indication as the proper mode of phenomenological concept formation and an intensive reading of the Pauline epistles, especially 1 and 2 Thessalonians, are the foci around which IPR forms an ellipse.

In the attempt to reinvent phenomenology in order fully to realize its radical potential, Heidegger is preoccupied with questions of method. He canceled MM in order to devote himself single-mindedly to such questions in his first "Basic Problems" course. It is just as well. On the basis of the notes he prepared for MM it is fair to assume that students coming to learn about medieval mysticism would have been disappointed to find themselves mired in abstract attempts to answer the question What is philosophy? That, indeed, is just what happened a year

---

[14] See n. 11.

later in IPR. The students complained, apparently to the dean, that there was nothing about religion in the course. So Heidegger had to break off his methodological reflections and turn to the reading of the Pauline epistles. He began with Galatians, but no sooner had he begun (pp. 67–74) than he returned to questions of method (pp. 75–86), and he began his expositions of 1 Thessalonians with more of the same (pp. 87–92).

If phenomenology as the hermeneutics of facticity is neither the immediacy of life nor scientific concept formation, what is it? In a word (or two): formal indication.[15] The presupposition of this methodological move is Heidegger's revision of Husserl's notion of intentionality. Husserl distinguishes two modes of meaning: empty intentions, such as memory or imagination, to which intuited presence does not belong, and fulfilled intentions, such as perception, in which the intended "object" is present to intuition. Heidegger speaks of sense in three dimensions: *Gehaltssinn,* or content sense; *Bezugssinn,* or relational sense; and *Vollzugssinn,* or enactment/fulfillment sense. The distinction between *Gehalt* and *Bezug* is (almost) the familiar Husserlian distinction between the content of an intentional experience (a red barn) and the mode of intentional relation to it (perception, memory, imagination, etc.). *Vollzug* hints at the Husserlian distinction between empty and full or fulfilled intentions. But in keeping with the challenge to the primacy of the theoretical posture, perception is not the model, so fulfillment is not the presence of the content to an observer but an execution, actualization, or enactment by an agent. Perception or intuition would be a particular, somewhat thin, mode of enactment. But because it is not a privileged mode, enactment has a temporal sense as a process rather than as a present moment. Whereas fulfillment is an achievement word for Husserl, it is a task word for Heidegger.

Equally important is the Kierkegaardian twist this triple schema is given. *Gehaltssinn* obviously concerns the What of experience. But Heidegger, echoing Johannes Climacus, insists that

---

[15] Kisiel argues that this notion, which goes back to KNS 1919, is the heart and soul of early Heidegger, including *Being and Time.* See *Genesis,* pp. 152, 172, and 218, and *Reading Heidegger from the Start,* p. 177.

both of the other two dimensions of meaning concern its How (p. 63; cf. pp. 110–11). Accordingly, his reading of the Pauline epistles maintains a constant focus on the How of the life of faith (pp. 72, 80, 82–83, 88, 99, 101–4, 106, 116–21, 124).[16] In this connection the question of motivation is always on the table.

Husserl's distinction between formalizing and generalizing is virtually useless in spelling out the meaning of formal indication for the simple reason that it remains mired in the prejudice of theory. For him as for so much of the tradition, the move to the universal is oriented toward transforming experience into science. In the process the emphasis falls on the *Was* of experience and the *Wie* (including both temporality and motivation) is overlooked (pp. 57–63). Accordingly, formal indication is not the attempt to render the What intelligible by moving to higher and higher levels of abstraction; it rather shifts attention entirely away from the What to the How.

Since the How is neutral with respect to the What of experience, formal indication avoids preconceived ideas that prematurely absolutize what turns out to be only relative (p. 55). Over against the tendency of factical life to fall into the current modes of objectivity, worldviews as ideologies, formal indication seeks to keep fundamental questions open, most especially about the temporality of life, which is falsified by objectivity (pp. 64–65). While remaining worldview neutral, phenomenological philosophy provides a way of access (*Weg des Zugangs*, cf. pp. 305–10) to prereflective experience. Anticipating his own later formulations of the hermeneutical circle, Heidegger argues that (1) it is the task of phenomenology to free philosophy from the prejudice of the primacy of theory, and (2) from the prejudice of uncritically absolutized worldviews, but (3) so far is the goal from being the elimination of all pre-understandings, that it is the task of formal indication with its concern for proper access to phenomena to help us find the right anticipation (*Vorgriff*) (p. 78).

---

[16] When Heidegger shortly turns his attention to Aristotle, the emphasis on the How remains equally strong. See "Phenomenological Interpretations with Respect to Aristotle: Indication of the Hermeneutical Situation," trans. Michael Baur, *Man and World* 25 (1992), pp. 355–93. As late as 1924, in the lecture *The Concept of Time*, trans. William McNeill (Oxford: Blackwell, 1992), the same is true.

We have already noted the emergence of Kierkegaard over Husserl and Dilthey as Heidegger's philosophical mentor. In formal indication as the shift of attention from *Gehaltssinn* to *Bezugssinn* and *Vollzugssinn*, construed as a move from the What to the How of experience, it is impossible not to hear echoes of Johannes Climacus's distinction of objectivity from subjectivity in just those terms. And when, in his reading of the Pauline epistles, Heidegger will focus on the strenuousness of existence before God, the echoes are even louder. So it is not surprising that formal indication should be assimilated to indirect communication. Van Buren introduces the comparison in the context of the Lutheran humility about what the believer does not (yet) possess. As described a year later than IPR (in GA 61), formal indication does not provide "a comfortable metaphysical island high above the flux, but rather these indications are only like rough provisional maps that make the individual thinker ready to leap. . . . Heidegger's formal indications are really questions indirectly communicated to others for their own quests and adventures toward the ever elusive things themselves." What matters is not his insights but their response.[17]

In a similar vein, Otto Pöggeler makes the comparison with indirect communication by noting that what is formally indicated is "in the first place, the *region* to which something belongs. . . . This means, secondly, that the matter indicated need not present itself in theoretical evidence; rather, the formal indication points to a *decision* (for example, a decision of faith) which itself remains outside thinking [as theory]."[18] The whole point of the distinction between objectivity and subjectivity, in whose service Climacus places indirect communication, is to locate the proper region for God talk so that the necessity of decision will not be politely overlooked in what he likes to call a world historical fit of absent-mindedness.

There is an important difference, however. Climacus recog-

---

[17] John van Buren, "The Ethics of *Formale Anzeige* in Heidegger," *American Catholic Philosophical Quarterly* LXIX (spring 1995), pp. 158, 167–68. Heidegger's comments on Kierkegaard at the end of his Jaspers review are interesting in this connection. See GA 9, pp. 41–43.

[18] Otto Pöggeler, in *Reading Heidegger from the Start*, pp. 140–42. Emphasis added.

nizes that Socratic Religiousness A and Christian Religiousness B take place in the same region, a region of decision unsecured by certainty and presence, by comparison with the speculative postures of Plato and Hegel. But he also insists on the radical difference between A as religious immanence and B as religious transcendence, precisely because he insists that the How of existence is inseparable from its What. It is the *Gehaltssinn* of Christianity that makes its *Bezugssinn* and *Vollzugssinn* so decisively different from anything found in ancient Greece. By contrast, Heidegger, who turns to the life world of Aristotelian ethics after exploring that of the Pauline epistles, is formal to the point of erasing the difference between the two. He fails to remark, as Caputo puts it, that "the biblical narratives are not at all oriented to the *phronimos*," that while Aristotle's was "a hermeneutics of the best and the brightest," it was "of just these well-to-do, respectable gentlemen that the biblical experience of life was most suspicious."[19]

The ambiguous character of Heidegger's separation of content from form can also be seen in its link to the methodological atheism of phenomenology. It is not until WS 1921–22 that Heidegger explicitly describes philosophy as "a-theistic in principle" (GA 61, pp. 196–97). Whereas he at first speaks simply of philosophy's *Atheismus*, three factors make it clear that this is a methodological and not a substantive atheism. First, in a second reference he describes philosophy as "*a-theistisch* in principle." Given the sustained critique of the theoretical posture, the hyphen makes the claim that philosophy is not-theistic echo both his earlier claim that it is worldview neutral (as distinct from both theism and atheism) and Climacus's claim that Christianity is not primarily a doctrine. Second, the two references to philosophy's atheism are embedded in notes about philosophy as skepticism, not as a dogma but as a posture of radical questioning (GA 61, pp. 196–98), echoing once again the claim in IPR that it is worldview neutral. Finally, Heidegger writes, "The questioning posture [*Fraglichkeit*] is not religious, but may nevertheless first lead into the situation of religious decision. I am not religious insofar as I philosophize, but as a philosopher I can

---

[19] *Demythologizing Heidegger*, pp. 62–63 in relation to p. 51.

also be a religious person. The trick [in that case] is to philo-
phize and thereby to be authentically religious" (GA 61, p. 197).

This triply methodological character of philosophy's atheism
has a Kierkegaardian rather than Nietzschean character (as it
indeed grows out of a period of intense reading of Kierkegaard
prior to the immersion in Nietzsche in the thirties). It echoes the
claim of Climacus's that he is not a Christian, though he seems
obsessed with rescuing Christianity from Hegel and all other
speculative thinkers. For him it is not a matter of affirming,
much less arguing for, Christianity, but rather of finding the
right region for any possible encounter with its claims. Seen in
this light, Heidegger's WS 1921–22 claim that philosophy is a-
theistic in principle is only a bold rhetorical reaffirmation of
what he had been saying all along, including the previous year
in IPR, about phenomenology as formal indication.

Heidegger will repeat that this notion of philosophy is atheistic.[20] Taken together with the notion that it is the right of philosophy to "correct" theology,[21] this claim will evoke a protest from
Jean-Luc Marion that Heideggerian philosophy is a form of intellectual imperialism. From a theological point of view, the impo-
sition of a philosophical a priori on our God talk is idolatrous
since it requires that God fit into categories developed atheisti-
cally, that is, without reference to God.[22]

The issue is too complex to be treated adequately here, but if
we read Heidegger's later declarations of philosophy's atheism
in the light of his 1919–23 Freiburg lectures, it is clear what his
basic line of defense will be. First, phenomenology does not
"correct" theology by dictating to the latter what its content
must be. Like Kierkegaard, it only "corrects" theology when it
wanders from its proper region (existence sphere or stage) to
become speculative theory, thereby cutting its link to preaching

---

[20] In "Phenomenological Interpretations with Respect to Aristotle," p. 367; in
History of the Concept of Time: Prolegomena, trans. Theodore Kisiel (Bloomington:
Indiana University Press, 1985), pp. 79–80 (GA 20, pp. 109–10); and in *The
Metaphysical Foundations of Logic,* trans. Michael Heim (Bloomington: Indiana
University Press, 1984), p. 140 (GA 26, p. 177). Cf. *The Concept of Time,* p. 1E,
"The philosopher does not believe."

[21] "Phenomenology and Theology," pp. 19–20.

[22] *God without Being,* trans. Thomas A. Carlson (Chicago: University of Chicago Press, 1991), chs. 2–3.

and thereby to the practice of faith. Second, phenomenology's notion of the proper region for theology is a priori in the sense of being prior to any specific theological claims. But it is not imposed from without. For Kierkegaard this concern is theologically motivated. In the case of Heidegger, who does not write (lecture) out of the same passionate faith commitment, the understanding of the proper region for God talk comes very largely from an intensive reading of the Pauline epistles and their *Wirkungsgeschichte* in such thinkers as Augustine, Luther, and Kierkegaard. Phenomenology and theology are linked by a kind of hermeneutical circularity.

Still, there is another way of reading these texts in which Heidegger looks less like Kierkegaard and more like those modern thinkers, *Aufklärer* like Lessing and Kant and romantics like the early Schleiermacher, who sought to make religion respectable to autonomous reason by separating the universal (natural, rational) kernel from the particular (confessional, dogmatic) husk. What are we to make of Caputo's suggestion that formal indication anticipates the program of demythologizing Heidegger would encounter in Bultmann when he moved to Marburg?[23] Or of the suggestions that the Heidegger of the twenties was but a secularized version of Luther or the New Testament?[24] Does phenomenology as formal indication slide down the slippery slope from methodological atheism to become a vaguely, and thus inoffensively, Christian worldview of its own? Is this the meaning of the report to Löwith, "I am a Christian theo*logian*"?

Later, when resisting the existentialist reading of *Being and Time,* Heidegger would say, in effect, "My phenomenology, unlike Sartre's, is not a Nietzschean, anti-Christian worldview. I am up to something quite different." We have already noticed the resources he has for making a similar claim about his early Freiburg lectures. But has he fully freed himself from the project, stretching from deism to demythologizing, that Dilthey expressed so clearly when he wrote to Count Yorck, "If the dogmas . . . are untenable in their restriction to the facts of Christian history, then in their universal sense they express the highest

---

[23] *Demythologizing Heidegger*, p. 10.
[24] See van Buren, *The Young Heidegger,* pp. 150 and 152.

living content of all history"?[25] Just as it is all but impossible not to read the distinction in "Phenomenology and Theology" between phenomenology as an ontological science and theology as an ontic science as a distinction between the deep and the superficial, the essential and the optional, so it is hard not to read the Freiburg lectures, including IPR, as implying the claim that phenomenology, as formal indication, puts us in touch with what is most important in the epistles of Paul and the theologies of Augustine and Luther. We do not find ourselves tempted in this way by Climacus, who never suggests that subjectivity is more profound than the Incarnation. He would never describe himself, as Heidegger does in IPR, as looking for the *Ewigkeits-wert* of early Christian eschatological notions that are manifestly *zeitgeschichtlich bestimmt* (p. 110).

If we turn our attention from formal indication to Heidegger's other focus, the reading of the Pauline epistles, which we have already anticipated, this issue does not entirely disappear. The official task is to understand the factical life experience of the early Christians by a kind of transcendental analysis, discovering formal conditions for the possibility of that experience that are not tied to its specific content but could be actualized in non-Christian modes of experience. (Why, then, the focus on Christian experience? Because we can only think "out of our own historical situation and facticity. . . . *Es gibt nur eine Geschichte aus einer Gegenwart heraus*" [pp. 124–25]. Again the hermeneutical circle.)

Heidegger's focus is on the expectation of the *parousia*, the second coming of Christ, in the epistles to the Thessalonians and on the way this hope challenges the complacency of everyday factical life. On the one hand, "They say" peace and security, "but you" are called to "keep awake and be sober" (p. 103; 1 Thess. 5:3–8). This is why, when the Thessalonians "turned to God from idols to serve a living and true God, and to wait for his Son from heaven" (1 Thess. 1:9–10), this involved an "absolute reversal" (p. 95). Noting that Paul's letters (as if inspired by Climacus) always make life harder rather than easier (pp. 107–8, 112, 120–21), Heidegger stresses the strenuousness of Christian

---

[25] Quoted by van Buren in ibid., p. 152.

life as *Bedrängnis, Leiden, Not, Trübsal*, and *ungeheure Schwierigkeit* (pp. 98, 100, 109, 111, 120–21, 124).

As phenomenologists, however, we neither become caught up in eschatological fervor nor become historians of chiliasm. "We leave the content completely aside" (p. 116) in order to indicate formally the meaning of Christian factical life. We discover just how formal formal indication can be when Heidegger tells us three times what the upshot of his Pauline studies is: "Christian religiosity lives temporality as such" (pp. 80, 104, 116). Everything specifically Christian has disappeared, as it is supposed to in formal indication, and we are on our way to *Being and Time,* where death will replace the second coming of Christ as the future that will certainly come (but at a time uncertain) and whose coming calls us out of complacent everydayness.

But is Heidegger simply playing the game by his own clearly announced rules? He tells us that Christian expectation is not ordinary expectation. One reason is that the When of the eschaton is not available to knowledge (p. 102). But that only means that it is more like waiting for the end of the war, whose conclusion we cannot predict, than like waiting for Christmas, when we know exactly how many shopping days are left. Another reason is that Christian expectation involves serving God, so that "each stands alone before God" (p. 112). No reader of Kierkegaard will underestimate the weightiness of such a situation. But even if awaiting the coming of God has an ultimacy that awaiting the soldier's return from war does not have, does it warrant the claim that we are dealing with a future (like death in *Being and Time*) that will never be present, that Christian expectation concerns only my present tasks before God *and not* a future event for which I long and which I expect some day to experience (pp. 114, 117)?[26]

There is a double problem here. First, there is a non sequitur. In order for Christian hope to motivate believers to "keep awake and be sober" today, it is not necessary to eliminate their belief that Christ will actually return on some tomorrow. As any child can tell us, even the coming of Santa Claus, whose arrival time can be known quite precisely, can motivate strenuous behavior.

---

[26] See Sheehan's summary, "Heidegger's 'Introduction,' " pp. 321–22.

"You'd better watch out. You'd better not cry. You'd better not pout. I'm telling you why. Santa Claus is coming to town." Second, this either/or (it is either about now or about some future event), which is false in itself, is entirely foreign to the texts Heidegger is reading; and he is methodologically committed, not to strong misreading, but to letting the text show itself from itself. The nagging suspicion is that an interpreter who was not guided by an agenda, a worldview if you like, quite different from and even hostile to Christian faith would not find it necessary to impose this either/or and deny that early Christian hope was the awaiting of a future event, however indefinite both its When and its What might be. Here it looks as if formal indication "corrects" theology's *Gehaltssinn*, anticipating Bultmann by insisting on an "existentialist" understanding of the *parousia* rather than an historical understanding. No one familiar with the debates set off by Bultmann's demythologized, existential theology can deny that the issues are substantive and not merely formal. Perhaps if Heidegger had taken his own emerging understanding of the hermeneutical circle more seriously he would have been less optimistic about the possibility of a content neutral formal indication. When he asks Jaspers "how far formal considerations prejudice the observation of concrete material" (GA 9, p. 27; cf. p. 42), his question comes back to haunt him.

It will be necessary to be brief about the Augustine course. In it Heidegger gives a double reading that seeks to rescue a Pauline, "Protestant" Augustine from a Plotinian, "Catholic" Augustine. Put slightly differently, Heidegger explores a tradition that runs from Augustine through Luther to Kierkegaard and includes the medieval mystics and that resists the onto-theological synthesis of early Christianity with either Plato or Aristotle (p. 159; cf. GA 58, p. 205; GA 9, p. 6).

At the same time he seeks to rescue Augustine from the historical objectivism of such modern readers as Troeltsch, Harnack, and Dilthey. The goal is to understand Augustinian subjectivity, which is sharply to be distinguished from Cartesian subjectivity, since the latter is but the flip side of the objectivism that hides the difficulty of factical life (pp. 298–99; cf. GA 58, p. 205).

The Augustinian subjectivity Heidegger seeks to rescue from both ancient metaphysics and modern historicism is the enactment of an understanding of life as *cura* (care, disquiet), as *ten-tatio* (trial), and as *molestia* (dissatisfaction). Factical life is "Bekümmerung um das *Sein* seiner selbst" (p. 245) or "radikale Selbstbekümmerung vor Gott" (p. 242). In Heidegger's droll summary, Augustine makes it clear "dass das 'Leben' kein Spaziergang ist" (205). It is important to recognize that these accounts come from a reading of Book X of the *Confessions*, where Augustine speaks not of the journey to conversion and faith but of the life of faith itself. The one who asks, "But what do I love when I love my God?" (ch. 6) and then "What, then, am I, my God? What is my nature?" (ch. 17), concluding "quaestio mihi factus sum" (ch. 33) is a believing soul, and indeed a bishop.

And yet, Heidegger thinks, Augustine opens himself to an invasion of Greek thinking that undermines this unrest when (1) he acknowledges his desire for the blessed life (*beata vita*), (2) he invokes the distinction between *uti* and *frui* (use and enjoyment) in this connection, suggesting an end to striving, and (3) he identifies the God of the blessed life with the highest truth, beauty, and goodness, suggesting an essentially contemplative relation. In doing so he succumbs to the fatal onto-theological interpretation of Romans 1:20 that had been the Trojan horse in which Greek theory had breached the walls of Christian factical life (pp. 264, 281).

Perhaps there are places where Plotinus crowds out Paul in Augustine's thought; but this is not one of them. It is true, his restless heart yearns for rest, but the eschatological motif is too strong to permit him to import it into this life in any mode more than partial and anticipatory, like the Pauline joy in the midst of suffering. He is consistently clear that the *beata vita* for which he longs is to be found in the life to come and not in the here and now. For Heidegger to begrudge him this hope is equivalent to saying that the only courageous soldier is the one without hope that the war will end, that the only way to be serious about the difficulty of factical life is to assume that it is the truth not only about time but about eternity as well. But surely this would be to allow what is supposed to be formal indication to dictate an essentially Nietzschean content to Christian faith.

Further, it is far from clear that Augustine's reading of Ro-

mans 1:20 is an onto-theological reading. For Paul, the point of
the claim that the invisible nature of God can be clearly seen in
the things God has made is not that philosophy's dream of total
intelligibility is possible but that idolatry is without excuse. Similarly, when Augustine invokes Romans 1:20 in *De Doctrina
Christiana*, a locus classicus (repeatedly cited by Heidegger) for
the distinction between using the world and enjoying God, the
point of the ascent from created things to their Creator is not
that thought can achieve its desired universality by means of
what is highest but rather that it would be foolish for us to seek
our happiness in anything lower than "that God of gods . . .
than which there is nothing better or more sublime."[27] The text
functions, for Augustine, to call us from our fallen absorption in
the good things of the world (a central theme of *Confessions*,
Book X), to the strenuous task of seeking a happiness beyond
the limited and temporary happiness they can provide.

Perhaps it is a *felix culpa* that Heidegger misreads Augustine
here. For it leads him to appeal to Luther's quite unambiguous
repudiation both of the synthesis of Greek philosophy with the
gospel of grace and of the reading of Romans 1:20 on which it is
based. Indeed, it is precisely to save Augustine from himself, as
Heidegger sees it, that he draws on his intensive reading of Luther in AN (pp. 67–68, 97, 281–82; cf. pp. 308–10 in MM). There
is something quite wonder-ful in seeing a philosopher who insists on the a-theistic character of philosophy appealing to perhaps the most vigorously anti-philosophical theologian prior to
Karl Barth to help him get straight about the right path for philosophy. But when we notice how Heidegger seeks to appropriate the anti-scholastic polemic of Luther's early commentaries
on Romans (1515–16) and Galatians (1519), along with the distinction between the theology of glory and the theology of the
cross from the Heidelberg Disputation of 1518, we understand
more fully how he could tell his hearers in IPR that while phenomenology is not theology, it opens a new way for theology (p.
67). First the theologies of Paul, Augustine, and Luther play a
key role in challenging philosophy's traditional flight from the

---

[27] Augustine, *Teaching Christianity*, trans. Edmund Hill, O.P. (Hyde Park, N.Y.:
New City Press, 1996), vol. I, pp. 3–7.

earth of factical life to the ether of pure theory; then the resultant phenomenological, a-theistic philosophy serves as a guide and prod to contemporary theology to remain faithful to its biblical origins and not sell its soul to Greek gazing. The goal of this circular relationship between theology and philosophy is to destroy by deconstructing the tendencies of both theology and philosophy to fall into onto-theological discourse, the *Gerede* of the learned.[28]

---

[28] I am indebted to John van Buren for helpful comments on an earlier draft of this essay.

3

Hermeneutics As Epistemology

Now no more useful inquiry can be proposed than that which seeks to determine the nature and scope of human knowledge. . . . Neither ought it to seem such a toilsome and difficult matter to define the limits of [human] understanding.

Descartes[1]

For I thought that the first step toward satisfying several inquiries the mind of man was very apt to run into, was to take a survey of our own understandings, examine our own powers, and see to what things they were adapted. . . . Whereas, were the capacities of our understandings well considered, the extent of our knowledge once discovered, the horizon found which sets the bounds between the enlightened and dark parts of things; between what is and what is not comprehensible by us, men would perhaps with less scruple acquiesce in the avowed ignorance of the one, and employ their thoughts and discourse with more advantage and satisfaction in the other.

Locke[2]

I know no inquiries which are more important for exploring the faculty which we entitle understanding, and for determining the rules and limits of its employment, than those which I have instituted.

Kant[3]

---

[1] *Rules for the Direction of the Mind,* in *The Philosophical Works of Descartes,* trans. Haldane and Ross (New York: Dover Publications, 1955), vol. I, p. 26 (discussion of Rule 8).

[2] *An Essay Concerning Human Understanding* (New York: Dover Publications, 1959), vol. I, p. 31 (introduction, section 7).

[3] *Critique of Pure Reason,* trans. Norman Kemp Smith (New York: St. Martin's Press, 1961), A xvi.

RICHARD RORTY ANNOUNCES the end of epistemology in part 3 of *Philosophy and the Mirror of Nature*, entitled "From Epistemology to Hermeneutics." He makes it clear that he is not offering, with help from Quine and Sellars, a new and better epistemology but a complete abandonment of the whole idea of a theory of knowledge, for which no legitimate task can be identified.[4]

What Rorty repudiates as epistemology he associates strongly with Descartes, Locke, and Kant. As is clear from the above citations, the three of them contribute toward identifying epistemology with the broad, generic task of reflecting on the nature and limits of human knowledge. It is entirely unclear why Rorty identifies as epistemology not this generic task but certain features of the specific way these three and others go about it; ultimately this identification is seriously misleading.

Among the most important of the specific notions that Rorty identifies with epistemology are the following:

- The notion of knowledge as accurate representation, as correspondence. It is here that the "mirror of nature" image plays its role.
- The demand for certainty in knowledge.
- The notion of epistemology as a neutral, a priori tribunal whose task is to show how to achieve the desired apodicticity of accurate representation.
- The special role of privileged representations as providing the foundations of knowledge so construed. Sellars's critique of the myth of the given and Quine's argument for the contingency of necessity, along with Kuhnian philosophy of science and its argument against the possibility of theory free data—these are all attacks on the notion of "representations which cannot be gainsaid."[5]

It is clear that where Rorty says "epistemology" one might just as well say "modernity" or, to be more precise, "the Enlightenment project" or, to be still more precise, "foundationalism."[6]

---

[4] Richard Rorty, *Philosophy and the Mirror of Nature* (Princeton: Princeton University Press, 1979), pp. 10, 180, 210, and 315.

[5] Ibid., p. 315.

[6] By 'foundationalism' I shall always mean the strong variety that requires foundational apodicticity from privileged representations "which cannot be gainsaid." See n. 9.

Over against the foundationalist epistemologies of modernity, whose twentieth-century paradigms are to be found in Russell's knowledge by acquaintance and Husserl's intuition of essences, Rorty offers a paradigm shift to an understanding of understanding that he calls hermeneutics. It is holistic, historicist, and pragmatic; it construes truth as conversational agreement, rationality as practical, self-corrective capacity, and intuition as linguistic capacity.

But hermeneutics, so conceived, is a reflection on the nature and limits of human knowledge; for it is no longer limited to the interpretation of texts but interprets all cognition as interpretation. In terms of the nature of knowledge, it emphasizes the embeddedness of knowledge in historically particular and contingent vocabularies (Rorty calls them "optional"); in terms of the limits of knowledge, it emphasizes our inability to transcend that embeddedness in order to become pure reason or absolute knowledge or rigorous science. In other words, *hermeneutics is epistemology*, generically construed. It is a species diametrically opposed to foundationalist epistemologies, but it belongs to the same genus precisely because like them it is a meta-theory about how we should understand the cognitive claims of common sense, of the natural and social sciences, and even of metaphysics and theology. By failing to distinguish the generic epistemological task from the specifically modern foundationalist projects, Rorty obscures the fact that hermeneutics is not the replacement of epistemology as such but the replacement of one type of epistemology with another.

The issue of self-reference arises here. Especially because Rorty denies that epistemological reflection can occur in a privileged space prior to that of first-order knowing and immune from the conditions of the latter, hermeneutics must be understood to be a theory about itself and not just about various kinds of first-order knowing. If hermeneutics presents itself as a particular language game whose truth consists not in accurate representation but in conversational agreement, it is hard to see how it falls immediately into performative or self-referential contradiction.

But isn't hermeneutics hopelessly relativistic? Yes and No. As already noted, hermeneutical historicism offers no hope that we can escape from the particular and contingent life world or language game to which our beliefs are relative into anything other than another particularity and contingency. Against Cartesian foundationalism it denies that we can start at some Alpha point from which it is possible to view the world *sub specie aeternitatis;* and against Hegelian holism it denies that we can achieve this same goal by arriving at some Omega point of transubstantiation in which the totality of particularity becomes universality and the totality of contingency becomes necessity.

Still, Rorty is not content to leave us with a "these language games are played" relativism. Hermeneutical understanding is needed not merely to illuminate conversations occurring within a given paradigm but especially to highlight the conditions under which conversations between apparently incommensurable paradigms can occur.[7] Hermeneutical "arguments" will not be foundationally constructed, but will be conversational attempts to generate anomalies for other paradigms. To say that this is a matter of rhetoric rather than of logic is simply to say that there is no neutral language game in which the conversation can be played.

Rorty is not the theme of this essay. My assignment is to discuss epistemological currents in continental philosophy, and I have chosen to do so by focusing on hermeneutical themes in Heidegger and then, briefly, on their "right-wing" development in Gadamer and their "left-wing" development in Derrida. Rorty serves as a useful introduction for two reasons:

1. By presenting hermeneutics as an alternative to epistemology he makes it easy to specify the sense in which it is rather an alternative epistemology. To repeat, *hermeneutics is epistemology.*[8]

2. Since the search for alternatives to foundationalism (in the strong sense that requires privileged representations to give security to the foundations and thus the whole edifice of knowledge) is widespread outside continental philosophy,[9] and since

---

[7] Rorty, *Philosophy and the Mirror of Nature,* p. 347.

[8] This is not to say that it is *only* epistemology or that for any given thinker it is *primarily* epistemology.

[9] For example, in his critique of classical foundationalism, Alvin Plantinga identifies three types of privileged representations: "The only properly basic propositions [according to classical foundationalism] are those that are self-evident or incorrigible or evident to the senses." Quine's critique of necessity

Rorty himself draws heavily not only on Heidegger but also on Wittgenstein, Dewey, Quine, Sellars, and Kuhn, starting with him points to the common problematic that runs through many different philosophical traditions, methodologies, and vocabularies. If the Enlightenment project is quintessentially modern, then not only is Gadamer as "postmodern" as Derrida, but analytic philosophy in many of its current forms is as "postmodern" as contemporary continental philosophy. As I turn to Heidegger, Gadamer, and Derrida, I hope to have given at least initial plausibility to the claim that although they do not describe themselves as epistemologists, they are addressing some of the same large questions discussed by those who do.

Heidegger's account of the hermeneutical circle at work in all understanding is a critique of "the myth of the given" and a repudiation of foundationalist epistemologies. It is not that Heidegger denies that knowledge has foundations; it is just that the kinds of foundations he discovers render the ideals of foundationalist epistemologies futile.

Originally the hermeneutical circle had to do with interpreting texts. One comes to a text with a sense of the whole (this is a poetic tragedy, this is a historical narrative) that guides the interpretation of specific passages. But the understanding of the whole is revised in the light of specific readings. At the very least, it becomes more specific and precise. But it may be modified quite dramatically. What at first seemed to be a children's story may turn out to be a political satire or a theological reflection, and an apparent historical narrative may turn out to be a hoax of some sort. What makes the relation circular is the fact that neither one's sense of the whole nor one's reading of the parts is an independent variable. X is (at least in part) a function of Y and vice versa.

We are familiar with such circles in postpositivist philosophy of science. Theories, of course, are supposed to be dependent upon observational data. But suppose there are no theory-free

---

addresses the first of these, while Sellars's attack on the given addresses the other two. See "Reason and Belief in God," in *Faith and Rationality: Reason and Belief in God*, ed. Alvin Plantinga and Nicholas Wolterstorff (Notre Dame, Ind.: University of Notre Dame Press, 1983), p. 59. See n. 6.

data because, as Hanson writes, "There is a sense, then, in which seeing is a 'theory-laden' undertaking. Observation of x is shaped by prior knowledge of x."[10] In that case the relation between theories and the data that suggest and confirm them would be circular. Each could be modified in light of the other.

This same circle is at work in what Rawls calls reflective equilibrium in ethical theory. We try to formulate general principles that will account for our firmest considered convictions about particular (types of) situations. These convictions are only "provisional fixed points" because "there is no point at which an appeal is made to self-evidence in the traditional sense either of general concepts or particular convictions."[11] In case the theory under consideration conflicts with our pretheoretical convictions, we may either revise the theory or amend our convictions. Since neither general theory nor particular judgment is an independent variable, the relation between them is circular; each is subject to modification in the light of the other.

Like Hanson and Rawls, Heidegger gives us a revised Kantianism. The hermeneutical circle is Kantian because it stresses the role of the a priori in all cognition. Nothing is simply given, pure and unaffected by our receptive posture: "By showing how all sight is grounded primarily in understanding . . . we have deprived pure intuition of its priority. . . . 'Intuition' and 'thinking' are both derivatives of understanding, and already rather remote ones" (p. 187/147).[12] Every cognitive act presupposes a prior understanding of the matter at hand. Heidegger details this pre-understanding in terms of fore-having, fore-sight, and fore-conception (*Vorhabe, Vorsicht,* and *Vorgriff*), concluding, "In-

---

[10] N. R. Hanson, *Patterns of Discovery: An Inquiry into the Conceptual Foundations of Science* (Cambridge: Cambridge University Press, 1961), p. 19. It is worth noting that Hanson, drawing on Gestalt psychology and Wittgensteinian analyses of seeing-as, makes the point about seeing in general. Scientific observation is but one case in point.

[11] John Rawls, *A Theory of Justice* (Cambridge: Harvard University Press, 1971), pp. 20–21; cf. pp. 48–51.

[12] Passages from Heidegger's *Being and Time* will be cited by A/B references in the text. A stands for the translation by Macquarrie and Robinson (New York: Harper and Row, 1962). B stands for the pagination in the seventh German edition, given in the margins of Macquarrie and Robinson and the more recent translation of Joan Stambaugh (Albany: SUNY Press, 1996). I will sometimes use or draw on Stambaugh's renderings.

terpretation is never a presuppositionless grasping of something previously given. . . . Any interpretation which is to contribute understanding, must already have understood what is to be interpreted" (pp. 191–92, 194/150, 152).

But this is a revised Kantianism because, by speaking of the circular structure of understanding and interpretation, Heidegger makes it clear that the a priori elements do not have the fixed and final character Kant gave to the forms and categories.[13] They are not simply given any more than the interpretations they make possible. At the same time, by insisting that this circularity is not to be construed as vicious, Heidegger makes it clear that he is simply abandoning the Euclidian, syllogistic models of knowledge (pp. 194–95/152–53). Rather, we are to see in the circle "a positive possibility of the most primordial kind of knowing" (p. 195/153).

But Heidegger's account of the hermeneutical circle is a far more radical revision of the Kantian scheme and thus of the Enlightenment project than we have seen to this point. On his view the a priori elements in knowledge are not only corrigible but also pretheoretical. According to Hanson's formula, "Observation of x is shaped by prior *knowledge* of x," which means that all seeing is "*theory*-laden" (emphasis changed). But Heidegger thinks the deepest levels of pre-understanding do not consist of knowledge or belief or representation. For this reason his account of the hermeneutical circle in terms of fore-having, fore-sight, and fore-conception "includes, but goes beyond, the insight of theoretical holism that all data are already theory laden."[14] He signals this by presenting knowing as a "founded

---

[13] For a similar account of the a priori from the same decade as *Being and Time*, see C. I. Lewis, "A Pragmatic Conception of the A Priori" in *Readings in Philosophical Analysis*, ed. Herbert Feigl and Wilfrid Sellars (New York: Appleton-Century-Crofts, 1949). This essay anticipates major themes in Quine's "Two Dogmas of Empiricism" in *From a Logical Point of View* (New York: Harper and Row, 1963) as well as Rorty's joint appeal to Heidegger and American pragmatism.

[14] Hubert Dreyfus, "Holism and Hermeneutics," *Review of Metaphysics* XXXIV (1980–81), p. 10. Where Dreyfus says "theoretical holism," we can read "a theoretical interpretation of the hermeneutical circle." Like Rorty, Dreyfus links hermeneutics to holism at least in part because in the absence of either a fixed a priori form or a given empirical content for knowledge, the whole fabric of knowing is in question whenever one of its parts is in question.

mode" of being-in-the-world in ¶13 of *Being and Time,* and by entitling ¶33 "Assertion as a Derivative Mode of Interpretation." If knowing is "founded" and assertion is "derivative," theoretical cognition has precognitive presuppositions that can nevertheless be called understanding and interpretation.

There is a religious background to Heidegger's protest against the primacy of the theoretical that dominates so much of the philosophical tradition. His philosophy of religion lecture courses of 1920–21 are a sustained argument that the life of faith is not primarily a concern over the correctness of assertions.[15] He summarizes his findings in a lecture first given in 1927, the year *Being and Time* was published. After quoting Luther, "Faith is permitting ourselves to be seized by the things we do not see," he claims that faith "is not some more or less modified type of knowing" and that theology "is not speculative knowledge of God."[16]

But in *Being and Time* he makes a more general argument for the founded character of knowing and the derivative nature of assertion. It involves a double movement from the secondary to the primary: from theory to practice and from theory to affect. For Husserl, the phenomenological reduction abandons the natural standpoint of empirical consciousness in the midst of a surrounding real world. By bracketing the question of the relation of thought to reality, the phenomenologist is to focus on the ways in which the contents of consciousness, whatever their ontological status, are given to pure or transcendental consciousness, that is, consciousness that intends a world of which it is not a part. But for Heidegger the task is not a move from the natural standpoint to a realm of pure consciousness where presuppositionless, apodictic intuitions of essences can occur; it is a move from all theoretical postures (scientific, theological, philosophical, etc.), now understood as abstractions from primordial, everyday experience, back to the fullness of the natural stand-

---

[15] *Einleitung in die Phänomenologie der Religion* (WS 1920–21) and *Augustinus und der Neuplatonismus* (SS 1921) in *Gesamtausgabe* (GA), vol. 60, *Phänomenologie des religiösen Lebens* (Frankfurt: Klostermann, 1995). See chapter 2 of this volume.

[16] "Phenomenology and Theology," in *The Piety of Thinking,* trans. James G. Hart and John C. Maraldo (Bloomington: Indiana University Press, 1976), pp. 10 and 15.

point, or to be more precise, to a reflective understanding of the natural standpoint in all of its practical and affective concreteness.

Following a tradition that goes back to Plato and his own Orphic-Pythagorean religious roots, Husserl's reduction is a rite of purification. By contrast, Heidegger's reduction is a rite of repentance and conversion, turning away from the cult of such self-purification. The tradition we can call Platonic, though it has a wide variety of footnotes, is a kind of Gnostic or Manichean dualism that treats embeddedness, the epistemological form of embodiment, as intrinsically evil. Heidegger's theological analogue is the Jewish or Christian affirmation that embodiment, and thus embeddedness, is good because it is part of God's creation. It is a sign of our finitude, but it is not evil; and every attempt to flee that finitude is a self-defeating, Luciferian hybris that says, "I will make myself like the Most High" (Isa. 14:14).

Heideggerian hermeneutics is a three-story universe in which assertion is doubly derivative; it rests upon interpretation that in turn rests upon understanding. In attempting to understand what it means to say that both understanding and interpretation are more basic than assertion, we can deliberately adopt two hypotheses to serve as heuristic pre-understandings to guide us. In the process, of course, they will be put to the test.

The first will be the hypothesis that Heidegger seeks to dethrone the theoretical in the same way that speech act theory does. In Austinian language, making an assertion is performing a constative speech act, one whose raison d'être and primary virtue relate to the truth of falsity of what is said. But this is only one of the many things we can do with words, one of the many illocutionary acts we can perform by the locutionary acts of uttering or inscribing sentences. Others, such as promising, commanding, comforting, complaining, and so forth, have different rationales and can fail to be apt other than by being false.

Heidegger's account has obvious affinities with speech act theory. He speaks the language of assertion (*Aussage*) and judgment (*Urteil*) rather than the Platonizing language of proposition (*Satz*). The foundation of language (*Sprache* = *langue* = language as system) is discourse (*Rede* = *parole* = language in use) and not the reverse (p. 203/160). The logos (semantic field, intelligible space) to which he links assertion is an earthly and temporal logos rather than a heavenly and eternal one (pp. 195–96/153–54). Furthermore, he makes it equivalent to "categorical statement" and "theoretical judgment," and in doing so links it tightly to constative speech acts and thus to truth as correctness (pp. 196/154, 200/157).

But there is a crucial difference. Speech act theory challenges the primacy of theoretical reason by making assertion or the constative speech act just one of the many things we can do with words. Among many other illocutionary acts, which do not have correct information or accurate representation as their essential mission, assertion has no special privilege. At the same time, there is nothing in speech act theory to resist the Husserlian move that makes theoretical intentions primary and basic to all nontheoretical intentions.[17]

But such a resistance is explicitly present in Heidegger's account, precisely when he insists that assertion is "a derivative form in which an interpretation has been carried out" and that "in concernful circumspection there are no such assertions 'at first' [zunächst]. . . . Interpretation is carried out primordially [ursprünglich] not in a theoretical statement but in an action of circumspective concern—laying aside the unsuitable tool, or exchanging it, 'without wasting words'. From the fact that words are absent, it may not be concluded that interpretation is absent" (p. 200/157); for the interpretation is expressed in the action even in absence of any assertion. Assertion is not just one mode of interpretation among many; it is less basic than some mode of interpretation it presupposes.

Heidegger immediately (re)introduces his distinction between the ready-to-hand (Zuhandenheit) and the present-at-hand (Vor-

---

[17] See Husserl's Logical Investigations, trans. J. N. Findlay (New York: Humanities, 1970), pp. 556, 636–40, and 648–51. Heidegger appropriately calls Logical Investigations "a phenomenology of the theoretical logos" (GA 9 35 = Wegmarken). See also Ideas Pertaining to a Pure Phenomenology and to a Phenomenological Philosophy, First Book, trans. F. Kersten (The Hague: Martinus Nijhoff, 1983), ¶¶116–21. It is difficult not to read Wittgenstein's critique of his own Tractatus as other than as at least the intention of such a resistance. See Philosophical Investigations, trans. G. E. M. Anscombe (Oxford: Basic Blackwell, 1958), section 23.

handenheit) as crucial to his point. If I see what is before me as merely present-at-hand or objectively present, I see it as a fact about which true or false assertions can be made.[18] If it see it as ready-to-hand, I see it, to use his most famous example, as a hammer available for my use, or perhaps for some reason unusable. The world initially gives itself to us in this latter mode, on Heidegger's view, and it requires a severe abstraction from experience to see things as objectively present, as what is merely the case, as facts or events waiting to be accurately represented: "The kind of dealing which is closest to us is as we have shown, not a bare perceptual cognition, but rather that kind of concern which manipulates things and puts them to use; and this has its own kind of 'knowledge' " (p. 95/67) or sight (pp. 98–99/69).[19]

In light of this distinction, Heidegger makes his point this way. If what we interpret

> becomes the 'object' of an assertion, then as soon as we begin this assertion, there is already a change-over in the fore-having. Something *ready-to-hand with which* we have to do or perform something, turns into something *'about which'* the assertion that points it out is made. Our fore-sight is aimed at something present-at-hand or objectively present in what is ready-to-hand. Both *by* and *for* this way of looking at it, the ready-to-hand becomes veiled as ready-to-hand. . . . Only now are we given any access to *properties* or the like. . . . The as-structure of interpretation has undergone a modification. (p. 200/157–58)

How shall we interpret this distinction and the "modification" it signals? If we take as our clue Heidegger's claim that prior to assertion is a mode of interpretation that can occur "without wasting words" and from which "words are absent," we can give ourselves a second heuristic hypothesis, this time from Rorty. In his attack on the "myth of the given," Sellars seems to argue that there is no prelinguistic awareness, and Rorty seeks to show why this is not "unfair to babies," since babies clearly have pains and some sort of awareness of colored objects. Sellars

---

[18] Where Macquarrie and Robinson translate *vorhanden* as 'present-at-hand', Stambaugh renders it as 'objectively present'. What Heidegger has in mind is very much like the facts of the early Wittgenstein, that which is simply the case, so I shall go with Stambaugh's translation from here on.

[19] The scare quotes are in the German original.

and Rorty distinguish "awareness-as-discriminative-behavior," which children, rats, amoebas, and even computers may be said to have, from awareness "in the logical space of reasons, of justi-fying and being able to justify what one says" (Rorty, quoting Sellars), which is found only among language users. "In this latter sense awareness is justified true belief—knowledge—but in the former sense it is the ability to respond to stimuli."[20]

It is Sellars's view that prelinguistic discriminative awareness is a causal condition of knowledge but not a justifying ground. On this view "there is no such thing as a justified belief which is nonpropositional, and no such thing as a justification which is not a relation between propositions. . . . [K]nowing what things are like is not a matter of being justified in asserting proposi-tions."[21] Knowing that such and such is the case presupposes linguistic competence; knowing what things are like does not.

Our second hypothesis can be that Heidegger makes assertion derivative because, like Sellars and Rorty, he wants to distin-guish linguistic interpretation from prelinguistic interpretation. Let us see if this is how to draw the line between assertion as derivative and the understanding and interpretation that are the a priori conditions for the possibility of assertion.

Interpretation is seeing-as. Every act of interpretation appre-hends something as something, as "a table, a door, a carriage, or a bridge" (p. 189/149). It comes as no surprise that a prior understanding is already at work in every interpretation. We've been going around in hermeneutical circles for a while now. What goes beyond the merely formal structure of the hermeneu-tical circle is Heidegger's claim that the understanding presup-posed by every act of interpretation is our understanding, not of the table, the door, the carriage, or the bridge, but of ourselves.

Heidegger calls this self-understanding a kind of 'knowing'

---

[20] Rorty, *Philosophy and the Mirror of Nature*, pp. 181–83. Heidegger's focus is on human understanding. He might be willing to extend his analysis of pre-assertive understanding to rats and amoebas, but would surely balk at comput-ers. But that will not be the issue here.

[21] Ibid., pp. 183 and 185. It is worth noting that in the previous paragraph Rorty ties knowledge to linguistic awareness, while here he refers to pre-lin-guistic awareness as "*knowing* what things are like" (emphasis added). He might well have put this latter 'knowing' in scare quotes. Heidegger will make a similar distinction between knowing and knowing. See nn. 19 and 22.

(p. 184/144; cf. p. 186/146).[22] But he repeatedly denies that it is theoretical knowing, the kind of knowing with which philosophy has been so preoccupied. Thus, understanding oneself does not mean "gazing at a meaning" (p. 307/263). Nor are we dealing here with the understanding, as distinct from explanation, with which neo-Kantianism sought to put the *Geisteswissenschaften* on the sure path to science (p. 182/143). Nor are we dealing with introspection, as if the self were some entity objectively present that could be known by an "immanent self-perception" in which the self would grasp itself thematically (pp. 183–85/143–45). Self-understanding is "not a matter of perceptually tracking down and inspecting a point called the 'Self' " as if, to repeat, the self were something objectively present to itself (p. 187/146–47).

Every act of interpretation presupposes our understanding of ourselves as thrown projection or thrown possibility in our concernful dealings with things and our solicitude for other persons. But we "know" ourselves as such, not by reflectively observing these characteristics inhering in us but by being them. To be a thrown projection for whom the beings we encounter in the world matter is to understand oneself as such, and all explicit acts of interpretation, including self-interpretation, presuppose this primordial understanding.

So far Heidegger would seem to be innocent of the "unfair to babies" charge. Nothing he has said about understanding as the most basic form of "knowing" requires linguistic competence. Between understanding and assertion there lies interpretation. Self-understanding as so far specified is mostly unspecified; it is vague and general. Like the pre-understanding of a whole text as belonging to a particular genre, it needs to be filled out and concretized with specific interpretations. Accordingly, Heidegger presents interpretation as the "development" of understanding in which the beings which matter to us are "explicitly" understood (pp. 188–89/148–49). As already noted, each specific interpretation is a seeing-as, an apprehension of something as something (pp. 189–90/149–50).

---

[22] The scare quotes are in the German original of both passages cited. See previous note.

But this "pre-predicative seeing" is not to be identified with assertion or judgment (pp. 189–90/149); for assertion has been defined, in part, as predication (p. 196/154). According to our working hypothesis, pre-predicative here means prelinguistic. Can we confirm the suggestion that assertion or judgment is derivative because it is a linguistic act that presupposes prelinguistic experience? Is it sufficient to point out that babies can interpret the mother's breast as a source of satisfaction and, when hungry, can interpret the pacifier as a poor substitute?

The answer depends on Heidegger's understanding of our primal encounter with things as ready-to-hand. What we encounter in this way we can call "Things 'invested with value' " or "equipment," but both of these expressions are liable to serious misinterpretation. What is ready-to-hand matters to us in modes more immediate and concrete than as being objectively present as possible topics for truthful assertions. As such they are not bare things, tractarian facts whose mission in life is simply to be the case. In the ways they matter to us they are value-laden facts, something welcome or unwelcome or irrelevant. But to speak of them as "invested with value" suggests a value-added interpretation of them as if we first encounter them as bare facts and only later endow them with value. It is not "as if some world-stuff which is proximally objectively present in itself were 'given subjective colouring'. . . . In interpreting, we do not, so to speak, throw a 'signification' over some naked thing which is objectively present, we do not stick a value on it; but when something within-the-world is encountered as such, the thing in question already has an involvement . . . which gets laid out by the interpretation" (pp. 101/71; 190–91/150).

Heidegger is aware of the broader Gestalt form of this argument: "It requires a very artificial and complicated frame of mind to 'hear' a 'pure noise'. The fact that motor-cycles and wagons are what we proximally hear is the phenomenal evidence that in every case Dasein, as Being-in-the-world, already dwells *alongside* what is ready-to-hand within-the-world; it certainly does not dwell proximally alongside 'sensations' " (p. 207/164).[23]

---

[23] In developing his hermeneutic understanding of natural science, Hanson (p. 9) makes a similarly general Gestalt appeal: "one does not first soak up an optical pattern and then clamp an interpretation on it."

There is also a danger with describing the ready-to-hand as "equipment" (*das Zeug*), that which is "manipulable in the broadest sense and at our disposal" (pp. 97–98/68–69), as distinct from the object of a theoretical gaze. First, in spite of Heidegger's famous example of the hammer, we must avoid identifying equipment with tools; for he also presents the room as equipment for dwelling and shoes as equipment for wearing. In addition, he tells us that Nature too first comes to us as ready-to-hand and not as "pure objective presence" (p. 100/70). Thus, for example, the honey is to be eaten, but the angry bees are to be avoided.

Reference to the angry bees, not a Heideggerian example, points to a second danger. Heidegger wants to define the ready-to-hand in terms of our activity, our practical behavior in the world (pp. 98–99/69). But by focusing on what is manipulable and usable he gives insufficient attention to negative instances where the value in which things come already wrapped is negative. It is stretching language too far to speak of angry bees as equipment.

If we avoid narrowing the notion of the ready-to-hand to that of tools or the positively useful, we have a concept of things, all the way from hammers to angry bees, that are meaningful to us in valuational terms in relation to our practices. We have seen that Heidegger describes the interpretation at work in these practices as pre-predicative and pretheoretical. Does this mean that it is prelinguistic?

We can see in what sense we must answer this question Yes and in what sense No if we return to a passage considered earlier: "Interpretation is carried out primordially not in a theoretical *statement* but in an *action* of circumspective concern—laying aside the unsuitable tool, or exchanging it [or rejecting the pacifier], 'without wasting words'. From the fact that words are absent, it may not be concluded that interpretation is absent" (p. 200/157, emphasis added). It is clear that interpretation is prelinguistic in that neither linguistic expression nor linguistic competence is required for it to occur. So far we must say, Yes, our hypothesis is confirmed.

But linguistic expression and, a fortiori, linguistic competence, may very well belong to interpretation; and this means that we must say No. If interpretation is not *necessarily* linguistic, neither is it *necessarily* prelinguistic. Immediately before the passage just cited, Heidegger writes that interpretation, being prior to assertion, does not have the form of the " 'categorical statement' . . . 'The hammer is heavy' " nor the form of a "theoretical judgment" such as "This Thing—a hammer—has the property of heaviness." But the practice-embedded interpretation of the hammer as too heavy "may take some such form as 'The hammer is too heavy', or rather just 'Too heavy!, Hand me the other hammer!' "[24]

According to Heidegger's epistemology, knowledge has foundations. But at the basis of the linguistic expressions that are the bearers of truth or falsity are not those representations that are epistemically privileged, guaranteed to be true by being given (Sellars) or necessary (Quine) or self-evident or incorrigible or evident to the senses (Plantinga). At the basis of our truth-bearing assertions are practices that are not truth bearing, whether or not they are accompanied by speech acts. Relative to such foundations, the dominant epistemological ideals of the philosophical tradition from Plato to Husserl, Russell, and the early Wittgenstein are pipe dreams.

The reason it has been both possible and necessary to speak of Heidegger as an epistemologist is that such claims plainly constitute a theory about the nature and limits of human knowledge. It is precisely because his theory opens up a realm of understanding and interpretation prior to that of truth in the usual sense that Heidegger looks for a more primordial conception of truth as unconcealment. Just as the claim that assertion is derivative is not meant to abolish assertions but to specify (in a kind of Kantian manner) the conditions under which they are possible, so the quest for a more fundamental notion of truth is not meant to replace the usual notion but to specify its conditions.[25]

---

[24] Cf. the opening paragraphs of Wittgenstein's *Philosophical Investigations,* where he critiques the primacy of the theoretical in the *Tractatus* in terms of a simple language game in which "Slab!" means "Bring me a slab!" It would seem that Heidegger is mistaken in suggesting that linguistic *communication* first arises at the level of assertion (pp. 197/155 and 203/160).

[25] See Section 44 of *Being and Time; On the Essence of Truth* (1930), in *Basic Writings,* ed. David Farrell Krell (New York: Harper & Row, 1977); and *Plato's Doctrine of Truth* (1942), trans. John Barlow, in *Philosophy in the Twentieth Cen-*

This account of the radically conditioned nature of our truth as correspondence, agreement, adequation, etc., is a humbling of philosophy's pride in the light of which the empiricist traditions appear less as the humblers of rationalist hybris than as corevelers in it.[26] While repudiating the value added understanding of the ready-to-hand, Heidegger insists, *"Readiness-to-hand is the way in which entities as they are 'in themselves' are defined ontologico-categorically"* (p. 101/71). The Kantian reference is unmistakable, and it means that our theoretical accomplishments, which reduce the world to objective presence, never get beyond appearances or phenomenal knowledge, whether we construe them in rationalist or empiricist terms.

Because of the way Heidegger makes practice foundational to theory, Dreyfus calls his hermeneutics a form of practical holism as distinct from the theoretical holism of, say, post-positivist philosophy of science.[27] This provides a nice segue to his own interest in the way Foucault will give foundational epistemological significance to social practices, similarly denying the autonomy of knowledge.[28] But it leaves us with a seriously incomplete account of Heidegger's "phenomenological reduction" from theoretical (constative, truth-asserting) modes of being-in-the-world to the primordial experience from which they are derivative. For Heidegger treats state of mind or attunement (*Befindlichkeit*) as equiprimordial with understanding and a prior condition of cognition. Since this is the ontological (a priori) structure that

---

tury, vol. 3, ed. William Barrett and Henry D. Aiken (New York: Random House, 1962).

[26] Hume's appeal to custom and the passions would be an exception. So would Hempel's reluctant acknowledgment that the verification criterion of meaning is a policy and not a truth. See "Problems and Changes in the Empiricist Criterion of Meaning" in *Semantics and the Philosophy of Language,* ed. L. Linsky (Urbana: University of Illinois Press, 1952).

[27] In doing so he links Heidegger to Wittgenstein and Merleau-Ponty. See "Holism and Hermeneutics," p. 7. He might well have followed Rorty and added Dewey to the list. See the passages cited from Hanson at nn. 10 and 23 above.

[28] See Hubert L. Dreyfus and Paul Rabinow, *Michel Foucault: Beyond Structuralism and Hermeneutics,* 2nd ed. (Chicago: University of Chicago Press, 1983). A brief introduction to this motif in Foucault is found in chapters 5–9 of *Power/Knowledge,* ed. Colin Gordon (New York: Pantheon Books, 1980).

expresses itself ontically (empirically) in moods, it becomes clear that Heidegger is an affective holist as much as a practical holist. His "reduction" is from theoretical cognition both to the practices in which beings are meaningful as ready-to-hand and to the moods in which an equally "primordial disclosure" takes place (p. 173/134).

We are *"delivered over"* to our moods. They are tightly tied to the *"thrownness"* of our existence as thrown projection, our *"facticity"* (pp. 173–74/134–35). In this respect Heidegger conforms to the tradition that identifies our affective life with passivity, with the passions. But where much of the tradition treats feeling and emotion as subjective addenda whose only cognitive significance is that they might interfere with clear thinking, Heidegger stresses the disclosive function of moods as a priori conditions of theoretical thought: they are *"prior* to all cognition and *beyond* their range of disclosure" (p. 175/136). In addition, they are conditions of the possibility that anything, including ourselves, should "matter" to us. *The mood has already disclosed, in every case, Being-in-the-world as a whole, and makes it possible first of all to direct oneself towards something"* (pp. 176–78/ 137–39). Intentionality presupposes mood.

We are not surprised when Heidegger tells us once again that the conditions for the possibility of theoretical (assertive, constative) engagement with the world are pretheoretical. This is because "the possibilities of disclosure which belong to cognition reach far too short a way compared with the primordial disclosure belonging to moods. . . . 'To be disclosed' does not mean 'to be known as this sort of thing' " (p. 173/124). We should not compare what is disclosed to one in moods with what one "is acquainted with, knows, and believes" or measure it "against the apodictic certainty of a theoretical cognition of something merely objectively present" (p. 175/135–36). It is when the world shows itself "in accordance with our moods, that the ready-to-hand shows itself. . . . By looking at the world theoretically, we have already dimmed it down to the uniformity of what is merely objectively present" (p. 177/138).

Does this primacy of mood over cognition mean that for Heidegger as for Hume reason "is and ought only to be the slave of the passions"?[29] Surely not if this means the attempt "to surrender science ontically to 'feeling' " (p. 177/138) in which phenomena are falsified by being "banished to the sanctuary of the irrational" (p. 175/136). The Stoics, and following them, Spinoza, emphasize the dependence of the passions on our beliefs.[30] Heidegger clearly wants to give a priority to the passions, but not simply by reversing this relationship so as to make the propositional content of our assertions a function of our moods. He has no interest in a world in which the cat is on the mat for happy folks but not for sad sacks.

His point is rather that theory commits the fallacy of misplaced concreteness, at least as traditionally conceived. The world comes to us as value-laden by our moods as by our practices, and we kid ourselves if we think we can reflect ourselves out of this condition, for "when we master a mood, we do so by way of a counter-mood; we are never free of moods" (p. 175/136). Theory has its own mood, just as it is a certain kind of practice. What is more, we kid ourselves if we think we would get closer to the way things "really" are if we could strip away our moods and our practices in order to become pure reason. As we saw at the conclusion of the previous section of this essay, if we wish to be in touch with things in themselves and not with mere appearances, we must let them show themselves to us in the light of our moods and our practices.

And in the light of our prejudices—which brings us to Gadamer. At the heart of Gadamer's hermeneutics is the claim that

> the fundamental prejudice of the Enlightenment is the prejudice against prejudice itself, which denies tradition its power. . . . The overcoming of all prejudices, this global demand of the Enlightenment, will itself prove to be a prejudice, and removing it opens the way to an appropriate understanding of the finitude which dominates not only our humanity but also our historical con-

---

[29] Hume, *A Treatise of Human Nature,* ed. L. A. Selby-Bigge (Oxford: Clarendon Press, 1960 reprint of 1888 edition), p. 415 (bk. II, pt. III, sec. III).

[30] For helpful discussion of the Stoics on this point, see Martha Nussbaum, *The Therapy of Desire: Theory and Practice in Hellenistic Ethics* (Princeton: Princeton University Press, 1994).

sciousness . . . *the prejudices of the individual, far more than his judgments, constitute the historical reality of his being.* (pp. 270, 276–77)[31]

Heidegger's account of the hermeneutic circle and of the fore-
structure of understanding is Gadamer's point of departure (p.
265). In urging us not to flee the hermeneutical circle, Heidegger
stresses its positive role: "In the circle is hidden a positive possibility of the most primordial kind of knowing" (p. 195). Gadamer shares this emphasis: "Prejudices are not necessarily
unjustified and erroneous, so that they inevitably distort the
truth. In fact, the historicity of our existence entails that prejudices, in the literal sense of the word [prejudgments], constitute
the initial directedness of our whole ability to experience. Prejudices are biases of our openness to the world. They are simply
conditions whereby we experience something."[32] The prejudices
Gadamer seeks to rehabilitate are not ugly attitudes toward people who are different from ourselves, but the pre-understandings presupposed by every understanding. Just as embodiment
is a condition for being either Jack the Ripper or Mother Teresa,
so prejudgment is a condition for seeing those who are different
from me either as inferior or as my sisters and brothers.

But there are at least two important differences from Heidegger. First, Gadamer stands in closer relation than Heidegger to
Kuhnian philosophy of science and Rawlsian reflective equilibrium. For rather than reflect on our affects and practices as conditions for the possibility of assertion or judgment, Gadamer
returns us to a theoretical holism in which prior to every judgment (*Urteil*) there is a prejudgment or pre-judice (*Vor-urteil*).
Thus, while Heidegger points to modes of pre-understanding
that are prior to assertion or judgment, Gadamer points to
modes of pre-understanding that already have the form of judgment (assertion, constative speech act).

In close relation to this first difference is a second. 'Tradition'
ceases to be a dirty word. In Robinson and Macquarrie's "Index
of English Expressions" in *Being and Time*, the only three sub-

---

[31] Gadamer references in the text will be to *Truth and Method*, trans. Joel Weinsheimer and Donald G. Marshall, 2nd ed. rev. (New York: Crossroad, 1991).

[32] *Philosophical Hermeneutics*, trans, David E. Linge (Berkeley: University of
California Press, 1976), p. 9.

headings are to the traditional conception of time, the traditional conception of truth, and traditional ontology. One need not know *Being and Time* very well to know that all three signify a danger from which we are to be rescued. Nor is this surprising in the light of what Heidegger says about tradition in general:

> When tradition becomes master, it does so in such a way that what it 'transmits' is made so inaccessible . . . that it rather becomes concealed. Tradition takes what has come down to us and delivers it over to self-evidence; it blocks our access to those primordial 'sources' from which the categories and concepts handed down to us have been in part quite genuinely drawn. . . . Dasein has had its historicality so thoroughly uprooted by tradition that . . . it has no ground of its own to stand on." (p. 43/21)

It is ironical to hear Heidegger sounding so much like Descartes. Gadamer wants to make a more radical break with the spirit of the Enlightenment by breaking not only with the substantive content of the Cartesian worldview but also with the repudiation of the authority of tradition that motivates Descartes's resort to method. For, to allow ourselves a bit of historical freedom, Gadamer views Descartes as following Kant's advice to grow up by shaking off his "self-incurred tutelage," the "inability of make use of his understanding without direction from another,"[33] only by adopting a thoroughly adolescent rebellion according to which whatever one's intellectual parents say is ipso facto discredited.

One of Gadamer's subheadings is "The Rehabilitation of Authority and Tradition" (p. 277). He might well have spoken of the authority of tradition, for on his view tradition has considerable, though not absolute, authority. His attitude is like that of Socrates to the laws of Athens as his parents. Even when one is sharply critical of tradition, as Gadamer is critical of the Cartesian/Enlightenment tradition, one must recognize one's embeddedness in tradition and one's indebtedness to it. Tradition is the primary source of the prejudices without which understanding, including critical understanding, would not be possible. When Rorty says that criticism is never possible in terms of eternal

---

[33] Kant, "What Is Enlightenment," in *On History*, ed. Lewis White Beck (Indianapolis: Bobbs-Merrill, 1963), p. 3.

standards but only in terms of those "of our own day,"[34] Gadamer will agree only if "of our own day" means not "those currently dominant in our culture" but "those currently available, thanks, for the most part, to tradition."

Gadamer's critics are usually willing to concede "that there are legitimate prejudices" (p. 277). But the weight he gives to tradition has led many, reviving a distinction from the aftermath of Hegel, to portray Gadamer as a "right-wing" Heideggerian, distinct from such "left-wing" developers of Heideggerian hermeneutics as Derrida and Foucault.[35] Both in the Gadamer-Habermas debate and in the Gadamer-Derrida debate,[36] Gadamer's opponents, failing to pay much attention to tradition as a source of critique, portray him as tilting too much away from critique in favor of tradition.

For example, Jack Caputo describes Gadamer's hermeneutics as "a reactionary gesture,"[37] too comforting in relation to the truth of tradition. He cites the passage from the section entitled "The Rehabilitation of Authority and Tradition" in which Margolis finds the key to Gadamer's "closet essentialism." That which has been sanctioned by tradition and custom has

> an authority that is nameless, and our finite historical being is marked by the fact that the authority of what has been handed down to us—and not just what is clearly grounded—always has power over our attitudes and behavior. . . . The real force of morals, for example, is based on tradition. They are freely taken over but by no means created by a free insight or grounded on reasons. This is precisely what we call tradition: the ground of their validity . . . tradition has a justification that lies beyond rational grounding and in large measure determines our institutions and attitudes. (pp. 280–81)[38]

---

[34] Rorty, *Philosophy and the Mirror of Nature*, pp. 178–79.

[35] By far the best accounts of Derrida and Foucault in this light are, respectively, Jack Caputo, *Radical Hermeneutics* (Bloomington: Indiana University Press, 1987), and Dreyfus and Rabinow, *Michel Foucault*.

[36] A good introduction to the former, with references to the primary sources, is found in Thomas McCarthy, *The Critical Theory of Jürgen Habermas* (Cambridge, Mass.: MIT Press, 1978). For the latter see Diane P. Michelfelder and Richard E. Palmer, eds., *Dialogue and Deconstruction: The Gadamer-Derrida Encounter* (Albany: SUNY Press, 1989).

[37] Caputo, *Radical Hermeneutics*, pp. 5–6.

[38] Quoted in Caputo's essay, "Gadamer's Closet Essentialism: A Derridian Critique," in *Dialogue and Deconstruction*, p. 258, from the older translation, which I have replaced with the second (1991) edition.

Is this equivalent to the claim that reason is and ought to be the slave of tradition? Any careful reading of this passage will notice that it is explicitly an "is" statement, describing what actually happens. It needs to be read in the light of Gadamer's warning in the second edition foreword to *Truth and Method*, "My real concern was and is philosophic: not what we do or what we ought to do, but what happens to us over and above our wanting and doing" (p. xxviii).[39] Also relevant here is Gadamer's very Heideggerian claim about the limits of reflection: "Reflection on a given pre-understanding brings before me something that otherwise happens *behind my back*. Something— but not everything, for what I have called the *wirkungsgeschichtliches Bewusstsein* is inescapably more being than consciousness, and being is never fully manifest."[40] In other words, the reflection that critically thematizes some presupposition will itself be guided by a pre-understanding not yet subjected to criticism. Gadamer agrees with the pragmatists that we can subject any of our beliefs to criticism, but not all at once. We are, as a matter of fact, always given over to our belonging to history, not so absolutely as to be but pawns, but so thoroughly that the dream of cognitive autonomy is a pipe dream and the anxiety of influence a neurosis: "Does being situated within traditions really mean being subject to prejudices and limited in one's freedom? Is not, rather, all human existence, even the freest, limited and qualified in various ways? If this is true, the idea of an absolute reason is not a possibility for historical humanity" (p. 276).

There is an "ought" implicit in this analysis. Since foundationalist justifications are unavailable, we ought not to seek them; and since our commitments always exceed what we can rationally justify in any absolute sense, we ought not to pretend differently.

So reason is and ought to be, not the slave of tradition, but honest about its ineluctable dependence on tradition. Finitude is

---

[39] Elsewhere I have shown that Gadamer repudiates the Hegelian strategy for achieving absolute knowledge as vigorously as he rejects the Cartesian strategy. See "Hegel and Gadamer" in *Hegel, Freedom, and Modernity* (Albany: SUNY Press, 1992). I am not convinced by Caputo's claim that Gadamer is more Hegelian than Heideggerian. See *Radical Hermeneutics*, p. 6 and "Gadamer's Closet Essentialism," p. 259.

[40] *Philosophical Hermeneutics*, p. 38.

not fate. I am not bound over inexorably to this tradition or that one. The hermeneutical circle always means that one's foundations, which cannot eliminate tradition in favor of pure insight, are contingent and corrigible. The earth rests on the back of a turtle, and it's turtles all the way down. Where is the excessive comfort in this unflinching acknowledgement of reason's inability to become self-sufficient by escaping the hermeneutical circle?

Finally, an all too brief look at Derrida's "left-wing" or radical hermeneutics.[41] Already with Heidegger, hermeneutics goes way beyond the interpretation of texts. Everything, including ourselves, our artifacts, and the world of nature, is apprehended in interpretation. The whole world is a text, or better, a library of texts. Gadamer makes explicit his own commitment to this ubiquity of interpretation in the opening essays of *Philosophical Hermeneutics*.[42] One of the ways Derrida affirms the universal scope of interpretation, and thus the textual character of the world, is in his (in)famous claim *"There is nothing outside the text."*[43]

There are two meanings to this thesis, one Kantian and one Hegelian. Neither implies that we are free to make up the world as we go; instead, both signify textuality as a limit within which we have whatever freedom we have. The Kantian sense is merely the affirmation of the hermeneutical circle in its theoretical dimension, the claim that before we say anything, "Being must always already be conceptualized." This " 'must always already' precisely signifies the original exile from the kingdom of Being . . . signifies that Being never is, never shows *itself*, is never *present*, is never *now*, outside difference (in all the senses today required by this word)."[44] In its Kantian form, this denial of

---

[41] For a much fuller treatment, see Caputo, *Radical Hermeneutics*.

[42] "The Universality of the Hermeneutical Problem" and "On the Scope and Function of Hermeneutical Reflection." The latter is an explicit response to Habermas's attempt to delimit hermeneutics.

[43] *Of Grammatology*, trans. Gayatri Chakravorty Spivak (Baltimore: Johns Hopkins University Press, 1976), p. 158.

[44] "Edmond Jabès and the Question of the Book," in *Writing and Difference*, trans. Alan Bass (Chicago: University of Chicago Press, 1978), p. 74. See "Différance," for the spatial and temporal meaning of this key term, in *Margins of*

presence (and the metaphysics of presence) is not a denial of the claim that there is a computer in front of me as I write. It is a denial of all philosophies according to which either meanings or facts can be merely and directly present to me, unmediated essentially (and not just causally) by that which is absent. There are no atomic facts, no instantaneous nows.

Of course, there are intuitions and there is acquaintance. But such cognitions lose their epistemic privilege when we pay attention to the mediations that make them possible and render their highly valued immediacy illusory. It goes without saying that Derrida's is a post-Kantian Kantianism in which those mediations are themselves diverse and contingent, like Rorty's optional vocabularies, not universal and necessary.

But when introducing his "nothing outside the text" thesis, Derrida focuses on the Hegelian meaning of his claim. The point is not primarily that we have access to, in this case, persons "only in the text," that is, in some particular interpretation of them, "and we have neither any means of altering this, nor any right to neglect this limitation. All reasons of this type would already be sufficient, to be sure, but there are more radical reasons." The more radical reasons concern the nature of the things themselves, not our access to them. "What we have tried to show . . . is that in what one calls the real life of these existences 'of flesh and bone,' beyond and behind what one believes can be circumscribed as Rousseau's text, there has never been anything but writing."[45]

What does it mean to say that "beyond and behind" the text of Rousseau's *Confessions*, through which we have access to Rousseau, Mamma, and Thérèse, they themselves, and whatever else gets written about or interpreted, are texts? Most simply put, "*The thing itself is a sign.*" Like signs, things essentially point beyond themselves. We must abandon the search for the transcendental signified and, what is the same, the distinction between sign and signified. For there is no signified that "would

---

Philosophy, trans. Alan Bass (Chicago: University of Chicago Press, 1982). The temporal sense of the term derives from the deconstructive reading of Husserl on internal time consciousness that Derrida gives in *Speech and Phenomena,* trans. David B. Allison (Evanston: Northwestern University Press, 1973).

[45] *Of Grammatology,* pp. 158–59.

place a reassuring end to the reference from sign to sign" by failing to refer beyond itself.[46] Things are not substances or atoms that stand alone. Their very being is constituted by their relations. This is the Hegelian theme that the English idealists labeled the doctrine of internal relations, and it is an important part of what Derrida means by calling his "mediation on writing" Hegelian.[47]

In summary, radical hermeneutics finds that "there is nothing outside the text," and this means both, epistemologically, that "Being must always already be conceptualized" and, ontologically, that "The thing itself is a sign."

This theory of double mediation signifies our exile from sheer immediacy, pure presence. But it leaves open the possibility of "two interpretations of interpretation."[48] One is associated with the rabbi and Rousseau, the other with the poet and Nietzsche. Both experience interpretation as exile, texts as a veil that separates them from Truth as directly and fully present. For both "we have ceased hearing the voice [of God] from within the immediate proximity of the garden. . . . Writing is displaced on the broken line between lost and promised speech. The *difference* between speech [immediacy, presence] and writing [mediation, absence] is sin, the anger of God emerging from itself, lost immediacy, work outside the garden."[49] Interpretation is what we do east of Eden, after the Fall, prior to the beatific vision.

But the world of the rabbi is that of a *"sacred text surrounded by commentaries."*[50] The task of interpretation is to retrieve the divine voice in the written word, to return as nearly as possible to the garden where truth is immediately present. The broken immediacy and the inevitable incompleteness of interpretation

---

[46] Ibid., p. 49. This notion that things refer in a signlike way is built into Heidegger's account of the ready-to-hand.

[47] Ibid., p. 26. Derrida immediately adds that his Hegelianism is without the closure that comes by moving from finite, signlike things to the infinite totality that would be the transcendental signified, in Spinoza's language, the only substance. Gadamer can also be described as an Hegelian without totality, without the Absolute.

[48] Derrida develops this theme both in "Edmond Jabès and the Question of the Book," p. 67, and in "Structure, Sign, and Play in the Discourse of the Human Sciences," in *Writing and Difference*, p. 292.

[49] "Edmond Jabès," p. 68.

[50] Ibid., p. 67. The phrase is quoted from Jabès.

evoke nostalgia, and even guilt, for Rousseau, but he "dreams of deciphering a truth or an origin which escapes play and the order of the sign." In other words, he dreams "of full presence, the reassuring foundation, the origin and end of play."[51] This is the (possibly regulative) ideal of the Transcendental Signified.

The Nietzschean poet, by contrast, rather than seeking to retrieve the voice of God, takes the silence of God to be an invitation to speak ourselves. God allowed the Tables of the Law to be broken "in order to let us speak . . . we must take words upon ourselves . . . must become men of vision because we have ceased hearing the voice from within the immediate proximity of the garden."[52] The silence or death of God is experienced, not in nostalgia and guilt but in "the joyous affirmation of the play of the world and of the innocence of becoming, the affirmation of a world of signs without fault, without truth, and without origin which is offered to an active interpretation. *This affirmation then determines the noncenter otherwise than as the loss of the center.* And it plays without security."[53]

If one understands that for Derrida the overcoming of metaphysics is not its abolition but its delimitation, one will not be surprised to find that he does not simply reject the first interpretation of interpretation in order to affirm the second. He thinks it is foolish to talk of choosing between them and talks instead of living them simultaneously and trying to discover their common ground.[54] For "there will always be rabbis and poets. And two interpretations of interpretation."[55] "Rabbinical" hermeneutics is indeed like metaphysics in the Kantian dialectic: it is a project we can neither accomplish nor abandon.

But the hermeneutical turn in both its nostalgic and its Nietzschean modes is a recognition that absolute knowledge is not in

---

[51] "Structure, Sign, and Play," p. 292. For Derrida play is more something that happens to us than something we do. It is the constant reference of signs, including things, from one point to another without any point being privileged as center or origin. For an attempt to counter widespread misreadings of this theme, see "Deconstruction and Christian Cultural Theory: An Essay on Appropriation" (ch. 9 below).

[52] "Edmond Jabès," p. 68.

[53] "Structure, Sign, and Play," p. 292.

[54] Ibid., p. 293.

[55] "Edmond Jabès," p. 67.

4

Appropriating Postmodernism[1]

ONCE UPON A TIME, not yesterday, but not so very long ago, I'm told, there was a minister in the Reformed tradition whose sermons all had three points. In itself that is not unusual, but in this case they were the same three points, regardless of the text. Each text was expounded in terms of (1) what it said against the Arminians, (2) what it said against the papists, and (3) what it said against the modernists.

It would no doubt be going too far to call this zealous preacher a postmodernist. But he certainly was persistent in expressing his suspicions of modernity. Moreover, he suggests that one might have theological reasons for such suspicions and that a Christian thinker might be sympathetic with postmodernism, which shares those suspicions.

But, the objection immediately arises, postmodernism is a radically secular movement. If by postmodernism you mean (as in fact I do) such philosophers as Derrida, Foucault, and Rorty, along with those aspects of Nietzsche and Heidegger they have appropriated, it is clear that the 'and' in 'Christianity and postmodern philosophy' can signify only an either/or without compromise. What has Athens to do with Jerusalem, or, to be a bit more current, what has Paris to do with Grand Rapids (aka the New Jerusalem)? Is not the task of the Christian thinker in the face of such godless projects of thought to inoculate the faithful against these diseases, first by warning them of the dangers posed by Nietzsche and his minions, and then by refuting their philosophies, wholesale if possible, but retail if necessary?

Before suggesting a different response, I note in passing the

---

[1] The following is a lecture presented on June 26, 1996, at Calvin College, Grand Rapids, Michigan, in connection with a Calvin College Faculty Summer Seminar in Christian Scholarship, a program funded by the Pew Charitable Trusts. The theme of the six-week seminar was Postmodern Philosophy and Christian Thought.

all too real possibility that such refutations will consist of arguments designed to persuade those within the circle of faith and will often come down to little more than "They are different from us." When apologetics lets this happen, it does not constitute a serious engagement with one's opponents and can even be construed, not without reason, as a refusal even to talk with them.

"Appropriating postmodernism" is the name I give to the alternative strategy I wish to propose, one that seeks a middle way between the total rejection of the refusenik and the equally uncritical jumping on the bandwagon of this month's politically correct fad.

One can think of appropriation as a doubly violent act. When, for example, Derrida appropriates Heidegger, he first distinguishes the wheat from the chaff and discards Heidegger's romantic/mystical tendencies as relics of the metaphysics of presence that both seek to overcome. Then he recontextualizes the features of Heidegger's attempt at the overcoming of metaphysics to which he is sympathetic, relocating them in his conceptual framework rather than in Heidegger's. In their new home they are recognizable, but not always immediately or easily, for their meaning is no longer quite the same, and the vocabulary in which they are expressed is often quite different.

Without forgetting the dual negativity of rejection and recontextualization, it is possible to think of such an appropriation as an invitation to conversation. The appropriator, after listening carefully to the appropriatee, responds by saying, "I find these aspects of your presentation quite compelling and illuminating. But for me they work better when recontextualized as follows. Of course, that changes the project somewhat and involves the abandonment of this or that aspect of your original proposal. But don't you agree that those ideas of yours I find compelling work better in the context I propose, or at least, since they can be fruitfully put to work there, that they are not inherently wedded to the larger goals of your project?"

Whether one thinks of appropriation as violence or invitation to conversation, I suggest that although it does not involve discovering any counterexamples, it is a form of philosophical counterargument. In another context, this was the strategy I adopted in response to the religion critiques of Marx, Nietzsche, and Freud. In a book called *Suspicion and Faith*, I argued that their accounts of the ways in which irreligious interests shape religious ideas and especially the uses to which they are put by the believing individual and community are genuine insights and that the task of the Christian thinker is not to refute them but to acknowledge their force. But I also argued that Marx, Nietzsche, and Freud are plagiarists, that this kind of critique has its origin in biblical religion itself, that its proper motivation is a religious fear of idolatry, and that its proper home is the communities of biblical faith. Although I did not try to refute the atheism of Marx, Nietzsche, and Freud directly, I did note that my recontextualization involved the abandonment of that aspect of their project, and I claimed to have shown that there is nothing inherently atheistic about their critique. That religious people are often, even always, idolatrous, worshipping a god created in their own image and in conformity with their own interests, does not mean that there is no God.

Since Marx and Freud are quintessentially modern thinkers, while Nietzsche is a posthumous postmodernist, it will obviously not do to identify postmodernism with their hermeneutics of suspicion. So how shall we identify what might be appropriated in the present context? Postmodernism is as difficult to define as, say, romanticism. Or more so. Just as romanticism is defined with reference to classicism, so postmodernism is defined with reference to modernity. But there are so many modernisms. We speak of modernism in music, literature, painting, and architecture. I shall not be concerned with these aesthetic modernisms nor with the various postmodernisms that stand over against them. We have already been reminded of theological modernism. That, too, is not my point of reference. But it brings us closer to what we want, for "modernism" was the early-twentieth-century American name for the liberal Protestant theology that developed during the nineteenth century in Germany, and that theology was an attempt to accommodate the message of Christianity to "the modern mind," to "modern man come of age."

It is this latter modernity (which was not particularly gender conscious) to which the philosophical postmodernism that concerns me is the aftermath. It is a philosophical attitude, expressed in a wide variety of philosophical theories, that might be described as a certain faith in reason, a reason that took scientific objectivity and method as its touchstones. The philosophers I have named, along with quite a few others, are united by a loss of that faith in that reason. It should be obvious, but needs to be noted, that their loss of faith represents a threat to moral and religious values just and only to the degree that those values have been wedded to modern or Enlightenment conceptions of reason.

Let me illustrate what I mean by this latter point with reference to three theologians I encountered a few weeks ago during my undergraduate studies. All wanted to base their theology on the authority of biblical revelation, and all thought the right account of that authority was the theory of biblical inerrancy. So it is clear that all were far too conservative to have any sympathy for theological liberalism. Yet two of them, ironically, had wedded their conservative theologies to precisely that modernity with which that liberalism had sought accommodation. In terms of theological content no one would have called their theologies modernistic. But the metaclaims they made about their theologies, to which, it should be noted, they gave theological status, were born of the Enlightenment, children of Athens rather than Jerusalem.

One of them said, "With the help of biblical revelation we can achieve a knowledge of God wholly on a par with God's own self-knowledge. Our knowledge does not extend as far as God's, of course, but what we know is not in any way inferior to God's knowledge of the same truths." This means that theological knowledge, with the help of revelation, achieves the ideal of objectivity and perfect correspondence that science was thought to achieve in relation to nature. This knowledge is entirely free from prejudice or perspective, is wholly unconditioned by interests and desires, and is relative to no human culture.

N.B. Our theologian is not saying this about the Bible, but about his own theology, at least in principle, at least when he gets it right.

As a hint toward the possibility of a theologically motivated postmodern protest against this metatheology, I remind you that it is not just Nietzsche but also Kierkegaard's Climacus who wages a sustained polemic against claims that human knowledge can operate *sub specie aeterni*, can peek over God's shoulder and see things from the divine perspective.

Our second theologian lectured on the perspicuity of scripture. He said, "It is not necessary for us to interpret the Bible. The Bible interprets itself. When we use the proper grammatico-historical method, the meanings that result are, if not untouched by human hands, at least uncontaminated by human cultures in their finitude and fallenness." Truth in advertising might have required that the lecture be titled "Cartesian hermeneutics."

N.B. Once again, by a curious osmosis, the absoluteness first claimed for biblical revelation has been claimed for a particular theology, at least insofar as it has been methodologically rigorous.

In its general form, this non sequitur is anything but rare. One does not even have to listen very closely to those who present themselves as defenders of Absolute Truth or Absolute Values to hear the all too frequent follow-up: "And since We are the defenders of Absolutes, it should come as no surprise that we are the ones in possession of them. Our theories are the Truth and our practices are the Good." One of the tasks of a theologically motivated appropriation of postmodernism is to challenge this move in all its forms, blatant and subtle. For just as I do not become purple by speaking about violets, so I do not become absolute by speaking about God. The divine character of revelation does not cancel out the human character of my attempt to say what it means.

If our first two theologians would be surprised to discover how thoroughly Cartesian they are, our third would be surprised to find himself linked to postmodernism. But he used to say, "The Bible is the divinely revealed misinformation about God." This means that his theology, based on biblical revelation, will never get it right, no matter how methodologically rigorous. His beliefs will never simply correspond to the object they intend; they will never be the *adequatio* of his intellect to the divine reality. He is a theologically motivated anti-realist, and just to that degree we can say, a bit anachronistically, that he has appropriated postmodernism.

This does not mean for a moment that he is an anything-goes theologian, to cite an all too standard straw-man critique of postmodernism. He was as concerned with theological methodology as our second theologian and as explicitly dependent on biblical revelation as the first. But he thought the goal of theological rigor was to think about God as humans should think about God rather than to think about God as God thinks about God. To think God's thoughts after God is not to see anything through God's eyes or to peek over God's shoulders. It is to be the best possible human approximation to a divine thought that always transcends our grasp of it.

In trying to think through the notion of the Bible as the divinely revealed misinformation about God I have often come back to this homely analogy. My three-year-old son is sucking on a quarter. I tell him not to put coins in his mouth. He asks why not. Since he lacks an understanding of viruses and bacteria, and doesn't even have those words in his vocabulary, I tell him, "Because they have little, invisible bugs on them that can make you sick if they get inside you. Remember how awful you felt last time you were sick?"

This is the parentally revealed misinformation about sucking on coins. It is false, but it is how the boy ought to think about the matter. But just for that reason, we probably shouldn't simply call it false. Rather, we should notice that a good epistemologist would give an anti-realist account of the boy's knowledge and suggest that his belief is phenomenally correct, by comparison with the belief that sucking on coins will cause the cat to die, but noumenally false, relative to adult human knowledge as the criterion of the in itself.

To describe postmodernism as a loss of faith in the Enlightenment project and the concept of reason it presupposes is to give a wholesale account. For a deeper understanding we would have to go retail. We would have to look at specific themes of postmodern philosophy, such as Nietzsche's perspectivism, Heidegger's overcoming metaphysics as onto-theology and technology, Derrida's deconstruction of the metaphysics of presence, Foucault's genealogy as the critique of discursive practices, and Rorty's claim that all our vocabularies are contingent and none final. This requires painstaking reading of texts that are often painful to read. I am not disposed to inflict that pain on you, and in any case there is not time. So I need to find a way of splitting the difference between wholesale and retail analysis.

The best way to do that, I believe, will be to take as a typically postmodern thesis the following claim: the truth is that there is no Truth. Although this formulation is too general and abstract to do justice to the thought of any of the five thinkers I have been naming, each of them has a detailed development of its basic idea in his own distinctive vocabulary and conceptual scheme. The advantage of making it our focus is that it will be possible to speak about all five at once; the disadvantage is that the distinctiveness of each will be lost.

The key to understanding the claim "The truth is that there is no Truth" is found in the second appearance of the key term, the one where "Truth" appears with a capital T. Modernity's faith in reason is faith in the human capacity to achieve such Truth. Ironically, this faith goes back at least to Plato. (The irony in the notion that modernity begins with Plato is mitigated at least somewhat if we remember that he is sometimes described as the high point of the Greek Enlightenment.) In any case, Plato's faith is that reason can be pure, that with the right discipline, which we can call either method or ascesis, reason can rise above its encavement to gaze directly upon eternal being. When he speaks in the *Phaedo* (65e ff.) of "the unaided intellect," he means a thought fully purified of dependence on the senses. Then he speaks (and this is quite clearly Plato and not Socrates speaking) about "the man who pursues the truth by applying his pure and unadulterated thought to the pure and unadulterated object." To do this "we must get rid of the body and contemplate things by themselves with the soul by itself." Thus the purification of the intellect leads to a heavenly orgy in which the totally naked soul and its totally naked object enjoy unmediated union. This is the moment of Truth.

By the time we get to modernity, both in its rationalist, Cartesian form and in its empiricist, Lockean form, the enemy is not so much the senses as tradition, opinions received from others in the cave (even if they claim to have just returned from Plato's party) rather than from one's own direct face-to-face with the real. We would not normally think of Descartes and Locke, in contrast to Plato, as ascetic priests. But by calling their faith in objectivity through method a form of the ascetic ideal, Nietzsche helps us to see their kinship with Plato and the appropriateness of lumping them all together as Enlightenment thinkers.

One does not break faith with their objectivism by becoming a fallibilist, for all three of them are already fallibilists. We do not always get it right. Much, if not most, of the time our beliefs are not True, are not the products of Method and thus of Pure Reason. But they can be, and when they are, they are Truth as Absolute Knowledge. For they are relative to nothing but the facts of the matter. The mind has become the mirror of nature, or supernature; however partially in extent, the ideals of adequation and correspondence have been completely achieved. And this we know to be Truth.

What is known in this way is perfectly known. Not even God could know it any better. There is thus good reason for Kierkegaard's religious postmodernism and Nietzsche's atheistic postmodernism to agree in identifying their target as the claim to know *sub specie aeterni*.

Postmodernists give a variety of reasons (yes, they give reasons, like a good philosopher should) for denying that we ever simply get it right, that we ever have Truth in this sense. They find us to be too deeply embedded in the cave to be able to extricate ourselves through any methodology or ascetic discipline. Among the features of cave life that hold us most tightly in their grip are time and culture (or history as concrete time).

It was time (in something like Husserl's sense of internal time consciousness) that made Kant distinguish the phenomenal from the noumenal and deny our access to Truth (at least in the realm of theory). To know things in themselves, things as they really are, would be to know them as God would know them. But since all the categories of human understanding are schematized in terms of time and since God sees everything under the aspect of eternity, there is a great gulf fixed between human and divine understanding, with the result that we can know things as they appear to us, but not as they are in themselves. We can call our beliefs true when we apprehend the world as we should; but they are not True, since that would require us to apprehend the world as we can't. Going back to our three-year-old's belief that coins have invisible bugs on them, we can say that his belief is true but not True.

Postmodernists, especially Heidegger and Derrida, are Kantians in their emphasis on the inescapably temporal character of human experience. We are always in medias res and can never stand at the Alpha or Omega point where Truth can be had. Every present has as part of its meaning both its whence and its whither, both of which have an indeterminability about them that renders our meanings in flux (Derrida will say undecidable) to such a degree that, while we may very well be able to get along quite well with daily tasks, any theoretical claims to Truth will already be vitiated at the level of meaning.

In their Kantianism, postmodernists are Humeans as well. To be more precise, they think the Humean lesson has not been well enough learned. Hume did not think we should stop making causal judgments. Nor did he deny that for all practical purposes they work quite well. What he denied was the appropriateness of a certain theoretical interpretation of those judgments. Similarly, in denying our access to Truth, postmodernists are not saying we should abandon the distinction between truth and falsity that, for all practical purposes, is both indispensable and fruitful; they are only denying the metaclaim that our truths are Truth. They are Kantians.

What ties us to the cave even more tightly than the abstract time of internal time consciousness is the concrete time of historical, cultural existence. With the possible exception of Nietzsche, our five postmodernists have all taken the linguistic turn, and their theories of culture will be theories of language. They make the following claims:

- All our experience is linguistically mediated. Whatever prelinguistic encounters with reality we may have, they are not the building blocks out of which knowledge is built.
- Every language is a language. It is a particular conceptual scheme or vocabulary and lacks the universality that Truth requires.
- Every language is contingent in the sense that it contributes to our interpretation of the world elements which derive from historical accident rather than from super-historical, direct encounter with the real.

- In short, every language is a perspective, and it is the plurality of vocabularies that make up human language that shows us most clearly the inescapability of Nietzsche's perspectivism, according to which there are no facts but only interpretations. For all our insights are relative to some frame of reference which is itself anything but absolute. In this relativity, our truths are never Truth.

The move from time to history or culture was from abstract to concrete. But we need to take another step in that direction, for the linguistic theory of culture just sketched is still too abstract. For the postmodernists as for Wittgenstein, languages are always language games in the strong sense of the term. This means not just that there are verbal rules and moves, but that forms of life are involved. In other words, our verbal practices, and thus our insights, are themselves always embedded in the social practices of our culture(s).

This final move to concretion has devastating consequences. For the abstract theory of time and the abstract dimension of the linguistic theory of culture belong to the hermeneutics of finitude. Because we cannot transcend the limited perspective of our location in time and in cultural history, knowledge can never be Truth. But cultural practices are not just finite and contingent; they are also fallen and corrupt, a point the postmodernists are not slow to point out (even if they don't speak the language of sin and the fall). This takes us from the hermeneutics of finitude to the hermeneutics of suspicion and introduces us to another whole class of reasons why Truth exceeds our grasp. As Nietzsche puts it, pure Truth is not exactly the highest priority of our will to power. This dimension of the postmodern critique of knowledge is (unwittingly) an extended homily on the Pauline account of those "who by their wickedness suppress the truth" (Rom. 1:18). Taken together, the hermeneutics of finitude and of suspicion tell us: We cannot attain to the Truth, and if we could, we would edit (that is, revise) it to suit our current agenda.

These are the kinds of considerations that lead postmodernists to say: The truth is that there is no Truth. But some would dismiss the whole discussion out of hand on the grounds that there is a fatal problem of self-reference, a performative contradiction in saying that there is no Truth. Consider the liar's paradox. Suppose I say, "What I'm telling you now is a lie." The problem is one of self-reference because the statement refers to itself. The paradox is that if it is true that the statement is a lie, then what I told you (that the statement is a lie) is not true, in which case the statement is not a lie. So the truth of the statement entails its falsity. This problem can be described as a performative contradiction, for the act of uttering the statement indirectly asserts its truth, while the statement itself asserts its falsehood. The contradiction is between what I do and what I say.

Now, when I say there is no Truth, do I not performatively commit myself to the Truth of this claim, while inconsistently denying at the same time that there is any Truth at all? In a word, no. The philosophies that postmodernism takes issue with say, The Truth is that there is Truth, and they assume that to disagree is to say, The Truth is that there is no Truth. No doubt there is a performative or self-referential problem with the latter assertion. But we were careful to notice that the postmodern claim is different, namely, The truth is that there is no Truth.

We can expand that to something like this. I understand that various philosophers (and cultural traditions stemming from them) have claimed Truth for our most properly validated beliefs. But from where I stand, it looks as if this is not possible. Here are some of the things I observe that lead me to that conclusion. Taken together, I suppose, they make up a theory about human knowledge. But I don't claim Truth for my philosophical theories any more than I do for my scientific or theological theories. Of course, this does not mean that I abandon the distinction between truth and falsity and say, Anything goes. Every viewpoint is just as good as every other—no matter how badly my critics wish I would say that. I think my theory is true in the sense that it is the theory we ought to hold and that the Platonic theory of truth is false because it does not do justice to what I see and to what I think you can see if you look carefully and honestly. Since the truth I claim for my theory is different from the Truth I deny to it and to every other theory, I fail to see the performative contradiction. Just as Humeans can debate what causal judgments we should make, while denying that the "right" ones express insight into necessary connection, so postmodernists can debate what theories we should adopt, while denying that any of them simply and finally gets it right.

If the self-reference objection had the force its proponents wish for, there would be nothing left of postmodernism to appropriate, at least not as a theory of Truth. But it doesn't have that force, and in that respect the path to appropriation remains open. I remain interested in appropriation because I find much in the postmodern hermeneutics of finitude and of suspicion to be compelling philosophically. Moreover, as a Christian thinker I find postmodernism's hermeneutics of finitude helpful in thinking about human createdness and its hermeneutics of suspicion helpful in thinking about human fallenness.

As promised, my appropriation will involve a double negation, a rejection and a recontextualizing. Both of these stem from the way the postmodern insights get expressed. It seems to me that the postmodern arguments are about the limits of human understanding and that they support the claim that we do not have access to Truth. But that is different from the claim that there is no Truth, which would be true only if there were no other subject or subjects capable of Truth. But one looks in vain for an argument, even a bad argument, for the claim that the conditions for human understanding are the conditions for any understanding whatever.

Secular postmodernism is guilty, I believe, of a non sequitur that is equal but opposite to the one we noticed earlier. That one slid from "There is something Absolute" to "Our speech about the Absolute must be absolute." Postmodernism tends to slide in the opposite direction, from "We have no absolute insight" to "There is no absolute insight." Hence the formulation, "The truth is that *there is no Truth*." But this is equivalent to the claim that since our understanding is not divine there is no divine understanding, a view that might be taken to exaggerate our importance in the overall scheme of things.

Kant, in the First Critique, is as stubborn as any postmodernist in denying our access to Truth. But he thinks it would be simple dogmatism to deny the reality of God and that only God's knowledge, unlike human knowledge, deserves to be called Truth. Similarly, in a context where Truth and System have been tightly linked by Hegelian theory, Kierkegaard's Climacus says

that reality is a system for God, but not for us as existing creatures. These two thinkers provide the theistic context into which
I would like to appropriate postmodernism's claim. In this case,
not surprisingly, recontextualizing means reformulating. The
version I want to propose is this:

> The truth is that there is Truth, but in our finitude and fallenness
> we do not have access to it. We'll have to make do with the truths
> available to us; but that does not mean either that we should deny
> the reality of Truth or that we should abandon the distinction be-
> tween truth and falsity. Moreover, the most we should claim for
> this claim itself is that it is true, that it is the best way for us hu-
> mans to think about the matter.

The rejection that accompanies this recontextualizing is fairly
obvious. It is the secular, atheistic project of some postmodernists that falls by the wayside. My claim is that the arguments I
am interested in appropriating neither presuppose nor entail a
godless world and that the links between those arguments and
the secular project with which they are usually associated by
friend and foe alike are merely biographical and not conceptual.
To repeat, this is because those arguments show, not that there
is no God, but simply that we are not God. Moreover, they do so
in ways that make it more difficult to agree that we are not God
and then go about our business, theoretical and practical, as if
we were.

In saying that we do not have access to the Truth, I am claiming that we do not possess it, that we do not preside over it, that
our knowledge fails to embody the ideals of adequation and
correspondence in terms of which Truth has traditionally been
defined. But this does not entail that the Truth has no access to
us, or that we should abandon the attempt to determine how
best to think about what there is. The boy who does not suck on
coins because his parents have told him about the bugs that will
make him sick does not have the Truth about the matter (defined, in the analogy, by superior parental knowledge). But he
does think about the matter as a boy with his intellectual limitations ought to think about it. Moreover, it is important to recognize from a theological point of view that his knowledge of the
truth of the matter, while neither Knowledge nor Truth, is suffi-

cient to keep him healthy (so far as coins are concerned) and to bring him into a grateful and obedient relation to his parents. It is not clear that we should ask our knowledge of God to do more than this.

I want to conclude with a remembrance of another pastor, this one my own, years ago. His preaching did not shy away in the least from kerygmatic boldness; and he never suggested that we replace the Ten Commandments with the Ten Suggestions. He wrestled hard with the biblical text in order that his sermons might be as faithful to it as possible. But with great regularity he ended his sermons with these words: I think it must be something like that. I like to think of him, anachronistically to be sure, as having appropriated postmodernism.

5

Christian Philosophers and the Copernican Revolution

SHOULD CHRISTIAN PHILOSOPHERS be favorably or unfavorably disposed toward Kantian idealism? I want to suggest that they should be favorably disposed, that there are important affinities between Kantian idealism and Christian theism—important resources in the former for expressing themes essential to the latter.

This is not a majority report. Christian philosophers, both Catholic and Protestant, have often felt a strong need to be realists and have exhibited a correspondingly strong allergic reaction to Kantian idealism in all its forms. No student of Art Holmes is likely to say that there is only one way to be a Christian philosopher; and so I do not wish to deny that realism has resources that can be put to good use by Christian thinkers. I wish only to suggest that the instinctive distrust of Kantian idealism is unfortunate and in need of being overcome.

A recent renunciation of Kant and all his works can be found in Alvin Plantinga's 1989–90 Stob Lectures, "The Twin Pillars of Christian Scholarship."[1] In disputing that repudiation of Kant, my quarrel is not with Plantinga in particular but with a widespread tendency among Christian philosophers to which he has given a powerful, simple, and typically witty expression.

Rejecting the view that human reason is worldview neutral, he claims that philosophical conflict is one form in which the battle between the *Civitas Dei* and the *Civitas Mundi* takes place. In the western intellectual world at present he sees two primary opponents to Christian theism: Perennial Naturalism, with its ancient roots in Epicurus, Democritus, and Lucretius, and Cre-

---

[1] Published as a pamphlet by Calvin College and Seminary, Grand Rapids, Mich., 1990. Cited in the text as TP.

ve Anti-realism, with its ancient roots in Protagoras and his claim that man (*sic*) is the measure of all things. But he makes it clear that the real locus classicus for this second major modern threat to Christian theism is Kant's *Critique of Pure Reason* (TP pp. 10, 14–15).

At issue is the epistemological core of the First Critique, to which he gave memorable expression in the preface to the second edition by calling it a second Copernican Revolution. Realism has assumed that "all our knowledge must conform to objects." His idealism will explore the alternative, "that objects must conform to our knowledge" (B p. xvi). Plantinga identifies precisely this move as the essence of Creative Anti-realism: "But the fundamental *thrust* of Kant's self-styled Copernican Revolution is that the things in the world owe their basic structure and perhaps their very existence to the noetic activity of our minds" (TP p. 15). I want to suggest that there are four fundamentally different kinds of Kantianism, and that only one of these merits the negative response Plantinga gives to Creative Anti-realism in general.

The epistemological claim of realists is that "knowledge must conform to objects" because such conformity (however difficult it may be to state wherein it consists) is both possible in principle and just what it takes to make our judgments or beliefs into knowledge. It is this claim that Kant seeks to qualify substantially. Much of what he counts as human knowledge is not our conforming to the way things are but their conforming to the way we apprehend them.

My experience in trying to teach Kant is that students are so deeply wedded to some sort of commonsense realism that they have a difficult time, not so much in accepting Kant's claim, as in first understanding what he is saying. So when I teach the First Critique I resort to homely examples. I ask how it is possible for me to know a priori, that is, before turning on the TV to watch the Evening News, that Dan Rather's tie will be various shades of gray. A typical answer will have an inductive character quite contrary to Kant's meaning. Dan Rather has been wearing gray ties all week, so I infer that he will do so again tonight. I insist that I have not been watching the news lately and have no observational basis for such an inference, but nevertheless know for sure that the tie will be gray tonight. Silence. Then, suddenly, a light goes on, and some student solves the puzzle. "You're watching on a black and white TV set." From there it is fairly easy to show that Kant thinks of the human mind as a kind of receiving apparatus whose "spontaneity" permits things, regardless of what they are actually like, to appear only in certain ways.

Crude as this model is, it illustrates several key elements in Kant's account. First, it attributes some but not all of the features I perceive the object to have to my receiving apparatus. I can know the tie's color a priori, for example, but not whether it will be polka dot or striped. For Kant the features due to the "spontaneity" of the human mind are formal, the forms of intuition and the categories of understanding: hence the appropriateness of describing the Copernican Revolution as attributing the "basic structure" of things in the world to "the noetic activity of our minds."

Second, this model helps us resolve the question whether they owe "their very existence" to that same activity. Plantinga's answer to the question of whether Kant makes such a claims is "perhaps."[2] It might be better to say, It depends. One way of talking about Dan Rather's tie is to say that there are two of them, the red and blue one I would see if I were in the studio and could see it without dependence on my black and white receiving apparatus, and the gray one I see while watching TV.

On the other hand, since I more naturally say I am watching Dan Rather than that I am watching his image on the screen (unless I am comparing two sets with higher and lower resolution), it might be better to speak of only one tie and of two ways of seeing it. In both cases I look at his red and blue tie, but in the studio I see it as it truly is, while at home watching TV I see it as it has been systematically distorted by a receiving apparatus that *simultaneously makes it possible for me to see the tie at all (since I'm not in the studio) and makes it impossible for me to see it as it truly is.*

Now, Kant often talks the first way, as if there were two

---

[2] In his discussion of Creative Anti-realism in his 1982 Presidential Address to the Central Division of the APA, Plantinga exhibits the same uncertainty. See "How to Be an Anti-realist," in *Proceedings and Addresses of the American Philosophical Association,* 1983, pp. 48 and 50.

worlds, a noumenal world of things in themselves and a phenomenal world of appearances. But a careful reading makes it
clear that this is just a *façon de parler,* a convenient, all but inevitable way of speaking about two ways of apprehending one set of
objects.

*epistemic
remedy of
Kant*

Both ways of speaking have their point, but as with the distinction between use and mention or between the material and
formal mode, it is important to be clear which one is operative
in any given context. It we are speaking the language of two
worlds, then it makes sense to say that "the things in the [phe-
nomenal] world owe their . . . existence to the noetic activity of
our minds." For without that activity there would be no such
world and no such things.

If, on the other hand, we are speaking of one object and two
modes of apprehension, it would be misleading to attribute the
existence of things to our noetic activity for just the same reason
that it would be silly to attribute the existence of Dan Rather's
red and blue tie to the "spontaneity" of my black and white TV
set. Without leaving this mode of thought, however, we could
say that the thing (the only tie there is, the red and blue one) *as
known by us* (and thus seeming to be gray) owes its existence to
the receiving apparatus, though the thing as it is in itself does
not. This way of speaking brings us so close to the language of
two objects and two worlds that the virtual inevitability of this
mode of speaking becomes clear.

A third advantage of our crude model is that it illuminates
Kant's theory of the thing in itself, and, in so doing, reveals the
realism at the base of his idealism. Two important points about
Kant's theory of the thing in itself are suggested by our model.
In the first place, by refusing to jettison the thing in itself as
later idealists from Fichte and Hegel to Husserl and Rorty have
wanted to do, he makes it clear that the world whose existence
is dependent on our apprehension is not *the* world. It is only *our*
world, the world of appearances, the world as known by us; and
the dependence of that world on our apprehension is tautolog-
ical.

In the second place, our model illustrates the fact that for Kant
the thing in itself, which is what it is independently of our noetic
acts, is not best identified merely by that independence. It is true

that the real tie, the red and blue one, is what it is without reference to the black and white TV sets through which it may appear. If all those sets were destroyed, it would still be there. But it is not necessary to identify the tie without any reference to its being observed. On the contrary, it is most easily identified as the tie as seen by those in the studio.[3]

For Kant, to be in the studio means, quite simply, to be God. Thus, for Kant, the thing in itself is the thing as apprehended by God.[4] In the aftermath of Kant there has often been debate over whether it makes any sense to speak of a world, of objects and properties, of facts and truths, independent of any and all apprehension of them. It is an interesting debate; but in view of the tight link Kant makes between the thing in itself and God's knowledge, it is a debate rendered not in the least necessary by the First Critique.

In that context, of course, Kant cannot simply help himself to God's existence, so the point must have a hypothetical character. The thing in itself is the thing as apprehended by the God of classical theism if there is such a God. But even in this hypothetical mode, Kant does not know how to identify *the* world, except by reference to God's knowledge. Kant is, we might say, a per spectivist, and unless God (or some viable surrogate) represents *the* perspective on the world, it is not clear that there is anything that deserves to be called *the* world.

Now it becomes clear how the Kantian version of Creative Anti-realism, so far from being one of the major modern threats to Christian theism, is itself an essentially theistic theory.[5] The

---

[3] If there are color-blind people in the studio, we need only apply our analysis of the TV set as a distorting apparatus to their biological sensing equipment. The tie in itself is the tie as apprehended by viewers whose cognitive equipment is properly functioning. But if I am watching a black and white TV instead of being present in the studio, the proper functioning of my cognitive equipment will avail nothing so far as seeing the thing as it is in itself.

[4] For a more detailed, textual presentation of this thesis and its implications, see my essay "In Defense of the Thing in Itself," *Kant-Studien* 59, no. 1 (1968), pp. 118–41.

[5] Thomas Aquinas writes, "Even if there were no human intellects, there could be truths because of their relation to the divine intellect. But if, *per impossibile*, there were no intellects at all, but things continued to exist, then there would be no such reality as truth." Plantinga quotes this passage from *De Veritate* Q. 1, A. 6 in "How to Be an Anti-realist" (p. 68) as part of his argument

whole point of the distinction between appearances and things in themselves is to distinguish between human and divine knowledge, between the way the world appears to God's infinite and eternal mind and the way it appears to our finite and temporal minds, *precisely when our cognitive equipment is properly functioning*. This distinction, in some form, would seem to me to be essential to any kind of Christian theism.

It is misleading, then, for Plantinga to treat 'Creative Anti-realism' as essentially interchangeable with 'Enlightenment Humanism' (TP pp. 10, 14). There are indeed humanist versions, and I shall shortly discuss two of them, but at its locus classicus Creative Anti-realism is an essentially theistic theory and not an enemy of theism. Plantinga sees Creative Anti-realism as a theory that "vastly overestimates" the place of human beings in the universe" because "we human beings, insofar as we confer its basic structure upon the world, really take the place of God" (TP p. 17). But according to Kant it is just where human cognition becomes creative or constitutive of the world (as apprehended) that we are cut off from Truth. For Kant, to paraphrase Protagoras, Man (*sic*) is the measure of human truth, but not of Truth, whose only measure is God.

The matter is somewhat more complicated with another phrase Plantinga uses as virtually synonymous with 'Creative Anti-realism,' namely, 'Enlightenment Subjectivism' (TP pp. 10, 14). On Kant's view, human cognition of the world, even when our epistemic equipment is properly functioning, is essentially different in certain important respects from God's. Since God's view is the standard of truth, reality, and hence, objectivity, human understanding is necessarily subjective.

---

that the best way to be an anti-realist is to be a theist. He affirms the anti-realist intuition that truth is not independent of minds or persons (pp. 67–70) and, summarizing Aquinas, whom he takes to speak here for the theistic tradition, he affirms "that truth is independent of our intellectual activity but not of God. . . . Creative anti-realism, I said, is the claim that truth is not independent of mind: and divine creative anti-realism is the view that truth is not independent of God's noetic activity" (pp. 68–69). As we have seen, this is Kant's view of Truth, although he also recognizes a second-order truth dependent on the properly functioning human mind. Unfortunately, Plantinga nevertheless associates Kant with the humanistic forms of Creative Anti-realism he rejects.

But to the transcendental idealism that affirms this subjectivity, Kant unites an empirical realism that confers upon it a certain objectivity and permits him to call it (human) knowledge.[6] For Kant distinguishes the way the world appears to a human mind that is properly functioning from the way it appears to a human mind that is not and is thus, as we would normally say, in error. There is, we might say, the thing as it is for God, the thing as it is for us, and the thing as it is for me; the distinction between us and me is obviously intended to express the distinction between properly and improperly functioning human minds. Now, what Kant calls the phenomenal world is the world for us. Relative to the world for God it is subjective, but relative to the world for me it is objective. So there is no contradiction in calling the cognitive correlative of the phenomenal world (human) knowledge, speaking in an empirically realistic tone of voice, while denying it the status of knowledge ("I have therefore found it necessary to deny *knowledge*"; B p. xxx), speaking in a transcendentally idealistic tone of voice. Under such circumstances the term 'Creative Anti-realism' is less likely to be misunderstood than 'Enlightenment Subjectivism.'[7] There are two kinds of truth that Kant does not allow to be dissolved by subjectivistic skepticism: the *Truth* represented by the knowledge of God, and the *truth* represented by the human mind, properly functioning.

Now, many commentators on Kant are not especially interested in theism, and some, I suppose, are positively allergic to it.

---

[6] The First Critique opens with the words "Human reason." Humanists (where humanism designates an alternative to theism) assume that the human point of view is *the* point of view; consequently, they have little reason to speak of human reason as distinct from simply reason. Theists, however, have good reason to distinguish human reason from divine reason. The theistic character of Kant's Critical Anti-realism appears in its first two words.

[7] The phrase 'Creative Anti-realism' is itself not entirely free of misleading implications. The Copernican Revolution says we are "responsible for the structure and nature of the [phenomenal] world." But on Kant's view we are responsible the way a virus is responsible for an illness and not the way an artisan is responsible for an artifact. So it could easily be misleading to refer to us as "architects of the [phenomenal] universe" (TP p. 14). Plantinga concludes his brief account of Kantian idealism by asking, "And if the way things are is thus up to us and our structuring activity, why don't we improve things a bit?" (TP p. 16). One hopes he has not taken the architect metaphor too literally, but rather is speaking in jest.

The result is that the theistic character of Kantian idealism is often overlooked entirely and almost never emphasized. Humanists often treat Kant as if he were a humanist. While this helps to explain the negative reaction Christian philosophers often have toward Kant, it does not justify it. For the humanist reading of Kant does great violence to the text, while a textually responsible reading develops an important theistic theme.

It is the general structure of the Copernican Revolution that I wish to commend to Christian philosophers, not necessarily its details. But I do want to look at a couple of "details" that play a significant role in Plantinga's critique, to try to clear away what I see to be misunderstanding. Still speaking about Kant, he writes,

> Such fundamental structures of the world as those of space and time, object and property, number, truth and falsehood, possibility and necessity—these are not to be found in the world as such, but are somehow constituted by our own mental or conceptual activity . . . they are not to be found in the things themselves. . . . Were there no persons like ourselves engaging in noetic activities, there would be nothing in space and time, nothing displaying object-property structure, nothing that is true or false, possible or impossible, no kind of things coming in a certain number— nothing like this at all." (TP pp. 14–15).[8]

The reference to truth and falsity makes it look as if Kant identifies truth with human truth after all, qualifying for the humanist designation and the opposition of theists. But what does Kant mean by saying that these characteristics are not to be found "in the world as such," that is, in the world as it really is? Nothing more than that the "world as such," which is to say, the world as God sees it, does not have the temporal characteristics of human experience. For all of the a priori features that define the phenomenal world and would be lacking in the absence of human knowers are essentially tied to the human experience of time: (1) Time, for Kant, is the sequential flow of inner and outer sense, without which there is no human experience at all. (2) Space is

---

[8] Although such terms as truth and falsity, object and property do not appear in Kant's table of categories, it is not difficult to identify the categories Plantinga expresses with these terms, reality and negation, inherence and subsistence respectively. (A 80 = B 106).

essentially temporal for Kant as well, since, to put it crudely, it takes time for perception to move from here to there. (3) Finally, all twelve categories, insofar as they constitute the world of human experience and are not merely formal features of judgment, are schematized with an essential reference to time. Thus the object and property that would disappear from the world in the absence of human knowers are not object and property per se, but substance and accident *as defined by human temporality.* ?
Similarly, the truth and falsity that would disappear derive from the categories of reality and negation *as essentially linked to our experience of time.* Thus we are back to the tautology that in the absence of human cognition, the world *as apprehended by human minds* would disappear.

All this leaves God free to apprehend objects and their properties and to distinguish truth from falsity in the manner proper to divine knowledge. On Kant's view (and Plantinga's, according to a recent essay), what we know about the nature of divine knowledge is somewhat overwhelmingly exceeded by what we don't know. But surely on the basis of what Kant has said we are not entitled to say with regard to such features of our world as object and property or truth and falsity that without us there would be "nothing like this at all."

My teacher, Wilfrid Sellars, used to talk about the thing in itself as in sprace and trime. Though no theist he, and wishing to put Kant to essentially humanist uses, he recognized that Kant assumes some kind of correlation between the phenomenal and noumenal worlds. Of course, he is not in a position to prove this or to specify the nature of what we might call the analogy between the two by translating the metaphors of sprace and trime (Sellars's metaphors, not Kant's) into the prose of the phenomenal world. The point is simply that nothing Kant says prohibits the assumption of such an analogy. Kant's doctrine only prohibits the claim that our knowledge and God's are univocal.

Objection—Kant's theism makes too sharp a distinction, more Platonic than biblical, between time and eternity. Today some theists want to move away from the *totum simul* tradition and to say that God is in some sense in time. That would seem to make Kant's move unnecessary.

Reply—(1) Even if God is in some sense in time, there might well be such a significant difference between divine and human temporality that the distinction between the world for God and the world for us remains necessary for the theist. (2) To say, on the other hand, that God's temporality is so nearly univocal to ours that the distinction is otiose is to stretch theism to its limits, or beyond; but in any case, the Kantian attempt to preserve the distinction would be an intra-theistic debate rather than the onslaught of the *Civitas Mundi* on the *Civitas Dei*.

Objection—But Kant's theory is not just about our knowledge of the world. It is also about our knowledge of God, and it entails that we cannot prove the existence of God, thereby depriving faith of its rational foundation.

Reply—(1) Kant's rejection of the ontological argument does not derive from the Copernican Revolution but from the quite different doctrine that existence is not a predicate. If he is mistaken about that, the ontological argument might work. (2) Kant's theory does nothing to preclude the moral argument for the existence of God and might be seen as paving the way for it. (3) Theistic proofs are not in any case an integral part of theism, only of certain theistic systems. Many theists reject some or all of the traditional proofs, and some go so far as to argue that the very project of trying to prove the existence of God is dangerous, if not to theism, then to the faith theism means to express. In short, the debate over theistic proofs is not the confrontation between the *Civitas Mundi* and the *Civitas Dei* either.

Objection—The previous objection raised the right issue but in the wrong way. It is our knowledge of God that is primarily at issue; but the issue concerns revealed rather than natural theology. Scriptural revelation, received in faith, gives us a knowledge of God fully on a par with God's own self-knowledge. But Kant's distinction between human and divine knowledge denies this possibility.

Reply—There is a considerable difference between the claim that biblical revelation teaches us things we need to know and, given our finitude and sinfulness, cannot discover on our own and the claim made for revelation by the objector, whose theism might well be described as hubristic theism. My teacher, Kenneth Kantzer (well known, like the objector, for his "high" view of Scripture), used to say that the Bible gives us the divinely revealed misinformation about God. That was his way of saying that revelation is incarnational, that it comes to us as we are rather than lifting us quite completely out of the human condition. Kant is no threat to this kind of theism; and if he is a threat to the hubristic theism of the objector, he is in good company. Was it not St. Paul who said that "we know only in part" and see even that part "in a mirror dimly" (I Cor. 13:9, 12)? Once again the Copernican Revolution is not the Trojan horse that the *Civitas Mundi* is trying to sneak into the *Civitas Dei*. It rather serves as a reminder to the citizens of the latter that the city of their love was not named after them.

Having promised to discuss four kinds of "Kantian" idealism, I turn briefly to three versions that differ in important ways from Kant's own. All of them reflect the fact that the history of the Copernican Revolution, in spite of the universalist character Kant gave to it, has been, from at least the time of Hegel on, particularist and pluralist. For Kant, the forms and categories that constitute the phenomenal world are at work in all human cognition, at all times and in all places. But almost immediately people began to notice the operation of historically specific a priories constituting a variety of human worlds.

I like to illustrate this variation on the Kantian theme with another homely illustration. Suppose I am a racist and I meet a member of a racial group I despise. I "know" a priori that this person will have a number of undesirable characteristics and will be inferior to me intellectually and morally. For my racism has turned my mind into a receiving apparatus that will only allow people of that race to appear in that way, just as the black and white TV allows red and blue ties to appear only as gray. This racism is no doubt shared by others, with whom I live together in a world constituted by our shared racist a priori. In that world persons of the race(s) in question appear of necessity to be quite different from what they are in themselves, that is, different from the way God, and, for that matter, humans whose cognitive apparatus is functioning properly, see them. It is quite easy to apply a Kantian analysis to the many different worlds (good, bad, and indifferent) that make up human history. We usually call them cultures (or subcultures).

It is at this point that *Humanist-Relativist Creative Anti-realism* enters the scene. Lacking any possible reference to God's perspective as the criterion of *the* world, and faced with the overwhelming variety of human worlds (even in the natural sciences, in the aftermath of Kuhn et al.), it is easy for the humanist to conclude "that there simply isn't any such thing as objective truth. . . . The whole idea of an objective truth, the same for all of us, on this view, is an illusion, or a bourgeois plot, or a silly mistake. Thus does anti-realism breed relativism and nihilism" (TP p. 18).

In his Stob Lectures Plantinga calls this view "deeply antagonistic to a Christian way of looking at the world" (TP p. 19; cf. p. 20). In his 1982 Presidential Address to the Central Division of the APA, he attributes this view to Richard Rorty and suggests that it represents an illegitimate inference from the true premise that there is "no methodical way to settle all important disagreements."[9] It is, we might say, like concluding from the fact that the jury is hung that the defendant was neither guilty nor innocent.

I agree with both of these assessments of this particularist Protagoreanism. I also find it both logically and theologically problematic. But I demur to the tag line, "Thus does anti-realism breed relativism and nihilism." For what drives this relativism is its humanism, not its anti-realism. The two together can give rise to views like Rorty's. But theism, combined with a bizarre reading of Genesis 11, has generated a theological rationale for apartheid in South Africa. Yet it would be strange to say, "Thus does theism give rise to racism." Plantinga's dire warnings should have been directed at this species of Creative Anti-realism, not at the entire genus. Only some mushrooms are poisonous.

There is another humanist variation on the Kantian theme. Let us call it *Humanist-Objectivist Creative Anti-realism.* It recognizes the plurality of human worlds (cultures, paradigms, language games) and even the absence of any neutral algorithm for resolving our deepest disputes about how the world is or ought to be. At the descriptive level it is as pluralist as the previous view. But it does not abandon the notion of objective truth.

Lacking God, it needs what was previously referred to as a viable surrogate for the divine perspective that would signify *the* world. It designates the consensus of the ideal (counterfactual)

---

[9] "How to Be an Anti-realist," pp. 62–64.

human community of investigators as the criterion of Truth. A classic expression of this view is Peirce's definition of truth: "The opinion which is fated to be ultimately agreed to by all who investigate, is what we mean by the truth, and the object represented in this opinion is the real."[10]

According to this view the distinction between appearances and the thing in itself returns. The thing in itself is the object of that ultimate consensus. Anything else is appearance. Thus we may (think we) have good reason to think that Newtonian physics is closer to the truth than Aristotelian, and relativity and quantum physics closer than Newtonian. But none of these can claim to be more than our best approximation to the Truth, our current truth. Since the idea of Truth functions as a regulative ideal, any current truth is phenomenal and not noumenal truth.

Habermas's notion of a consensus reached by an ideal speech community or in accordance with the counterfactual norms implicit in ordinary discourse is an extension of this idea to normative as well as factual truth. Its explicit purpose is to retain, in the face of various forms of ethical relativism, an objective truth for ethics analogous to what is available for science.[11] Here, too, the clear implication is that while all our judgments, whether of fact or of right, are open to challenge and revision, these truths are answerable to the Truth.[12]

Since this is a humanist view, the theist will find it inadequate. But once again it is important to locate the disagreement correctly. The proper theistic complaint against this view is that it

---

[10] *Collected Papers of Charles Sanders Peirce*, ed. Charles Hartshorne and Paul Weiss (Cambridge, Mass.: Harvard University Press, 1931–35), vol. 5, p. 407.

[11] Habermas does not treat all value judgments as objective. Some remain matters of taste, so he distinguishes the right from the good. Drawing the line is a difficult and hotly disputed task. But the point is that Habermas is an ethical as well as a factual objectivist. In the midst of de facto moral pluralism, he holds that our judgments about what is right are responsible to a norm independent of what we or anyone else at any given moment may happen to think. See especially "Discourse Ethics: Notes on a Program of Philosophical Justification," in *Moral Consciousness and Communicative Action*, trans. Christian Lenhardt and Shierry Weber Nicholsen (Cambridge, Mass.: MIT Press, 1990).

[12] Habermas is more explicit than Peirce about the humanist character of his view. This comes most fully to expression in his theory of the linguistification of the sacred, the substitution of human language for God. See *Theory of Communicative Action*, trans. Thomas McCarthy, 2 vols. (Boston: Beacon Press, 1984, 1987), vol. II, pp. 77 ff.

is humanist, not that it is an anti-realist. For it is the former and not the latter that links this theory to the *Civitas Mundi*.

At the same time, the theist has reason to appreciate several features of this view in spite of its humanism. First, the PH (for Peirce-Habermas) version of Creative Anti-realism can recognize at the descriptive level the unsurpassable plurality of human perspectives without abandoning the notion of objective truth. Unlike relativistic anti-realism, it doesn't conclude from a hung jury that the defendant neither did nor did not commit the crime. Thus it can avoid the temptation, to which the Enlightenment succumbed, of having to make excessive claims for human reason's actual ability in order to preserve the notion of objectivity.

Second, it can nevertheless reflect critically about the criteria and the methodologies by which our efforts to know the real are shaped. The goal, ideal *human* consensus (which the humanist will call Truth, the theist truth), may well enable us to specify norms with whose help our progress is more likely to be in the right direction than without them. For the humanist this will primarily concern science (the realm of objective fact) and ethics/politics (the realm of objective value). For the theist it will also include theology, and the theologian (whose proper goal is also an ideal *human* consensus) might well learn from the philosophy of science and from critical social theory lessons that will help to develop a sounder hermeneutics for interpreting the data of experience and biblical revelation. The task of finding a middle ground between arrogant objectivism and cynical relativism is just as difficult for theology as for science and ethics.

Finally, the theist can appreciate and appropriate from the PH version of Kantianism its strong sense of the penultimate (at best) character of our current theories and of the de facto pluralism of perspectives from which we find ourselves unable to extricate ourselves other than by fiat. The reminder that our best theories to date, including our theologies, are in their very structure and not just in their details fallible, open to critique, and revisable can be welcomed by the theist, who is committed to taking both human finitude and human sinfulness seriously.

This reference to sinfulness brings us to our fourth and final version of Kantianism. It is a theistic view that equates the thing in itself with the thing as known by God. Thus it holds to an

objectivist notion of truth. Its idealistic interpretation of hu1
understanding differs from Kant's and agrees with the two .
manist variations we have examined by giving a pluralist account of the phenomenal world. The a priories that define
human cultures, paradigms, language games, and so forth are
legion. We can call this view *Theist-Pluralist Creative Anti-realism*
to distinguish it from Kant's own *Theist-Universalist* version. It
also differs from Kant's view by making sin rather than finitude
the primary barrier between human and divine knowledge. For
my money Kierkegaard is the best proponent of this view.

Our racism example is helpful here. In it we encounter a
human world that has two important characteristics. First, it is
one of many different worlds constituted by human patterns of
apprehension. Thus the worlds of white racism, black racism,
anti-Semitism, nationalism, sexism, and so forth represent distinctively different ways in which the human receiving apparatus requires others to appear. Second, it is a result of human
sinfulness. If for Kant the primary barrier between God's view
of the world and ours is our finitude, more particularly, our temporality, for Kierkegaard it is our sinfulness. While Kant points
to differences that obtain when our cognitive equipment is properly functioning, Kierkegaard, in the tradition of Paul, Augustine, Luther, and Calvin, points to the fact that it never is, that
with respect to at least some kinds of truth, including above all
else the truth about God, we are disposed to "suppress the
truth" and thereby to become those whose "senseless minds
[are] darkened" (Rom. 1:18, 21). Paul, whose words these are,
immediately connects them to idolatry (v. 23), to the gods who
are created in the human image, that is, constituted by the
human mode of apprehending them.

Plantinga notices that Creative Anti-realism can talk this way
about the divine. In contrast to simple atheism it takes the essentially Feuerbachian view "that there is such a person as God, all
right, but he owes his existence to our noetic activity—[a view
that] seems at best a bit strained" or "seems at best a piece of
laughable bravado."[13] Would that it were only laughable bravado that we have to do with here, and not the inveterate human
tendency toward idolatry!

---

[13] "How to Be an Anti-realist," pp. 49 and 54.

In spite of his professed Calvinism, Plantinga fails to recognize in what he calls, aptly, creative theological anti-realism a cogent and powerful account of the noetic effects of sin. We might say that he is so devoted to giving an account of human knowledge in terms of the proper functioning of our cognitive equipment that he tends to ignore its persistent propensity toward malfunctioning.

Or we might say that he has failed to make the kind of distinctions between various forms of anti-realism to which this essay is devoted. In a humanist context, the view that we create God in our own image is the whole story about God and is but a sophisticated version of atheism. But in a theist context, it is the recognition that in spite of what God truly is, our sinfully corrupted receiving apparatuses generate gods conveniently suited to our demands.

We may be looking at the red and blue God present in nature or in scripture, but we see one of the many gray gods that make up the story of human religion. This is not to say that we create these gods out of whole cloth. Kantianism never confuses the phenomenal world with fiction. Thus idolatry is perhaps better thought of in terms of edited gods than of fabricated gods, just as propaganda is most effective when liberally laced with truth.

This means that the God we actually worship, the phenomenal God constituted by the sinful "spontaneity" of our receiving apparatus, may be (1) all comfort and no demand (Freud), (2) the justifier of our position of social privilege and power (Marx), or (3) the justifier of our resentment and revenge against our enemies (Nietzsche).[14]

In short, where the humanist finds a sophisticated version of atheism, the theist *can and should* find a powerful expression of prophetic monotheism and its protest against the human tendency, even among God's covenant people, to idolatry. Such a warning, it seems to me, should be an essential part of every epistemology that purports to be guided by Christian theism,

---

[14] For a detailed study of these three masters of the hermeneutics of suspicion as presenting an essentially prophetic critique of religion from a secular perspective, see my *Suspicion and Faith: The Religious Uses of Modern Atheism* (New York: Fordham University Press, 1998).

and this is the most important reason why Christian philosophers should take the Copernican Revolution seriously.

In other words, Kierkegaardian Kantianism is more important than Kantian Kantianism. Why? Kant's version helps the theist to express the limitations of human knowledge due to finitude, whereas Kierkegaard's helps to express those due to sin. Both are important, but epistemic finitude seems to get itself expressed more easily without help from the Copernican Revolution than does epistemic fallenness.

Take the cases of Aquinas and Plantinga (who may be more a Thomist than a Calvinist). Both give anti-realist accounts of Truth, making Truth and God's knowledge necessarily coextensive.[15] But when it comes to human knowledge, the matter is different. Aquinas gives a classically realist account, and Plantinga treats all forms of Creative Anti-realism as assaults on the Kingdom of God. Neither has trouble expressing the finitude of human knowledge vis-à-vis the divine; though neither of them notices the "Kantian" implications of the distinctions they draw. Finally, neither of them is very sensitive to the noetic effects of sin. Compared to Augustine, Luther, and Calvin, for example, Aquinas does epistemology as if in the Garden of Eden. And Plantinga, as already noted, has an epistemology all but entirely oriented toward the proper functioning of the human mind. He is unable to see in "creative theological anti-realism" anything more than what it is in the hands of humanists.

Could it be that realism/hostility toward anti-realism in our account of human knowledge tends to blind us to the noetic effects of sin, and encourages us to treat as episodic (empirical) error what needs to seen as systematic (a priori) suppression of the truth? If so, then Christian philosophers would do well to start out by making friends with the Copernican Revolution.

---

[15] See the passage from Aquinas, quoted by Plantinga in n. 5. His own view comes down to the claim that "the fundamental anti-realist intuition—that truth is not independent of mind—is correct. This intuition is best accommodated by the theistic claim that necessarily, propositions have two properties essentially: *being conceived by God* and *being truth if and only if believed by God*. So how can we sensibly be anti-realists? Easily enough: by being theists." See "How to Be an Anti-realist," p. 70.

6

Totality and Finitude in Schleiermacher's Hermeneutics

Flower in the crannied wall,
I pluck you out of the crannies,
I hold you here, root and all, in my hand,
Little flower—but *if* I could understand
What you are, root and all, and all in all,
I should know what God and man is.

Alfred, Lord Tennyson

WE CAN TAKE "root and all, and all in all" to be poetic longhand for 'completely' and "God and man" to be a synecdoche for 'all there is, the totality of being'. The poet says, in effect, "If I could understand the tiniest part *completely*, I would understand the whole show." On the other side of this coin we find the holist, telling the poet, "Yes, and unless you know the totality of being and know it completely, you cannot understand any of its parts aright."

Like Spinoza and Hegel, Schleiermacher is a holist par excellence, especially by virtue of his hermeneutical circles. The relation of mutual determination between whole and part is utterly fundamental to his theory of interpretation. But I say circles, plural, because (with apologies to Howard Cosell) one finds a veritable plethora of circles in his writings on hermeneutics, not just that of whole and part. If we imagined them as a kind of entourage, he would rival that Gilbert and Sullivan character who was accompanied by "his sisters and his cousins, which he reckons by the dozens, and his aunts."

There is, for example, the way in which both grammatical and technical or psychological interpretation depend upon the other member of this pair for their own completion. Thus, "*Under-*

standing is only a being-in-one-another of these two moments" (p. 9).[1] In abbreviated form, "Grammatical. Not possible without technical. Technical. Not possible without grammatical." To separate the two is to engage in "complete abstraction" (p. 94). Or again, "Just as both methods are necessary to obtain complete understanding, so every combination of the two must proceed in such a way that the initial result of the one method will be supplemented by further applications of the other" (HHM p. 191).[2] *N.B.* While Schleiermacher is talking about what is necessary for complete understanding, he does not posit that completion but rather talks of an "initial result" that is to be "supplemented," not completed, by applications of the other method. We will return to this issue.

Schleiermacher describes this reciprocal dependence in terms that evoke the structuralist distinction between *langue* and *parole.* Thus, *"every utterance has a dual relationship, to the totality of language and to the whole thought of its originator. . . .* The individual is determined in his thought by the (common) language and can think only the thoughts which already have their designation in his language. . . . [L]anguage determines the progress of the individual in thought. For language is not just a complex of single representations, but also a system of the relatedness of representations . . . and every individual is only a location in which the language appears" (pp. 8–9).

On the other hand, "every utterance is to be understood only via the whole life to which it belongs" (p. 9). The author "collaborates in the language: for in part he produces something new in it . . . in part he preserves what he repeats and reproduces" (p. 91). The relation of the utterer to the language is this: "he is its organ and it is his. . . . The grammatical side puts the utterer in the background and regards him as just an organ of the lan-

---

[1] Page numbers not otherwise identified in the text are from Friedrich Schleiermacher, *Hermeneutics and Criticism and Other Writings,* ed. Andrew Bowie (New York: Cambridge University Press, 1998). When citations are from Schleiermacher's *Hermeneutics: The Handwritten Manuscripts,* trans. James Duke and Jack Forstman (Missoula, Mont.: Scholars Press, 1977), the page numbers will be preceded by HHM.

[2] These last two quotations are, respectively, from the notes of 1805 and from the first Academy Address of 1829. See also pp. 5, 24, 60, 88–89, 229, 254, 257, and 267.

guage. . . . The technical side, on the other hand, regards the utterer as the real-ground of the utterance and the language merely as the negative limiting principle" (pp. 229–30). It is in making the latter point that Schleiermacher identifies the hermeneutical task as "to understand the utterance at first just as well and then better than its author" (p. 23; cf. pp. 33, 228, 266).

Within grammatical interpretation there is at least one further circular relationship. Within a single sentence or proposition there are the subject and the predicate, "which mutually determine each other" (p. 61). "The subject must receive its final determinacy via the predicate and the predicate via the subject" (p. 239).[3]

Then, on the side of technical/psychological interpretation there are a couple of circular relations that do not appear to be variations on the whole/part scheme. One is the relation between the objective and subjective in a given utterance: "There is nothing purely objective in discourse; there is always the view of the utterer, thus something subjective, in it. There is nothing purely subjective, for it must after all be the influence of the object which highlights precisely this aspect." Since the utterer is at once "in the power of the object" and "outside this power, inhibiting, interrupting it," the reconstructive task of interpretation "rests primarily on understanding the relationship of both functions and the way they interlock" (pp. 257–58; cf. pp. 260–61). Thus, for example, we interpret love in the light of what the poet says about it, but we interpret that subjective presentation in the light of what we already (somehow) know about love.

A second circle (no doubt in hermeneutical hell for those who lust greedily for the pleasures of unilateral determination and are angry when their sloth is disturbed by the strenuous tasks imposed by circularity) is found between divinatory and comparative methods, which *"because they refer back to each other, also may not be separated from each other. . . .* Both refer back to each other. . . . Both may not be separated from each other," because divination gets its confirmation from comparison, and compari-

---

[3] Although subject and predicate "mutually condition" each other, they do so "not completely" because each is also determined by the adjectives, adverbs, prepositions, and so forth (p. 50).

son gets its unity from divination (pp. 92–93).[4] And just to keep things interesting, Schleiermacher tells us that both operations in their mutual dependence are "necessary for each side, for the grammatical as well as for the psychological" (HHM p. 205), which, as we have already seen, form a circle of their own.

We might see these relationships as a form of contextualism.[5] Seminarians, while being trained to preach, are often told that a text without a context is a pretext, as in the juxtaposition of the gospel texts that read: "and Judas went out and hanged himself . . . go and do thou likewise" (Matt. 27:5, Luke 10:37). In the pairs we have just looked at, Schleiermacher presents each partner as the context for the other. But the most basic form of text-context relation in his hermeneutics is that of part to whole. This is the paradigmatic hermeneutical circle. Thus interpretation is a two-fold task, "namely to understand the unity of the whole via the individual parts and the value of the individual parts via the unity of the whole" (p. 109). For, to repeat, as Schleiermacher is not bashful about doing, "on the one hand the whole can only be understood via the particulars, and on the other hand . . . the particulars can only be understood via the whole" (p. 148). When he repeats this idea once again in his second Academy Address, he adds, "This principle is of such consequence for hermeneutics and so incontestable that one cannot even begin to interpret without using it" (HHM p. 196).

It should come as no surprise that the whole/part circle is not one but rather many circles, as we shall see shortly. But before looking at their concentric/eccentric structure, we should eliminate, if possible, an important misunderstanding (a task Schleiermacher can hardly object to). It is while speaking of the whole/part relation that Schleiermacher says, "Complete knowledge is always in this *apparent* circle" and "This *seems* to be a circle" (pp. 24, 27, emphasis added).

We need to read this passage in connection with another: "If we are to understand the whole via the particular and the particular via the whole we find ourselves in the situation of *mutual determination*" (p. 149, emphasis added). It is mutual determina-

---

[4] Cf. pp. 100, 262, and HHM pp. 189–92.
[5] Schleiermacher speaks the language of context at pp. 54 and 231–36.

tion that makes the relations we have looked at so far circular rather than unidirectional or unilateral. Not only is there nothing *apparent* or *seeming* about this, but Schleiermacher never suggests that there is. So why does he suddenly speak that way about his most fundamental circle, that of part and whole?

It might be that he envies the confidence with which the classical foundationalists set sail from their point of departure, something that is either self-evident, or evident to the senses, or incorrigible,[6] but in any case not something provisional that awaits correction and revision in the light of that to which it leads. In the presence of any thought that is relative to its presuppositions, he may share the vertigo that leads to foundationalism as the attempt to render thought presuppositionless, or, to say essentially the same thing, to make sure that its presuppositions are premises that themselves are absolute and not relative.

In the context of Heideggerian pre-understandings and Gadamerian pre-judgments (pre-judices), it is common to speak of presuppositions and their provisional character. Schleiermacher does not often speak of presuppositions, but in the passage just cited about "mutual determination," he does. He continues:

> If we now posit the same hermeneutic principles for the achievement of this task as well, but posit a difference of the underlying presuppositions, then different results will emerge. [Enter the vertigo of relativity.] The sameness of the results points back to the sameness of presuppositions. Admittedly, if we can now say that the rightness of the results depends purely on the application of the right hermeneutic principles, then on the other hand the right results must often first decide which presupposition is the right one, for the result has been arrived at via this presupposition.

After noting that the interpreter uses presuppositions as foundations "one after the other" and needs to be careful in so doing, Schleiermacher continues, "The result which, if one begins with the various presuppositions, most corresponds with the immediate context of a text will be the correct one. But without trying

---

[6] I take this account of classical foundationalism from Alvin Plantinga. See *Faith and Rationality: Reason and Belief in God*, ed. Alvin Plantinga and Nicholas Wolterstorff (Notre Dame, Ind.: University of Notre Dame Press, 1983), pp. 58–59.

this out one cannot say that one has a safe foundation" (pp. 149–50).

Just how safe a foundation Schleiermacher hopes to end up with remains to be seen, but we must notice first of all that it is something he ends up with, not something he starts out with. Still, if his procedure is one that starts out with provisional presuppositions that lose this character at the end, leaving one with a safe foundation, one might be tempted to say that interpretation is only apparently or seemingly circular. But that is not what happens in this text. In the first place, it begins by affirming "mutual determination," the essence of circularity. Then, so far from seeking to eliminate this feature, Schleiermacher reiterates it, insisting that the result depends on the presupposition but also that "the right results must often first decide which presupposition is the right one."

Whatever the "safe foundation" may be, for which Schleiermacher hopes, there is no attempt to render circularity itself merely provisional. So why does he speak of an apparent, seeming circle? I think it must be admitted that even if this diction does not represent a failure of nerve on his part, it is misleading and likely to arouse false hopes in the faint of heart.

But a charitable reading of the passages in question is possible, as follows. There is no escaping the hermeneutical circle of whole and part (or any of the other hermeneutical circles). No matter how stable any given state of reflective equilibrium may appear (and here the language of seeming is not misleading), it retains its circular character. We are puzzled, as when we think of the two famous ladies who made their living by taking in each other's wash; and we are anxious lest we get the hermeneutical equivalent of feedback screech, as when the output of an amplifying system becomes its input. But this puzzlement and this anxiety need not be paralysis. Even if we can never get out of the circle, we can get in. As Heidegger puts it, "What is decisive is not to get out of the circle but to come into it in the right way."[7]

So perhaps Schleiermacher is just calling our attention to his

---

[7] Martin Heidegger, *Being and Time*, trans. John Macquarrie and Edward Robinson (New York: Harper & Row, 1962), p. 195 (¶32).

account of how to get in in the right way. We want to interpret a text. But in order rightly to read any part we must know the whole, but how can we know the whole, since we have not yet interpreted the parts from which alone such knowledge can arise? The answer, of course, is simple, straight out of Mortimer Adler's *How to Read a Book*. On the basis of a "cursory reading" (p. 27) or a "provisional read-through" (62) we formulate a "provisional overview" (p. 257; cf. p. 92). In this "general overview" (pp. 31, 90, 152, 258–59) of the whole (pp. 61–62) we have the whole "provisionally understood as a sketch" (p. 232; cf. p. 238). On the basis of this anticipation of the whole, provisional and sketchy as it may be, it is possible to begin interpreting the parts, anticipating that the results will correct and concretize our vision of the whole, which in turn will provide new guidance for interpreting the parts. We're in! We're off and running!

But it's not that simple. On the linguistic side, the text is but one of many wholes that are presupposed by the interpretation of their respective parts. The smallest unit of understanding is the sentence or proposition. But it is a whole that must be understood in terms of its parts, and vice versa (pp. 28, 30, 35, 44, 56, 61; HHM pp. 197, 202).

But sentences, too, must be understood, not just in terms of their parts but as themselves parts of a larger whole, namely, a text (pp. 27, 35, 44; HHM pp. 197, 202). Of course, a text may be made up of texts: "Be careful to distinguish the limits of the whole. Truly mad ideas have come via this into poetics: that the Iliad was regarded as being originally a whole, the Pentateuch, Joshua as well. In the same way a book can, although it is otherwise a unity, consist of many wholes, which one must separate from each other" (p. 99).

The next largest whole, of which the text is a part, is a genre, and Schleiermacher continually reminds us to pay attention to these contexts and the presuppositions they embody (pp. 25, 92, 240, 246, 254, 262–64). I find this a particularly good site at which to illustrate the logic of whole and part. Suppose I pick up *Gulliver's Travels* and from the title anticipate that the whole is an ordinary travelogue. My attempt to make sense of the parts on this presupposition will rather rapidly encounter difficulties. On the basis of my encounter with the parts, I will revise my provisional overview. Now I take the book to be a novel, or, more particularly, children's fiction, and interpretation will go more smoothly. But for a reader with some knowledge of Swift and English history, technical interpretation will intersect with grammatical, and a further revision of my genre presupposition will be necessary. I will discover that I can make fullest sense out of the text only if I take it to be political satire in the guise of children's fiction. Thus the whole is continuously revised in terms of parts.

But a literary genre is but a part of a language; so if we would understand a genre, and texts that are its parts, and the sentences that are the text's parts, we must know the language as a whole, in particular, "the language area which is common to the author and his original audience" (p. 30). But this can be a very complex whole. For example, the New Testament is written in Greek; so its interpreter must know the Greek common to its authors and their first readers. But to know this one must know the Aramaic in which many of the recorded events first took place, and that was the mother tongue of some of the authors and readers. In addition, one needs to know the Greek of the Septuagint into which the Old Testament background of both the events and the writings themselves had been translated. In both of these ways, one must pay special attention to the presence of Hebrew patterns of thought that are present in the Greek language of the writers and their audience (pp. 39–43, 47, 50, 85).

By now we should expect to be reminded that the complex whole that is Koine Greek is itself but a part of the whole history of the Greek language. Nor does Schleiermacher disappoint us. For its completion, grammatical interpretation must place sentences, texts, genres, and even that "certain period of a language" that the author shares with the original readers (p. 236) within the whole history of the language. And so, for example, the New Testament language "must be subsumed under the totality of the Greek language" (pp. 37–39, 247).

The wholes we must encompass to make sense out of the parts become parts of larger wholes with such blinding speed that we become dizzy. And we've just been looking at the grammatical side of the task. The technical or psychological side still lies before us. To repeat, *"every utterance has a dual relationship, to the totality of language and to the whole thought of its originator"* (p. 8). The second part of this dual task means that "every utterance is to be understood only via the whole life to which it belongs," not just the language but the language users "in the determinedness of all the moments of their life, and this only from the totality of their environments . . . via their nationality and their era" (p. 9; cf. p. 24).

Again we move in ever widening circles. We cannot restrict ourselves to that portion of the author's life from which most immediately the text arises but must ask, "what relationship does it have to his whole life and how does the moment of emergence relate to all other life-moments of the author?" (p. 107). Of special interest, of course, will be the whole of the author's life as author. We must grasp "the literary totality of a person" (p. 94).

I shall never forget the awe and wonder with which I once heard a distinguished literary critic announce the death of the New Criticism. As part of a series of lectures to incoming freshmen on exciting new developments in various disciplines, he was describing the cutting edge of literary theory (a special hermeneutics, I suppose). With the solemnity only possible in an academic context, he announced to the bright and eager new collegians, "We have discovered that if we are trying to understand a poem, and if the author of that poem has written other poems, it helps in understanding that first poem to read the other poems." What a breakthrough! Would Schleiermacher be pleased to see his wheel reinvented, or dismayed that it could be presented as avant-garde thinking?

I don't know. But in either case, he would not have been satisfied to stop with this textual totality. He is concerned about the "whole sphere of life" (p. 27) to which a text belongs, and this means, in the first place, that we must know the writer "in the totality of his life as a historical person" (p. 142) and not just as a writer.

But we do not have to wait for Schleiermacher to tell us that this richer, more concrete totality is but a part that needs to be understood in the context of the whole to which it belongs: "The writer is therefore only to be understood via his age" (p. 100).

The "history of the era of an author" is the whole in terms of which the author must be understood (p. 24). This can be understood in the first instance as "the literary life of the people and of the age" (p. 144), but once again we cannot stop there; we must go on to a more encompassing horizon. Thus, with reference to classical philology, Schleiermacher tells us that the interpreter needs to grasp "the spirit of classical antiquity" (HHM p. 211); and the New Testament exegete must contextualize the biblical text in "the total state of Christianity in the Apostolic era" (p. 152), and in an even larger whole, "the world from which the N[ew] T[estament] immediately arose" (p. 231).

The import of this prodigious holism, it seems to me, is independent of what one thinks about the degree to which the interpretation of Schleiermacher's interpretation of interpretation by Dilthey and Gadamer needs to be corrected along lines suggested by Frank and Bowie.[8]

My own view, for what it is worth, is that there is more than a little psychologism or "Romanticism" in Schleiermacher's texts, but that his concern to reconstruct the inner life experience of the author is only of penultimate significance for his hermeneutics, which has as its ultimate goal what Gadamer would call the *Sache*, the "object" or subject matter of which the writer speaks. In the attempt to escape the narrow isolation of one's own first-hand experience of love or God or whatever, one seeks to encounter the *Sache, not as die Sache selbst but as re-presented by another in a text.* It is to understand this content that one seeks to understand the text, and to understand the text one must have a vast array of both linguistic and historico-psychological knowledge and skills. Reconstruction of the life experience from which

---

[8] For this "debate" see Wilhelm Dilthey, "The Rise of Hermeneutics" and other essays on Schleiermacher in *Hermeneutics and the Study of History* (vol. IV of *Selected Works*), ed. Rudolf A. Makkreel and Frithjof Rodi (Princeton: Princeton University Press, 1996); Hans-Georg Gadamer, *Truth and Method*, trans. Joel Weinsheimer and Donald G. Marshall, 2nd rev. ed. (New York: Crossroad, 1991); Manfred Frank, *Das Individuelle-Allgemeine: Textstrukturierung und -interpretation nach Schleiermacher* (Frankfurt: Suhrkamp, 1977); Manfred Frank, *The Subject and the Text: Essays in Literary Theory and Philosophy*, ed. Andrew Bowie (Cambridge: Cambridge University Press, 1997); Andrew Bowie, *Aesthetics and Subjectivity: From Kant to Nietzsche* (Manchester: Manchester University Press, 1993); and Bowie, *From Romanticism to Critical Theory: The Philosophy of German Literary Theory* (London: Routledge, 1997).

a text arises is but a means to encountering the presence of the *Sache* in the text.

Although Schleiermacher does not quite use this Gadamerian language of the presence of the *Sache* in the text's re-presentation,[9] he often makes it clear that the telos of interpretation is "the object, that by which the author is moved to the utterance" (p. 90). It is the idea of the author that "vouches for his significance, not his individuality, but *the way in which he presents the idea* does vouch for his individuality" (p. 98, emphasis added).[10] Thus, in theological interpretation the goal is "supersensuous things via the understanding of human discourse" (p. 228) or, more specifically, "the being and the spirit of Christ" (p. 157).

But we can leave aside for now the otherwise important debate about how best to construe Schleiermacher's concern with reconstructing the life experience of the author. For on any account our author will remind us of the prophet who saw wheels within wheels.[11] Ours sees circles within circles within circles. And he is a prophet of gloom and doom in two important respects. In the first place, his hermeneutics spells the end for foundationalist strategies in any domain in which knowledge has the form of interpretation.

In my experience, the term 'foundationalism' is often misleadingly used to signify either of two metaphysical views rather than the epistemological thesis that I take to be its proper signification. I understand metaphysical realism to be the view that the real is and is what it is independent of our cognitions and construals (except, of course, for our cognitions and construals, which are also real).[12] And I understand theism to be (in part) the view that there is a personal creator who stands in an asymmetrical dependence relation to the world: the world depends for its actuality (both essence and existence) on God, but God is

---

[9] See *Truth and Method,* pp. 113, 127, 143, 149, 153.

[10] For other relevant passages, see pp. 103, 137, 139, 230, and 257–58.

[11] Ezekiel 1:15–21 and 10:9–14.

[12] Kant holds this view. That is what the thing in itself is all about. Any realism that wants to distinguish itself from the anti-realism of Kant and the host of subsequent variations on his transcendental idealism must add the epistemic claim that we can know the independently real as it is in its independence, that our knowledge exactly corresponds to or mirrors what is "out there" without in any way altering or distorting it.

not so dependent on the world. Since creation is a free choice, God is actual whether or not there is an actual world. When these are called foundationalist views, it is presumably because for metaphysical realism the world is an independent foundation for our knowledge, and for theism God is an independent foundation for the world. In both cases foundation has a causal sense.

But the point of calling these views foundationalist is usually to suggest that they have been discredited by the broad, contemporary consensus against foundationalism, its widely announced collapse. This is frightfully misleading, for that consensus is not directed against either metaphysical realism or theism but rather against an epistemological thesis that is neutral with respect to both. It is a claim about the structure of our knowledge, whatever its content.

In its soft form it is merely the claim that while some parts of our knowledge depend epistemically upon others, there are parts that do not, that stand on their own. This view, while vigorously challenged by some, is just as vigorously defended by others. Announcements of the collapse of foundationalism concern a stronger claim, namely, that those parts of our knowledge that do not depend on other parts but stand on their own can be a *fundamentum inconcussum* for the whole edifice of knowledge by virtue of their certainty and finality.[13] We can begin with parts that can be known prior to our grasp of the whole and that will not require revision as we build the whole on them as foundation. Epistemically these parts are atomic in nature rather than holistic. Neither do they presuppose the whole to which they eventually belong, nor are they liable to correction as that whole emerges into view.

It is clear that the relation of mutual determination that Schleiermacher finds between whole and part is incompatible with both of these claims. Schleiermacher belongs, if we may speak a bit anachronistically, to the contemporary consensus against (strong) foundationalist strategies in epistemology, at least, to repeat the qualifier, in any domain in which knowledge has the form of interpretation.

---

[13] See n. 6 above.

But how much of a qualifier is that? Dilthey, supported by Weber, Ricoeur, and others, has extended hermeneutics beyond the world of texts to the world as text, at least the human world as studied by the *Geisteswissenschaften*.[14] More dramatically, no doubt, Kuhnian philosophy of science gives a hermeneutical cast to the natural sciences. What else is a scientific revolution but a revision of our picture of the whole of (some domain of) nature in the light of our study of its parts?[15] Both Heidegger and Wittgenstein, each in his own way, teach us how to see all seeing as seeing-as, all cognition as construal. So perhaps the qualifier is left with no real work to do.

There is a second sense in which Schleiermacher, with his circles in circles in circles, is a prophet of epistemic gloom and doom. For if knowledge as interpretation has no fixed and stable Alpha, it is equally devoid of a final and all-inclusive Omega. Right at the start, Schleiermacher tell us that "criticism should come to an end, but hermeneutics should not" (p. 4). The totality required for a final interpretation "is never completed; the task is therefore strictly infinite and can only be accomplished by approximation" (p. 235).

There are three components to this last claim. First, the task is never completed because neither of its mutually dependent tasks, the grammatical and the technical/psychological, can be completed: "No language is completely present to us, not even our own mother tongue" (pp. 14–15; cf. p. 55). But this is only half the story. The hermeneutical Omega Point would require "a complete knowledge of the language, in the other case a complete knowledge of the person. As there can never be either of

---

[14] See Dilthey, *Hermeneutics and the Study of History;* the discussion by and about Weber (and others) in *Understanding and Social Inquiry,* ed. Fred. R. Dallmayr and Thomas A. McCarthy (Notre Dame, Ind.: University of Notre Dame Press, 1977); and Paul Ricoeur, *Hermeneutics and the Human Sciences,* ed. and trans. John B. Thompson (New York: Cambridge University Press, 1981).

[15] See Thomas S. Kuhn, *The Structure of Scientific Revolutions,* 2nd enlarged ed. (Chicago: University of Chicago Press, 1970); Robert P. Crease, "The Hard Case: Science and Hermeneutics," in *The Very Idea of Radical Hermeneutics,* ed. Roy Martinez (Atlantic Highlands, N.J.: Humanities, 1997); and the debate between Gyorgy Markus, "Why Is There No Hermeneutics of Natural Sciences? Some Preliminary Theses," and Patrick Heelan, "Yes! There Is a Hermeneutics of Natural Science: A Rejoinder to Markus," in *Science in Context* 1, no. 1 (1987) and 3, no. 2 (1989), respectively.

these, one must move from one to the other, and no rules can be given for how this is to be done" (p. 11).

With reference to these two gargantuan circles, Schleiermacher asks, "But who could dare completely to accomplish this task!" Then he immediately continues, "In the meantime [while awaiting the consummation never to be expected, however devoutly wished] one does not ever have to want to completely accomplish this task, but in most cases only to accomplish it to a certain extent" (p. 38).[16] This is the second point. Because the to-ing and fro-ing between whole and parts both within and between the two most basic circles is always ongoing, final interpretation is but a regulative idea. The goal is *"complete understanding of style,"* but this objective *"is only to be achieved by approximation"* (p. 91; cf. pp. 235, 240, 267; HHM p. 201). It is always provisional (p. 257; HHM pp. 200, 203), ever open to correction (pp. 25, 92, 98, 259).

In the third place, there is another way of seeing hermeneutics as an infinite task, complementary to the image of the hermeneutical circle as the horizon that ever recedes from our advance and leading to the same conclusion about approximation, provisionality, and correctability. The three key terms are individuality, intuition, and indeterminateness. Schleiermacher emphasizes that the goal of hermeneutics is an individual, and this, we might note, will be true whether we think of a text as an event in the history of a language, or of a text as an event in the experience of its author, or of a text as a representation of its "object." But, as Kant reminds us, concepts give us universality; only intuitions give us the individual. The infinite task of interpretation is to achieve the intuition in which individuality is grasped as such (pp. 96–98).

This is the context, I believe, to understanding what Schleiermacher says about determinacy and indeterminacy. He writes that "in every case there is construction of something finitely determinate from the infinite indeterminate. Language is infinite because each element is determinable in a particular manner via

---

[16] Schleiermacher adds a warning against sloth: "But precisely where we do not strive for complete thoroughness we often overlook what we should not overlook."

the rest of the elements. But this is just as much the case in relation to the psychological side. *For every intuition of an individual
is infinite"* (p. 11, emphasis added). In other words, parts are
indeterminate not only by virtue of their relatedness to the context, the whole to which they belong (pp. 30–31), but also by
virtue of their inherent concreteness as individuals. Individuality is apeironic. As such is remains "the infinite indeterminate"
relative to all our "finitely determinate" articulations. Interpretation is always approximation.

There are, to be sure, passages in which Schleiermacher talks
about the "successful completion" of interpretation (HHM p.
193) and even of its necessity (pp. 110, 229). Sometimes reference
is to both grammatical and psychological interpretation (pp. 11,
89, 229), sometimes to both comparative and divinatory interpretation (HHM p. 193). Often these references occur in contexts
immediately adjacent to reminders that this completion is not
possible, that what is being talked about is what we would have
if we could fully grasp the relevant infinities of totality and individuality, or what we would have to have in order to declare
our work done (pp. 11, 31, 91). Given Schleiermacher's emphatic
insistence on interpretation as an infinite task and the reiteration
of this theme when talking about completion, it is fairly clear
that even in those passages where he speaks of completion without such an explicit reminder (pp. 29, 89, 101, 110, 229; HHM p.
193), we should take it as tacitly present. Talk about complete or
final interpretation, even if expressed in the indicative, will always be partly imperative and even more basically subjunctive.
Thus, when he speaks of the "divinatory certainty which arises
when an interpretation delves as deeply as possible into an author's state of mind" (HHM p. 185), we will hear the "as deeply
as possible" as a reminder that the "certainty" is not absolute
but approximate, provisional, correctable.

There is, however, one passage from the second Academy Address that possibly merits special attention.

> When we consider the task of interpretation with this principle
> [of whole and parts] in mind, we have to say that our increasing
> understanding of each sentence and of each section, an under-
> standing which we achieve by starting at the beginning and mov-

ing forward slowly, is *always provisional*. It becomes more complete as we are able to see each larger section as a coherent unity. But as soon as we turn to a new part we encounter new uncertainties and begin again, as it were, in the dim morning light. It is like starting all over, except that as we push ahead the new material illumines everything we have already treated, *until suddenly at the end every part is clear and the whole work is visible in sharp and definite contours.* (HHM p. 198, emphasis added)

I shall never forget the shock with which I first read this passage. Is this a failure of nerve of the sort Heidegger attributes to Kant?[17] Has Plato's great German translator succumbed to the charms of Diotima's account of the suddenness of the "final revelation" that comes to the one initiated into the mysteries of Love, when "there bursts upon him that wondrous vision which is the very soul of the beauty he has toiled so long for" and now "at last he comes to know what beauty is . . . beauty's very self . . . the heavenly beauty face to face"?[18]

I think not. Schleiermacher proceeds immediately to reiterate the provisional, imperfect, approximate, hypothetical character of interpretation (HHM pp. 200–207). He sees all too clearly that his analysis of what we might call the logic of interpretation signifies a finitude that cannot be suddenly sloughed off. When, then, are we to make of the claim that *"suddenly at the end every part is clear and the whole work is visible in sharp and definite contours"*? A charitable reading will find in it a somewhat hyperbolic but nevertheless illuminating account of the move from one presentiment of the whole to a qualitatively different one. No doubt our view of the whole changes quantitatively as we fill in more details gathered from the parts. This change is gradual and incremental. But then there are those changes which are paradigm shifts. No new epicycles for a Ptolemaic astronomy, but the abandonment of circular orbits for elliptical ones. No deepened appreciation of a children's entertainment, but the awareness of *Gulliver's Travels* as a biting political satire for adults. These changes have a Gestalt-switch character to them,

---

[17] See Martin Heidegger, *Kant and the Problem of Metaphysics*, 5th enlarged ed., trans. Richard Taft (Bloomington: Indiana University Press, 1997).

[18] Plato, *Symposium* 210e–211e, Joyce translation.

and Schleiermacher's account of how things suddenly make new sense can be confirmed from such hermeneutical moments. We simply need to be reminded, as Schleiermacher himself recognizes, that his "at the end" also signifies a new beginning, a new phase of a task that remains infinite.

With this account of interpretation, Schleiermacher parts company decisively with his major Berlin contemporary and, as some would have it, rival—Hegel. Hegel, too, is a holist; as such he consistently repudiates atomistic, foundationalist strategies in knowledge. But he would rather label regulative ideas and infinite tasks the Bad Infinite of Unhappy Consciousness than abandon the claim to Absolute Knowledge that belongs to Platonism (as distinct from Socratism) and the history of the footnotes thereto. So, with equal consistency, he affirms in various ways (phenomenological, logical, and ultimately historical) our ability to grasp the whole, not just in presentiment and anticipation, but in a definitive and final way. Those who seek to weaken his claims in this respect by noting, for example, that he was willing to revise his Logic fail to recognize that just to the degree that he acknowledges, in anticipation of the wicked question of Johannes Climacus,[19] that the System is not complete, he falls back into the Bad Infinite of Unhappy Consciousness he has so disdainfully purported to surpass. If his grasp of the whole is provisional and penultimate, this contaminates the whole of speculative science and undermines the claim to reach "the goal where it can lay aside the title 'love of knowing' and be *actual knowing*," where "Spirit has made its existence identical with its essence . . . and the separation of knowing and truth is overcome," where "knowledge no longer needs to go beyond itself" because we have reached "the *completion* of the series, where 'appearance becomes identical with essence, so that its exposition will coincide at just this point with the authentic Science of Spirit," which will "signify the nature of absolute knowledge itself."[20]

---

[19] Climacus has satirical fun at Hegel's expense with his readiness to bow down and worship the System if only he can be assured that it is complete. See Kierkegaard's *Concluding Unscientific Postscript*, trans. Howard V. Hong and Edna H. Hong (Princeton: Princeton University Press, 1992).

[20] *Hegel's Phenomenology of Spirit*, trans. A. V. Miller (Oxford: Clarendon Press, 1977), pp. 3, 21, 51, 50, 57.

Schleiermacher sides with Kant, rejecting the purported Hegelian *Aufhebung* of critical idealism into speculative idealism. This means that he relegates human understanding to the realm of appearances rather than things in themselves, phenomena rather than noumena. He is what today would be called an anti-realist. Of course, he does not use this Kantian or contemporary language. But over against Hegel he affirms an unsurpassable finitude of human knowledge—I am assuming here that we extend his hermeneutics beyond the realm of the textual, as suggested above—and over against Descartes, for example, he gives a qualitative rather than quantitative analysis of that finitude. This makes him a kissing cousin to Kant.

Consider Descartes's analysis of human cognitive finitude. It is twofold. On the one hand is the fact of error. By contrast with a divine, perfect knowledge that never errs, we sometimes get it wrong. On the other hand, there is incompleteness. There are, to speak the language of propositions, true propositions whose truth we do not know and of which, in some cases, we have never even imagined. But when we get it right, when we know the truth of a true proposition, there is no incompleteness about that knowledge. We know that fact as well as it can be known, as well as any divine or infinite knower knows it. Neither the meaning nor the truth of that proposition is dependent upon a context not yet articulated. In this propositional atomism, the growth of knowledge will add new pieces to these pieces of knowledge, but the original pieces (since by hypothesis we got them right) will not be revised or corrected in the process.

As holists, both Schleiermacher and Hegel reject this picture. For them T. S. Eliot's "In my end is my beginning"[21] comes to mean that I truly know my epistemic point of departure only at the journey's conclusion when the to-ing and fro-ing between part and whole has ceased, not temporarily because I am tired or because I have no practical need to pursue it further, but permanently because we have achieved the final paradigm and understood the parts (at least in principle)[22] in the light of this final whole.

---

[21] T. S. Eliot, "East Coker" in *Four Quartets*.

[22] Hegel has no difficulty acknowledging the empirical finitude of human knowledge, and he rightly refuses the demand of Herr Krug to deduce his

The idea of this completion is the touchstone of Schleiermacher's hermeneutics. He differs from Hegel only in one little detail: he insists that we can never occupy this Beulah Land of the Spirit, having crossed the Jordan that separates finitude from infinity, human from divine, the church militant from the church triumphant. In the Hegelian church, realized eschatology is orthodoxy, and it is because he is a heretic on just this point that Schleiermacher is a Kantian.[23]

For Kant, the distinction between appearances and things in themselves is the difference between the way the world (the only world there is) is apprehended by finite human minds and an infinite, divine, creative intellect.[24] While Schleiermacher doesn't employ the Kantian vocabulary, his hermeneutics articulates essentially the same distinction, namely, between finite minds that can never encompass the totality except provisionally and an infinite knowing, unavailable to us, that could bring the process to completion. On Kant's view, our attempt to grasp the Unconditioned by grasping the totality of the conditions results in dialectical illusion. Schleiermacher's view, at least in his hermeneutics, is milder. Our failure to grasp the whole adequately results in penultimacy rather than paralogism, anticipation rather than antinomy. But in either case, the inadequacy means that our knowing never achieves truth in its classical sense as *adaequatio rei et intellectus*.

Kant sees human knowing in rather static terms, while Schleiermacher's view lends itself to a more historical (Hegelian, Kuhnian) understanding of understanding. But for both of them, what counts as truth among us at any given time can only be truth with a small t, in Kantian language phenomenal knowl-

---

pen within the System. See Hegel's 1802 essay "How the Ordinary Human Understanding Takes Philosophy (as Displayed in the Works of Mr. Krug)," in *Between Kant and Hegel: Texts in the Development of Post-Kantian Idealism,* trans. George di Giovanni and H. S. Harris (Albany: SUNY Press, 1985). See also *Hegel's Philosophy of Nature,* trans. A. V. Miller (Oxford: Clarendon Press, 1970), p. 23n. (Note the Remark to ¶250 of the *Encyclopedia*.)

[23] It is not too difficult to argue that Schleiermacher is a Kantian both in his *Reden* and in his *Glaubenslehre*. But a careful analysis will show, I believe, that he works out his finitist epistemology quite differently in those texts both vis-à-vis each other and vis-à-vis his hermeneutics.

[24] See my essay "In Defense of the Thing in Itself," *Kant-Studien* 59, no. 1 (1968), pp. 118–41.

edge, knowledge of appearances rather than of things in themselves. Or, to put the point bluntly: We never get it right. Lacking that final, unrevisable vision of the whole, we never fully understand the flower in the crannied wall. And our failure is qualitative and not quantitative. It is not that we know a few things adequately, while being ignorant of many other facts. We know nothing adequately, everything (at best) only approximately. Our very highest cognitive achievements, Newtonian science in Kant's case, fail to mirror nature (or supernature).

I once argued to the Maritain Society that Aquinas was a Kantian. Since I lived to tell about it, I have become bolder. So I shall conclude with the suggestion that Schleiermacher is not only a Kantian but also a Derridean. Derrida, of course, is a holist. In an early, now classic, exposition of deconstruction, he writes, "Yet all that Hegel thought within his horizon, all, that is, except eschatology, may be reread as a meditation on writing."[25] Derrida is telling us that he, like so many others, is a Hegelian without the Absolute, without totality, without eschatological closure.

Nothing links Derrida to Hegel more closely than his holism. The point about privileging writing is simply that, according to a classical theory, written signs point beyond themselves to other signs that, by virtue of being themselves signs, point beyond themselves. To say *"There is nothing outside of the text"*[26] is to say that everything points beyond itself to its other, without which it cannot be understood. In semantics this is a holist theory of meaning, analogous to the structuralist notion that one must know the entire unabridged dictionary to really understand any of the words in it. But it is an ontological as well as a semantic thesis. Derrida writes, *"The thing itself is a sign,"*[27] and whether we want to speak of things, or facts, or events, he is an Hegelian who tells us that all finite realities point essentially beyond themselves—this is the so-called doctrine of internal relations—to other finite things and ultimately to the totality of their complex interrelation.

But, of course, Derrida is an Hegelian without the eschatology,

[25] Jacques Derrida, *Of Grammatology*, trans. Gayatri Chakravorty Spivak (Baltimore: Johns Hopkins University Press, 1976), p. 26.

[26] Ibid., p. 158.

[27] Ibid., p. 49.

which means that the totality (semantic or ontological), while always presupposed and always required, is never actually present. This is the heart of deconstruction as the critique of the metaphysics of presence. Nothing is ever simply and fully present because the totality of the others that are essential to its meaning and to its being is never present except as presentiment. Thus, for example, Derrida rejects what he calls the "transcendental signified," by which he means "a concept signified in and of itself, a concept *simply present* for thought, independent of a relationship to language, that is, of a relationship to a system of signifiers." Such a meaning "would exceed the chain of signs, and would no longer itself function as a signifier. On the contrary . . . every signified is also in the position of a signifier," that is, every meaning essentially points beyond itself to other meanings.[28]

When Schleiermacher tells us, in the context of his own holism, "No language is completely present to us, not even our own mother tongue" (pp. 14–15), we hear the affinity with Derrida and draw the conclusion that no word, no sentence, no text, etc., is ever completely present to us for just this reason. By the same token, as we have already seen, we would have to have a universal history, eschatologically fulfilled, to be able to have fully present to us any author in the context of his or her historical era.

Among the other Derridean themes appresented with this critique of simple or pure presence we can mention two: deferral and undecidability. The (in)famous neologism *différance* was created to signify not only the importance of difference, as in the need to attend to meanings and things different from the ones we would understand if we should understand them, but also deferral, the fact that the definitive articulation of any meaning, thing, fact, or event is perennially postponed until eschatalogical

[28] Jacques Derrida, *Positions*, trans. Alan Bass (Chicago: University of Chicago Press, 1981), pp. 19–20, emphasis altered. If one traces the terms 'simply' and 'pure' throughout *Positions*, one will discover an essential nuance that is often overlooked in reading Derrida. He writes, "I have never ceased calling into question the motif of 'purity' in all its forms (the first impulse of what is called 'deconstruction' carries it toward this 'critique' of the phantasm or the axiom of purity, or toward the analytical decomposition of a purification that would lead back to the indecomposable simplicity of the origin)"; *Monolingualism of the Other or The Prosthesis of Origin*, trans. Patrick Mensah (Stanford: Stanford University Press, 1998), p. 46.

closure is achieved and the part is fully present because its whole (which is no longer itself but a part) is fully present.[29]

Closely linked to this notion of deferral is that of undecidability.[30] Because "a context is never absolutely determinable,"[31] semantic or ontological entities, which are essentially contextual, are never absolutely determinable either. Abstracted from their context, as they necessarily are, both for atomists who take them to be externally related to their others and for holists who recognize their internal relatedness but cannot absolutely determine their context, they have about them a certain indeterminacy or undecidability. Things might go this way or that; it is too early to tell for sure (and it will still be too early tomorrow). Of course, undecidability doesn't mean that we cannot and do not make decisions, provisional and risky as they may be, or that we are free to construe things however we please, without any constraints. But it does mean that our current truths (lowercase t) are decision relative in a way both Descartes and Hegel are desperate to deny.

It is not too difficult to see Schleiermacher's affinity with these motifs. As the hermeneutical circle ripples ever wider, it becomes increasingly clear that it will be tomorrow, and tomorrow, and tomorrow before we reach fully determinate meaning. When he tells us that "in every case there is *construction of something finitely determinate from the infinite indeterminate. . . . For every intuition of an individual is infinite*" (p. 11, emphasis added),[32] we suspect that he has been reading Derrida on the sly.

Hegel would not be pleased. Where are the thought police when you need them?

---

[29] See "Différance," in *Margins of Philosophy*, trans. Alan Bass (Chicago: University of Chicago Press, 1982).

[30] Derrida alludes to Gödel's theory as a model of the kind of undecidability he has in mind. See *Dissemination*, trans. Barbara Johnson (Chicago: University of Chicago Press, 1981), p. 219, and *Writing and Difference*, trans. Alan Bass (Chicago: University of Chicago Press, 1978), p. 162. Cf. *Positions*, p. 43, and John D. Caputo, *Deconstruction in a Nutshell: A Conversation with Jacques Derrida* (New York: Fordham University Press, 1997), pp. 37–38.

[31] Jacques Derrida, "Signature Event Context," in *Margins*, p. 310.

[32] Derrida's strong misreading of *Fear and Trembling* in *The Gift of Death*, trans. David Wills (Chicago: University of Chicago Press, 1995), with its slogan *tout autre est tout autre* (every other is wholly other), can be read as a meditation on the infinity of the individual as such.

7

Positive Postmodernism As
Radical Hermeneutics

HERMENEUTICS is the form in which epistemology lives on. In one sense epistemology is dead. As the attempt to provide human knowledge with solid foundations, to prove that it can transcend the limitations of its perspectives and be adequate to the reality it intends, it is widely perceived to have failed. As the extravagant claims for clarity, certainty, and completeness necessary for *Episteme* or *Wissenschaft* have proved chimerical even for the paradigms of mathematics and mathematical physics, the notion that epistemology is a bad habit that needs to be broken has increasingly carried the day. But as an investigation into the nature and limits of human knowledge (with special emphasis on its limits), epistemology lives on, frequently under the name of hermeneutics, signifying both the interpretative character of pre-philosophical human understanding and, correspondingly, interpretation as the central theme of a certain mode of epistemological reflection.

THE INESCAPABILITY OF HERMENEUTICS

Hermeneutics is inescapable. Human life is cultural and not merely natural. We remain unable to spell out this distinction as clearly as we would like, but it remains undeniably the case that even the most mindless couch potato does not live by instinct alone. Our lives are embedded in ideas (and thus texts) and practices (and thus institutions) that are handed down to us and that we make our own, thus giving form and content to our existence, by (re)interpreting them.

Corresponding to the categorical necessity of hermeneutics at this level is a certain hypothetical necessity. It is not necessary

that there should be *Geisteswissenschaften*. They are cultural artifacts, and much of human history has preceded their invention.
But if there are to be sciences of human life itself as cultural
artifact, they will necessarily be hermeneutical sciences, exhibiting the same hermeneutical circle as the ideas and practices that
are their subject. They will be interpretations that presuppose
interpretations, (re)interpretations of (re)interpretations.

From Aristotle through Ayer, empiricists have sought to make
perception a matter of nature untainted by nurture, freeing
knowledge from history while keeping it tied to the earth. But
without success. As it has become increasingly clear that all
seeing is "seeing as," it has become increasingly unclear how
to deny, convincingly, the cultural, hermeneutical character of
perception. The Hegelian claim that consciousness is less basic
than spirit means that I perceive even physical nature as We have
learned to perceive it. (Even the ability to perceive the world as
physical nature is learned, and the concept of physical nature is
a cultural artifact.)

Corresponding to the categorical necessity of hermeneutics at
this level is another hypothetical necessity. It is not necessary
that there should be *Naturwissenschaften*. They are cultural artifacts, and much of human history has preceded their invention.
But if there are to be sciences of physical nature, they will necessarily be hermeneutical sciences, exhibiting the same hermeneutical circle as the perceptions to which they make their ultimate
appeal; in the absence of theory-free data, they will be interpretations that presuppose interpretations, and their objects will be
(theoretical) (re)interpretations of the (perceptual) (re)interpre-
tations that constitute their evidence. Since the work of Thomas
Kuhn and others, the hermeneutical character of the natural sciences has been increasingly acknowledged.

Corresponding to this fourfold necessity of hermeneutics,
doubly categorical and doubly hypothetical, is a third hypothetical necessity. It is not necessary that there should be philosophy
as epistemological reflection. It is a cultural artifact, and much
of human history has preceded its invention. But if there is to be
second-order reflection on human life both in its prereflective
(but interpretive) everydayness and in its first-order (interpretive) reflection in the sciences, it will necessarily be hermeneuti-

cal, exhibiting the same hermeneutical circle as all four regions of its subject matter (a classification that is itself an interpretation). It will be a (re)interpretation of (re)interpretations that presupposes prior interpretations. If it is not naive, it will know itself to be such. Very likely it will call itself philosophical hermeneutics.

In these senses hermeneutics is inescapable. When philosophers like Habermas and the late Heidegger—and, following the latter, Foucault and Derrida—speak of being beyond hermeneutics, they do not deny the inescapability thesis I have just sketched. They rather mean that their philosophical hermeneutics differs in some important respect from someone else's, usually the early Heidegger's or Gadamer's or Ricoeur's, which they perceive as remaining too Cartesian or too Hegelian. But they do not deny that all seeing is "seeing as," that philosophical reflection and its subject matter is hermeneutical "all the way down." Thus it is appropriate that John Caputo should give the title *Radical Hermeneutics* to his challenging, largely Derridean answer to the question "What is philosophy?

THE CONCEPT OF RADICALITY AS A MIXED METAPHOR

But what does it mean for hermeneutics as a mode of philosophical reflection to be radical? If, as we are often told today, concepts are a certain kind of metaphor, the concept of radicality can be described as a mixed metaphor. It combines two quite distinct meanings. Etymologically it means getting to the root of things, or, to use a virtually synonymous metaphor, getting to the heart of the matter. To be radical is the opposite of being superficial; it is to break through the surface appearances to the reality they hide or disguise. Even the Nietzschean claim that appearances are all there is is radical in this sense, for to reach this "truth" it is necessary to break through the "superficial" view that the distinction between appearance and reality makes sense.

It may seem strange that one moment it is superficial to be satisfied with surface appearances and radical to seek the reality they hide or disguise, while the next moment it is superficial to seek such a reality and radical to recognize that deep down there is nothing but surface. Who is radical, Plato or Nietzsche?

This puzzling situation loses the appearance of paradox when we remember that the concept of radicality is a mixed metaphor and turn our attention from its spatial to its temporal dimension. Temporally speaking, to be radical is to make a decisive break with the status quo. It is to go beyond the critique of the status quo that is itself part of the status quo. The loyal opposition is also critical of the status quo, but the radical is critical of the status quo constituted by the currently dominant forces and their one or more loyal oppositions. From a radical perspective, the loyal opposition is too loyal. It is reformist rather than revolutionary because it shares important common ground with the dominant forces of any given historical present. To be radical is to be revolutionary in the sense of rejecting the framework in which the current debate and struggle for power take place. Thus, Marxism is radical in relation to the conservatisms and liberalisms that have defined Anglo-American politics, Merleau-Ponty was seeking a radical politics in *Humanism and Terror* when he rejected both Communism and anti-Communism, and Thomas Kuhn is radical vis-à-vis the debate between "creation science" and traditional Darwinism.

It is clear that in this sense the concept of radicality is situation relative. The concept of human rights that was radical in the eighteenth century (as defined by the French and American Revolutions), and in many contemporary contexts still is (as defined by the United Nations and Amnesty International), is viewed in other contexts, for example, by feminists, who not surprisingly call themselves radical, as part of the status quo that needs to be questioned. They see the totalitarian-authoritarian societies that violate human rights and the liberal democracies that (by comparison, at least) honor human rights as sharing patriarchal assumptions that either represent the neglect and violation of important human rights or render the very concept of human rights hopelessly ideological. (Does the spatial metaphor of penetrating to the heart of the matter have androcentric, agonistic assumptions that render the very concept of radicality hopelessly ideological? Is there a receptive radicality?)

It is not difficult to see how the mixed metaphor we know as the concept of radicality came to be. Those who stand outside the two or more sides of the debate that defines a particular status quo will easily find all parties, including the loyal opposition, to share a common superficiality. The entire debate, and not just this side of the question or that, must be rejected; for the question itself fails to get to the root of things, to the heart of the matter. The spatial metaphor of penetration is taken up into the service of the temporal metaphor of revolution.

Thus, to use one more example, morality is always radical in relation to technology and the assumptions of its instrumental reason that (1) means are justified by their effective production of (2) ends (such as economic growth) that are themselves self-evident and not subject to moral evaluation. Conversely, instrumental reason is always radical in relation to morality because it rejects all debates about what ends we should seek and about what means are legitimate, as distinct from efficient, in achieving them.

If military-industrial instrumentalism is the most concrete product of the radical revolution known as modernity, to be radical as the twentieth century comes to a close would be to adopt a moral posture that challenges, not just this strategy or that for achieving economic growth or national security, but the very framework that defines the fundamental human task as finding the most effective strategies for achieving greater wealth and power for one's own nation state.

THE HERMENEUTICAL TURN AS ALREADY RADICAL

We can now see that what it would mean to develop a radical hermeneutics will depend on how we interpret (since hermeneutics is inescapable) the status quo, our here and now. I shall adopt the fairly widespread practice of naming our here and now 'modernity' and accept the implication that (for us) to be radical means to be postmodern; and I shall interpret the dividing line between modernity and its sequel so as to make it clear that postmodern radicality is far from being the monopoly of French poststructuralism. It will turn out that Gadamer's philosophical hermeneutics and Derrida's deconstruction are both postmodern, but also that each represents only a minimally radical hermeneutics.

We might begin our interpretation with the military-industrial instrumentalism already suggested as the most concrete expression of modernity. This would put the question of ethics front and center. But we might do better, in Hegelian fashion, to make concreteness our terminus ad quem rather than our terminus a quo. I find those interpretations of modernity most convincing and illuminating that begin more abstractly with what is sometimes called the Enlightenment project. It can be identified in terms of three ends and one means. The ends have been to replace *mythos* with *logos,* tradition with critique, and authority with autonomy. The means has been one variety or another of a foundationalist epistemology in terms of which *logos,* critique, and autonomy are defined. Thus, to begin abstractly is to begin with epistemology rather than with ethics, but it is to realize that postmodern challenges to modernity will eventually have to be ethical if they are not to remain lost in abstraction.

Epistemologically speaking, the break with modernity begins when we begin to see foundationalism as a particular culture's *mythos* about the *logos,* to see how deeply dependent on the authority of scholastic metaphysical traditions is Descartes's attempt to free himself from all authority and tradition, to see how quickly the Enlightenment project itself becomes a tradition whose authority is to be taken for granted, and to see the account of autonomy in terms of "the rights of man" and of "man come of age" as embodying an older, patriarchal tradition whose authority is likewise not to be questioned. All such seeings are insights into the ways modernity deconstructs itself and gives rise to the postmodern.

But we mustn't move too quickly to the postmodern. For modernity, like virtually every other status quo, is a complex reality with its loyal opposition and corresponding debates. Two such debates, internal to modernity, require special attention. For the postmodern is not only the rejection of the Enlightenment project and its foundationalism, but of the entire framework in which it debates and, for the most part, defeats, its loyal opposition.

The first of these debates is between Enlightenment and Romanticism. While the former seeks to escape the tutelage of historical existence through the forward-looking movement to majority and the autonomy of adulthood, the latter, finding childhood and adolescence equally intolerable, longs for a return to the womb of some past Eden. (How's that for a mixed metaphor?) Freud's contempt for Romain Rolland's oceanic feelings, at the outset of *Civilization and Its Discontents,* gives us this debate in a nutshell. Emergence vs. immersion, progress vs. nostalgia, discursive reason vs. intuitive faith.

And yet Romanticism is distinctively modern, the loyal opposition rather than a radical alternative to the Enlightenment project. For it shares with its opponent (1) a keen sense of the historicality of its existence, (2) an unwillingness to tolerate the essentially incomplete character of a life so richly mediated, and (3) the desire to transcend the mediations that constitute its minority, its always-on-the-way-but-never-there character, through the attainment of some kind of immediacy. The debate is over the nature of this immediacy, whether it is to be found in the protocol sentences of some rationalist or empiricist foundationalism or in an affective realm whose expression can only be through the metaphors and images of art. To the participants the debate is a ferocious fight, but it presupposes a huge agreement that is all but definitive of modernity.

The second debate is between Enlightenment foundationalism and Hegelian holism. The latter repudiates immediacy in all its forms, thereby setting itself over against both Enlightenment and Romanticism. It is tempting to call it the first form of postmodernism.

Yet Hegel remains distinctively modern. For in spite of repudiating the immediacy that unites the other parties in the parliament of modernity, he retains with the Enlightenment the ideal of absolute knowledge. But in his case one is to get beyond the mediated incompleteness of historical minority not by withdrawal to immediacy but by advance to complete mediation. This totalizing strategy, worked out conceptually in the Logic and historically in the Philosophy of Spirit, is at once an alternative to foundationalism and the transformation of the ideal of progress into a realized eschatology, fleeing the incompleteness of historical existence even faster than the incrementalism of the

Enlightenment, which is willing to content itself with piecemeal eschatology.

If we ask what unites Enlightenment and Romanticism on the question of immediacy in spite of their disagreement over absolute knowledge, we find it to be the same thing that unites Enlightenment and Hegel on absolute knowledge in spite of their disagreement over immediacy. It is an allergic reaction to the intertwined *Unterweglichkeit* and *Unheimlichkeit* of historical existence and the corresponding desire at every moment to have already arrived, to experience no gap between essence and existence. Modernity is Platonism run amuck. It seeks to suppress the fears of childhood and the anxieties of adolescence by being always at home. In the language of Hegel's Logic, the three modes of modernity operate at different levels of categoreal complexity: Romanticism at the level of Being, Enlightenment at the level of Essence, and Hegel himself at the level of the Concept. Thus it is easy to overlook their essential kinship.

In relation to modernity so conceived, the hermeneutical turn is already radical, and the term 'radical hermeneutics' is a pleonasm. For hermeneutics is the claim that all forms of modernity are superficial, and that if one digs deeply enough to get to the heart of the matter, one discovers that immediacy and totality are equally chimerical. We are never at home, or, to be more precise, we are always at home (never without Gadamerian prejudices, a world or life world of established meanings and facts), but every home is provisional and penultimate (never beyond Derridean difference). Our existence is necessarily nomadic. The *Unterweglichkeit* and *Unheimlichkeit* of our historical odyssey are unsurpassable. They demarcate our existence because they belong to the essence of our being in the world. To flee them is to undertake a self-defeating project, and this is fortunate, since to succeed, *per impossibile*, would be to take leave of ourselves. Unfortunately, we take leave of ourselves simply by engaging in such flight, no matter how futile it always turns out to be.

GADAMER AND DERRIDA AS EQUALLY RADICAL

The argument of the preceding section implies that the hermeneutics Gadamer develops out of the early Heidegger is just as radically postmodern as the deconstruction Derrida develops out of the late Heidegger. There are important and interesting differences between them, but in relation to modernity the important thing is their mutual denial of both immediacy and totality, their mutual affirmation that we never stand at either the Alpha or the Omega point of our experience. Whether we speak of language or the world, it has always begun when we arrive on the scene, and neither has completed its historical journey when it comes our time to speak. We are always in medias res.

Gadamer's strategy is to reprise Hegel's arguments against immediacy in terms of linguistic and historical mediation and then to allow these elements of Hegel's thought to deconstruct his claims to achieve absolute knowledge by means of either logical or world historical totality (closure). Because there is so much of Hegel in Gadamer's refutation of Hegel's essential link to modernity, he is often accused of having made only a half-hearted break with Hegelian modernity. But if immediacy and totality are impossible, they are impossible, and nothing Derrida can say will make them, to speak ungrammatically, more impossible.

Derrida's strategy is to develop an argument against immediacy (presence) more deeply indebted to structuralism than to Hegel, and then to allow this critique to undermine any subsequent claims to totality. One learns things from Derrida that one does not learn from Gadamer, but the opposite is equally true, and, to repeat, Derrida does not render immediacy and totality more impossible than Gadamer does; he just renders them impossible.

Of course, Gadamer is dependent on Hegel in the process of deconstructing him, but Derrida is no less dependent on structuralism in deconstructing it, and structuralism belongs as much to modernity as does Hegelianism. It is a species of the Enlightenment project. In keeping with Descartes's practice and in opposition to his profession and promise, Gadamer and Derrida jointly acknowledge the dependence of their thought on the traditions they seek to criticize. For both of them criticism is necessarily internal criticism. It always has something of an ad hominem character.

Like Derrida, Gadamer sides with Nietzsche against Hegel.

Unlike the Enlightenment, which often sought unity by an un-historical denial of plurality, Hegel acknowledges the plurality of perspectives generated by the historical process but seeks unity nevertheless by integrating all of them into an organic totality. His formula, taken from the Kantian table of categories, is simple: Plurality + Unity = Totality. But if asked to solve the following formula for x, Plurality = Totality = x, the answer can only be Nietzsche. His perspectivism is the result of ac-knowledging historical plurality with Hegel while denying his claim to surpass it by means of a totalizing unity. In these terms Gadamer is as much a Nietzschean as Derrida is. For both of them affirm a plurality of perspectives that is beyond our power to totalize and thus unify in any final view from nowhere. For both of them the truth is that we have no Truth. They represent two variations on the theme of perspectival finitism.

It is widely thought that Derrida is a more radical thinker than Gadamer. Against this received wisdom I have suggested that vis-à-vis modernity, at least, they are more or less equally radical. Why has it seemed otherwise to so many? No doubt it is largely a matter of rhetoric, style, and emphasis, which may in turn be due to national character. French intellectuals seem to feel a deep need to shock and scandalize. Derrida's rhetoric and his styles are shaped by this tradition and addressed to readers whose expectations have been shaped by it as well. Correspond-ingly, he emphasizes all but exclusively what we cannot do and cannot have, given the collapse of the Enlightenment project and its loyal oppositions.

By contrast, Gadamer is willing to talk about what we can do and have even if immediacy and totality are not among them. While Derrida hammers away on undecidability, Gadamer notes that while no fusion of horizons (perspectives) can be complete or permanent, there can be a mutuality of understanding and agreement (*Verständigung*) sufficient for cooperative life to-gether.

Gadamer does not deny that ultimately and theoretically un-decidability reigns, since there can be neither immediacy nor totality; and Derrida does not deny that penultimately and prac-tically we can find ways to live together. For one the glass is half full; for the other, half empty. It is this difference of emphasis that gives the appearance of greater radicality on the part of Derrida (especially to English-speaking readers caught up in the French tradition of shock and scandal). But those emphases lie on the surface, and that view is superficial. At the heart of the matter, Gadamer and Derrida are equally postmodern.

The Incompleteness of the Hermeneutics of Finitude

William James is said to have complained that for his colleague Josiah Royce, the world is real but not so very damn real. In that spirit we can say that the hermeneutical turn is radical but not so very damn radical. If we wish to make it more radical, to break more decisively with modernity, what is needed is not more shock and scandal rhetoric, but a more penetrating analysis of the failure of the Enlightenment project and its Romantic and Hegelian alternatives.

Modernity wanted to own the Truth and thereby always to be at Home. It wanted life to begin not with "Once upon a time" but with "And they lived happily ever after." As perspectival pluralism, the hermeneutical turn recognizes modernity's self-understanding as a wish-fulfilling fantasy, Descartes's dream in the Freudian sense. With Kant, but ultimately against Kant, it makes finitude an epistemological category in a far more radical sense than did classical empiricism. Being situated in our bodies, in our language, and in our social history, we are caught between the Eden of originary presence and the Eschaton of organic totality.

But this finitude is not the only barrier to our possessing the Truth and being always at Home. The hermeneutics of finitude becomes more radical when it becomes the hermeneutics of suspicion by making sin, in addition to finitude, an epistemological category.

To make sin an epistemological category is to call attention not merely to the influence of desire upon cognition but more particularly to the influence of precisely those desires that we cannot acknowledge because we have sufficient conscience to be ashamed of them. This means that while the hermeneutics of suspicion involves the unmasking of false consciousness and

self-deception, not every such unmasking involves the hermeneutics of suspicion. For not every false consciousness is motivated, that is, not every distortion of self-consciousness is rooted
in desire; and not every self-deception, which is by definition
motivated, is motivated by desires of which the self involved is
morally ashamed.

We can find an example of the first case in Merleau-Ponty.
His critique of Descartes in the section of *The Phenomenology of
Perception* entitled "The Cogito" includes an analysis of false
love. This is clearly a case of false consciousness, but he sharply
distinguishes it from deceitful love that must be understood in
terms of an inner conspiracy of the self against itself. As motivated false consciousness, deceitful love is the self-deception in
which I persuade myself of something I know to be false. By
contrast, false love is not so much motivated from within as
something that overtakes me from without. I am seized by powerful affections. In my inexperience and not knowing any better,
I identify them with love. I am mistaken, but my false consciousness, being unmotivated, is not a case of self-deception. I am not
mistaken in the service of some need not to recognize the truth.
Although Merleau-Ponty's politics regularly employs a full-
fledged hermeneutics of suspicion, his phenomenological ontology remains, here as elsewhere, within the hermeneutics of finitude.

We can find an example of the second case in the account of
Dasein's Being-toward-death with which Division II of Heidegger's *Being and Time* opens. There is no question but that the
"evasive concealment" and "tranquilized everydayness" with
which I confront death as my ownmost possibility is motivated
from within and is a case of self-deception in which I try to persuade myself of what I know isn't so. Heidegger identifies the
motive as "cowardly fear," and it is just this motive that distinguishes Heidegger's analysis from the hermeneutics of suspicion, where the motive would better be described as guilty
shame. Heidegger exposes a self-deception whose purpose is to
comfort, while the hermeneutics of suspicion exposes those self-
deceptions whose purpose is to justify a plea of not guilty in
spite of the presence in me of desires, feelings, or actions I do
not and cannot morally condone. Cowardly fear may be a vice,

but it is not that, on Heidegger's example, that I am trying to hide from myself. It is the certainty of my death, my finitude and not my fault.

If we compare Heidegger's analysis with Freud's interpretation of his dreams of Irma's injection and the uncle with the yellow beard, this difference in motivation will emerge clearly. Freud makes sin an epistemological category, whereas Heidegger's analysis, even of self-deception, does not. In the former case we lack the humility to acknowledge our faults; in the latter we deceive ourselves because we lack the courage to face our fate.

Ricoeur, through his studies of Freud and Marx, and Foucault, through his genealogical strategy derived from Nietzsche, represent the best examples of the hermeneutics of suspicion within contemporary philosophical discussions. By making sin an epistemological category, in fact if not in name, they are more radical than Gadamer and Derrida.

Foucault's analysis of the will to power, for example, does not focus our attention on those would-be *Übermenschen* who shamelessly seek to exploit and control others, but rather on those who (1) achieve domination (2) without noticing that they have done so because (3) their professed morality does not approve of domination. He directs our attention to wolves in sheep's clothing, practicing masters with slave superegos. For Nietzsche the paradigm of that kind of will to power is the priest, and what Foucault gives us is a series of variations on the theme of priestly power, whether the priests be quite literally clergy from the church, or, as modernity's secularism establishes itself, doctors and therapists from the Ministry of Health, philosophers and social scientists from the Ministry of Truth, and correctional officers from the Ministry of Justice.

Far from being an alternative to the hermeneutics of finitude, such a hermeneutics of suspicion presupposes and sometimes even develops on its own the standard analyses of situation epistemology. But it goes beyond those analyses to pinpoint problems even more threatening to modernity than finitude. For, in its Enlightenment form, at least, modernity thought it could handle finitude. We need only think of Descartes's distinction between finite and infinite substance or Kant's distinction between phenomena and noumena. But all forms of modernity are deeply committed to a Pelagian anthropology that is seriously put into question by the Augustinian assumptions underlying the hermeneutics of suspicion. (If Marx and Nietzsche, two of its paradigmatic practitioners, have eschatological hopes for a restoration of primal innocence, so does Augustine. Against Kant, and with Augustine, they would agree that human life this side of apocalyptic change is not capable of regeneration without grace.)

The Incompleteness of the Hermeneutics of Suspicion

The hermeneutics of suspicion is a powerful weapon against illusions, including the mystifications of modernity. But it is not a very good resting place. In the first place, it easily becomes a form a moral megalomania. For if we practice it only against "them," whether "they" are Cartesians, communists, or whatever, we become the ultimate Pharisees. We become like the Sunday School teacher who concluded a lesson about the self-righteous Pharisee, whose prayer consisted in thanking God that he was not like other people, by saying, "Now children, let us fold our hands, close our eyes, bow our heads, and thank God that we are not like that Pharisee."

If, on the other hand, we make a point of including ourselves among the targets of suspicion, things are not necessarily any better. For with sustained suspicion directed against ourselves the thrill of discovery quickly dissolves into the agony of despair. Such a discipline may be good for our spiritual health, but by itself it is like a diet of nothing but ex-lax. It helps to purge us of putrid waste that has been deprived of whatever nourishment it may once have had (since illusions are seldom wholly without truth—they only render the truth they retain poisonous to their believers). But it satisfies no spiritual hunger, and our spiritual bulimia guarantees that we remain malnourished as well.

Of course, despair may be the ultimately philosophical passion, the affect that best fits the truth about our situation. It is just such a belief, I suspect, that makes so much of modern and

postmodern philosophy little more than thinly disguised Sto-
icism. But even if despair is a vice and not a virtue, it is not the
most dangerous consequence of sustained suspicion. It has an
essentially unstable chemistry, and it turns into cynicism much
more easily than into hope. As despair turns cynical, the bulimia
of the spirit turns into the anorexia of the spirit. Turning from a
feast and purge strategy that leaves one as exhausted as hungry,
the spirit is no longer willing to risk any nourishment at all. The
irony is that this cynicism is peculiarly modern, for the criterion
of its negations is modernity's concept of Truth. Instead of offering a less arrogant and possibly more human concept of truth, it
is content to tell us what we can't have, measured by modernity's quite possibly neurotic needs for certainty and finality.

The point I am trying to make is simply this. Our analysis to
this point has identified radicality with negativity. It threatens
to leave us between the devil and the deep blue sea, between the
illusions of modernity and the cynicism of postmodernity. In
response to this threat, I want to suggest that postmodern epistemology as the hermeneutics of finitude combined with the hermeneutics of suspicion need not be cynical, however tempting it
may be to accentuate the negative in the quest for radicality. Of
course, radicality is by definition negative; but it is not by definition wholly negative. From the premise that we have no Truth
it is not necessary to conclude that everything is false, and, thus,
that everything is permitted.

If we do draw this inference, there is really no good reason
not to sell our souls to the military-industrial instrumentalism
that can reward us so handsomely, especially if we are white,
and male, and smart. We can define nihilism as, first, this cynical
inference from the failure of modernity (everything is false) and,
second, the cynical pact with the Devil that goes with it (everything is permitted). It is, to repeat, a possible path for those who
see modernity as malaise rather than as mankind's (sic) majority.
And it is undeniably a radical response to modernity.

But if nihilism is both possible and radical, I want to suggest
that it is neither necessary nor so very damn radical. If we are
really serious about a radical hermeneutics, we must go beyond
the negations of both the hermeneutics of finitude and the hermeneutics of suspicion. I have in mind not the abandonment of

these negations through a desperate defense of realism (usually a defense of extravagant epistemological claims masquerading as a metaphysical claim) but their *Aufhebung,* their teleological suspension, their incorporation into a larger whole of which they are but parts, however crucial. It is clear that the whole in question cannot be composed by adding new negations, on pain of merely intensifying the cynicism we seek to avoid. A truly radical hermeneutics must reply to the positivity of modernity with an alternative positivity that is distinctively postmodern by virtue of presupposing the negations involved in seeing our thinking as both situated and sinful.

POSITIVE POSTMODERNISM

I find in Kierkegaard and Nietzsche the best examples of such a radical hermeneutics. So I want to claim that in relation to modernity Gadamer and Derrida offer a measure of hermeneutical radicality, that Ricoeur and Foucault offer a more radical hermeneutics, and that Kierkegaard and Nietzsche offer a still more radical hermeneutics. Without claiming that theirs is a hermeneutics than which a more radical hermeneutics cannot be conceived, I do not find myself in a hurry to go beyond them. The challenge they present to us is so deep and so comprehensive that we could do worse than work on it and let it work on us for a while. The kind of hermeneutics they offer to us is anything but a mastered moment.

Both thinkers are decisively postmodern. Both have taken the hermeneutical turn, and each has developed his own sophisticated hermeneutics of finitude, supplemented by a devastating hermeneutics of suspicion. What makes them distinctively postmodern, however, is their positivity. Without retracting the relentless negativity of their thinking, both are willing to affirm an ontology, a metaphysics, a *Weltanschauung*—call it what you will—in terms of which human life can be meaningful by virtue of goals worth sacrificing for. Each is the self-appointed prophet of a god he finds worthy of worship in the forms of celebration, surrender, and imitation.

Their gods, of course, are as different as can be. Kierkegaard's is the God of the Bible: of Abraham, Isaac, and Jacob; of Peter, James, and John—the God who became human in Jesus of Nazareth. Nietzsche's deity is Dionysus, the God of madness, the myrtle, and, above all, the maenads—another God human enough to die, and divine enough to rise again. But the modes of this death and resurrection are as different from those of Jesus as the moralities taught to the followers of these faiths are different. Kierkegaard would have no quarrel with the slogan Nietzsche uses to conclude *Ecce Homo, "Dionysus versus the Crucified."*

It may seem all too inevitable that the positivity of these postmodernists should take the form of religious faith. After all, an important part of the modernist project was to bring religion within the limits of reason alone (think of Kant, Schleiermacher, and Hegel for the three modes of modernity discussed above). If, during the heyday of modernity, many of its own devotees (please note the irony) concluded that such a task was impossible and that religion must be rejected as irrational, is it not even more obvious in the collapse of the entire modernist project that reason cannot ground any positivity, sacred or secular, and that faith as arbitrary choice is the only alternative to the nihilism of cynical negativity?

Interestingly, neither Kierkegaard nor Nietzsche sees it that way. In spite of the former's talk about the leap and about the subjectivity of truth, and in spite of the latter's talk about truth as useful lies and about the irreducible plurality of perspectives, both are eager to give reasons for their faith. Both are clear that giving reasons cannot have the meaning modernity would have wished, a pure gaze at naked truth by means of a recollective withdrawal from earthbound situatedness. But both, unlike modernity and its cynical critics, reject the either/or of absolute reasons or no reasons at all. Each spends a great deal of time and effort spelling out an interpretation of human existence in terms of which his faith makes sense. They know full well, and never let us forget, that those interpretations are just that, interpretations, and that they necessarily lack both the immediacy and the totality that might satisfy modernity's question for certainty (epistemologically speaking) and security (existentially speaking). Because these interpretations are thoroughly phenomenological, in the descriptive sense, each is able to invite us to try his on and see whether it does not fit our own experience better than the alternatives.

I want to draw these reflections to a close (temporarily, that is, without closure) by giving my own reasons, which do not claim to be absolute, for preferring Kierkegaard's faith to Nietzsche's and for concluding that radical hermeneutics is best exemplified in the complex authorship of the melancholy Dane. Since this entire essay is but the sketch of an argument, each part of which needs and could easily be given detailed development, I make no apology for giving little more here than theses that I believe are capable of detailed defense.

In the midst of his most sustained witness to his Dionysian faith, at the very beginning of *Thus Spoke Zarathustra*, Part III ("The Wanderer"), Nietzsche writes, "in the end, one experiences only oneself." No text in his entire corpus gives greater support to the Heideggerian thesis that Nietzsche is the *Vollendung* of metaphysics, and thus of modernity, rather than its *Überwindung*. It is Nietzsche's loneliness rather than his madness that is the existential correlate to this thought. The triumph of Platonic intuition over Socratic conversation has given a monological cast to the metaphysical tradition of the west that modernity did not (even try to) overcome, even in Hegel, whose dialectic is eventually not dialogical. In its allergic reaction to *Unterweglichkeit* and *Unheimlichkeit*, inherited from Plato (hence all those footnotes), modernity turns out to be allergic to alterity as well. On this crucial point, Nietzsche remains, *malgré lui,* more the child than the enemy of modernity, not just in the passage cited, but throughout his writings. For they are the quest for a form of autonomy far more extensive than anything modernity ever dreamed of.

By contrast, Kierkegaard's authorship is the sustained attempt to spell out the conditions of the possibility of encountering the genuinely other. The individualism for which he is famous is only penultimate. It seeks to expose the crowd (Nietzsche's herd) as a strategy for collectively warding off anything truly other, in order to open the essentially relational self, who is neither a Spinozistic substance nor a Leibnizian monad, to the thoroughgoing otherness of God and neighbor. If he focuses especially on the God relationship, it is because God is better able than my neighbor to resist the variety of strategies by which I or We might try to reduce the other to the same, thereby retaining my Cartesian or our Hegelian self-sufficiency.

It is this will first to permit and eventually to welcome the other into one's life that makes Kierkegaard seem to me more radically postmodern than Nietzsche. In relation to two themes left dangling earlier in this essay, this reading of their relationship has two important corollaries. Although I have pointed to military-industrial instrumentalism as the most concrete expression of modernity, implying that a truly radical postmodernity would have a morality capable of challenging the will to power of the nation state, I have kept the discussion focused on more abstract, epistemological issues.

I think it can be shown that Nietzsche does not have the resources for developing such a moral critique of modernity, not because of his epistemological negations but because of his allergy to alterity. It may well be that the Nazis' use of his statements on war and cruelty rest on unsophisticated readings that overlook his interest in spiritualizing or sublimating our instincts of hatred. But no one has ever found in him a critique of the honestly hostile heart, or accused him of being a philosopher of peace rather than, like Heraclitus before him and Heidegger after him, of *polemos*.

By contrast, Kierkegaard, who knows as well as Nietzsche how easily professed virtues are really splendid vices, does not give up on compassion and neighbor love but seeks to show how their true form is essential to human flourishing. By virtue of his fundamental willingness to find that decentered selfhood that can experience the other as truly other, Kierkegaard has the basic moral resources needed for a critique of modernity's moral Cartesianism, the placing of the self, individual and collective, at the center, thereby making wealth and power, personal and national, the overriding goals of life. Like the Hebrew prophets before him and Levinas after him, Kierkegaard is a philosopher of *shalom* rather than of *polemos*.

The other corollary concerns the question whether there can be a receptive radicality or whether the image of penetrating beneath the surface to the inner core of being is hopelessly andro-phallo-centric. I would not be so foolish as to call Kierkegaard a feminist. But I believe his openness to otherness, expressed in the priority he gives, in contrast to Nietzsche, to *agape* over *agon*, lays the groundwork for a receptive radicality that can include the feminist critique of modernity. And no critique of modernity that incorporates a thoughtful feminist component will ever be able to say, "In the end, one experiences only oneself."

Modernity is an escapist refusal of the ontological relativity defined by *Unterweglichkeit* and *Unheimlichkeit* and the moral relativity defined by the unconditional claims of both the divine and human other upon me as an individual and upon us as a people. Much of secular postmodernism, inspired by Greek sources, sees this multiple decentering of the self as a fate nobly to be borne. By contrast, Kierkegaard sees it as a task humbly to be accepted, the task that makes life at once human and worth living. In doing so he points the way to a postmodernism of *shalom*, one that undermines the foundations of war between nations, classes, races, and genders. Those of us who are interested in radical hermeneutics could do worse than to linger thoughtfully with him awhile.

8

Father Adam and His Feuding Sons: An Interpretation of the Hermeneutical Turn in Continental Philosophy

THE STORY of the hermeneutical turn in continental philosophy can be told in almost biblical terms. In the place of Father Adam (or Father Isaac) we have Father Heidegger, and in the place of the feuding sons, Cain and Abel (or Jacob and Esau), we have, at least according to one telling, the reactionary son, Gadamer, and the radical son, Derrida.[1]

I find this reactionary/radical dichotomy at least as misleading as it is illuminating.[2] It is perhaps one of those hierarchical dyads that needs to be deconstructed. But, following the old preacher's adage, "a text without a context is a pretext," which isn't the worst hermeneutical theory I've ever run across, I'd like to take a running start at the troika whose hermeneutical reflections dominate so much of contemporary discussion, for their prehistory is an essential part of their story.

Actually, it seems to me that there are two prehistories. The standard story sees the emergence of philosophical hermeneutics in Heidegger and Gadamer as the critical heirs of Schleiermacher and Dilthey.[3] The critical side involves a double

---

[1] See John D. Caputo, *Radical Hermeneutics: Repetition, Deconstruction, and the Hermeneutic Project* (Bloomington: Indiana University Press, 1987), pp. 5–6, 81–82, 96, 108–119. Cf. Caputo's "Gadamer's Closet Essentialism: A Derridean Critique," in *Dialogue and Deconstruction: The Gadamer-Derrida Encounter*, ed. Diane P. Michelfelder and Richard E. Palmer (Albany: SUNY Press, 1989).

[2] For one account of why, see "Positive Postmodernism as Radical Hermeneutics" (chapter 7 above).

[3] See, for example, Richard Palmer, *Hermeneutics: Interpretation Theory in Schleiermacher, Dilthey, Heidegger, and Gadamer* (Evanston: Northwestern University Press, 1969); Paul Ricoeur, "The Task of Hermeneutics," in *Paul Ricoeur:*

rejection. First there is a move away from the psychologistic tendencies of nineteenth-century hermeneutics, according to which the task of understanding is to reconstruct and reexperience precisely the authorial experience that gave rise to the text. Writing is the outward expression of inward experience; reading is the reverse movement that uses the expression as a means to relive the experience. Thus, for Schleiermacher, "every act of understanding is the reverse side of an act of speaking, and one must grasp the thinking that underlies a given statement."[4] One "must be able to step out of one's own frame of mind into that of the author."[5] Comparative grammatical study is essential to this task, but ultimately it depends on divination: "By leading the interpreter to transfer himself, so to speak, into the author, the divinatory method seeks to gain an immediate comprehension of the author as an individual."[6]

Dilthey, we are told, does not ground *Verstehen* "in empathy and intuition," but instead of speaking of *Einfühlen* speaks rather of *Nacherleben* and *Nachfühlen*, "neither of which refers to a unifying projection of the self into the other."[7] But this is only to reformulate the psychologism of romantic hermeneutics, not to abandon it.

The idea that the ultimate goal of interpretation is to recon-

---

Hermeneutics and the Human Sciences, ed. and trans. John B. Thompson (New York: Cambridge University Press, 1981); and Joseph Bleicher, *Contemporary Hermeneutics: Hermeneutics as Method, Philosophy, and Critique* (London: Routledge, 1980).

[4] F. D. E. Schleiermacher, *Hermeneutics: The Handwritten Manuscripts,* ed. Heinz Kimmerle and trans. James Duke and Jack Forstman (Missoula, Mont.: Scholars Press, 1977), p. 97. Henceforth *HHM*. Implicit in passages of this kind is the assumption that thought is prior to and independent of language, which is related to it only accidentally and externally. In his introduction Kimmerle argues that Schleiermacher moves toward such a view from an earlier view where thought and language are inseparable.

[5] Ibid., p. 42.

[6] Ibid., p. 150. Cf. p. 113: "Before the art of hermeneutics can be practiced, the interpreter must put himself both objectively and subjectively in the position of the author."

[7] Rudolf A. Makkreel, *Dilthey: Philosopher of the Human Studies* (Princeton: Princeton University Press, 1975), pp. 5–7, including nn. 3–5. Cf. pp. 252–53, n. 5. Makkreel argues that Dilthey's movement is away from psychologism toward a hermeneutic focused more on the expressions of *Geist* than on the underlying experiences. In other words, he moves in the opposite direction from Schleiermacher as interpreted by Kimmerle. See n. 4 above.

struct and reexperience the intention of the author is the link between the psychologism of Schleiermacher and Dilthey and a second feature of their hermeneutics rejected by Heidegger and his sons, namely, its objectivism. Objectivism in this context is the claim that interpretation can mimic the natural sciences by producing judgments of universal validity, namely, judgments not relative to some particular standpoint and valid only within it. Schleiermacher knew that interpretation is an art (*Kunst*), but he wanted hermeneutics to be a science (*Kunstlehre*). The basic ingredients of the objectivism he shares with Dilthey are two:

1. Hermeneutics can be a science only if it has a determinate and unchanging object (for which role the author's intention is a splendid candidate). Two major twentieth-century heirs of this objectivism are E. D. Hirsch, Jr., and Emilio Betti. Seeing that objectively valid interpretation requires a certain kind of object, Hirsch writes,

> When, therefore, I say that a verbal meaning is determinate I mean that it is an entity which is self-identical. Furthermore, I also mean that it is an entity which always remains the same from one moment to the next—that it is changeless. Indeed, these criteria were already implied in the requirement that verbal meaning be reproducible.... Verbal meaning, then, is what it is and not something else, and it is always the same. That is what I mean by determinacy.[8]

Betti makes much the same point when he makes "the autonomy of the object" the first canon of his hermeneutic.[9]

2. Hermeneutics can be a science only if it spells out a normative methodology, a strategy for gaining objectively validated knowledge of its determinate and unchanging object in terms of rules or canons. From Descartes down to the more experimental methodologies of the natural sciences, the goal of method has

---

[8] *Validity in Interpretation* (New Haven: Yale University Press, 1967), p. 46.

[9] *Hermeneutics as the General Methodology of the Geisteswissenschaften*, ed. and trans. Josef Bleicher, in *Contemporary Hermeneutics*, p. 58. Like Hirsch, Betti links this autonomy tightly to the author's intention. Friedrich August Wolf, in dialogue with whom Schleiermacher developed his hermeneutic, had already written that the aim of hermeneutics is "to grasp the written or even spoken thoughts of an author as he would have them to be grasped." Quoted in Palmer, *Hermeneutics*, p. 81.

been to free knowledge from tradition, bias, or any other kind of particular perspective and render its validity universal.

If the hermeneutical turn we seek to understand is a turning away from psychologistic tendencies and methodological aspirations, both in the service of objectivism, it is also the appropriation of two important themes from Schleiermacher and Dilthey. The first of these is a generalized hermeneutics. Schleiermacher bemoaned the fact that there was no general theory of interpretation but only the specialized hermeneutics associated with three groups of normative texts: biblical hermeneutics, legal hermeneutics, and the hermeneutics of classical philology. He insisted on seeing these as special cases of a more general account that would apply to any text whatever (spoken or written). In seeking to make hermeneutics the methodology of the *Geisteswissenschaften*, Dilthey enlarges the range of interpretation and understanding to include all expressions or objectifications of the human spirit, including nonverbal works of art, historical events, social practices and institutions, and so forth. It is now textual interpretation as such, and not, for example, biblical interpretation, that is seen as a special case.

This double generalization, or *"deregionalization"* of hermeneutics, as Ricoeur calls it,[10] is assumed by the hermeneutical turn we are exploring. Heidegger and Gadamer will seek to express it by saying they are doing ontology rather than methodology. We have already seen briefly what this "rather than" means negatively. What "ontology" signifies positively is that interpretation belongs as a fundamental feature to the being-in-the-world of the being that each of us is. The understanding that arises from interpretation is who we are. Ricoeur calls this the *"radicalisation"* of hermeneutics. But the turn to ontology is not, as Ricoeur suggests, a turn away from epistemology. For, first, deregionalized hermeneutics remains a reflection on the nature and limits of human knowledge, and, second, what makes Heidegger and Gadamer radical relative to Schleiermacher and Dilthey is their epistemological reading of the hermeneutical circle.[11]

---

[10] "The Task of Hermeneutics," p. 44.

[11] Ibid., p. 44. Cf. "Hermeneutics as Epistemology" (chapter 3 above). Rorty's slogan of the end of epistemology in *Philosophy and the Mirror of Nature*

The hermeneutical circle is the other theme that carries over into the hermeneutical turn of the twentieth century. Already propounded by Schleiermacher's immediate predecessor, Friedrich Ast, it is a circle of part and whole. But already in Schleiermacher it means more than that the meaning of the whole of a text must be constructed from meanings of the parts *and vice versa.* For the whole in terms of which any given passage must be interpreted is not just the whole of the text in which it appears but the whole of the language in which it is written and the whole of the life of the author who wrote it.[12]

This means that the task of interpretation is infinite, for the two wholes that are the context of any text are themselves both infinite. We can have a "presentiment" of the whole, but every interpretation will be "imperfect," "only an approximation," in short "provisional . . . until suddenly at the end every part is clear and the whole work is visible in sharp and definite contours."[13] By itself this passage suggests that hermeneutical totality can be achieved; but elsewhere when stressing the infinity of the interpretative task, Schleiermacher makes this "end" of interpretation sound more like a regulative ideal. To complete the task "it would be necessary to have a complete knowledge of the language . . . [and] to have a complete knowledge of the person," which in both cases is "impossible."[14] Because of the infinity of the task, "inspiration" is needed.[15] But from this inspiration we should not expect necessary insight of the sort that results from proofs.[16] It would seem that we are back to a presentiment of the whole that will remain provisional.

It is a shorter step from Schleiermacher's infinite to Derrida's undecidability than might be immediately evident to those who share the *Sehnsucht nach der Wissenschaft* that links romantic hermeneutics to its reiteration in Dilthey, Betti, and Hirsch. But Heidegger and Gadamer, and not only Derrida, will find in this

---

(Princeton: Princeton University Press, 1979) is misleading. The hermeneutical turn is in the end only one particular way of reflecting on the nature and limits of human knowledge.

[12] *HHM,* pp. 98–99, 202.
[13] Ibid., pp. 198–203.
[14] Ibid., p. 100.
[15] Ibid., p. 112.
[16] Ibid., pp. 183–86.

notion that the hermeneutical circle poses an infinite task for interpretation the basis for deconstructing that yearning (which is not the same as abolishing or abandoning it). In order to appreciate more fully the radical implications of the hermeneutical circle for our troika and those who have taken the hermeneutical turn with them, it will be helpful to trace the other prehistory of that turn.

This second story moves from Kant through Hegel and Kierkegaard to Nietzsche. Within the hermeneutical circle the presentiment of the whole functions as an a priori, as a condition for the possibility of interpreting any part. The Copernican revolution of the First Critique is the discovery that interpretations dependent on a priori guidelines are relative to the standpoint constituted by those guidelines and that, unless it can be legitimately claimed that such a standpoint is the absolute standpoint (today, following Thomas Nagel, we might call it the view from nowhere), the resultant knowledge will not be Absolute Knowledge. Since the forms and categories that make possible human experience constitute the human standpoint, not the divine, the former can give only phenomenal knowledge (appearance), while only the latter can give noumenal knowledge (the thing in itself). Even within the limitations of the phenomenal, our inability to specify the totality of the conditions of any phenomenon make the ideal of knowledge a regulative ideal.[17]

One might reply that there is no hermeneutical circle in Kant since we do not revise our a priori principles in the light of experience. True enough, and while he insists that (noumenal) Truth and Knowledge are not available to us, the (phenomenal) truth and knowledge he thinks we can have depend for their objectivity on our having universally valid and unrevisable anticipations of experience. But what if human knowledge is historical and its presentiments labile as Schleiermacher and Dilthey presume (at least for the *Geisteswissenschaften*)?

---

[17] My reading of Kant's Copernican Revolution as essentially theistic has been developed in more detail in "In Defense of the Thing in Itself," *Kant-Studien* 59, no. 1 (1968), and "Christian Philosophers and the Copernican Revolution" (ch. 5 above). Its relevance to hermeneutics is discussed in my "Post-Kantian Reflections on the Importance of Hermeneutics," in *Disciplining Hermeneutics: Interpretation in Christian Perspective*, ed. Roger Lundin (Grand Rapids, Mich.: Eerdmans, 1997).

Hegel to the rescue. First, he recognizes both phenomenologi-
cally and logically that there is a plurality of human interpretative standpoints, defined by different a priori, categoreal
structures. Then he recognizes that this synchronic plurality
shows itself historically in a diachronic plurality. Next he notes
that the relativity inherent in this plurality can be overcome only
if the totality of perspectives can be integrated into an organic
whole, which would then define a perspective no longer relative
to any alternative. Finally, he makes the audacious claim to have
achieved that integral totality by which Absolute Knowledge is
constituted. His Logos is God before the creation of the world,
to which all finite things are relative but that itself is relative to
nothing other than its own internal moments. Better than the
merely human objectivity that Kant thought was possible
through the ahistorical (noncircular) character of human understanding, Hegel offers a Divine Objectivity in two easy steps:
first, acknowledge the historical diversity and revisability of interpretative standpoints that make the hermeneutical circle a reality; then escape the circle by completing the infinite task it
poses, by achieving totality.

The aftermath to Hegel is largely the story of Hegelians without the Absolute, philosophers with too much of a sense of
human historicality to take seriously any strategy but Hegel's,
but with too much of a sense of human finitude and diversity to
take that strategy itself seriously. History without totality renders null and void not only the Divine Objectivity offered by
Hegel but even the human objectivity offered by Kant.

This is already the case for Kierkegaard. He and his pseudonyms often argue like this:

> It is often said that Christianity is unreasonable. Some, like Les-
> sing, conclude that it must be rejected on these grounds. Others,
> like Hegel, conclude that it must be reinterpreted beyond recogni-
> tion in order to become reasonable. Christian apologists respond
> by trying to show that their faith is reasonable after all. My "de-
> fense" of Christianity is quite different. I admit, nay insist, that it
> is unreasonable. But I reserve the right to inquire just who "Rea-
> son" might be and who appointed it to be the ultimate arbiter of
> the True and the Real.

Upon examination "Reason" turns out to be doubly defective.

On the one hand, it is radically finite. It is always human understanding that takes to itself this honorific title. But for Christianity, human understanding is not Divine Understanding and can never be the ultimate touchstone of Truth. Kant was right about that.

But Hegel helps us to see that it is worse than that. Human understanding is not timeless, unchanging, and universal. It is always some contingent, particular point of view, shared by a certain group of people at a certain time. But especially when "Reason" claims to be the integrated totality of all such perspectives and insists on the uppercase R in its name, impatiently dismissing as unenlightened (Lessing) or immature (Hegel) anything that dares to differ from it, it becomes clear that "Reason" is not just the shared assumptions of some human group but the self-congratulatory self-legitimation of some Established Order. Kant was right in denying the power of totality to human understanding; but that means that what Hegel shows us (against his intentions) is what Marx would say clearly: "Reason" is ideology.

But why should Christianity have to prove its respectability by showing that it conforms to the Idols of the Tribe? When it is objected that Christianity is unreasonable, people of faith should reply, "It is just as you say, and the amazing thing is that you think that it is an objection."[18] "Reason" is a Wizard of Oz who has cowed people far too long. It's long since time to go behind the screen and see the discrepancy between the image and the reality.

So far as I can see, there is only one difference between Kierkegaard's demythologizing of "Reason" and Nietzsche's perspectivism. Kierkegaard thinks that there is an Absolute Perspective (at once the view from everywhere and from nowhere), available to God but not to us. Nietzsche thinks there is no such thing. But they are in profound agreement about the nature and limits of human understanding:

- Its *presuppositions* always constitute a finite and contingent *perspective.*
- This *perspective* is always one of many, conflicting *points of view.*[19]

---

[18] *Philosophical Fragments/Johannes Climacus,* trans. Howard V. Hong and Edna H. Hong (Princeton: Princeton University Press, 1985), p. 52.

[19] The visual perception of a physical object is perspectival. But it is not radi-

- The resultant relativity of truth claims to the *point of view* or *paradigm* which is the a priori condition of their plausibility and verifiability cannot be overcome by Hegel's totalizing strategy but signifies the nature and limits of human understanding.
- The present age, whether it thinks of itself as Modernity, flying the flag of Reason, or Christendom basking in its demonstrated reasonableness, is the self-deceived, self-deifying denial of these (to it) humiliating reminders that it is neither God nor the Kingdom of God.

This story, or something very much like it, is the other prehistory of the hermeneutical turn, the context in which the hermeneutical circle was taken over by Heidegger and his sons and *interpreted* against Schleiermacher and Dilthey. It is not that Dilthey did not know the story. He writes,

> The finitude of every historical phenomenon, . . . the relativity of every kind of human apprehension of the totality of things is the last word of the historical *Weltanschauung*. . . . And over against this both the demand of thought and the striving of philosophy for universal knowledge assert themselves. The historical *Weltanschauung* liberates the human spirit from the last chains that natural science and philosophy have not yet broken. *But where are the means to overcome the anarchy of opinions which then threatens to befall us?*[20]

But Dilthey's objectivist response to this question shows that he is still enthralled by "the striving of philosophy for universal knowledge" and only partly unchained from natural science. His critique of historical reason is free from the assumption that *Geist* must become the object of knowledge in just the same way as *Natur*, but not from the assumption that it must have a separate but equal objectivity so as to satisfy "the striving of philosophy for universal knowledge."[21]

---

cally perspectival because the view from here and the view from there complement rather than contradict each other. The mutual incompatibility of perspectives is crucial to the radical perspectivism of Kierkegaard and Nietzsche. This is obvious enough when Christianity is seen as incompatible with "Reason" or Dionysian Overman, but it is often left implicit in more general discussions, leaving careless readers to see perspectivism as trivial.

[20] Quoted in Makkreel, *Dilthey*, p. 3, emphasis added.

[21] Bleicher describes Dilthey's "scientistic territory" in this way: "Empiricistically he focuses on something 'given,' the ultimate unit of experience which

It is the abandonment of this assumption in understanding the significance of the hermeneutical circle that constitutes the hermeneutical turn and its radicality in twentieth-century continental philosophy.[22] Heidegger's interpretation of the circle in terms of pre-understanding in *Being and Time* and Gadamer's construal in terms of prejudice in *Truth and Method* have broken decisively with "the striving of philosophy for universal knowledge." We are too embedded in our historical locality, our language, our culture, our practices, and, of course, the interpretations these make possible for philosophy's striving to be anything but futile, its dream anything but a pipe dream.

What then about Dilthey's question, "But where are the means to overcome the anarchy of opinions which then threatens to befall us?" It is Gadamer more than Heidegger who addresses this issue, and his answer is quite direct: not methodological objectivity but open and honest dialogue.[23] It is possible, he believes, to come to an understanding with those who start with different prejudices from our own. There can be a fusion of horizons. Of course, these understandings and these fusions are never total nor permanent, but they are not nothing either.

It is this aspect of Gadamer's work that leads many to see his as a conservative or even reactionary hermeneutic, especially in comparison with Derrida. This seems to me mistaken.[24] In the first place, the claims Gadamer will make about the limited and fragile possibility of mutual understanding making it (sometimes) possible for us to live together without violence are not

---

in the sphere of hermeneutics is the 'lived experience'. Equally, 'reliving'—a concept Dilthey never seemed able to free himself from—functions as the equivalent to observation: 'both fulfill on the empirical level the criterion for a copy theory of truth; they guarantee, it seems, the reproduction of something immediate within an isolated consciousness that is free of any subjective elements' "; *Contemporary Hermeneutics*, pp. 23–24. The final quotation is from Jürgen Habermas, *Protestbewegung und Hochschulreform* (Frankfurt: Suhrkamp, 1969), p. 226.

[22] For very similar developments within the Anglo-American "analytic" traditions, see Rorty, *Philosophy and the Mirror of Nature,* and Nancey Murphy, *Anglo-American Postmodernity* (Boulder: Westview Press, 1997).

[23] Habermas enters the scene with a theory of the rules for such a dialogue. But these are more nearly moral norms than the rules that constitute a methodology. For Gadamer and for Habermas the task of coming to an understanding is more basically a moral than a theoretical task.

[24] See n. 2 above.

claims Derrida finds it necessary to contest. In the second place, like Heidegger before him and Derrida after him, Gadamer has seen the radical implications of Schleiermacher's recognition that the infinite whole(s) in terms of which the parts must be interpreted set for interpretation an infinite task that it can never complete. All construals will be provisional—but not in the way in which our vision of a physical object is provisional, since there is an infinite number of perspectives from which we might view it, and we will always have occupied only a finite subset of these. Like Heidegger before him and Derrida after him, Gadamer understands Dilthey, when he says that "the relativity of every kind of human apprehension of the totality of things is the last word of the historical *Weltanschauung*," to signify not just that our presentiments of the totality are just that, anticipations of experience we have not yet had; their relativity also signifies that they are embedded in and constituted by conflicting a prioris, pre-understandings, prejudices, which cannot simply be added together to give us an increasingly determinate and stable common object.

The differences have to be negotiated; that is the infinite task of understanding. Every understanding, the one I start with and the one you and I reach through a dialogical fusion of horizons, is open to deconstruction and further dialogue, open to the claim, not just that it has left something out, but that it has construed things wrongly and needs to be revised, not just supplemented (or perhaps that supplementation is always *Aufhebung*, the recontextualization that changes even what it retains).[25]

In other words, before Gadamer becomes the evangelist of the gospel of *Horizontverschmelzung*, he is, like Heidegger before him and Derrida after him, a prophet of epistemological gloom and doom. And he is hopelessly protestant. He has given up all hope of a universal Mother Church, whether in the temples of Reason or the basilicas of Christendom. In a world of dangerous difference, the most he can hope for is a bit of ecumenism, a modus vivendi based on dialogue rather than violence and manipula-

---

[25] See Jacques Derrida, "From Restricted to General Economy: A Hegelianism without Reserve," in *Writing and Difference*, trans. Alan Bass (Chicago: University of Chicago Press, 1978).

tion. But the presence of this hope doesn't cancel out his radical resistance to the sirens of science who seduced Schleiermacher and Dilthey. Nor does it make him a reactionary any more than Paul is a Pelagian because after preaching sin he preaches salvation. Just as Pauline soteriology presupposes and does not erase his hamartiology, so Gadamer's politics of dialogue presupposes and does not erase his radical reading of the hermeneutical circle. Neither of texts nor of the world are methodologically validated objective interpretations available to us.[26] We have always already presupposed what has not (yet) been methodologically validated and what is at odds with the presuppositions that lead others to make conflicting construals. In short, the hermeneutical turn is inherently radical. It says a decisive No to "the striving of philosophy for universal knowledge."

It is not necessary to huff and puff arguments to show that Derrida's reading of the hermeneutical circle is radical. Perhaps he has been reading Schleiermacher in addition to Saussure when he tells us that "the book is never finite."[27] But without denying the infinite task of hermeneutics, it is possible to understand that infinity in two quite different ways: "The original opening of interpretation essentially signifies that there will always be rabbis and poets. And two interpretations of interpretation" (p. 67). The comparison of the rabbi and the poet is an important chapter in the hermeneutical turn we are exploring and therefore

---

[26] By speaking simply of the world and not the human world, this formulation assumes that the distinction between the *Geisteswissenschaften* and the *Naturwissenschaften* cannot be sustained and that the natural sciences are also caught up in a hermeneutical circle. Since Thomas Kuhn's *The Structure of Scientific Revolutions*, 2nd ed. (Chicago: University of Chicago Press, 1970), this latter claim has had to be taken seriously. For a sense of the discussion, see Mary Hesse, *Revolutions and Reconstructions in the Philosophy of Science* (Brighton: Harvester Press, 1980), and Robert P. Crease, "The Hard Case: Science and Hermeneutics," in *The Very Idea of Radical Hermeneutics*, ed. Roy Martinez (Atlantic Highlands, N.J.: Humanities Press, 1997). In ¶14 of *Beyond Good and Evil*, Nietzsche had already written, "It is perhaps just dawning on five or six minds that physics, too, is only an interpretation and exegesis of the world (to suit us, if I may say so!) and *not* a world-explanation."

[27] "Edmond Jabès and the Question of the Book," in *Writing and Difference*, p. 75. Subsequent references to this essay will be given parenthetically in the text.

worthy of our exploration. For like Jabès, the author of the text on which he comments in this essay, "adding pitiful graffiti" (p. 74) as he puts it, Derrida sees the Jew and the poet as "at once so united and disunited" (p. 67).[28]

They are united by a similarity so deep that the Jew is at once a metonym and exemplar of the poet. For both the scene of writing is exile. They "are not born *here* but *elsewhere*. They wander, separated from their true birth . . . sons of the Land to come" (p. 66). But just because they share "the very form of exiled speech" they also share "the necessity of exegesis, the interpretive imperative," or, to put it a bit differently, "In the beginning is hermeneutics" (p. 67).

The nature of this shared exile and its link to the infinite task of interpretation is not immediately clear. It becomes clearer when Derrida supplements one Old Testament metaphor with another and identifies the scene of writing, east of Eden but west of the New Jerusalem, as the desert, describing it this way:

> God no longer speaks to us; he has interrupted himself: we must take words upon ourselves. We . . . must entrust ourselves to traces, must become men of vision because we have ceased hearing the voice from within the immediate proximity of the garden. . . . Writing is displaced on the broken line between lost and promised speech. The *difference* between speech and writing is sin, the anger of God emerging from itself, lost immediacy, work outside the garden. (p. 68)

Derrida, of course, does not think there is a deep difference between speech and writing. But a philosophic tradition going back at least to Plato and Aristotle does, and he employs the distinction (as here) in the process of deconstructing it. Thus, when he says that all language is writing, he is not denying the obvious fact that we sometimes speak and sometimes write; he is saying that speech also has the derivative character attributed by the traditional theory (sometimes called logocentrism) only to writing.

---

[28] The essay takes the form of quotations from Jabès's *Le Livre des questions* and commentary thereon, which takes the form both of explication and of extrapolation, leaving it unclear where Jabès leaves off and Derrida begins. To this observation Derrida might well reply, "Bingo! Is it not always so?"

What, then, is the "immediacy" or "immediate proximity" whose possession constitutes the garden and whose loss constitutes exile into the desert that is, for rabbi and poet alike, the necessity of interpretation? It is, of course, the presence presupposed by the western tradition insofar as that tradition is the metaphysics of presence. This presence is of two sorts: the sheer presence of the mind to meanings is what makes it possible for (spoken) words to be the bearers of clear and distinct ideas, while the sheer presence of the mind to objects or facts is what makes it possible for the mind to be the mirror of the world. Where meanings have such clarity and truths such certainty, interpretation is not necessary.

On the logocentric version of the metaphysics of presence, speech is the immediate outward expression of an inner intuition in which the mind is directly and fully present to its meanings, and, when not in error, just as directly and fully present to the objects or facts referred to in terms of those meanings. Both meaning and reference are without ambiguity or indeterminacy. The object of the mind's intentionality, whether it be meaning or fact, concept or thing, is a transcendental signified, in which the mind comes to rest. (Hence the language of intuition.) It is a signified that is not also a signifier, pointing beyond itself to other signs in terms of which it must be interpreted. It is not necessary to go beyond the given.[29]

There is another way to see how interpretation is not necessary on this model. Spoken words are the postal system that enables, by means of divination or deciphering, the reconstruction or reexperiencing in another mind of the intuitions (sheer presences to meaning or fact) of the first mind. If the original intuition renders interpretation unnecessary in the inner speech that is thought, the repetition of intuition makes interpretation unnecessary in the context of communication. The idea seems to be this: If the postal system malfunctions and there is misunderstanding, it can be easily remedied because, first, in the typical, face-to-face situation the hearer can ask, Do you mean this? and

---

[29] Derrida's fullest account of logocentrism in terms of the transcendental signified is found in *Of Grammatology*, trans. Gayatri Chakravorty Spivak (Baltimore: Johns Hopkins University Press, 1976). Also see n. 32 below.

the speaker can reply, No, I mean that,[30] and, second, given the postal system model, there is nothing inherently calling for construal, but only for repetition.

For logocentrism, spoken signs signify or point to meanings (essences) and facts or objects (existences) but not to other signs. Written signs, by contrast, being derivative from speech, signify or point to other signs, possibly other written signs (intertextuality) but ultimately to spoken signs. Thus, they never signify a transcendental signified in which the mind can come to rest, but always other signs, which point beyond themselves. But suppose, as Derrida does, that all signs did this; suppose all language is "writing" in this sense. Then all language calls for interpretation, because all signs point beyond themselves to other signs in terms of which they are to be interpreted.[31] To live away from the "intimacy of the garden . . . between lost and promised speech" (p. 68) is to experience absence where logocentrism promises presence, to live in the desert where writing is possible and interpretation necessary.

Where the immediate presence of speech, as traditionally construed, has been replaced by writing and the absence it involves, "Encounter *is* separation" (p. 74). In other words, presence is (also) absence (cf. Heidegger: unconcealing is also concealing). It should not be necessary to say, but it probably is, that Derrida's emphatic denial of presence is not the denial that I am now (as I write) present to my computer but absent to the Taj Mahal.[32]

---

[30] It is pointless to object that some speech situations (radio broadcasts, press conferences, or lectures without opportunity for questions) are not face to face in the specified sense, while some forms of writing (students passing notes in class) are. Derrida has far deeper reasons for challenging the traditional distinction, which rests in any case on their typical forms in which the speaker is present to the hearer and the writer absent to the reader.

[31] This way of putting it suggests a link between Derrida and classical American anti-intuitionist theories of interpretation as found in Royce, Whitehead, and Peirce. For an attempt to distance Peirce from Derrida, see Umberto Eco, "Unlimited Semeiosis and Drift: Pragmaticism vs. 'Pragmaticism'," in *Peirce and Contemporary Thought*, ed. Kenneth Laine Ketner (New York: Fordham University Press, 1995).

[32] I was about to qualify this sentence by the insertion of the phrase "in the commonsense meaning of the terms [presence and absence]," but part of what Derrida wants to resist is the way in which the theoretical interpretation he opposes has insinuated itself into common sense so that we come to philosophy with a bias in favor of the "myth of the given." He writes, "Now, 'every-

What he disputes is the philosophical theory that this kind of presence or introspective presence to my own meanings is ever *sheer* presence, presence not essentially accompanied by absence.[33] That is why he speaks so frequently of traces, which are precisely presences that essentially point beyond themselves to what is not present.

Derrida preaches a brief, two-point sermon on the text "Encounter *is* separation." First, this statement "contradicts 'logic,' breaks the unity of Being . . . by welcoming the other and difference into the source of meaning" (p. 74). The point is as simple as its implications are disturbing. If signs and things always point beyond themselves to other signs and things that point beyond themselves, etc., then the task of determining meaning or fact is an infinite task that could only be stopped arbitrarily or by means of Hegelian totality. To call this "welcoming the other and difference into the source of meaning" is to note that the meanings from which any meaning differs are an essential part of its own meaning and that the others from which any object is distinguished are essential parts of its being.[34]

The second point comes in the form of an objection and a reply. *Objection:* "But . . . Being must always already be conceptualized in order to say these things . . . and especially in order to say that encounter *is* separation." *Reply:* "Certainly, but 'must

---

day language' is not innocent or neutral. It is the language of Western metaphysics, and it carries with it not only a considerable number of presuppositions of all types, but presuppositions inseparable from metaphysics, which although little attended to are knotted into a system"; *Positions*, trans. Alan Bass (Chicago: University of Chicago Press, 1981), p. 19. Wilfrid Sellars's attack on the "myth of the given" in *Empiricism and the Philosophy of Mind* (Cambridge, Mass.: Harvard University Press, 1997) belongs to the story of "analytic" postmodernism. See n. 22 above.

[33] According to Derrida, by maintaining "an essential and juridical distinction" between signifier and signified, Saussure, with the tradition to which he belongs, "leaves open the possibility of thinking a concept signified in and of itself, a concept *simply* present for thought, independent of a relation to language, that is of a relationship to a system of signifiers. . . . He accedes to the classical exigency of what I have proposed to call a 'transcendental signified,' which in and of itself, in its essence, would refer to no signifier, would exceed the chain of signs, and should no longer itself function as a signifier"; *Positions*, pp. 19–20, emphasis changed.

[34] For the classical statement of this point in the language of difference, see Derrida's essay "Différance," in *Margins of Philosophy*, trans. Alan Bass (Chicago: University of Chicago Press, 1982).

always already' precisely signifies the original exile from the kingdom of Being, signifies exile as the conceptualization of Being, and signifies that Being never is, never shows *itself*, is never *present*, is never *now*, outside difference" (p. 74). Careless and hostile readings will omit the last two words of this claim and attribute sheer nonsense to Derrida. But the claim that everything includes difference, that every itself includes an other, that every presence includes an absence, and that every now includes a then is not nonsense; it is rather a strong doctrine of internal relations.[35]

The 'must always already' reminds us again of the hermeneutical circle. The construal of any phenomenon as something (along with the assertion that it *is* something) contains an implicit reference (presentiment, pre-understanding, presupposition, prejudice, paradigm) to the totality of the differences and alterities that Derrida has welcomed into the origin of meaning. Because this totality is never present, never now, we never understand anything as itself, as it is in itself. For it *is* itself, not in splendid isolation from everything else but only in its essential relatedness to everything else. The poet thinks if he really understood the flower in the crannied wall he would understand everything else (or at least "what God and man is").[36] Derrida reverses this; unless we understand everything else, we do not understand the flower. It has not yet showed *itself*.

Not even, or perhaps, especially not God. Ever mindful of the theological ramifications of these issues, Derrida adds, "Whether he is Being or the master of beings, God himself is, and appears as what he is, within difference, that is to say, as difference and within dissimulation" (p. 74). In Thomistic language, our knowledge of God in this lifetime, whether by reason or by revelation, is not to be confused with the beatific vision. In Pauline language, we do not now see God face to face.

If the rabbi and the poet carry on the task of interpretation in

---

[35] This very strong doctrine of internal relations, but without closure or totality, is what enables Derrida to write, "Yet all that Hegel has thought within this horizon, all, that is, except eschatology, may be reread as a meditation on writing. Hegel is *also* the thinker of irreducible difference"; *Of Grammatology*, p. 26. In Derrida's deconstruction, Hegel is hoisted with his own petard.

[36] Alfred, Lord Tennyson, "Flower in the Crannied Wall."

the arid exile of this perennial penultimacy, they nevertheless do so differently. The rabbi belongs to "the Jewish community which lives under heteronomy and to which the poet does not truly belong." The symbol of this heteronomy is a *"sacred text surrounded by commentaries"* (p. 67).[37] N.B. What defines rabbinic heteronomy is not the denial of exile; for the rabbi, like the poet, has made the hermeneutical turn. It is rather the claim that what we interpret in the desert is a sacred text, a repository of divine truth that may exceed our grasp (or what's a heaven for), but that is real nevertheless, nay, more real than any interpretation. The rabbi gives a Kierkegaardian interpretation to human finitude.

The poet, by contrast, is a Nietzschean, for whom God is dead:

> Poetic autonomy, comparable to none other, presupposes broken Tables. . . . Between the fragments of the broken Tables the poem grows and the right to speech takes root. Once more begins the adventure of the text as weed, as outlaw far from *'the fatherland of the Jews,'* which is a *'sacred text surrounded by commentaries.'* . . . The difference between the horizon of the original text and exegetic writing makes the difference between the rabbi and the poet irreducible. (p. 67)[38]

For the poet's task is to produce an original text, not a commentary, and the presupposition of this is the story of Exodus 32, in which the tables of stone on which God wrote the covenant are smashed to smithereens. The rabbi, but not the poet, reads Exodus 34, in which the broken tables are replaced by new ones. For the poet, "God separated himself from himself, in order to let us speak, in order to astonish and to interrogate us. He did so not by speaking but by keeping still, by letting silence interrupt his voice and his signs, by letting the Tables be broken" (p. 67).

This is why it is possible to describe Jabès's book as "the poetic revolution of our century, the extraordinary reflection of man finally attempting today—and always in vain—to retake possession of his language (as if this were meaningful) by any means, though all routes, and to reclaim responsibility for it against a Father of Logos" (p. 73).

---

[37] This phrase is italicized because Derrida takes it directly from Jabès.

[38] On these italics, see previous note.

This would be good, orthodox Nietzscheanism except for that nagging little phrase "and always in vain." Is the earlier acknowledgment that "there will always be rabbis and poets" (p. 67) something other than the regret of the intellectual elite that, like the poor, the hermeneutical hoi polloi (along with their scriptures and their classics) will always be with us? Is the poetic interpretation of interpretation ultimately futile?

With these questions in mind, we turn to Derrida's comments on the book in the closing pages of his essay. Faith in the book, he warns us, is not to be simply identified with faith in the Bible. The rabbi, with his *sacred* text, now becomes a metonym for all who believe "that Being is a Grammar; and that the world is in all its parts a cryptogram to be constituted through poetic inscription or deciphering; that the book is original, that everything *belongs to the book* before being and in order to come into the world . . . and that always the impassible shore of the book is *first*" (pp. 76–77).

To believe in the book is to believe both that intelligibility and truth precede empirical existence and human language and that to understand the latter is to decipher it by seeing it as an external manifestation of and occasion for recognizing in it that prior ideality. Plato and Hegel should be sufficient to remind us that this view of interpreting the (book of the) world is not tied to belief in the Bible; and Schleiermacher, along with Dilthey, Betti, and Hirsch, should suffice in the same way when it is a matter of interpreting texts.

The crucial move here is the construal of interpretation as deciphering. Suppose I want to ask my wife a question without the kids understanding it. I say, Al-shay e-way o-gay oo-tay ac-may onalds-day? If she understands me, she will decode my pig Latin message to read, Shall we go to McDonalds? We started with a fully determinate and unambiguous statement in my mind; I gave it external expression in a linguistic form wholly external to its prior meaning; and Mom understood me when she deciphered it back into its original form, so that now the meaning in her mind and the meaning in mine are identical. This is precisely the interpretation of interpretation that is abandoned by all who take the hermeneutical turn with Heidegger, Gadamer, and Derrida. Thus, for example, when Gadamer suggests that interpretation is translation, he emphasizes that translation is not this kind of deciphering: "Not occasionally but always, the meaning of a text goes beyond its author. That is why understanding is not merely reproductive but always a productive activity as well. . . . It is enough to say that we understand in a *different* way, *if we understand at all.*"[39]

In other words, rabbinic hermeneutics, practiced by people of the book, whether that book be the Bible or not, knows itself to live in an exile from the immediacy of sheer presence that makes interpretation necessary; but it construes interpretation as discovering a pre-empirical, prelinguistic intelligibility through deciphering the texts (including the world) in which it has been encoded. With or without an appeal to method, it interprets interpretation along the lines of Schleiermacher, Dilthey, Betti, and Hirsch rather than radicalizing the hermeneutical turn with Heidegger and his quarreling sons.

We are prepared for Derrida's question: "What if the Book was only . . . an *epoch* of Being (an epoch coming to an end . . .)? If the form of the book was no longer to be the model of meaning?" But perhaps we are not quite ready for the dramatic turn it takes: "If Being was radically outside the book . . . If the Being of the world, its presence and the meaning of its Being, revealed itself only in illegibility, in a radical illegibility which would not be the accomplice of a lost or sought after legibility, of a page not yet cut from some divine encyclopedia?" (p. 77).

This illegibility is "radical" because it is "original" (p. 77). In Heidegger's language the foundation (*Grund*) turns out to be the abyss (*Abgrund*). In the language of Kierkegaard's Climacus, the risk of meaning always occurs at sea, with 70,000 fathoms of brine separating the speaker from a terra firma that could be reached only by drowning. But radical, original illegibility "is not irrationality, is not despair provoking non-sense, is not everything within the domains of the incomprehensible and the illogical that is anguishing. Such an interpretation . . . already belongs to the book" (in accord with the notion that skeptics are always disappointed Platonists) but "original illegibility is

---

[39] Hans-Georg Gadamer, *Truth and Method*, 2nd ed., trans. Joel Weinsheimer and Donald G. Marshall (New York: Crossroad, 1991), pp. 296–97.

therefore the very possibility of the book and, within it, of the ulterior and eventual opposition of 'rationalism' and 'irrationalism' '' (p. 77).

This is not the time or place to go into Derrida's theory of the quasi transcendentals that are at once the condition of possibility and the condition of impossibility of that to which they give rise.[40] What is important for us about this little meditation on the death of the Book, the passing of its epoch, is the strong denial, in the form of rhetorical questions to be sure, of meaning or intelligibility prior to and outside the world of the text and the text of the world (the humanly interpreted world). It looks like a homily on one of Derrida's most famous texts, *"There is nothing outside of the text,"*[41] especially when Derrida adds, "Every exit from the book is made within the book" (p. 75).

But there is another side to this meditation on the book. What about these exits from the book? No doubt they are the putative excursions beyond language to a prelinguistic intelligibility that are thought to be possible by those who have not fully made the hermeneutical turn. So we should forget about them. But no! Derrida assumes that we can and must undertake such exits, even if they are not possible, even if they can only be made within the book. Can this be the meaning of the "and always in vain" with which Derrida earlier qualified the poetic project of autonomy, taking over responsibility for language from the Father of Logos, the Author of the Book?

If there is nothing outside the text, and human writing, as Derrida assumes, is the only writing there is, the poet's patricide would be unproblematic. But just after he speaks of exiting from the book, Derrida writes, "If writing is not a tearing of the self toward the other within a confession of infinite separation, if it is a delectation of itself, the pleasure of writing for its own sake, the satisfaction of the artist, then it destroys itself. . . . It is true that to go toward the other is also to negate oneself" (pp. 75–76).

---

[40] Rodolphe Gasché introduced this term in *The Tain of the Mirror: Derrida and the Philosophy of Reflection* (Cambridge, Mass.: Harvard University Press, 1986). John D. Caputo uses it extensively in *The Prayers and Tears of Jacques Derrida* (Bloomington: Indiana University Press, 1997).

[41] *Of Grammatology*, p. 158. For a double reading of this claim as both Kantian and Hegelian, see "Hermeneutics as Epistemology" (ch. 3 above).

It may be, as Derrida writes elsewhere, that "the notion of an Idea or 'interior design' [interior to the mind of some author or Author] as simply anterior to a work [text or world] which would supposedly be the expression of it, is a prejudice." But we must not forget that if creative writing

> is not the purely transparent expression of this form, it is nevertheless, simultaneously, revelation. If creation were not revelation, what would happen to the finitude of the writer and to the solitude of his hand abandoned by God? Divine creativity, in this case, would be reappropriated by a hypocritical humanism. If writing is *inaugural* it is not so because it creates, but because of a certain absolute freedom of speech, because of the freedom to bring forth the already-there as a sign of the freedom to augur. A freedom of response which acknowledges as its only horizon the world as history and the speech which can only say: Being has always already begun. To create is to reveal.[42]

N.B. The poet's creative freedom is not freedom to create ex nihilo. It is a "freedom of response" to Being that "has always already begun." Whatever play means in Derrida, it does not mean making it up as we go along and as we please. To write is to engage the other, not just other writers but something outside the text: "Just as the end of writing passes beyond writing, its origin is not yet in the book" (p. 76).

Before we get too excited, Derrida repeats his sober reminder, "But—and this is the heart of the matter—everything that is exterior in relation to the book, everything that is negative as concerns the book, is produced *within the book*. The exit from the book, the other and the threshold, are all articulated *within the book* . . . the book is not in the world, but the world is in the book" (p. 76).[43]

The exit from the book is impossible (as achievement) because everything we say about what might be outside the book, prior to our language and its prejudices, is shaped by our language and its prejudices. But the exit from the book is also necessary (as attempt) because in our finitude we can never be the Father

---

[42] "Force and Signification," in *Writing and Difference*, pp. 11–12.

[43] It would seem that Derrida means text as human writing rather than book as pre-empirical, prelinguistic divine intelligibility.

of Logos, the mind in which intelligibility precedes worldly or textual existence. With common sense, we must assume that the world is out there. But, having taken the hermeneutical turn, we must acknowledge that we can never get out there for a naked romp with Being in which, having shed the latest style (and all others) of prejudices, we can coax Being to disrobe before our voyeuristic gaze.

The hermeneutical turn is the Copernican Revolution—updated by a nineteenth-century appreciation of history and a twentieth-century appreciation of language. In its original version, that revolution says, "Human reason has this peculiar fate that in one species of its knowledge it is burdened by questions which, as prescribed by the very nature of reason itself, it is not able to ignore, but which, as transcending all its powers, it is also not able to answer."[44] In its Derridean version it is the similar reminder that we must seek to exceed the text, for that is the meaning of our finitude, knowing all the while that such attempts are "always in vain" precisely because of our finitude.

This same paradoxical situation reappears when Derrida revisits the "two interpretations of interpretation," this time associated with Rousseau and Nietzsche, in an essay that has been used to date the transition from structuralism to poststructuralism in Europe:[45] "The one seeks to decipher, dreams of deciphering a truth or an origin which escapes play and the order of the sign, and which lives the necessity of interpretation as an exile. The other, which is no longer turned toward the origin, affirms play and tries to pass beyond man and humanism, the name of man being the name of that being who . . . has dreamed of full presence, the reassuring foundation, the origin and the end of play."[46]

---

[44] Opening sentence, preface to the first edition, *Critique of Pure Reason*.

[45] "Structure, Sign, and Play in the Discourse of the Human Sciences," in *Writing and Difference*. Less sympathetic than I to this development, Roger Lundin, who sees this essay as the transition to poststructuralism, also says that it "proved to be a deadly opening salvo in the Continental invasion of American universities"; *The Culture of Interpretation* (Grand Rapids, Mich.: Eerdmans, 1993), p. 189. For our differing interpretations of "Structure, Sign, and Play," see Lundin's chapter 8 and my "Deconstruction and Christian Cultural Theory (ch. 9 below).

[46] "Structure, Sign, and Play," p. 292. In the Jabés essay, both the rabbi and

It is easy to read this as a call to abandon one interpretation of interpretation for the other. But the text won't allow this. Derrida reminds us that these two hermeneutical postures "are absolutely irreconcilable even if we live them simultaneously and reconcile them in an obscure economy." But he does not advise us to flee the tension of this irreconcilability. On the contrary, "For my part, although these two interpretations must acknowledge and accentuate their difference and define their irreducibility, I do not believe that today there is any question of *choosing*."[47]

Derrida goes on to give his reasons, suggesting that we neither can nor should try to choose between these "absolutely irreconcilable" alternatives. For him the hermeneutical turn is not from the rabbi to the poet or from Rousseau to Nietzsche but from such either/ors to the tension of both/and. We might put it this way. The real is too "weak" to determine or govern our construals of it. This leaves to human language an enormous freedom that the poet celebrates as autonomy. At the same time, we cannot but think of ourselves as seeking to articulate (reveal) a real that is not a product of our construals, for we are finite and not God. This is the heteronomy the rabbi experiences as responsibility.

I have tried to be prescriptive in this paper while being descriptive; and I have tried to describe the hermeneutical turn that separates Heidegger, Gadamer, and Derrida from Schleiermacher, Dilthey, Betti, and Hirsch with sufficient sympathy to suggest that it is philosophically compelling. We should make that turn, if we have not already done so, at least to the degree of recognizing the double impossibility signified by Derrida's suggestion that we are not to choose between the two interpretations of interpretation. The rabbi reminds the poet in us that we are not God. The world, including the world of the text, is not simply a function of our interpretations; our task is to reveal

---

the poet seem to experience "the necessity of interpretation as exile." But just to the degree that the rabbi construes hermeneutics not only in terms of sacred texts and commentaries but also as deciphering, he thinks he can escape the desert.

[47] Ibid., p. 293.

what is already there. At the same time, the poet reminds the rabbi in us that neither by immediate intuition nor by deciphering inference do we have access to structures of intelligibility innocent of and uncontaminated by contingent and particular systems of human meaning.

To make the hermeneutical turn in its most radical sense is to be willing to construe human cognitive finitude as the inability to be either simply the rabbi or simply the poet. Rather than choosing between these alternatives, we choose to live the tension of their inseparability, allowing each to be interrupted and delimited by the other.

But can we, as Christians, make such a choice? I don't see why not. I see nothing in the gospel of Jesus Christ that requires us to be wed to the objectivism that is abandoned when we acknowledge that just because we are not the Creator, there is a creative aspect to all our construals that resists our attempts to reduce interpretation to decoding or deciphering. This means that our knowledge is finite not just in a quantitative sense but in a qualitative sense as well. There is much we do not know, to be sure; but even what we do know is perennially penultimate because of its relativity to perspectives that are themselves particular and penultimate. But for the Christian it is God who is Absolute and Infinite, not we; nor does our knowledge lose its relativity and its finitude by being about God, any more than we become purple by thinking about grapes. Just as we are not saved by good works morally speaking, we are not saved by good works epistemically speaking, by attaining to a knowledge of God and of God's will that is adequate (in the philosophical sense of the term *adequatio intellectus et rei*) to its intended object.[48] It's OK to see in a mirror dimly, or, if like me you prefer the King James here, to see in a glass darkly. Just as God's ways are not ours, so God's thoughts are not ours. As theists, Kant and Kierkegaard remind us of this biblical truth. Should we re-

---

[48] Obviously ideas that are not "adequate" in this technical philosophical sense of the term can be adequate to any number of important tasks: pointing us in the right direction, evoking worship, obedience, and service—in short, bringing us into the kind of relation with God and the world that is appropriate to human creatures in this life.

sist being reminded once again by Heidegger, Gadamer, and Derrida, just because they do not share our faith?

No doubt Derrida, with whom we have concluded, is the hardest case. Should we not reject his system of thought because of its atheism, because it entails claims we cannot accept: there is no God, there is no Truth, there is no revelation, etc? In a word, No, we should not.

To see why not, let's look at the matter of Truth. I think it fair to say that Derrida's "system" of thought "entails" that Truth and Knowledge as classically defined are illusory. But this conclusion follows from two distinct premises.[49] First, there is an analysis of the embeddedness of human understanding in particular systems of meaning that undermine philosophical aspirations to universality, objective certainty, correspondence, *adequatio*, etc. Second, there is the atheistic premise to the effect that there is no divine intellect in which is to be found (as Kant and Kierkegaard supposed) the Truth and Knowledge that exceed human grasp. The conclusion is that Truth and Knowledge are not to be found anywhere.

Surely the atheistic premise is unacceptable to theists, along with the conclusion about Truth and Knowledge it helps to support. But to reject these is not to reject the first premise and its analysis of human finitude as embedded relativity. That part of the package is not conceptually tied to the atheistic part. The Gospel is not threatened when we examine it on its own philosophical merits without theological prejudice. It presents itself as an account of human finitude, a theme to which we also are committed precisely by our belief in creation. It may well provide insights that can be appropriated for Christian thought, recontextualized by being separated from the atheistic premise and joined to theistic and more specifically Christian themes.

But, it will be argued, Christians are committed to the claim that God spoke to us by the prophets and by a Son and that God speaks to us today through the Bible, which is the Word of God, and by the inner testimony of the Holy Spirit, which enables us

---

[49] Although Derrida offers arguments, he does not employ the rhetoric of premises, entailment, and so forth. But I think we can use that language for purposes of analysis.

to understand what God has said and is saying to us,[50] while there is no room for this in Derrida's scheme. If there is no God, there is surely no revelation in salvation history, in Scripture, or by means of the witness of the Holy Spirit. Fair enough. But does it follow that Christians, who do not look to Derrida for these themes in any case, might not appropriate his analysis of our finitude into a context in which revelation motifs are pivotal?

I think we can formulate the issue quite sharply. If by revelation we understand an event by which we are caught up to the third heaven (2 Cor. 12:2–7) and enabled to see God face to face (Ex. 33:17–23, 1 Cor. 13:12) or, to put it in somewhat different language, if revelation enables us to see the real, including God, *sub specie aeternitatis,* it will be difficult to incorporate a Derridean interpretation of interpretation into our Christian thought.

But what if revealed truth is a treasure we hold in clay jars (2 Cor. 4:7)? What if revelation occurs, not when we are lifted out of the cave, but precisely when God kenotically enters our world and speaks to us under the conditions of our encavement? What if that is what it means to see in a mirror dimly (1 Cor. 13:12)? That, I believe, is what Thomas Aquinas thought when he denied that we have quidditative knowledge of God, whether by reason or revelation, but only analogical knowledge.[51] That, I believe, is what John Calvin thought when he suggested that "as nurses commonly do with infants, God is wont in a measure to 'lisp' in speaking to us. Thus such forms of speaking do not so much express clearly what God is like as accommodate the knowledge of him to our slight capacity. To do this he must descend far beneath his loftiness."[52]

There are substantial biblical and theological motivations for

---

[50] Nick Wolterstorff is right, I believe, to protest against the reduction of divine discourse to revelation. See *Divine Discourse: Philosophical Reflections on the Claim That God Speaks* (Cambridge: Cambridge University Press, 1995), especially chs. 2–4. God speaks to us for many purposes, and self-revelation is not always primary. I focus on revelation here because in this context it is revelatory speech acts that are especially important.

[51] See John Wippel, "Quidditative Knowledge of God," in *Metaphysical Themes in Thomas Aquinas* (Washington, D.C.: Catholic University of America Press, 1984).

[52] *Institutes* 1.13.1. Cf. Ford Lewis Battles, "God Was Accommodating Himself to Human Capacity," in *Readings in Calvin's Theology,* ed. Donald K. McKim (Grand Rapids, Mich.: Baker Book House, 1984).

thinking of revelation as divine kenosis rather than human apotheosis. The fully radical hermeneutical turn can be fruitfully appropriated for Christian thinking in such a frame of reference.

Finally, it will be argued in more general terms that it is always dangerous to go to the Philistines to sharpen one's tools (1 Sam. 13:19–21). After all, to mix biblical metaphors, the gold taken when Israel spoiled the Egyptians ended up in the golden calf. No doubt some of it did. Appropriation is inherently dangerous. But some of that gold ended up in the tabernacle as well, and it is that possibility I hope to keep open.

9

Deconstruction and Christian Cultural Theory: An Essay on Appropriation

THE PROSPECTS do not seem bright for an appropriation of post-modern insights in the service of a Christian interpretation and critique of contemporary culture. Philosophical postmodernism is widely seen as being, at best, the moral equivalent of leprosy and, at worst, the moral equivalent of AIDS. The need to demonize runs deep. How else do we persuade ourselves, in spite of the evidence to the contrary, that we are really good, the last, best hope of the world? So it is that the temptation to lump postmodernism together with Hitler and Stalin is simply irresistible to some.

For example, Michael Howard is enthusiastic about the "devastating attack on the forces of post-modernism in academic studies, literary, philosophical and historical" that he finds in Gertrude Himmelfarb's *On Looking into the Abyss*. She portrays postmodernists as the spiritual successors of John Stuart Mill's vision of a "value-free society" and of the Bloomsbury group that "poured mockery on the whole concept of moral commitment and regarded history, philosophy and literature as vehicles purely for private pleasure." Sandwiching a reference to Jacques Derrida, probably the most widely influential of the French poststructuralists on the North American scene, we find this summary: "We know what happens when people actually put these 'value-free' principles into practice; we saw it only a generation ago on a horrific scale in the Holocaust. . . . At best [these people] are frivolous game-players who make a virtue of their moral irresponsibility. At worst, they are set on destroying the standards that not only make their own activity possible but also enable society to survive at all."[1]

---

[1] Michael Howard, "Facing the Monsters," *The New York Times Book Review*, March 6, 1994, pp. 11–12.

Apparently in dealing with the bad guys one is permitted to be scurrilous rather than scrupulous. When an Oxford historian praises a CUNY colleague for deriving fascism from Mill's vision of a liberal society, it would seem that the academy is truly in deep peril—to say nothing of the curious portrayal of Hitler's gang as a "value-free" society. I had thought their problem was in assuming that the quite particular values of which they took themselves to be the embodiment were absolute values; and I was reminded of Arthur Schlesinger's address in which he reminded us that the atrocities of modernity have been committed by moral absolutists.

A certain Francis Duke from Los Angeles was thinking along the same lines. His reply to the Howard review points out that the Holocaust, like the Inquisition and slavery, was perpetrated by those who took the values legitimating their power to be quite absolute. Acknowledging his own reservations about postmodernism, he adds, "But implicitly they are asking the right question: How do we make sure another Holocaust doesn't occur while we are busy listening to Bach and Mozart and congratulating ourselves on our wonderful eternal values?"[2]

Literary theorist Roger Lundin is as eager as historians Howard and Himmelfarb to protect the world from the postmodern menace. His defenses are activated by the suggestion that "postmodernism can be seen as an extended meditation on several Pauline themes whose repudiation all but defines modernity" as the claim to absolute knowledge. Reference is to the notion that we do not now see the eternal "face to face" but only "in a mirror, dimly" (1 Cor. 13:12) and that we hold the truth of the gospel "in clay jars" (2 Cor. 4:7), to say nothing of our tendency as sinners to "suppress the truth" (Rom. 1:18). "Philosophically speaking, the main motifs of modernism are the attempt to have done, once and for all, with Paul and his gloomy followers, from Augustine through Luther and Calvin to Kierkegaard and Barth."[3]

Lundin duly notes that the suggestion alleges an affinity between the hermeneutics of finitude and the hermeneutics of sus-

---

[2] Letter to *The New York Times Book Review,* March 20, 1994, p. 31.

[3] Quoted from Merold Westphal, "The Ostrich and the Boogeyman," *Christian Scholar's Review* 20, no. 2 (Dec. 1990), pp. 115–16.

picion to be found in postmodernism and the Pauline understanding of the radical limits of our cognitive equipment. But rather than explore this curious convergence, he warns against misreading poststructuralist intentions and counters:

> To say that postmodernism is an extended meditation on Pauline themes is like saying that because Joseph Stalin shared Winston Churchill's fear and loathing of the Nazis, the Russian dictator's speeches to rally his countrymen were extended reflections on political democracy and economic freedom. It is accurate to say that, like Derrida, Augustine would assail the tenets of modernism, but it is misleading to imply that since the two of them would spurn Descartes, they would be eager to embrace each other.[4]

Presumably Lundin does not intend for us to correlate Paul (and Augustine) with Stalin, leaving Derrida to play the role of Churchill.

In this Wonderland as in an earlier one, things get "curiouser and curiouser." First of all, nothing was said about the intentions of the poststructuralists, whose radical secularism is obvious enough, while on the other hand, their "Pauline" dimension is something neither their friends nor their foes are eager to notice. One might have hoped that "can be seen as an extended meditation" would not be immediately translated as "is an extended meditation" in the sense that implies that this is the writers' intention. What about the possibility that what they help us to see exceeds their intentions?[5] That a hermeneutics of finitude will illumine the epistemic meaning of creaturehood, and that a hermeneutics of suspicion will illumine the epistemic significance of sin, even if developed by those who do not speak the language of Creation and Fall? What happened to the notion that all truth is God's truth, even truth from the pens of atheists?

---

[4] Roger Lundin, *The Culture of Interpretation* (Grand Rapids, Mich.: Eerdmans, 1993), pp. 205–7.

[5] My strategy in dealing with philosophical postmodernism is the same as my strategy for reading the hermeneutics of suspicion in Marx, Nietzsche, and Freud. In *Suspicion and Faith: The Religious Uses of Modern Atheism* (Grand Rapids, Mich.: Eerdmans, 1993), I argue that, contrary to their atheistic intentions, their critiques of religion echo and illumine the biblical critiques of instrumental religion and make good Lenten reading for Christians willing to engage in serious self-examination.

Nor was there the slightest suggestion that Augustine and Derrida would be "eager to embrace each other," only that the (not so obvious) similarity of substance between their critiques of what Augustine calls philosophical "presumption" (*Confessions* VII, 20) is worth noticing and exploring, and not just the (quite obvious) difference of motivation that underlies it. If there really is a similarity of substance, then the simile of Stalin only serves to obscure the possibility that those of us who trace our lineage through Augustine might find insights worth appropriating from Derrida in the pursuit of our own project.

Lundin is a serious scholar, not a talk show host trying to raise ratings or a televangelist trying to raise money with rhetorical reassurances that he will protect us from the bad guys. I assume the same about Howard and Himmelfarb. Why are they then so quick to link Hitler and Stalin with postmodernism? This assimilation of postmodernism to totalitarianism is especially ironic since the former is a sustained critique of the violent, totalizing discourses that absolutize their own insights, thereby legitimizing the violent, exclusionary practices congruent with those discourses.

Perhaps part of the reason is political: postmodern critique does not find such discourses and practices only in such safe places as communism and fascism. (The habit of labeling anyone who dares to criticize the West as either communist or fascist dies hard.) But the stated reason is ethical: postmodernism is seen as a nihilistic threat to what is good in our way of life, as a loss of moral compass that reinforces the moral wasteland of contemporary culture rather than challenging it.

Lundin, in particular, sees Derrida as providing philosophical aid and comfort to the therapeutic ideals so devastatingly analyzed by Rieff, Bellah, and MacIntyre. According to the last named, the implicit moral philosophy of a therapeutic culture is "emotivism," the view "that all evaluative judgments and more specifically all moral judgments are *nothing but* expressions of preference, expressions of attitude or feeling, insofar as they are moral or evaluative in character."[6]

---

[6] Alasdair MacIntyre, *After Virtue,* 2nd ed. (Notre Dame, Ind.: University of Notre Dame Press, 1984), p. 11. Cf. Philip Rieff, *The Triumph of the Therapeutic: Uses of Faith after Freud* (New York: Harper & Row, 1966), and Robert Bellah et

We are familiar with emotivism from the logical positivism of the forties and fifties (even if most denizens of our therapeutic culture are not).[7] But postmodernism is not positivism. Both traditions are skeptical, to be sure, of the grand claims to absolute knowledge that accompany the metaphysical foundations of morality in much of the philosophical tradition. But beyond their irreverence toward metaphysical pretensions, there are at least two striking differences. The postmodern critique applies to all human knowledge, and not just to ethics and metaphysics. It is miles removed from the scientism of the positivist tradition. More importantly, in the present context, the positivists were the ones who insisted that their theories entailed moral subjectivism, while in the case of the postmodernists, it is their enemies who make this claim.

At least some postmodernists continue to think that while the Enlightenment project of providing absolute justifications for our ethical beliefs has self-destructed, their own work still has the character of morally significant critique, both of theory and of practice. Like almost everyone else these days, they reject the positivists' all or nothing approach: *either* we have absolute knowledge in ethics, *or* we have nothing at all and ethics is nothing but personal preferences, any one of which is as good as any other. Moreover, echoing Kierkegaard's lament that "the system has no ethics" and paraphrasing Kant's claim "I have had to deny knowledge in order to make room for faith," they argue, in effect, "We have had to deny absolute knowledge in order to make room for moral responsibility." Then they add, "If we are to oppose the physical violence of political totalitarianism, we must oppose the epistemic or 'interpretative' violence of totalizing discourse."[8]

---

al., *Habits of the Heart: Individualism and Commitment in American Life* (Berkeley: University of California Press, 1985).

[7] For classic statements, see A. J. Ayer, *Language, Truth and Logic* (New York: Dover, 1946); Charles L. Stevenson, *Ethics and Language* (New Haven: Yale University Press, 1944); and Paul Edwards, *The Logic of Moral Discourse* (New York: Free Press, 1955).

[8] An especially lucid presentation of the first of these claims is to be found in John D. Caputo, *Against Ethics* (Bloomington: Indiana University Press, 1993). On the notion of "interpretative violence," see Jacques Derrida, "Force of Law: The 'Mystical Foundation of Authority,' " in *Deconstruction and the*

In this context, to assimilate the postmodernists to the positivists is doubly problematic. First, it attributes to them a position they explicitly repudiate; second, by assuming that since they deny we can have everything they must mean we have nothing, it invites the suspicion that one accepts the positivists' all or nothing approach, that one's own ethics stands or falls with claims to absolute knowledge that would have made the apostle Paul's hair stand on end. But why should a seriously Christian ethics be tied in this way to the epistemological extravagances of the not noticeably evangelical projects of Plato, Descartes, and Hegel? Why not agree with Paul that we see "through a glass darkly"?

I do not wish to claim that my account fits every thinker to whom the postmodern label has been applied. Perhaps there are some for whom the parallel with the positivists is perceptive.[9] Surely there are epigones who relish the image of local intellectual terrorist and who pose as moral nihilists. But I believe my account does fit, among others, Foucault and Derrida, the two French poststructuralist philosophers with the widest North American influence. (Derrida, it will be remembered, was the one assimilated first to Hitler and then to Stalin above.)

In his famous essay "What Is Enlightenment?" Foucault insists that his own brand of critique is "rooted in the Enlightenment." But, he says, "I have been seeking to stress that the thread that may connect us with the Enlightenment is not faithfulness to doctrinal elements, but rather the permanent reactivation of an attitude—that is, of a philosophical ethos that could be described as a permanent critique of our historical era."

Possibility of Justice, ed. Drucilla Cornell, Michel Rosenfeld, and David Gray Carlson (New York: Routledge, 1992), especially pp. 6–7 and 13–14. Given as a lecture at Cardozo Law School, 1989.

[9] Caputo suggests as much in distinguishing heteromorphic from heteronomic postmodernism. See especially chapter 3 of *Against Ethics* and *Demythologizing Heidegger* (Bloomington: Indiana University Press, 1993), p. 59, where he speaks of "a certain prophetic postmodernism." Cf. pp. 187 and 201–5. A similar distinction is found in Peter Sloterdijk's *Critique of Cynical Reason,* trans. Michael Eldred (Minneapolis: University of Minnesota Press, 1987). I suggest a Kierkegaardian reading of the distinction in "Postmodernism and Religious Reflection," *International Journal for Philosophy of Religion* 38, nos. 1–3 (December 1995), pp. 127–43. Reprinted in *God, Reason and Religions: New Essays in the Philosophy of Religion,* ed. Eugene Thomas Long (Dordrecht: Kluwer, 1995), pp. 127–43.

Seeking to characterize that ethos positively, he writes, "But if the Kantian question was that of knowing what limits knowledge has to renounce transgressing, it seems to me that the critical question today has to be turned back into a positive one: in what is given to us as universal, necessary, obligatory, what place is occupied by whatever is singular, contingent, and the product of arbitrary constraints? The point, in brief, is to transform the critique conducted in the form of necessary limitation into a practical critique that takes the form of a possible transgression."[10]

If we ask, What are we being invited to transgress? the answer is clear: the arbitrary constraints in which the singular and contingent, for instance, the German will to empire and fascist anti-Semitism, are taken to have ultimate validity. This genealogical form of critique is not emotivism but the hermeneutics of suspicion developed by Marx, Nietzsche, and Freud as an (unintended but theologically profound) commentary on the Pauline notion that sin produces distorted truth. It highlights one way this happens: the confusing of our particular interests with the universal good. And, like the Pauline version of this theme, the postmodern version resists the comforting assurance that this happens to "them" but not to "us."

In a similar fashion, Derrida takes his stand with the Enlightenment, at least with regard to the necessity of critique: "We cannot and we must not—this is a law and a destiny—forgo the *Aufklärung,* in other words, what imposes itself as the enigmatic desire for vigilance, for the lucid vigil, for elucidation, for critique and truth, but for a truth that at the same time keeps within itself some apocalyptic desire . . . to demystify or, if you prefer, to deconstruct apocalyptic discourse itself."[11]

---

[10] Michel Foucault, "What Is Enlightenment," in *The Foucault Reader,* ed. Paul Rabinow (New York: Pantheon Books, 1984), pp. 42–45. Cf. "The Subject and Power," Foucault's afterword to Hubert L. Dreyfus and Paul Rabinow, *Michel Foucault: Beyond Structuralism and Hermeneutics,* 2nd ed. (Chicago: University of Chicago Press, 1983).

[11] Jacques Derrida, "Of an Apocalyptic Tone Newly Adopted in Philosophy," in *Derrida and Negative Theology,* ed. Harold Coward and Toby Foshay (Albany: SUNY Press, 1992), p. 51. The French original was first given as a lecture in 1980 and published in 1981. On p. 59 Derrida writes, "So we, *Aufklärer* of modern times. . . ."

Even more dramatic is the claim that what is at work in the negations of deconstruction is nothing other than justice. In a lecture given at Cardozo Law School in 1989, Derrida argues that although positive law at its best seeks to be the embodiment of justice, it is always a human construction and thus liable to deconstruction: "The fact that law is deconstructible is not bad news. We may even see in this a stroke of luck for politics, for all historical progress." Historical progress! So much for the notion that since nothing historical is absolute and final, everything historical is of equal value. Derrida continues, "Justice in itself, if such a thing exists, outside of beyond the law, is not deconstructible. No more than deconstruction itself, if such a thing exists. Deconstruction is justice. . . . The undeconstructibility of justice also makes deconstruction possible, indeed is inseparable from it."[12]

The language of "justice in itself" evokes both Plato's and Kant's notions of what is truly transcendent. Derrida finds such a notion highly problematic—hence the "if such a thing exists." But he also finds that he cannot work without it. What is important to notice here is that he is working with a distinction between positive law and a justice to which it is responsible. He is claiming, in effect, that the natural law tradition survives the collapse of excessive epistemological claims ("we hold these truths to be self-evident") traditionally accompanying it.[13] Perhaps this is why Derrida can say, "Nothing seems to me less outdated than the classical emancipatory ideal," teasing Habermas, as it were, to see deconstruction as akin to his own critical theory, a parallel attempt to salvage the Enlightenment commitment to philosophy as critique after the fall of absolute knowledge.[14]

Like the laws, I am responsible as an individual to that which precedes my desires and even my insights. In another recent essay, Derrida invokes Levinas's notion of the trace. The trace

---

[12] Jacques Derrida, "Force of Law," pp. 14–15.

[13] For an analysis of Derrida's relation to this tradition, see "Derrida as Natural Law Theorist" (ch. 11 below). In this essay the similarity and difference between Derrida's justice in itself and Kant's regulative ideas is briefly explored.

[14] "Force of Law," p. xxx.

recalls Gilbert and Sullivan's modern major general who is not now an orphan, and moreover never has been; it signifies something at work in my thinking that is not now and never has been fully present to my thinking. No matter how far back I go in memory or (Platonic) recollection, it has always already been there and departed: "Language has started without us, in us and before us. This is what theology calls God. . . . Order or promise, this injunction commits (me), in a rigorously asymmetrical manner, even before I have been able to say *I* [so much for the primacy of the self and its desires], to sign such a *provocation* in order to reappropriate it for myself and restore the symmetry. That in no way mitigates my responsibility; on the contrary. There would be no responsibility without this *prior coming* (*prévenance*) of the trace, or if autonomy were first or absolute. Autonomy itself would not be possible, nor would respect for the law . . . in the strictly Kantian meaning of these words."[15]

A full gloss on this passage would involve a detailed analysis of Levinas and of Derrida's appropriation of him.[16] But this much is immediately clear: (1) the reference to Kant makes it clear that we are talking about ethical and not just grammatical responsibility; (2) Derrida associates himself with the Levinasian thesis that heteronomy precedes autonomy;[17] and most importantly, (3) the deconstruction of Kantian ethics seeks to preserve moral responsibility, not obliterate it. Derrida joins Levinas in saying, "We have had to deny autonomy in order to make room for responsibility."

How is it possible for presumably responsible scholars to find Hitler and Stalin in this?

Well, that isn't exactly what happens. When demonization is

---

[15] Jacques Derrida, "How to Avoid Speaking: Denials," in *Derrida and Negative Theology*, p. 99. Originally published in 1987.

[16] Key texts would include Emmanuel Levinas, *Totality and Infinity*, trans. Alphonso Lingis (Pittsburgh: Duquesne University Press, 1969); Jacques Derrida, "Violence and Metaphysics: An Essay on the Thought of Emmanuel Levinas," in *Writing and Difference*, trans. Alan Bass (Chicago: University of Chicago Press, 1978); and a second round of discussion, Levinas's "Wholly Otherwise" and Derrida's "At This Very Moment in This Work Here I Am," the opening essays of Robert Bernasconi and Simon Critchley, eds., *Re-Reading Levinas* (Bloomington: Indiana University Press, 1991).

[17] Cf. the discussion in Caputo's *After Ethics* of "heteronomous" postmodernism.

taking place, the silence on these themes in thinkers like Foucault and Derrida is deafening. In the case of Derrida, attention is almost invariably directed to his notion of play. Thus, in Howard's summary of Himmelfarb, postmodernists are "frivolous game-players who make a virtue of their moral irresponsibility."[18] Similarly, Lundin dates the "deadly opening salvo in the Continental invasion of American universities" to Derrida's lecture "Structure, Sign, and Play in the Discourse of the Human Sciences."[19] According to Lundin's Derrida, "there is nothing behind or beneath [language] save the *free play of desire.*" His (Derrida's) ideal is "a world in which intellectual history becomes a great video arcade, and every character or idea in that history is but one more game meant to heighten the pleasure of *the postmodern player at the controls.*"[20]

Just about everything is wrong with this account. In the first place, nothing is more distinctive of postmodern analyses than the vigorous denial that we are or can be in control: with Freud, who describes psychoanalysis as a "most bitter blow" to human self-love because it endeavors to show "to the 'ego' of each one of us that he is not even master in his own house";[21] with Heidegger, for whom "die Sprache spricht" in and through the human speaker, who is a kind of mouthpiece;[22] and with the structuralist account of how it is that language speaks and not "man," postmodernism is a sustained assault on the dialectical illusion of a self in control. Under such headings as "the death of the author," the death of man," and "the end of humanism," it seeks to show the variety of ways in which we are not in charge, especially in the realm of language.[23] Unless the video

---

[18] Howard, "Facing the Monsters," p. 12.

[19] Lundin, *Culture of Interpretation*, p. 189. Derrida's lecture was given at the Johns Hopkins University in 1966 and published (in French) in 1967. Its English translation appeared in 1978.

[20] Lundin, *Culture of Interpretation*, pp. 192 and 194, my emphasis.

[21] Sigmund Freud, at the conclusion the eighteenth lecture of his *Introductory Lectures on Psychoanalysis, Standard Edition*, vols. XV and XVI.

[22] Martin Heidegger, *Poetry, Language, Thought*, trans. Albert Hofstadter (New York: Harper and Row, 1971), pp. 197–98; cf. *On the Way to Language*, trans. Peter D. Hertz (New York: Harper and Row, 1971), p. 124.

[23] For an overview of this theme in relation to "the death of the author" in Barthes, Foucault, and Derrida, see my "Kierkegaard and the Anxiety of Authorship," *International Philosophical Quarterly* XXXIV, no. 1 (March 1994), pp. 5–22.

arcade image is meant to evoke the frustration rather than the pleasure of the player who is at the controls but unable to control what happens on the screen, it is highly misleading.

More specifically, in Derridean diction the human subject is not the subject of the verb to play. Thus, in the essay cited by Lundin, Derrida speaks of "the *play* of the structure" and "the play of the world" but not of the play of the subject of desire.[24] Ironically, Lundin quotes both of these passages,[25] one of them twice; but this does not keep him from offering an interpretation of Derridean play wholly at odds with their import.

For Derrida as for Gadamer, play is out there. The game is happening, and if we become players it is because we are drawn into a game we did not originate and cannot control.[26] Derrida does indeed bring the "play of the structure" into relation to human desire. But instead of speaking of the free play of desire, he portrays desire as hostile toward the play of the structure and the play of the world. Desire is for "a reassuring certitude, which itself is beyond the reach of play." This certitude is to be the cure for the anxiety that is "invariably the result of a certain mode of being implicated in the game, of being caught by the game, of being as it were at stake in the game from the outset." The subject for whom the controls are a means to personal pleasure is not the postmodernist who rejects the notion of "a full presence which is beyond play," but the devotee of the metaphysics of presence, one name for the tendency of the philosophical tradition to seek a fixed center for every structure that "permits the play of its elements . . . [but] also closes off the play." In short, play is not the fulfillment of the subject's desires but precisely

---

[24] Jacques Derrida, "Structure, Sign, and Play in the Discourse of the Human Sciences," in *Writing and Difference*, pp. 278, 292.

[25] Lundin, *Culture of Interpretation*, pp. 190, 194, 200.

[26] For Gadamer's interpretation, see Hans-Georg Gadamer, *Truth and Method*, trans. Joel Weinsheimer and Donald G. Marshall, 2nd ed. rev. (New York: Crossroad, 1991), especially pp. 101–31. For discussion see Fred Dallmayr, "Hermeneutics and Deconstruction: Gadamer and Derrida in Dialogue," and Neal Oxenhandler, "The Man with Shoes of Wind: The Derrida-Gadamer Encounter," in *Dialogue and Deconstruction: The Gadamer-Derrida Encounter*, ed. Diane P. Michelfelder and Richard E. Palmer (Albany: SUNY Press, 1989). Cf. Martin Heidegger, *The Principle of Reason*, trans. Reginald Lilly (Bloomington: Indiana University Press, 1991), p. 14.

what must be brought to a halt if those desires for control and security are to be fulfilled.[27]

Similarly, when Derrida speaks of the "play of the world" it is to present play as "the disruption of presence" and what presence signifies, the "reassuring foundation" in which we can assume the godly position above the play of the world, standing at "the origin and the end of play" as its Alpha and Omega. In short, the play of the world, so far from putting the postmodern player at the controls, is what deprives us of the security of being in control. *It is what makes it clear that we are not God.*[28]

Among the other early essays of Derrida that reinforce this understanding of play is "Plato's Pharmacy."[29] There one finds reference to the play of schemas, of thematic oppositions, of traces or supplements, of differences, of chains of signification, and of language. Writing will be the subject of the verb to play, but the subject of desire who would be seated at the controls of the world shows up only as the Platonism that is "the repression of play."[30]

It can come as no surprise that Derrida is no friend of Plato's demand and promise of absolute, pure presence, meanings and truths apprehended in an eternal now above the possibility and need of revision that comes in the wake of time. But it will come as a surprise to those who read Derridean play as a commentary on the "God is dead—everything is permitted" theme to hear (whoever has ears to hear, let them hear) how emphatically he denies that he is engaged in some "back-to-the-sophists" proj-

---

[27] "Structure, Sign, and Play," pp. 278–80. These passages are the immediate context of the passage about the "play of the structure" that Lundin quotes.

[28] Ibid., p. 292. Again, these passages are the immediate context of the cited passage about the "play of the world."

[29] Jacques Derrida, "Plato's Pharmacy," in *Dissemination,* trans. Barbara Johnson (Chicago: University of Chicago Press, 1981). This essay was first published in 1968. I emphasize the early dates of these two essays (see n. 19 above) because some would suggest that the reasonably tame, Enlightenment, and responsibility-loving Derrida of the eighties (see nn. 8, 11, and 15) is a move, under pressure, away from the dangerous, wild, irresponsible Derrida of the sixties. My countersuggestion is that this latter Derrida is a figment of the imagination of those whose readings of his work from the sixties is wildly irresponsible. This is wonderfully ironic, for whatever one ultimately makes of his work, one cannot deny that he is a meticulous reader of the texts he deconstructs.

[30] Ibid., p. 156.

ect. What interests him is the possibility of "some entirely-other of *both* sophistics *and* Platonism, some resistance having no common denominator with this whole [opposition between Platonism and sophistry]."[31] Derrida explicitly rejects the assumption, apparently shared by his critics and attributed to him against the evidence, that we have to choose between Platonic absolutism (in some form, the history of metaphysics) and sophistic relativism. From the very beginning, his project, whether one calls it humanism or anti-humanism, is the attempt to find an alternative to sophistry that does not forget that we are not God. For he sees the history of metaphysics as a set of variations on the Platonic theme, each of which demands and promises an absolute knowledge in which we would be able to see the world *sub specie aeternitatis*, to peek over God's shoulder from a standpoint securely outside the play of the world, above the temporal flow of both signifiers and signifieds that, like a rolling stream, bears all its sons (and daughters) away. It is ironic that this flight from incarnation is sometimes carried out in the name of the Word who became flesh and lived among us.

At the outset I spoke of the possibility of appropriating postmodern insights in the service of a Christian interpretation and critique of contemporary culture. If the argument to this point is convincing, it has shown that what we might call the immoralist objection to even the possibility of such appropriation is unsound, at least, first, with reference to the general posture of some postmodernists, who present themselves as moralists rather than immoralists, and, second, more specifically with reference to the Derridean theory of play, which is sometimes seen as evidence that deconstruction reduces all morality to arbitrary preference.

But even if this and other a priori arguments against the possibility of learning something from postmodernism can be deflected,[32] there remains the question whether there is anything

---

[31] Ibid., p. 108.

[32] My own sense is that the other attempts to dismiss postmodernism or, more specifically, Derrida wholesale are variations on the immoralist objection and rest on the same kind of misreading. This is not to suggest that Derrida and company should be considered immune from critique, but that such critique will have to occur at the retail level and on the basis of careful reading.

worth appropriating. If I am asking whether a certain food will be good for me, I need a stronger answer than "Well, it won't kill you." Since the focus to this point has been on Derrida, I will stay with him as I suggest an affirmative answer to the question.

Derrida regularly insists that the issues he is discussing are theological, and we have already seen that *deconstruction is the denial that we are divine.* At the heart of the metaphysical tradition Derrida sees a Heraclitophobia that begins with Parmenides and Plato. Like both Nietzsche and Kierkegaard, he sees the flight from flux and flow as endemic to the speculative impulse of Greek and Hellenized Christian thought, a flight rooted in anxiety in the face of a world, whether factual or semantic, too changeable to be under our control. The longing for Absolute Knowledge, which presents itself as the love of Truth, is less a desire to submit one's thought to the way things are than a desire to compel the world to submit to our conceptual mastery. The attempt to put a halt to the play of the world or the play of our structures of signification is the attempt to find a location for our own discourses outside of that play that is primarily, but not exclusively, the flow of time. This is a theological issue, because the identity of Thought and Being that is both required and promised as Absolute Knowledge is one of the classical definitions of God, who sees everything in an Eternal Now unconditioned by either past or future. As the desire and demand to see things *sub specie aeternitatis,* metaphysics is the not terribly subtle desire and demand to be God: and *deconstruction is the continuous reminder that we are not God.* In fact, it claims, we cannot even peek over God's shoulder.

Derrida's arguments are quasi-transcendental arguments about the conditions of the possibility of human meaning. They are Kantian arguments in the sense that they show, when they are successful (which I think is quite frequently), that we cannot have Absolute Knowledge, cannot stand at the Alpha or Omega points that look in on time from the security of a *pou sto* outside of it. Properly construed, they have Kantian limits. They show us something about human thought and language, but nothing about what else, if anything, there may be. Derrida ought to speak like Kierkegaard's Johannes Climacus, who knows that may very well be a system for God even if it cannot be for

t Derrida does not speak this way. He does not so much argue for the unreality of God as assume it, so when he shows that we are not the Alpha and Omega he talks as if he has shown that there is no Alpha and Omega. This is a non sequitur, and my primary criticism of Derrida is that he regularly falls into it. My complaint is not that he assumes atheism, but that he forgets that he has done so. He has the same right to assume that no one inhabits the Eternal Now as Kierkegaard has to assume that someone does. That either must first prove theism or atheism before thinking within that framework is a prejudice of Enlightenment evidentialism. But then they need to remember that conclusions into which their assumption essentially enters remain hypothetical.

When Derrida forgets to make this distinction and talks as if he has shown that there is no Alpha and Omega, we could point out that he has not established this and reject deconstruction as bad philosophy. But that would be to throw out the baby with the bathwater. What if he has strong quasi-Kantian arguments that do show that we are not God?[34] Might not Christian thinkers draw on them in their own work? Would it not be useful in the interpretation and critique of contemporary culture to be on the lookout for its "Luciferian" dimensions, the ways in which its Day Star brilliance says, in effect, "I will make myself like the Most High" (Isa. 14:14)?

"But we already know this. And if, from time to time, we need to be reminded, can we not turn to Augustine, Luther, Calvin, and, if all else fails, Kierkegaard?" The point is well taken insofar as it points out that Derridean thought is scarcely the Columbus who first (or second) discovered this truth. Moreover, it raises the important question whether Derrida's way of showing and saying that

---

[33] Søren Kierkegaard, *Concluding Unscientific Postscript,* trans. Howard V. and Edna H. Hong (Princeton: Princeton University Press, 1992), vol. I, 118.

[34] The Kantian character of Derrida's thought is especially emphasized in Rodolphe Gashé, *The Tain of the Mirror: Derrida and the Philosophy of Reflection* (Cambridge, Mass.: Harvard University Press, 1986); and Irene E. Harvey, *Derrida and the Economy of Différance* (Bloomington: Indiana University Press, 1986).

we are not God is sufficiently distinct to merit our attention and possible appropriation, we who trace our lineage through Augustine.[35]

I want to suggest three ways of saying yes to this last question. First, with reference to the acknowledgment that we are not God, Derrida is especially sensitive to the difference between the saying and the said (Levinas), the how and the what (Kierkegaard), the *modus significandi* and the *res significata* (Aquinas). He knows how easily the propositional content of such a saying is undermined and for all practical purposes neutralized by the performative mode of our speech act. If irony ("For Brutus is an honorable man") is the cancellation of what is said by the how of its being said, Derrida knows that irony and self-deception easily accompany each other, or, in other words, that not all irony is intentional. We can manage not to notice that in and through the very act of saying that we humans are not God we can enact the Luciferian project.

We do this, for example, (1) when we treat the theological framework within which we place this affirmation as final and ultimate, (2) when we react defensively/aggressively to criticisms of our own framework and tradition, (3) when we seek to deflect such criticisms by discrediting the critic (denying in effect that all truth is God's truth and committing the genetic fallacy at one and the same time), (4) when cultural theory becomes the vehicle for making "them" look bad in relation to "us"—in short, (5) when we act (no matter what we say) as if our own religious culture were an impregnable fortress from which to sally forth against the enemies of the Good to be found in secular culture (or in religious cultures different from our own).

"But we speak, however fallibly, on the basis of the infallible Word of God to a culture that simply ignores the Word of God." This objection leads us to a second reason to look especially closely at Derrida's version of the "we are not God" thesis. Of course, Derrida doesn't think there is any infallible Word of God. But his arguments, if successful, only establish a weaker claim about

---

[35] I see Aquinas, Luther, Calvin, and Kierkegaard as representing different species of Augustinianism and focus on the Protestant forms in this essay addressed primarily to a Protestant readership.

divine revelation that, properly formulated, would go something like this: "It is not that the voice of God is nowhere to be
heard, but only that this voice [if there is such a thing] is always
and already couched in human terms."[36] This distinction, which
echoes Barth's between religion and revelation and Levinas's between the saying and the said,[37] is the stubborn refusal to allow
the objector's "however fallibly" to function as a vacuous shibboleth. It is the reminder that even if God has spoken to us,
whenever we try to say what we have heard the formulation is
our own, and thus human, all too human. Just as the legislation
that sincerely seeks to enact justice results in positive law that is
deconstructible, so the theology that sincerely seeks to echo the
Word of God may be a somewhat muffled sound. It is a bit like
that game in which a statement is whispered from one person to
another to see how it gets transformed in the transmission.

The distinction between those who seek to speak on the basis
of the Word of God and those who do not is beyond challenge.
The problem is that it is no reliable index of who is right. The
secular critics of Christian anti-Semitism, slavery, and apartheid,
for example, were right. And those who purported to speak on
the basis of the infallible Word of God but tolerated or champi-
oned these evils were wrong. As Allen Verhey puts it, secular
culture

> may challenge and judge certain claims made on the basis of
> Scripture. Scripture has, after all, been used to justify racial and
> sexual discrimination; it has been used to justify 'holy wars,' cru-
> sades, and inquisitions; it has been used to justify the abuse of
> power and the violation of the rights and integrity of others in
> order to pursue what has been taken to be God's cause. Secular
> moral wisdom, and especially the principle of justice, has some-
> times challenged such uses of Scripture and led the church to con-
> sider particular practices and to repent of them. We must note

---

[36] Caputo, *Demythologizing Heidegger*, p. 100. This formulation derives from
Caputo's attempt to read Heidegger against Heidegger, but I believe it fits just
as well into my attempt to read Derrida against Derrida.

[37] Karl Barth, *Church Dogmatics*, vol. I, p. 2, trans. G. T. Thomson and Harold
Knight (Edinburgh: T. & T. Clark, 1956), p. 17, "The Revelation of God as the
Abolition of Religion"; Emmanuel Levinas, *Otherwise than Being or Beyond Es-
sence*, trans. Alphonso Lingis (Dordrecht: Kluwer, 1991).

that it is not the authority of Scripture itself that comes under criticism and review here, but authorizations for the use of Scripture in moral argument and moral claims made employing such authorizations. In the churches Scripture itself has sometimes finally corroborated the judgments of secular morality and has been vindicated against both its detractors and its so-called defenders in such cases.[38]

Perhaps we once learned from a rather Kierkegaardian Karl Barth, "It was the Church, not the world, which crucified Christ."[39] Today we can be reminded of this by a somewhat Nietzschean Derrida. He is a thinker, in the Enlightenment tradition, for whom interpretation and critique cannot be separated, and for whom the culture of the critic is just as vulnerable to critique as any other culture the critic may wish to critique.

So far the Derridean argument that we are not God is a double reminder that a Christian interpretation and critique of contemporary (secular) culture is an open invitation to the critique of Christian culture itself, its theories, practices, and institutions. First, there is the distinction between the propositional content and the performative mode of saying that human beings are not God. Second, there is observation that the sincere attempt to express some transcendent Truth or Justice does not elevate us above the human condition. We do not become God by purporting to base our discourse on divine revelation. Nor are we anything but confused when we act as if our attempt to point to the Absolute somehow made our pointing absolute. This confusion is perhaps the greatest temptation of Christian intellectuals. And there stands St. Jacques, working his hardest to protect us from Wormwood and Screwtape!

This second point can be phrased as a gloss on the (in)famous

---

[38] Allen Verhey, *The Great Reversal: Ethics and the New Testament* (Grand Rapids, Mich.: Eerdmans, 1984), p. 193.

[39] Karl Barth, *The Epistle to the Romans*, trans. Edwyn C. Hoskyns (New York: Oxford University Press, 1977), p. 389. In the preface to the fourth edition (pp. 20–21), Barth notes that "the literary organ of the Dutch Reformed Church" warned its readers against his book on the grounds that it was "foreign to their piety." For an interesting juxtaposition of Barth and Derrida, see Walter Lowe, *Theology and Difference: The Wound of Reason* (Bloomington: Indiana University Press, 1993).

Derridean claim *"There is nothing outside of the text."*[40] It would go something like this: if there is anything, such as God or Justice in itself, that might be said to be outside the text, saying that or anything else about it would bring it within the text. This is the Kantian point that we have only phenomenal language for talking about any possible noumenal world, and it is the reason for the discussion about the relation of deconstruction to negative theology.[41]

But the textuality of Derridean thought means more than that anything we talk about thereby gets incorporated into human discourse, explosive as that truism may be. Derridean textualism is an extension of the notion of text beyond language in the usual sense.[42] Like Paul Ricoeur, who extends the notion of text so as to treat meaningful action as text,[43] Derrida extends the notion of writing so that "things" we would not normally refer to as texts can be seen to have textual structures.

One advantage of this strategy for cultural theory is that it provides a common frame of reference for discussing such different cultural artifacts as theories, practices, and institutions; and, within cultural theory in the narrower sense, it provides a common grid for discussing explicitly textual practices such as philosophy, literature, and history, alongside practices that transcend textuality in the usual sense, such as theater, cinema, music, painting, sculpture, and architecture.[44]

But what especially concerns me here is the relational or contextual character of textual structure. To be (in) a text is to be inextricably interrelated, and in many directions at once.[45] Here

---

[40] Jacques Derrida, *Of Grammatology*, trans. Gayatri Chakravorty Spivak (Baltimore: Johns Hopkins University Press, 1974), p. 158.

[41] For an introduction to this issue, see "Faith as the Overcoming of Ontological Xenophobia" (ch. 12 below).

[42] After quoting *"There is nothing outside of the text"* in its immediate context, Barbara Johnson makes this point nicely in her introduction to *Dissemination*, p. xiv.

[43] See "The Model of the Text: Meaningful Action Considered as a Text," in Paul Ricoeur, *Hermeneutics and the Human Sciences*, trans. John B. Thompson (New York: Cambridge University Press, 1981).

[44] There is also the danger of neglecting the import of the differences among the various forms of cultural expression.

[45] Simon Critchley's reading of *"There is nothing outside of the text"* makes it equivalent to "There is nothing outside of some context." See *The Ethics of Deconstruction: Derrida and Levinas* (Oxford: Blackwell, 1992).

we meet a third way in which Derrida's way of saying that we are not God deserves the careful attention of Christian scholars. He joins Hegel and structuralism in denying the maxim of Bishop Butler that G. E. Moore liked to quote, "Everything is what it is, and not another thing."[46] The semantic principle of Spinoza, that every determination is a negation, becomes the semantic/ontological principle that everything (at least everything finite) has its meaning and its being by virtue of its relation to the others that it is not; these others, consequently, enter essentially into the meaning and the being of the selfsame. The same does not merely stand over against the other but has the other essentially within it. Nothing stands alone. Nothing (at least nothing finite) is a Spinozistic substance that exists in itself and is conceived through itself. Everything is and is understood through its others.[47]

The importance of this for cultural theory is that it helps to underscore the radical relativity of everything finite, and thus of all cultural processes and artifacts. They are and they mean only in contexts they neither create nor control. And since these contexts are in continuous historical flux, the being and the meaning of culture and its components is never final or finished.[48] The term 'cultural relativity' is pleonastic, for to be or belong to a culture is to be inextricably related.

But Derrida refuses to identify this relativity with relativism. He does not withdraw his repudiation of the sophists. He sees that unless one distinguishes the relativity ("textuality") of all phenomena from the relativism that seeks to render arbitrary preference immune from critique (and thus reduce human life to a conflict among various wills to power), one will have no

---

[46] G. E. Moore quotes this maxim on the frontispiece of *Principia Ethica* (Cambridge: Cambridge University Press, 1962), and again on p. 206.

[47] For classical theism finite creatures are relative because they are essentially related to God; but God is absolute because the divine being is not essentially related to creatures, since creation is a free act, and thus contingent. Hence the qualifier "at least nothing finite." This notion that the other is internal to the same is developed by Levinas in *Otherwise than Being* and by Ricoeur in *Oneself as Another*, trans. Kathleen Blamey (Chicago: University of Chicago Press, 1992).

[48] On this point Derrida is more Hegelian than structuralist. This is one reason why he can describe himself as an Hegelian without closure or totality. See *Of Grammatology*, p. 26.

alternative to that relativism but some variety of Platonism. Absolute Knowledge (in some form) will become such a necessity, that its impossibility will be overlooked, no matter how much bad faith that takes. Even when we deny it propositionally, we will affirm it performatively. If we wish to escape nihilism, we will have to play God. But, Derrida says, we are not God, and any genuine overcoming of nihilism will have to be honest about the human condition. Does this preclude grace? No, but it does preclude realized eschatology, the claim that we have reached the heavenly city, have put the journey behind us, and now see Truth face to face.

The deconstructive theory of textuality is, perhaps above all else, an attempt to point toward an overcoming of nihilism that is willing to remain human. To that end it seeks to articulate the coexistence of relativity and critique. In terms of its own critique of finality it can hardly expect to be or be taken to be the last word on this problem. But it is not a theory that Christian cultural theory needs to fear and to demonize. There just may be some gold to be mined in them thar hills.

10

Laughing at Hegel

EARLY IN *Of Grammatology*, Derrida tells us that he is an Hegelian—of sorts:

> The horizon of absolute knowledge is the effacement of writing in the logos, the retrieval of the trace in parousia, the reappropriation of difference, the accomplishment of what I have elsewhere called the *metaphysics of the proper*.
>
> Yet all that Hegel thought within this horizon, all, that is, except eschatology, may be reread as a meditation on writing. Hegel is also the thinker of irreducible difference.[1]

One of the places where Hegel is a thinker of difference is in his critique of immediacy. The famous chapter on Sense Certainty in the *Phenomenology* contains one version of this critique. The beginning of his *Lectures on the Proofs of the Existence of God* contains another.[2] For present purposes, however, we can direct our attention to *The Encyclopedia Logic*.[3]

There mediation is defined as "having already left a first behind, to go on to a second" (EL 86R). Thus the pure concept of being lacks determination, "for determination requires both one and another; but at the beginning we have as yet no other" (EL 86A). Mediation involves otherness; immediacy is its absence. It is as a philosopher of mediation that Hegel is a philosopher of difference.

---

[1] Jacques Derrida, *Of Grammatology*, trans. Gayatri Chakravorty Spivak (Baltimore: Johns Hopkins University Press, 1976), p. 26.

[2] These lectures are found in vol. 17 of *Werke in zwanzig Bänden*, ed. Eva Moldenhauer und Karl Markus Michel (Frankfurt: Suhrkamp, 1969), and in vol. 3 of *Hegel's Lectures on the Philosophy of Religion*, trans. E. B. Spiers and J. Burdon Sanderson (New York: Humanities, 1962). I have discussed their critique of immediacy in chapter 11 of *Hegel, Freedom, and Modernity* (Albany: SUNY Press, 1992).

[3] *The Encyclopedia Logic* (Indianapolis: Hackett, 1991). Citations in the text will be to EL, followed by the paragraph number. A = Addition (*Zusatz*), and R = Remark (*Anmerkung*). An earlier version of the present critique of Jacobi can be found in *Faith and Knowledge* (Albany: SUNY Press, 1977).

ıt he does not deny immediacy; he denies only that it stands in an either/or relation with mediation: "Not only does the immediacy of knowing not exclude its mediation . . . but they are so far connected that the immediate knowing is even the product and result of the mediated knowing" (EL 66; cf. 70). More dramatically, in the *Science of Logic*, Hegel insists "that there is nothing, nothing in heaven or in nature or mind or anywhere else which does not equally contain both immediacy and mediation, so that these two determinations reveal themselves to be *unseparated* and inseparable and the opposition between them to be a nullity."[4]

It is especially the doctrine of Essence that "deals with the essential self-positing unity of immediacy and mediation" (EL 65). Thus "we want to see the thing in question duplicated as it were: first in its immediacy and secondly in its ground, where it is no longer immediate. This is indeed the simple meaning of the so-called principle of sufficient reason or ground. This principle only asserts that things must essentially be regarded as mediated" (EL 121A).

But this also means that the apostles of immediacy are right. There is immediate knowledge. Sometimes we are directly aware of this or that. There is no need for argument, for evidence, for reflection. We just "see" that it is so. It is self-evident.

Well, not quite. It is not self-evident in itself. It is self-evident for us. Or, to be more precise, it has come to be self-evident for us through a double mediation that we can call ontogenetic and phylogenetic. The target of Hegel's critique is Jacobi, who, in response to Kant, claims that we do not need the proofs of God's existence because we have immediate knowledge of God. Just as we directly see that there are physical objects, we directly see that there is a God. We can speak in both cases of faith (*Glaube*), and doubt about God's reality is as silly and unwarranted as doubt about trees and houses.

In response, Hegel calls attention to the role of (in this case) "Christian education" in the religious beliefs Jacobi seems to

---

[4] *Hegel's Science of Logic*, trans. A. V. Miller (New York: Humanities, 1969), p. 68. Cf. EL 12R, where, although immediacy and mediation "*appear* as distinct, *neither of them* can *be wanting*, and they are *inseparably* bound together."

have in mind. "This means that, for all that religious and ethical life are a matter of *believing*, or *immediate* knowing, they are radically conditioned by mediation, which is called development, education, and culture" (EL 67). This is an illustration of the more general truth that immediacy is a fact as a *"psychological phenomenon"* (Hegel's emphasis) in which truths,

> which we know very well to be the result of the most complicated, highly mediated studies, can present themselves immediately in the consciousness of those who are *well versed* in that kind of cognition. Like anyone who has been *instructed* in a science, a mathematician has solutions at his fingertips that were arrived at by a very complicated analysis; every *educated* human being has a host of general points of view and principles immediately present in his knowing, which have only emerged from his meditation on many things, and from the life experience of many years. (EL 66, emphasis added)

Immediacy is the product of socialization. But the socializing institution is itself the product of historical mediation: "The Christian faith implies an authority that belongs to the church" (EL 63R). Whether the teaching agency is the church, the university, the guild, or, more generally, the laws and customs of one's people, that Hegel will call *Sittlichkeit*, what it passes on is what has emerged in its own development or *Entstehungsgeschichte*. Thus ontogenetic or psychological mediation is itself the product of phylogenetic or historical mediation.[5] Appeals to immediacy are abstract just when and to the degree that they abstract the phenomenon of immediacy from its dependency on this double mediation.

But every immediacy presupposes synchronic as well as diachronic mediation. Suppose Jacobi insists that it is some "natural" knowledge of God that it has in mind, one not mediated by socialization into the Christian church or any such institution. Hegel's reply is that Kant was right both in his claim that intuition is our immediate relation to objects (A19 = B33) and that "intuitions without concepts are blind" (A51 = B75). Taken in

---

[5] Hegel presents his own version of the notion that ontogeny recapitulates phylogeny in *Hegel's Phenomenology of Spirit*, trans. A. V. Miller (Oxford: Clarendon, 1977), p. 16.

full seriousness, "the immediate knowing of God" turns out to be the claim "*that* God is, not *what* God is . . . and the content of religion is reduced to a minimum" (EL 72).

Or worse. *Either* Jacobi's faith has a specific content, in which case its intuitions are mediated by the concepts in which they are articulated, *or* it is "so indeterminate" that it becomes undecidable whether the Christian trinity or "the Dalaï Lama, the bull, the ape, etc., is God" (EL 63R). The door of truth is opened to "all superstition and idolatry"—a dangerous tolerance since "natural desires and inclinations automatically deposit their interests in consciousness, and immoral purposes are found in it quite immediately. . . . Being totally abstract, [immediacy] is *indifferent* to *every content* and, just for that reason, it is receptive to any content; so it can sanction an idolatrous and immoral content just as easily as the reverse" (EL 72, 74). Immediacy's altar *"to the unknown God"* does not only reflect "the poverty of the times" (EL 73R);[6] it stands as an open invitation to ideology, the religious sanctification of all that is unholy.[7] Sheer immediacy is not only immune to doubt but also to critique.

Does Hegel's critique of immediacy justify Derrida's claim that he "is also the thinker of *irreducible* difference" (emphasis shifted)? Well, yes and no. Yes, because there is no sheer immediacy. Immediacy is "abstract self-relation and hence it is abstract identity" (EL 74A) because it abstracts things and thoughts from the other things and thoughts through which they are mediated. It suppresses difference. But difference and otherness are everywhere present, and neither ontologically nor semantically does anything have the characteristics of Spinoza's substance, "that which is in itself and is conceived through itself."[8]

But we must also say No. There is an eschatology (closure, totality, parousia) in which difference, while not disappearing, loses its irreducibility: "Only the insight that the content is not independent, but is *mediated through an other*, reduces it to its

---

[6] Cf. ibid., pp. 7–8, on the poverty of the times.

[7] Here Hegel sounds very much like the Hume of *The Natural History of Religion*. See my discussion in chapter 4 of *Suspicion and Faith: The Religious Uses of Modern Atheism* (Grand Rapids, Mich.: Eerdmans, 1993).

[8] *The Ethics*, part I, def. 3.

finitude and untruth" (EL 74). This means that only for finitude is difference irreducible and that a philosophy of irreducible difference, like Derrida's, would be a philosophy of irreducible finitude. But Hegel proceeds immediately (as if we were in doubt!) to point in a different direction: "But a content can only be [re]cognized as what is true, inasmuch as it is not mediated with an other, i.e., is not finite, so that it mediates itself with itself, and is in this way both mediation and immediate self-relation all in one" (EL 74). As self-mediating totality beyond the finitude of mediation through an other, the Infinite is a new immediacy, achieved through the *completion* of mediation rather than through its *suppression*. This Infinite is substance in Spinoza's sense, even if, as Spirit, it is more than substance. Neither in its being nor in its intelligibility does it refer beyond itself. As both ontological and semantic totality, there is no beyond to which it could refer.[9] If abstract immediacy occurs when (it seems) "we have as yet no other," true rational, immediacy occurs when we have no longer any other.

If there is any truth to the notion of thesis, antithesis, and synthesis in Hegel's thought, it is to be found in the following, rather more complex triad: abstract self-relation, mediation through an other, and the self-mediation of the totality.

For Kant, it was precisely the attempt to achieve the Unconditioned in the form of Totality that led to the expulsion of metaphysics from the Eden where physics and mathematics luxuriated. And his name for the paralogisms and antinomies that made the landscape east of Eden so barren and desolate was dialectic.

But Hegel is *also* the philosopher of dialectic, and thus once again, it would seem, of irreducible difference. Kant's discovery of the antinomies "has to be considered one of the most important and profound advances of the philosophy of modern times" (EL 48R). But he spoiled his discovery in two ways. First, in an excessive "tenderness for the things of the world" he insisted

---

[9] Accordingly Hegel sustains an unrelenting polemic against philosophies that imply a "beyond." EL 28A, 36A, 38A, 38R, 45A, 60A1, 94A, 213A. Closely related to this is the polemic against the "ought." See 6R, 38R, 45A, 60, 94, 94A and my discussion in "Hegel's Angst vor dem Sollen," *The Owl of Minerva* 25, no. 2 (spring 1994).

that "the stain of contradiction" could not belong to the world but "has to belong *only* to thinking reason." Second, Kant could only find four antinomies, whereas they are rather to be found "in *all* objects of all kinds, in *all* representations, concepts, and ideas" (EL 48R).[10]

Things and thoughts are not only externally conditioned or mediated; they are internally incoherent. Accordingly, "the finite is not restricted merely from the outside; rather it sublates itself by virtue of its own nature, and passes over, of itself, into its opposite. Thus we say, for instance, that man is mortal . . . the proper interpretation is that life as such bears the germ of death within itself, and that the finite sublates itself because it contradicts itself inwardly" (EL 81A1). I don't have to be murdered to die. Dialectic shows us "what everything finite is; its own sublation" (EL 81R).

In addition to human mortality, Hegel cites the following examples of what he means: "'*Summum ius summa iniuria*,' which means that if abstract justice is driven to the extreme it overturns into injustice. Similarly, in politics, it is well known how prone the extremes of anarchy and despotism are to lead to one another . . . we find the consciousness of dialectic in those universally familiar proverbs: 'Pride goes before a fall', 'Too much wit outwits itself', etc." (EL 81A1).

With origins in both Plato and Kant, dialectic is the properly negative moment of reason, the true form of skepticism (EL 81R). It is not merely a matter of doubt; "rather, it is completely certain about its central point, i.e., the nullity of everything finite. . . . Skepticism proper . . . is complete despair about everything that the understanding holds to be firm" (EL 81A2).[11] By contrast with modern, Humean skepticism that holds fast to the sensible in order to place the supersensible in question, dialectic is akin

---

[10] Earlier he had united these points: "But the usual tenderness for things, whose only care is that they do not contradict themselves, forgets here as elsewhere that in this way the contradiction is not resolved but merely shifted elsewhere, into subjective or external reflection generally"; *Science of Logic*, p. 423.

[11] This passage echoes Hegel's earlier account of the phenomenological dialectic as a journey of doubt (*Zweifel*) and despair (*Verzweiflung*) that brings "conscious insight into the untruth of phenomenal knowledge"; *Phenomenology of Spirit*, pp. 49–50.

to "the high ancient skepticism" of Sextus Empiricus, for example, which puts the (common) sensible in question (EL 81A2; cf. 39R and 24A3).[12]

Everything finite is its own sublation. Thus dialectic shows the might, or even the wrath, of God: "We say that all things (i.e., everything finite as such) come to judgment, and in that saying we catch sight of the dialectic as the universal, irresistible might before which nothing can subsist, however firm and secure it may deem itself to be" (EL 81A1).

Contrary to appearances, this is good news, and doubly so. First, it is only the finite that is thus brought to judgment; the Infinite has an alibi. Second, the verdict is guilty, but the punishment is sublation, *Aufhebung*. This is cancellation, to be sure; but it is also preservation in something higher. The finite does not simply disappear; it is recontextualized as part of the whole. It is not the organizing principle of this whole, but it plays an essential part.

Dialectical skepticism is thus the ally and propaedeutic to philosophy. It is "only the finite and abstract thinking of the understanding that has anything to fear from skepticism . . . philosophy, on the other hand, contains the skeptical as a moment within itself—specifically as the dialectical moment. But then philosophy does not stop at the merely negative result of the dialectic" (EL 81A2), but rather goes on to the positive mode of reason whose name is speculation.

The new triad is Understanding, Dialectic (reason in its negative, skeptical mode), and Speculation (reason in its positive mode). It is the movement from the affirmation of the finite, to the denial of the finite, to the *Aufhebung* of the finite in the Infinite. Once again the truth of thesis-antithesis-synthesis turns out to be more complex than that formula can adequately express.

More importantly, once again Hegel shows himself both to be and not to be a philosopher of "irreducible difference." The dialectical stage corresponds to the stage of mediation through another. Here internal difference complements external differ-

---

[12] Hegel first developed this contrast in the journal he co-edited with Schelling. See "Relationship of Skepticism to Philosophy," *Between Kant and Hegel: Texts in the Development of Post-Kantian Idealism,* trans. George di Giovanni and H. S. Harris (Albany: SUNY Press, 1985).

ence, and abstract self-identity proves as chimerical as abstract self-relation. The difference that emerges here, which Derrida might call the impropriety of the proper, is irreducible by being inescapable. Contrary to the assumption of Bishop Butler and G. E. Moore, no thing is what it is and not another thing.

Except the Infinite. The semantic totality of thoughts is the truth, and the ontological totality of things is the rationally real. If the dialectical moment (like other-mediation) is the Hegelian version of what Derrida calls writing, the trace, and difference, the speculative moment (like self-mediation) is the metaphysics of the proper, the eschatalogical event in which judgment becomes salvation. Hegel is *also*, but only penultimately, a philosopher of irreducible difference.

This is why Hegelian skepticism is only penultimate. Nothing breeds skepticism, including moral and religious skepticism, quite as effectively as an experienced pluralism of beliefs and practices. But the movement in which other-mediation becomes self-mediation and dialectical difference becomes speculative totality allows Hegel to affirm skepticism in the confidence that it will be *aufgehoben* in absolute knowledge, scientific system, the Idea. Eschatological closure is the secret to a pluralism that begins but does not end in skepticism and to an historicism that begins but does not end in relativism.

We see this movement concretely at work in Hegel's treatment of philosophical differences. Sounding a bit like Richard Rorty, if only for a sentence, he says that the *"external history"* of philosophy

> gives the form of a *contingent* succession to the stages of the Idea's development, and it gives a kind of mere *diversity* to the principles and their exposition in the various philosophies of these stages. But the master workman of this labour of thousands of years is the One living Spirit. . . . With regard to philosophies that *appear* [emphasis added] diverse, the *history of philosophy* shows, on the one hand, that there is only One philosophy at diverse stages of its formation, and, on the other, that the particular *principles* on which each system is grounded one by one are only *branches* of one and the same whole. . . . The science of [the Idea or the Absolute] is essentially a *system*, since what is *concretely* true is so only in its inward *self-unfolding* [emphasis added] and in taking and

holding itself together in unity, i.e., as *totality*. Only through the distinguishing, and determination of its distinctions, can what is concretely true be the necessity of these distinctions and the freedom of the whole. (EL 13–14; cf. 15–19)[13]

This freedom of the whole is distinctively Spinozistic. "Freedom is only present where there is no other for me that is not myself" (EL 24A2); it "consists precisely in my not having any absolute other over against me, but in my being dependent upon a content that is just myself" (EL 38A; cf. 161A). In response to "Love means never having to say you're sorry," Hegel says, "Freedom means never having an other."

But he qualifies this so as to cut short any hint of isolationism, of abstract identity and immediacy achieved through absolution of the finite from all relationship. If I am to be free, my other cannot be absolute; it must be myself. This is why, in good Spinozistic fashion, finitude lives under the sign of necessity, and only the Whole is free. For it is only the Whole that is "the activity of positing itself over against itself, in order to be for-itself, and to be, in this other, only at home with itself" (EL 18). While the "spurious infinity" is the endless progression through space, or time, or the sequence of integers, the "genuine Infinite . . . consists rather in remaining at home with itself in its other, or (when it is expressed as a process) in coming to itself in its other" (EL 94A).[14]

This home is apparently not a home on the range, where never is heard a discouraging word. Other-mediation and dialectic are discouraging words, even despairing words in relation to finitude's aspirations toward autonomy. But they are like the emotions generated by a James Bond movie in which we know that

---

[13] This repeats an argument given in the *Phenomenology of Spirit*, pp. 1–4.

[14] It is in terms of this language of being at home in one's other that Hegel regularly expresses his view of the relation of thought to being. See EL 20R, 23, 24A2, and 28A. The phenomenological journey achieves "the totality of its moments" as absolute knowledge and as the infinity of Spirit when self-consciousness is "in communion with itself in *its* otherness as such"; *Phenomenology of Spirit*, p. 479. Hegel's text says that self-consciousness "also in *seinem* Anderssein als solchem bei sich ist"; *Phänomenologie des Geistes,*ed. Johannes Hoffmeister (Hamburg: Felix Meiner, 1952), p. 549. Like EL, the Baillie translation renders *bei sich* as "at home." See *The Phenomenology of Mind* (London: George Allen & Unwin), p. 790.

however hopeless the situations seems, our hero will not only escape but end up in the arms of his lady love. We love being scared, but all the time we know, as the Germans say, that *die Geschichte ist happy geendet*.[15]

How can we escape the security of such narratives? This question immediately evokes another, Why would anyone want to run away from so reassuring a home to a world in which the bad guys so frequently win? In the aftermath to Hegel there has been no shortage of prodigal sons who have found the Hegelian homestead inhibiting. Each of these runaways has had his own motivation and, corresponding to it, his own strategy, for showing the paterfamilias to be a tyrant and the manor house at once a dungeon and a house of cards: Hegel as the Wizard of Oz.

But the different strategies have in common the charge that Hegel's alleged totality has left out something too important to ignore. In the case of Marx, the fatal omission is the suffering and hope of the proletariat, while in the case of Kierkegaard it is the suffering and hope of the knight of faith, to cite only two of the most familiar prodigals. Hegel's defenders can, of course, point to texts in which economic and religious suffering are mentioned; but the charge is not that Hegel failed to mention them but that he failed to do justice to them, that in his hurry to get to the place where James Bond and his damsel-no-longer-in-distress can live happily ever after, he defined real problems out of existence. He confused the real world with a Hollywood screenplay of which he was the author. This retreat to fiction leaves the real world in the hands of the spirit, to be sure, but this *Weltgeist* is the satanic spirit "that is now at work among those who are disobedient" (Eph. 2:2), whether this Pauline language is cashed in in terms of the spirit of capitalism or the spirit of complacent, bourgeois, Christendom.

While it is true that for Kierkegaard and Marx *die Geschichte ist noch nicht happy geendet*, they agree that there is a happy ending to be awaited and that "the sufferings of this present time are not worth comparing with the glory about to be revealed to us" (Rom. 8:18). Their challenge to the eschatology by which Hegel moves from other-mediation to self-mediation and from

---

[15] This comes verbatim from a German TV guide.

dialectic to speculation concerns its timing. They do not share Hegel's allergic fear of any *Jenseits* and the "Angst vor dem Sollen" that is the trembling that accompanies this fear.[16] For this reason they have no qualms about placing "the glory about to be revealed to us" in the future or about describing the arduous tasks and inescapable suffering that accompany, in each case, this hope.

Hope. Ay, there's the rub. As different as they are from each other and as deep as their disagreements with Hegel's realized eschatology may be, Marx and Kierkegaard are eschatological thinkers. Since Derrida says that it is the eschatological move that separates deconstruction from speculation, we must ask, Which eschatology? Is it precisely the realized eschatology of Hegel? Or is it eschatology as such, meaning that between Hegel and these two Oedipal sons of Hegel Derrida sees only nine cents and not a dime's worth of *différance?*

In his essay on Bataille, Derrida seems to give the second, more radical answer. Derrida's concern is that we take Hegel too lightly: "Misconstrued, treated lightly, Hegelianism only extends its historical domination, finally unfolding its immense enveloping resources without obstacle."[17] Derrida does not identify this historical domination of Hegelianism, but given Hegel's persuasion that the Owl of Minerva flies from east to west, he may very well have in mind those features of itself that the West sees as making it the goal of history: capitalism, democracy, and the moral order that undergirds these practices, with special emphasis on the rights of individuals.[18] Perhaps the self-evidence of liberal society to Richard Rorty would be an example of Hegel's hegemony extending itself among those who treat it too lightly.

This includes, Derrida fears, even "the best readers of Bataille" insofar as they think they can dissipate Hegel's self-evi-

---

[16] See n. 9 above.

[17] Jacques Derrida, "From Restricted to General Economy: A Hegelianism without Reserve," in *Writing and Difference,* trans. Alan Bass (Chicago: University of Chicago Press, 1978), p. 251. Subsequent page numbers in the text are to this essay, even where Derrida is quoting Bataille or Hegel.

[18] Such a reading would not be without irony, given Hegel's highly qualified enthusiasm for capitalism, democracy, and individual rights.

dence with a casual reference to Nietzsche or Marx or, we might add, Kierkegaard (p. 251). So listen up! Derrida will give us a reading of Bataille and his "aneschatology" (p. 271) even better than those offered by his "best" readers, one that will offer a more genuine escape from the tentacles of Hegel's "historical domination."

Like other prodigals, Derrida's Bataille points to what Hegel has left out, what he regularly refers to as Hegel's blind spot. His anti-Hegelian strategy will be first to locate this blind spot and then to laugh—loudly. Ought we to associate this laughter with the satirical wit with which Kierkegaard's Johanneses (de Silentio and Climacus) skewer the System?[19]

At first it seems so, when this laughter is equated with awakening from dream. Hegelian reason (with its passage from other-mediation to self-mediation and from dialectic to speculation) is a kind of sleep, "the slumber that engenders monsters and then puts them to sleep. . . . The slumber of reason is not, perhaps reason put to sleep, but slumber in the form of reason, the vigilance of the Hegelian logos. Reason keeps watch over a deep slumber in which it has an interest. . . . To laugh at philosophy (at Hegelianism)—such, in effect, is the form of the awakening" (p. 252). There can be little question but that Johannes Climacus would have loved this notion that Hegelian reason dialectically generates monsters only to put them speculatively to sleep in order to be able to remain asleep itself.

But if Bataille's laughter is to free us from the eschatology that Kierkegaard shares with Hegel, in spite of their far from trivial quarrel over the timing of the parousia, it must distance itself from Kierkegaard as well as from Hegel. This happens when Bataille equates his laughter not only with awakening but also with anguish (pp. 252, 257, 259). For this anguish is not the unhappiness of the Unhappy Consciousness, the fear and

---

[19] For the intimate relation between these two pseudonyms, see my "Johannes and Johannes: Kierkegaard and Difference," in *International Kierkegaard Commentary: Philosophical Fragments and Johannes Climacus*, ed. Robert L. Perkins (Macon, Ga.: Mercer University Press, 1994). Climacus refers us to "a thesis propounded by Lord Shaftesbury that makes laughter the test of truth"; *Concluding Unscientific Postscript*, trans. Howard V. and Edna H. Hong (Princeton: Princeton University Press, 1992), vol. I, p. 512.

trembling constitutive of Silentio's knight of faith and the suffering that is the essential expression of religious passion for Climacus. Hegel's Unhappy Consciousness and the two Kierkegaardian versions of it just mentioned are miles removed from a crisis of meaning. They intend a meaning they take to be Absolute Meaning. The pain in their lives comes from the fact that this intention is not fulfilled in intuition. They are walking by faith and not by sight (2 Cor. 5:7). They are nomads, sojourners, pilgrims. They have a home; they just aren't there. Yet.

For Bataille, by contrast, "Absolute comicalness is the anguish experienced when confronted by expenditure on lost funds, by the absolute sacrifice of meaning: a sacrifice without return and without reserves" (p. 257). It is in terms of an economy of expenditure without return that Bataille seeks to distinguish the sovereignty of postmodern laughter from the lordship of Hegel's phenomenological divine comedy, the key, as he sees it, to everything Hegelian. As we look at the difference between sovereignty and lordship, it becomes clear that it is eschatology as such and not just the realized eschatology of the Hegelian system that is the object, not of mirth, but of an anguished laughter that sounds a lot like "Eli, Eli, lema sabachthani?" (Matt. 27:46; see p. 262).[20]

In the background of Bataille's reading of Hegel is his own notion of sacrifice as unproductive expenditure. Over against the "pecuniary interest" that seeks "expenditure regularly compensated for by acquisition," Bataille places the *potlatch*, where the ideal "would be to give a *potlatch* and not have it returned."[21] Here I do not give in order to get, and my expenditure is not an investment in search of a profitable return. This is the meaning of an expenditure "without reserve."

---

[20] Jesus' cry from the cross is a quotation in Hebrew of Psalm 22:1, "My God, my God, why have you forsaken me?" On p. 262 Derrida quotes a reference by Bataille to this text.

[21] "The Notion of Expenditure," in *Visions of Excess: Selected Writings, 1927–1939*, ed. Allan Stoekl (Minneapolis: University of Minnesota Press, 1985), pp. 116–22. For Bataille, the point is that "human life cannot in any way be limited to the closed systems assigned to it by reasonable conceptions. The immense travail of recklessness, discharge, and upheaval that constitutes life could be expressed by stating that life starts only with the deficit of these systems" (p. 128).

We know from Marx that there are two forms of profit-seeking investment. One is quantitative and spends a given amount of exchange value in search of a greater amount of exchange value. This is the M-C-M form of exchange. The other, which Marx labels the C-M-C form, is qualitative and exchanges a use value for a different and more highly desired use value.[22] Bataille interprets Hegelian *Aufhebung* as an instance of the latter. The moment of negativity is the sacrifice, giving up, expenditure of something valued, but with an eye to getting something different but even more valuable in return. Thus in the famous struggle for recognition that generates lordship (*Herrschaft*) over against bondage in the *Phenomenology*, the risk of death is a rational risk in the C-M-C form. Life is the risk capital ventured in search of something better than mere life, namely, recognition.

Bataille is less concerned with the particulars of this phenomenological moment than with the very structure of every phenomenological experience (p. 256) and beyond this, to the very structure of negativity and *Aufhebung* in Hegel's thought in general. As both cancellation and preservation, dialectic is a negativity in the service of positivity. "The putting at stake of life is a moment in the constitution of meaning" (p. 254), whether the life that is risked is biological, phenomenological, or logical. The task of the negative is to "collaborate" in the genesis of meaning (p. 259). It is clear that Bataille uses 'meaning' as the generic term for the profitable return promised in the investment brochures from Hegel, Inc.

Hegel is careful to exclude death itself from being philosophically significant. So we read:

> To rush headlong into death pure and simple is thus to risk the absolute loss of meaning. . . . One risks losing the effect and profit of meaning which were the very *stakes* one hoped to *win*. Hegel called this mute and nonproductive death, this death pure and simple, *abstract negativity*, in opposition to "the negation characteristic of consciousness, which cancels in such a way that it preserves and maintains what is sublated . . . and thereby survives its being sublated." (p. 255)[23]

---

[22] See *Capital*, vol. 1, ch. 4, "The General Formula for Capital."

[23] In the *Phenomenology* Hegel gives philosophical significance to the death of Jesus as the death of divine transcendence, but dismisses his own death and

Bataille laughs. The "absolute loss of meaning" associated with death as abstract negativity is Hegel's blind spot, and having found it, Bataille breaks into a deep belly laugh. Sovereignty distinguishes itself, in the anguish of this laughter, from the serious work of lordship, the labor of the negative that gives birth to new meaning. The difference between sovereignty and lordship is "the *unique* interval which separates meaning from a certain non-meaning" (p. 254). Sovereign laughter is "an absolute renunciation of meaning," and its burst "is the almost-nothing into which meaning sinks, absolutely" (p. 256). Or should we call it the absolute-nothing into which meaning sinks, almost? In any case Hegelian *Aufhebung* is laughable in its "blinding itself to the baselessness of the nonmeaning from which the basis of meaning is drawn, and in which this basis of meaning is exhausted" (p. 257). The Alpha-and-Omega of meaning is nonmeaning. The *Grund* of meaning is an *Abgrund*.

If death is one "sign" of nonmeaning as the horizon of even dialectically constituted, Hegelian meaning, play is another. Here, as elsewhere in Derrida's writings, play is not something we do but something that happens so much against our will that we are always looking for ways to control it. Hegelian *Aufhebung* is one such effort to master play, "limiting it and elaborating it by giving it form and meaning" (p. 255). But sovereign laughter makes "the seriousness of meaning appear as an abstraction inscribed in play" (p. 256).

Now, an abstraction, in Hegelian terms, is something isolated, removed, from its proper context. To (re)inscribe an abstraction in something is to return it to its proper home, to (re)contextualize it. In this (re)inscription of meaning within play "I absolve myself of absolute knowledge, putting it back in its place as such, situating it and inscribing it within a space which it no

---

that of his reader as an *abstract negativity* that is of no concern to philosophy. The passage quoted by Derrida from the *Phenomenology* is found on pp. 114–15 of the Miller translation. Speaking of the "power of the negative" shown by the analytic Understanding, Hegel writes, "Death, if that is what we want to call this non-actuality, is of all things what is most dreadful. . . . But the life of Spirit is not the life that shrinks from death and keeps itself untouched by devastation, but rather the life that endures it and maintains itself in it. It wins its truth only when, in utter dismemberment, it finds itself"; *Phenomenology*, p. 19.

longer dominates" (p. 270). If that space is the abyss of non-meaning of which Bataille has been speaking, this would be the *Aufhebung* of the *Aufhebung*. For Hegelian preservation always recontextualizes finite meanings in larger and more inclusive networks of meaning until one arrives at the all encompassing network that can be called Idea, System, or Absolute Knowledge. If this ultimate network of meaning must be recontextualized within the horizon of nonmeaning from which its *exitus* arises and to which its *reditus* returns, this would be a negativity that is not exactly a moment in the constitution of meaning.[24]

Is play, like death, such a horizon of nonmeaning? It would seem so:

> In interpreting negativity as labor, in betting for discourse, meaning, history, etc., Hegel has bet against play, *against chance* [emphasis added]. He has blinded himself to the possibility of his own bet, to the fact that the conscientious suspension of play . . . was itself a phase of play; and to the fact that play *includes* the work of meaning or the meaning of work, and includes them not in terms of *knowledge*, but in terms of *inscription*: meaning is a *function* of play [= chance], is inscribed in a certain place in the configuration of a meaningless play [= chance]. (p. 260)[25]

Derrida is interested in a discourse "which can open itself up to the absolute loss of its sense, to the (non-)base of the sacred, of nonmeaning, of un-knowledge or of play, to the swoon from

---

[24] This paragraph perhaps best indicates where my reading of Derrida's essay differs from that of Joseph Flay in "Hegel, Derrida, and Bataille's Laughter," in *Hegel and His Critics*, ed. William Desmond (Albany: SUNY Press, 1989). Flay rejects the view that "the *Aufhebung* rules all and proscribes rupture of any sort" on the grounds that "a particular 'taking up' of a negation would rupture the previous economy" (p. 167). Thus the transition from Self-consciousness to Reason is a rupture that goes beyond the dialectic of master and slave. "The 'economy' of mastery is here broken" (pp. 168–69). But Derrida's Bataille does not deny this or present us with a ubiquitous master–slave dialectic. What is ubiquitous is the structure of that dialectic, the movement from one meaning to a new and richer meaning. That the ultimate movement might be to nonmeaning is, for Derrida's Bataille, the significance of death and the contingency signified here by play.

[25] In case we missed the point, Derrida repeats it: "Far from suppressing the dialectical synthesis, it inscribes this synthesis and makes it function within the sacrifice of meaning. It does not suffice to risk death if the putting at stake is not permitted to take off, *as chance or accident*, but is rather invested as the work of the negative" (p. 261, emphasis added).

which it is reawakened by a throw of the dice" (p. 261). He has reversed his metaphors. This swoon is not the complacent slumber of Hegelian meaning, but stands in apposition to "nonmeaning" and "un-knowledge." Hence this awakening is not sovereign laughter but the (forgotten) passage from the darkness of nonmeaning to the sunlight of meaning. In saying that this happens "by a throw of the dice," Derrida reiterates his earlier equation of play with chance. Play signifies the contingency that (shall we say necessarily?) underlies all the necessities of dialectical meaning.

This explains, of course, why the logic of *Aufhebung* is an attempt to control and limit play (p. 255). Sovereignty resists this attempt, but so far is its laughter from being a carte blanche to "play without rules" that "given over to 'play without rules,' poetry [or writing in general] risks letting itself be domesticated, 'subordinated,' better than ever. This risk is properly *modern*" (p. 261). In other words, the radical subjectivism often attributed to deconstruction in particular and postmodernism in general is better conceived as the flip side of modernity's objectivism. Logical positivism, where scientific objectivism and moral/metaphysical subjectivism become Siamese twins, is a modern, perhaps *the* modern, ideology.[26]

> There are things that even the wise fail to do,
> While the fool hits the point.
> Unexpectedly discovering the way to life in the midst of death,
> He burst out in hearty laughter.[27]

If we cannot equate Bataille's laughing at Hegel with Kierkegaardian satires because the former expresses a more radical crisis of meaning, perhaps it is akin to Zen laughter, which has been described as "loud, uproarious, unrestrained" and even "near-demonic."[28] Christmas Humphreys says, "There is more

---

[26] Cf. the similar argument in the opening chapters of MacIntyre's *After Virtue*.

[27] Quoted from Sengai in Conrad Hyers, *Zen and the Comic Spirit* (Philadelphia: Westminster Press, 1973), p. 37. For other discussions of Zen laughter, see R. H. Blyth, *Oriental Humour* (Tokyo: Hokuseido, 1959), pp. 87–97, and D. T. Suzuki, *Sengai, the Zen Master* (New York: New York Graphic Society, 1971), pp. 1–17.

[28] Hyers, *Zen and the Comic* Spirit, pp. 35 and 27.

honest 'belly laughter' in a Zen monastery than surely in any other religious institution on earth"—and the faithful chant before Maitreya, the Messianic Buddha whose avatar is a clown:

> When the big belly thunders with loud roars of laughter,
> Thousands of white lotuses rain through all the worlds.[29]

Is Bataille's laughter an "expression" of *satori?* Very possibly, but we must proceed carefully. Although we are dealing with an "absolute unknowledge" that is "the absolute excess of every *episteme*" (p. 268), we are sternly forbidden to construe sovereignty as a new mysticism (pp. 269, 272). In the first place, although "sovereignty can enounce nothing, except in the form of *neither this, nor that*" (p. 273), it is not a kind of negative theology that posits in and through its negations "a 'superessentiality' . . . a supreme being and an indestructible meaning" beyond "the categories of beings" (p. 271). Its rejection of mediation is not a retreat to an immediacy where it can "pleasurably consume an absolutely close presence" (p. 273).[30]

Still, sovereign laughter is intimately related to "the sovereign silence which interrupts articulated language." Is this a mystical silence? Not quite. "Since it excludes articulated language, sovereign silence is therefore, *in a certain fashion,* foreign to difference as the source of signification." In what fashion? In the fashion of "a sovereign operation transgressing the limit of discursive difference" (p. 263). The loud silence of sovereign laughter is the transgression rather than the erasure of meaning. To be more precise, the mode of writing that points to this laughing silence is the interruption of articulated language—linguistically.

Derrida describes this kind of writing in terms of excess, (re)inscription, and dislocation or displacement. Sovereignty is to be inscribed in discourse, but the only writing that can do this will be one that "exceeds the logic of philosophy" (p. 259). But

---

[29] Quoted in ibid., pp. 35 and 48.

[30] Derrida develops this argument in relation to his own work in "Différance," in *Margins of Philosophy,* trans. Alan Bass (Chicago: University of Chicago Press, 1982) and in "How to Avoid Speaking: Denials," in *Derrida and Negative Theology,* ed. Harold Coward and Toby Foshay (Albany: SUNY Press, 1992).

just as Johannes de Silentio sees faith as the paradox that *"after* having been in the universal [the single individual] as the single individual isolates himself as higher than the universal,"[31] so Derrida's Bataille interrupts the prevailing logos only after graduating from its schools. "Unknowledge is, then, superhistorical, but only because it takes its responsibilities from the completion of history and from the closure of absolute knowledge, having *first* taken them seriously and having *then* betrayed them by exceeding them" (p. 269, emphasis added). The question posed by Bataille is this: "how, *after* having exhausted the discourse of philosophy, can one inscribe in the lexicon and syntax of a language, our language, which was also the language of philosophy, that which nevertheless exceeds the oppositions of concepts governed by this communal logic?" (pp. 252–53, emphasis added).

The answer to the question How is this exceeding or transgression possible? is in terms of dislocation or displacement and reinscription. In Bataille,

> a complicity without reserve accompanies Hegelian discourse, "takes it seriously" up to the end, without an objection in philosophical form, while, however, a certain burst of laughter exceeds it and destroys its sense, or signals, in any event, the extreme point of "experience" which makes Hegelian discourse dislocate *itself* . . . all of Bataille's concepts are Hegelian. We must acknowledge this without stopping here. For if one does not grasp the rigorous effect of the trembling to which he submits these concepts, the new configuration into which he displaces and reinscribes them . . . one would conclude . . . that Bataille is Hegelian or anti-Hegelian, or that he has muddled Hegel. One would be deceived each time. (p. 253)[32]

Dislocation, displacement, reinscription—are these not the very sorts of recontextualizing that constitute Hegelian *Aufhebung?* If so, we could speak (as we did earlier in this essay) of Bataille as the *Aufhebung* of the Hegelian *Aufhebung.* At the end

---

[31] Søren Kierkegaard, *Fear and Trembling/Repetition,* trans. Howard V. and Edna H. Hong (Princeton: Princeton University Press, 1983), p. 55, emphasis added. Silentio repeats this theme on pp. 56, 69, and 99.

[32] The theme of displacement reappears on pp. 254, 257, and 275.

of his essay Derrida poses this question explicitly and calls attention to a crucial difference. The Hegelian *Aufhebung* occurs in a restricted economy where meaning circulates *"within* the circle of absolute knowledge, never exceeds its closure, never suspends the totality of discourse, work, meaning, law, etc." (p. 275). This is why Bataille "can only utilize the *empty* form of the *Aufhebung*, in an analogical fashion, in order to designate, *as was never done before*, the transgressive relationship which links the world of meaning to the world of nonmeaning. This displacement is paradigmatic [for a certain form of writing]. . . . This movement then makes philosophy appear as a form of natural or naive consciousness (which in Hegel also means cultural consciousness)" (p. 275).

Is Bataille, then, a Zen Buddhist? I shall not insist on the comparison, but leave it to the reader for what it may be worth. I would note only that when Derrida glosses his denial that Bataille is a mystic, he supports rather than undermines the comparison. For neither Zen nor Bataille should be thought of in terms of the negative theologian consuming the absolutely close presence of the superessential deity. The Mahayana emptiness, of which Zen is an heir, is not to be confused with the Hindu Brahman/Atman. Moreover, the kind of writing that uses language to point to the radical limits of language has an obvious affinity with the Zen *koan*, even if in its French versions it lacks the art of Asian brevity.

Derrida's essay on Hegel and Bataille appeared in 1967. More recently, he has shown an interest in Marx and Kierkegaard that would not be easy to derive from his reading of Bataille.[33] It involves no turn to eschatological hope. Derrida's Marxism is a messianism without a messiah, and his interest in Kierkegaard's Abraham does not extend to the God of Abraham or to the

---

[33] For Marx, see *Spectres of Marx: The State of the Debt, the Work of Mourning, and the New International*, trans. Peggy Kamuf (New York: Routledge, 1994). For Kierkegaard, see *The Gift of Death*, trans. David Wills (Chicago: University of Chicago Press, 1995), and John D. Caputo's essay "Instants, Secrets, and Singularities: Dealing Death in Kierkegaard and Derrida," in *Kierkegaard in Post/Modernity*, ed. Martin J. Matûstîc and Merold Westphal (Bloomington: Indiana University Press, 1995).

promise of eternal happiness. Still, there is an appeal to moral meaning that, to repeat, would not be easy to derive from Derrida's very sympathetic appropriation of Bataille.

The turn (or is it a return?) is neither new nor sudden. Derrida's thought has never been a God-is-dead-everything-is-permitted amoralism. But as we move from the sixties toward the nineties, normative considerations of an ethical and political nature do become more nearly central to Derrida's writing. Among the possible explanations for this we can list the following: (1) a desire to integrate the ethico-political concerns that were never missing from Derrida's thought more closely into his deconstructive epistemology; (2) a desire to respond to those critics who could find nothing but moral nihilism in his understanding of the limits of human knowledge; and (3) the influence of Levinas.

All but simultaneous with the recent discussions of Marx and Kierkegaard is Derrida's attempt to present deconstruction as a form of natural law theory.[34] Of course, he does not use this language; I use it out of a certain perverse desire to discomfit his admirers and his detractors, both of whom are more sensitive to the divergence between Derrida and, say, Aquinas or Locke, than to the convergence.[35]

When Derrida says that law (a fundamental form of meaning) has its origin in "a violence without ground" and that it is "constructible and so deconstructible,"[36] we hear echoes of the notion that nonmeaning is the horizon of meaning and that contingent throws of the dice lie at the foundation of our lofty principles. But when, in the same passage, he insists on distinguishing justice from law, he sings a different tune: "Justice in itself, if such a thing exists, outside or beyond law, is not deconstructible. . . . Deconstruction is justice." Our (legal) meanings retain their contingency and deconstructibility. But now their horizon, not sim-

---

[34] "Force of Law: The 'Mystical Foundation of Authority,' " in *Deconstruction and the Possibility of Justice,* ed. Drucilla Cornell, Michel Rosenfeld, and David Gray Carlson (New York: Routledge, 1992).

[35] I explore this divergence and convergence in my review of the book mentioned in the previous note, entitled "Derrida as Natural Law Theorist" (ch. 11 below).

[36] "Force of Law," pp. 14–15.

ply affirmed, not quite postulated, but ineluctably presupposed, is something beyond the ecstasy of construction and the agony of deconstruction.

Derrida has become a species of Unhappy Consciousness along with Marx and Kierkegaard. He intends a meaning he takes to be absolute (not deconstructible), though he insists not only that it is not fulfilled in intuition, but also that it cannot even be clearly and distinctly intended. Derridean thought remains without hope, anticipating no future time in which we will be simply present to a fully just world or even a definitive concept of justice. But his despair is not a despair over meaning, and we might describe his more recent thought as a moral argument for meaning, the reflection of a moral faith seeking understanding.

This moral faith is not the faith of the intellectually elite, but the faith of all who assume that the distinction between justice and injustice is not *merely* convention and construct. It is by siding with common sense (and Plato) against the sophists on this issue, formulated in this limited way, that Derrida associates himself with the natural law tradition. By virtue of his lack of hope he remains further from Hegel than either Marx or Kierkegaard. But if Hegel stands for the ultimacy of meaning and Bataille for the ultimacy of nonmeaning, Derrida would seem to have moved beyond laughing at Hegel to a place where he and Hegel work together, however differently, in the vineyard of meaning.[37] In this respect the prodigal son is a chip off the old block. It is just possible that Hegel has the last laugh.

---

[37] This way of putting it would narrow rather than widen the gap between Derrida and Gadamer.

11

Derrida As Natural Law Theorist

POSTMODERN PHILOSOPHY in general and Derridian deconstruction in particular are rightly perceived as the most sustained critique of metaphysics since logical positivism. Since it is within the natural law traditions, ancient, medieval, and modern, that ethics is most unabashedly metaphysical, the title of this essay will appear to many as simply oxymoronic.

But there is a difference between positivism and postmodernism that must not be lost sight of. In the former case it was the proponents and practitioners of the position who insisted that the overthrow of metaphysics was also the end of ethics in any objective sense, leaving ethics to be a matter of personal preference and ethical language to be the expression or evocation of emotion. In the latter case this double negation, or, more precisely, the claim that the critique of metaphysics entails the overthrow of ethics, is to be found all but exclusively among the opponents of the position. Its practitioners frequently talk as if they are engaged in a morally significant critique of a variety of theories, institutions, and practices. Levinas combines a dramatic and creative account of how ethics is possible with a devastating critique of western ontology, and even Derrida goes so far as to say, "Nothing seems to me less outdated than the classical emancipatory ideal."[1] He insists that "a deconstructivist approach . . . does not necessarily lead to injustice, nor to the effacement of an opposition between just and unjust." It is not "a quasi-nihilistic abdication before the ethico-politico-juridical

---

[1] Jacques Derrida, "Force of Law: The 'Mystical Foundation of Authority,' " in *Deconstruction and the Possibility of Justice,* ed. Drucilla Cornell, Michel Rosenfeld, and David Gray Carlson (New York: Routledge, 1992), p. 28. Page references in the text will be to this essay. In addition to this very important essay by Derrida, this volume of over four hundred pages contains thirteen diverse and illuminating essays on its title topic by scholars in law, government and political science, African American studies, comparative literature, and philosophy.

question of justice" in spite of the fact that "certain people have an interest in spreading this confusion" (p. 19).

No one has ever doubted that Derrida has ethical or ethically significant political commitments. But it has often been claimed that these are externally or contingently related to deconstruction, understood as a strategy of reading linked to a kind of Gödelian epistemology or semantics of finitude that can be read as a kind of skepticism.[2] A "weak defense" of Derrida would try to show that his ethical commitments are not undercut by deconstruction, that it is not the "everything is permitted" open invitation to ethical nihilism or cynicism that it has sometimes been said to be. A "strong defense" would try to show that there is an affirmative ethical significance to deconstruction.

The strong claim has been recently developed in books by Simon Critchley and Drucilla Cornell. Critchley claims both that deconstruction as a certain way of reading texts "can, and indeed should, be understood as an ethical demand," and that there is "an unconditional ethical imperative, which . . . is the source of the injunction that produces deconstruction."[3] Derrida himself seems closer to the second formulation when he says, "I mean that deconstruction is, in itself, a positive response to an alterity which necessarily calls, summons or motivates. Deconstruction is therefore vocation—a response to a call."[4]

Critchley himself quotes at length from another passage in which Derrida responds to a question about the relation of his critique of apartheid to deconstruction:

> In the different texts I have written on (against) apartheid, I have on several occasions spoken of "unconditional" affirmation or of "unconditional" "appeal." This has also happened to me in other "contexts" and each time that I speak of the link between decon-

---

[2] Derrida himself calls attention to the Gödelian aspect of his thought. See *Disseminations,* trans. Barbara Johnson (Chicago: University of Chicago Press, 1981), p. 219; *Writing and Difference,* trans. Alan Bass (Chicago: University of Chicago Press, 1978), p. 162; Rodolphe Gasché, *The Tain of the Mirror: Derrida and the Philosophy of Reflection* (Cambridge, Mass.: Harvard University Press, 1986), pp. 240 ff.

[3] Simon Critchley, *The Ethics of Deconstruction: Derrida and Levinas* (Oxford: Blackwell, 1992), p. xi.

[4] Richard Kearney, *Dialogues with Contemporary Continental Thinkers* (Manchester: Manchester University Press, 1984), p. 118.

struction and the "yes." Now, the very least that can be said of unconditionality (a word that I use not by accident to recall the character of the categorical imperative in its Kantian form) is that it is independent of every determinate context. . . . Not that it is simply present (existent) elsewhere, outside of all context; rather, it intervenes in the determination of a context from its very inception, and from an injunction, a law, a responsibility that transcends this or that determination of a given context. Following this, what remains is to articulate this unconditionality with the determinate (Kant would say, hypothetical) conditions of this or that context; and this is the moment of strategies, of rhetorics, of ethics, and of politics. The structure thus described supposes both that there are only contexts, that nothing *exists* outside context, as I have often said, but also that the limit of the frame or the border of the context always entails a clause of nonclosure. The outside penetrates and thus determines the inside.[5]

That this notion of a law that transcends every context and renders hypothetical every contextualized expression of the law, whether in a written code or oral tradition, belongs to the natural law tradition is clear in Drucilla's attempt to articulate the "ethical aspiration" at the heart of Derrida's thought. She portrays deconstruction as the philosophy of the limit that "exposes the quasi-transcendental conditions that establish any system, including a legal system . . . [and] demonstrates how the very establishment of the system as a system implies a *beyond* to it, precisely by virtue of what it excludes." It is precisely this limit, this beyond, that "serves as the limit to any attempt to collapse justice into positive law."[6]

This opposition to legal positivism as well as to any communitarianism that seeks "to resolve ethical, political, and legal questions of the day by invoking the current conventions of a given society" is what permits Cornell to speak of the "shared presuppositions" that link Derrida to the liberal jurisprudence of Rawls

---

[5] "Toward an Ethic of Discussion," afterword to *Limited Inc*, trans. Samuel Weber and Jeffrey Mehlman (Evanston: Northwestern University Press, 1988), pp. 152–53. Critchley suggests that this "nothing *exists* outside context" is the best commentary on the infamous Derridian *"There is nothing outside of the text"*; *The Ethics of Deconstruction*, pp. 31–44.

[6] Drucilla Cornell, *The Philosophy of the Limit* (New York: Routledge, 1992), pp. 1–2.

and Nagel.[7] If we remember that Dworkin has astutely shown how Rawls's theory of justice "presupposes a deep theory that assumes natural rights,"[8] and that natural rights theory is a branch of natural law theory, the title of this essay may begin to sound, if not yet plausible, at least not totally perverse.

If sympathetic interpreters are right in giving what I have called the "strong defense" of Derrida, it can only be because there are grounds for such an interpretation in his own text. Nowhere are such grounds more explicit than in his essay "Force of Law."[9] He realizes that to speak of "Deconstruction and the Possibility of Justice"[10] is to raise the question "Does deconstruction insure, permit, authorize the possibility of justice?" (p. 4). He points to texts in which he overtly thematizes ethical and political matters, discussing, for example, Levinas, Hegel's *Philosophy of Right,* or Nelson Mandela and apartheid. But he realizes that this will constitute only a weak defense unless he can show that deconstructive employments of such notions as undecidability, singularity, and difference are "at least obliquely discourses on justice" (p. 7). If deconstruction destroys the space in which ethical commitments can be anything more than subjective preferences, it will be the enemy of justice no matter how politically correct its practitioners are with reference, for example, to apartheid.

Derrida seeks to show that deconstruction is not such a destruction. The most pervasive assumption of the entire essay is that justice cannot be identified with positive law (*droit*). He wants "to insist right away on reserving the possibility of a justice, indeed of a law that not only exceeds or contradicts 'law' (*droit*) but also, perhaps has no relation to law, or maintains such a strange relation to it that it may just as well command the '*droit*' that excludes it" (pp. 5–6). This assumption, which links Derrida to the natural law tradition(s), is what enables him to

---

[7] Ibid., p. 8.

[8] Ronald Dworkin, *Taking Rights Seriously* (Cambridge, Mass.: Harvard University Press, 1977), p. 177 in the context of pp. 168–83.

[9] See n. 1 above.

[10] The title of the conference at which he first gave his paper as a lecture, which was held in 1989 at Cardozo Law School, as well as of the volume growing out of the conference.

say that deconstruction perhaps belongs more to the fields of law and theology than to literature, where it has become most popular (p. 8). But the question remains: Is this natural law posture contingently, even perhaps inconsistently, added on to deconstructive theory and practice, or does it find a rationale for itself precisely in them?

Derrida's claim that the latter is the case is bold: "Deconstruction is justice" (p. 15). But this is not to say that it is natural law theory in its usual guise. In its most familiar forms, natural law theory is, first, the ontological claim that there is a higher law, rooted in that which is most truly real, by which all human encodings or inscriptions of law are to be judged, and, second, the epistemological claim that human reason has the capacity to know this law in the strong sense that philosophy has traditionally designated with such terms as *episteme, scientia, Wissenschaft*, and self-evidence, as in "we hold these truths to be self-evident."

Any claim to knowledge of this sort is problematic for Derrida. He sees it as expressing a metaphysics of presence that presupposes both an atomistic semantics that isolates meaning from context and an intuitionist epistemology that promises the human knower direct and complete presence to such meanings. Derrida seeks to deconstruct this Platonism, to which so much of the western tradition is but a series of footnotes, by showing both the unsurpassable contextuality of meaning and the closely intertwined temporality of understanding that leaves the all-presentness of pure presence as a wish-fulfilling illusion.[11]

This is why, when Derrida says that "Deconstruction, while seeming not to 'address' the problem of justice, has done nothing but address it," he immediately adds, "if only *obliquely* . . . one cannot speak *directly* about justice, thematize or objectivize justice, say 'this is just' or even less 'I am just,' without immediately betraying justice, if not law (*droit*)" (p. 10; cf. pp. 7, 17, 23). There are two quite different claims here. Plato would have no

---

[11] See, for example, "Différance," in *Margins of Philosophy*, trans. Alan Bass (Chicago: University of Chicago Press, 1982); *Speech and Phenomena*, trans. David B. Allison (Evanston: Northwestern University Press, 1973); and *Limited Inc*, noting especially the essay "Signature Event Context," which is also found in *Margins*.

problem with the notion that we can never call anything or anyone just, since participation is always partial. But just to the degree that he thinks the soul can free itself of the body in order to "contemplate things by themselves with the soul by itself,"[12] he believes it is possible to speak directly about justice itself.[13]

But suppose he is wrong. Suppose there is something profoundly right about the varied but widespread arguments, going back not just to Kierkegaard and Nietzsche but even to Hume and Reid, that call into question the foundationalism, the intuitionism, and the totalism so dear to tradition, and, in each case, cast doubt on the transcendence of human temporality by human knowledge. One can tie the notion of natural law so tightly to the classical ideals of *episteme, scientia,* and *Wissenschaft* that every attempt to articulate the situated finitude of human knowledge will become, in effect, the ally of legal positivism and ethical relativism; or one can seek to articulate the idea of a higher law to which every human code is answerable in a conceptual framework not constituted (or constricted) by those ideals. It is clearly the latter alternative that Derrida has embarked upon.

Because he is a natural law theorist he cannot ignore the crucial distinctions between *nomos* and *physis* or, more particularly, between "positive law and natural law." But he cannot simply help himself to them either, since the assumption of an unambiguous boundary between them presupposes our direct access or pure presence to nature as that which is outside or independent of every human text or context. So deconstruction will be an "interrogation" or a "problematization of the foundations of law, morality, and politics," directed toward "destabilizing or complicating" these distinctions (p. 8). To show that the difference between nature and convention or art is not as neat as tradition would have it, Derrida will seek to show how much of what we take to be nature is the product of convention *and* how what we recognize as convention is not devoid of nature at work in it. In making the first of these moves, Derrida links himself with

---

[12] Phaedo 66e.

[13] This is an important reason why John Wild is right to include Plato as one of the founding fathers of the natural law tradition. See *Plato's Modern Enemies and the Theory of Natural Law* (Chicago: University of Chicago Press, 1953).

the sophists. By refusing to stop at that point and by insisting on the second move, Derrida decisively distances himself from them. In this way he rejects the classical either/or (that bears the name of Plato) between sophistry, subjectivism, conventionalism, emotivism, relativism, and so forth, on the one hand, and Knowledge as *episteme, scientia,* and *Wissenschaft,* on the other.[14]

Since Derrida's account of how nature is at work in convention presupposes his account of how convention often masquerades as nature, we must look at both moments. First the latter. The laws and customs of a people, at least their most basic ones, are often taken to be expressions of nature—discoveries, not inventions. But in the beginning of these laws and customs is an "originary violence" that marks them indelibly as inventions and conventions (p. 6).

Derrida is not simply repeating, though of course he is not denying, the Augustinian point about the violent origin of the state. He recognizes "the differential character of force" (p. 7) and knows that force can be "direct or indirect, physical or symbolic, exterior or interior, brutal or subtly discursive and hermeneutics, coercive or regulative, and so forth" (p. 6), and his focus is on the non-physical, the hermeneutical violence at the origin of law. He is engaged in linguistic rather than military analysis, which is why he calls the founding violence "mystical. Here a silence is walled up in the violent structure of the founding act" (p. 14).

The point is not that physical violence is extra-linguistic, but rather that language itself has a limit: "The very emergence of justice and law, the founding and justifying moment that institutes law implies a performative force, which is always an *interpretative force* . . . the operation that amounts to founding, inaugurating, justifying law (*droit*), making law, would consist of a *coup de force,* of a performative and therefore *interpretative violence*" (p. 13, my emphasis). What makes the original interpretation an act of violence? The fact that it has force without justification. Rather than being a direct reading of the nature of

---

[14] In *The Concept of Irony* Kierkegaard presents the negativity of Socratic ignorance and Socratic irony as a third possibility over against Platonic speculation on the one hand, and sophistic nihilism on the other.

things, this act occurs in an epistemic state of nature where "no justice and no previous law . . . could guarantee or contradict or invalidate [it]. No justificatory discourse could or should insure the role of metalanguage in relation to the performativity of institutive language or to its dominant interpretation" (p. 13).

In other words, law is a construct. But just because it is constructible, it is deconstructible: "The fact that law is deconstructible is not bad news. We may even see in this a stroke of luck for politics, for all historical progress." How so? "Deconstruction is justice" (pp. 14–15). In other words, the disruptive force that reveals the originary violence that constitutes "the mystical foundation of authority" is not sophistry trying to pry itself loose from the constraints of nature, but justice unmasking the claims of contingency to be necessity, of convention to be nature, and of positive law to be justice. This is how Derrida sees nature to be at work in convention, precisely by countering its claims to be nature.

To say that deconstruction is justice at work in the world, justice as judgment, we might say, is to present an alternative to the Platonic account according to which justice in itself is first directly apprehended (but definitely not constructed) by the philosopher king and then applied to the construction of social institutions, functioning like an artisan's blueprint. On the alternative account nature is at work in convention not through the pure insight that justifies the construction but through the insight into impurity that deconstructs the justifications.[15] The Derridean battle hymn goes something like this:

> No eyes have had a vision of the glory of the Lord;
> But he's trampling out the vintage where the grapes of wrath are stored;
> He hath loosed the fateful lightning of his deconstructive sword;
> His justice marches on.

Of course, Derrida does not speak of God as the source of justice. Still, while it is clear that his version of natural law theory

---

[15] Drucilla Cornell sees Adorno as a founding father of philosophical postmodernism. The chapter of *The Philosophy of the Limit* devoted to him bears the title "The Ethical Message of Negative Dialectics" and expresses the Derridean argument very succinctly.

is an alternative guided by epistemological disagreement with the tradition, we can ask about its ontological dimension. Just before he says, "Deconstruction is justice," he says, "Justice in itself, if such a thing exists, outside or beyond law, is not deconstructible" (p. 14). Derrida is careful about language, and just as he speaks of an "unconditional" appeal in order deliberately to evoke Kant, here he speaks of "justice in itself" in order to evoke Plato. He wants to express his agreement with Plato that while positive law is constructible and therefore deconstructible, justice itself is not.

But Derrida is not quite a Platonist, and a ringing "if" interrupts what might have been part of a Platonic credo: "Justice in itself is not deconstructible." The qualification is explosive: "if such a thing exists, outside or beyond law." For in the deconstructive texts that are at issue here, he makes clear that this assumption is counterfactual. We have already seen him say, speaking of that Kantian "unconditional" imperative, "Not that it is simply present (existent) elsewhere, outside of all context; rather, it intervenes in the determination of a context from its very inception. . . . The structure thus described supposes both that there are only contexts, that nothing *exists* outside context, as I have often said, but also that the limit of the frame or the border of the context always entails a clause of nonclosure. The outside penetrates and thus determines the inside." In other words, the outside is at work inside, but does not simply exist outside.

Derrida, it would seem, is clearly committed to saying that justice in itself does not exist. But, in keeping with his search for an alternative to both Plato and the sophists, he makes it clear that he cannot do without the idea of justice in itself. Deconstruction as a challenge to "the self-authorization of [positive] law" is possible "as an experience of the impossible, there where, even if it does not exist (or does not yet exist, or never does exist), *there is* justice" (p. 15).

Is Derrida perhaps groping for the notion of a regulative idea, an idea we cannot do without but that does not correspond to anything that can be given in our experience? Not quite. He does not find this a welcome suggestion (pp. 25–26). For Kant, the problem with a regulative idea was not that we could not give a clear and stable definition of it, but rather that nothing was capable of both being experienced and satisfying the concept. For Derrida there is no such confidence at the conceptual level. Deconstruction is rather "an interrogation of the origin, grounds and limits of our conceptual, theoretical or normative apparatus" (p. 20). It is not just our practices and institutions, but our concepts and theories as well that are perennially penultimate.

Still, the idea of justice in itself functions as a quasi-regulative idea for Derrida. It is not some thing that exists outside of every human context, and it is not an ideal essence to which we can give a fixed and final meaning. It is a bit like what Kierkegaard had in mind when he spoke of "thoughts which wound from behind."[16] Though we cannot get them out in front of us where they are fully present to us and we can master them, they nevertheless insinuate themselves into our thinking, disturbing its complacency in ways we can neither predict nor control. They ambush our absolutes. On Derrida's view it is precisely as deconstruction that the idea of justice in itself wounds our legal systems, both as theory and as practice, from behind.

The current philosophical scene is largely dominated by the search on many different fronts for an alternative to the classical either/or: Plato or the sophists. Caught between an absolutism that seems to many no longer theoretically defensible and a relativism that seems to many to be morally intolerable in its flirtation with cynicism and nihilism, much of contemporary philosophy is the quest for an escape from this dilemma. In terms of ethics in general and of legal theory, more specifically, Derrida's theory of natural law represents a serious contribution to the ongoing conversation. His essay "Force of Law" and the collection of essays published with it deserve the careful attention of those engaged in this pursuit, as well as of those happily perched on one horn of the traditional dilemma.

---

[16] The title of part III of Kierkegaard's *Christian Discourses*, trans. Walter Lowrie (Princeton: Princeton University Press, 1971), is "Thoughts Which Wound from Behind—for Edification."

12

Faith As the Overcoming of Ontological Xenophobia

"MY PA CAN LICK YOUR PA!" Thus, once upon a time, did aspiring machismo seek vicarious victory over its enemies.

There is something of an echo of this boast in the claim "My God is more radically other than your God!" The wording may not be as fully explicit in the second case, but the transfer of excellence from the greater to the lesser is, if anything, more satisfying. For when I make this claim I not only bask in the transcendent glory of this glorious transcendence—I take credit for seeing and saying this otherness better than you. Thus I claim to be holier than thou when I claim, throwing grammar to the winds, that my God is wholier other than thine.

Philosophically speaking, nothing is quite as PC today as alterity. The result is that when we present our God as the *ens alterissimum*, we may feel compelled to write *ens* with a *kreuzweise Durchstreichung* or *sous rature*; but the term *alterissimum* is that than which a more literal and univocal term cannot be conceived.

By pointing to the trendiness of our theme I do not mean to dismiss it. It has been around too long and has engaged too many thinkers of the first order to be nothing but a con*temporary* blip on the scene of history, condemned to disappear like hula hoops and leisure suits. But in the life of the mind fads and the lure of the avant-garde are always at least as dangerous as the resistance to new ideas, minimally by wasting time reinventing the wheel, and maximally by naively taking as self-evident what is merely con*temporary* orthodoxy.

One danger at the present moment is that in our hurry to define the otherness of the indefinable we may forget what is at issue. Or, to put the point more precisely, in our eagerness to attain the philosophical goals of overcoming onto-theo-logy, the metaphysics of presence, logocentrism, and so forth, we may forget to reflect on the religious significance of the project. When and to the degree that we do this, we make our philosophical goals at once autonomous and abstract and invite the Pascals of the world to ask whether we have not made ourselves irrelevant to the believing soul, whether we have not made ourselves into a Socrates whom Euthyphro has no reason to take seriously.

Accordingly, I want to pay attention not only to how we spell out the otherness of God but also to the kind of religious life that goes with each spelling. In this context otherness often means unknowability, and I will begin by focusing on ways of speaking of the ineffability of God. Hegel and Feuerbach remind us of two ways in which this theme can be highly problematic from a religious perspective. In response to the idea that we can know with certainty *that* God exists but have no articulable knowledge of *what* God may be, Hegel claims that this is an open invitation to fill in the content arbitrarily so that, as he is fond of saying, the Dalai Lama or even a cow can be said to be God. Thus he accuses Jacobi, with whom he associates this form of the unknowability thesis, of a "deification of the subject."[1] Others might call this subjectivism fideism or decisionism.

Feuerbach's reading of the unknowability thesis is a bit darker. He suspects that moral fault may underlie such a philosophical fallacy. Declaring God unknowable permits those who wish both to forget God and to salve their religious conscience to have their cake and eat it too. They affirm God's existence: "But this existence does not affect or incommode [them]; it is a merely negative existence, an existence without existence, a self-contradictory existence,—a state of being which, as to its effects, is not distinguishable from non-being. . . . The alleged religious horror of limiting God by positive predicates is only the irreli-

---

[1] G. W. F. Hegel, *Faith and Knowledge,* trans. Walter Cerf and H. S. Harris (Albany: SUNY Press, 1977), p. 149. Cf. p. 97 and ¶¶ 63 and 72 of the "Lesser Logic." Hegel's most sustained discussion of this matter comes in the first four of his "Lectures on the Proofs of the Existence of God," found in vol. III of his *Lectures on the Philosophy of Religion,* trans. E. B. Spiers and J. Burdon Sanderson (New York: Humanities, 1962). Cf. my discussion in *Hegel, Freedom, and Modernity* (Albany: SUNY Press, 1992), ch. 11, and, for context, *Hegel's Lectures on the Philosophy of Religion,* ed. Peter Hodgson (Berkeley: University of California Press, 1984), vol. I, pp. 159–63, 260–68, and 407–13.

gious wish to know nothing more of God, to banish God from the mind."[2] In short, negative theology is as inherently ambivalent as the Freudian symptom. Its dialectic is not simply that of theoretical affirmation and denial. In the context Feuerbach describes the theoretical negation is in the service of a practical denial that renders the theoretical affirmation hollow and impotent.

Without denying the force of these warnings, we can acknowledge the genuinely religious meaning of the following prayer:

> I shall never want to define You, O God, for I cannot worship what I comprehend.[3]

It reminds us both that one of the important religious concerns we need to keep front and center is the question of what is worthy of worship, and that negative theology or, more generally, epistemological expressions of the otherness of God can have as their motive and proper function the protection of the believing soul from idolatry, from domesticating the divine by rendering it too easily and too fully at the disposal of our conceptual schemes.

Although Heidegger's critique of onto-theo-logy belongs primarily to a thinking of Being he is careful to distinguish from the life of faith, he is not unaware of its religious import. The "onto-theo-logical constitution of metaphysics," as he understands it, means that God enters into philosophy, but only on philosophy's terms. God must be the unity of the universal and the highest in order to be *das Erste* and *das Letzte* as *ratio* and as

---

[2] Ludwig Feuerbach, *The Essence of Christianity,* trans. George Eliot (New York: Harper & Brothers, 1957), p. 15. Cf. Derrida's discussion of the possibility that "those who have nothing to say or don't want to know anything" might mimic negative theology: "How to Avoid Speaking: Denials," in *Derrida and Negative Theology,* ed. Harold Coward and Toby Foshay (Albany: SUNY Press, 1992), p. 75. In this passage he both acknowledges the possibility Feuerbach describes and suggests that the negative theology he wants to discuss is up to something else.

[3] Leslie F. Brandt, *Psalms/Now* (St. Louis: Concordia, 1973), p. 175. Cf. Meister Eckhart, "If I had a God whom I could understand, I should never consider him God"; Sermon 83 in *Meister Eckhart: The Essential Sermons, Commentaries, Treatises, and Defense,* trans. Edmund Colledge, O.S.A., and Bernard McGinn (New York: Paulist Press, 1981), p. 207. Eckhart purports to be quoting, but seems to be paraphrasing, with evident approval.

Λόγος. In other words, God must not merely be an all-encompassing principle in and for Godself, but in and for the totalizing project of human thought. God must be Alpha and Omega in order that the human thinker can stand at the beginning and end of all things, including all in a comprehensive gaze. Thus the problem with causal talk about God is not that it reduces God to a kind of cosmic billiard ball; for, especially in the ex nihilo tradition, metaphysics has by no means forgotten the difference between infinite, creative causality and finite, efficient causality. The problem is rather that God is conceived as *causa prima* and *causa sui* in order to satisfy demands of a particular, human intellectual project, one that culminates, anything but innocently, in modern technology.[4]

I needn't remind you that Heidegger sees this project as danger. But it may be worth recalling the degree to which he identifies this danger as religious. In this misinterpretation of the unconcealed, "even God can . . . lose all that is exalted and holy, the mysteriousness of his distance."[5] When the will to power becomes the project of total dominion of a world totally at its disposal, God and the gods are indeed dead: "God is still not a living God when we persist in trying to master the real without taking God's reality seriously." In the "insurrection" or "uprising" in which humankind claims "unlimited" and "unconditional" dominion over the earth, not only Being but God as well is reduced to a value in Nietzsche's sense of the term—namely, whatever serves as means or condition for the enhancement and preservation of human life: "The ultimate blow against God and against the suprasensory world consists in the fact that God, the first of beings, is degraded to the highest value . . . not that God is held to be unknowable, not that God's existence is demonstrated to be unprovable, but rather that the god held to be real is elevated to the highest value." Heidegger reminds us that this

---

[4] This paragraph is an interpretative summary of Heidegger's *Identity and Difference*, trans. Joan Stambaugh (New York: Harper & Row, 1969), pp. 55–61.

[5] "The Question Concerning Technology," in *The Question Concerning Technology and Other Essays*, trans. William Lovitt (New York: Harper & Row, 1977), p. 26. Heidegger adds, "in the light of causality, God can sink to the level of a cause, of *causa efficiens*. He then becomes, even in theology, the god of the philosophers."

"elevation," which often occurs in the name of intelligibility, does not come from atheism, but "from the believers and their theologians who discourse on the being that is of all beings most in being . . . seen from out of faith, their thinking and their talking is sheer blasphemy if it meddles in the theology of faith."[6]

Sounding a lot like Luther, Pascal, and Kierkegaard, Heidegger interprets the onto-theo-logical constitution of metaphysics, or, if you like, the metaphysical constitution of onto-theo-logy, as a degradation of God and a danger to the life of faith; and, in a crucial passage, he frames this analysis as a plea for a rediscovery of the divine alterity. As he articulates the danger, including the religious danger, of Enframing, the project in which humans become at once lords of the earth and raw materials or standing reserve, he speaks of "one final delusion: It seems as though man everywhere and always encounters only himself. . . . *In truth, however, precisely nowhere does man today any longer encounter himself, i.e., his essence* [or true self]." Even Enframing is a "claim," but in failing to recognize this being spoken to, exhorted, addressed, he fails to see that he "*can never* encounter only himself."[7]

This is one point at which the difference between Heidegger's critique of metaphysics and Nietzsche's comes most sharply into focus. While confessing his Dionysian faith, Zarathustra claims that "in the end one experiences only oneself."[8] In Heidegger's view one could not more eloquently express the danger that the metaphysical tradition represents; and by leaving Zarathustra's

---

[6] "The Word of Nietzsche: 'God Is Dead,' " in *The Question Concerning Technology*, pp. 99–107.

[7] "The Question Concerning Technology," p. 27. On the issue of humanity as answer or response to claims placed upon it, cf. *Identity and Difference*, pp. 31–34.

[8] Friedrich Nietzsche, *Thus Spoke Zarathustra*, part III, "The Wanderer." Derrida calls attention to a passage where Kant raises the question whether the voice of the moral law "comes from man, from the perfected power of his own reason, or whether it comes from an other, whose nature is unknown to us and speaks to man through this, his own reason," only to dismiss the question as "only speculative." "Of an Apocalyptic Tone Newly Adopted in Philosophy," in *Derrida and Natural Theology*, p. 47. The passage, which comes from the essay whose title Derrida transposes, is at the very heart of Kant's philosophy of religion, and it shows how much his moral theology resembles Nietzsche's immoralist anti-theology in its allergy to alterity.

credo unchallenged, Nietzsche shows that he more nearly belongs to the onto-theo-logical tradition than to its overcoming. To use language to which I shall return, Nietzsche is a Neoplatonist in the grips of ontological xenophobia, while Heidegger is, if not an instance of the Augustinian faith that overcomes this fear of meeting a stranger, at least someone who deliberately holds open the space for such a possibility.

I want to present this Neoplatonist/Augustinian typology as an alternative and corrective to the Augustinian/Thomistic distinction presented by Tillich in his famous essay "The Two Types of Philosophy of Religion."[9] But first I want to limit the field of discussion to positions that are genuinely religious and thus are directly concerned with the otherness of God. Not all theological negation is negative theology. To try to clarify this point I turn more specifically to Derrida's insistence that deconstruction is not negative theology, a claim I find to be both well grounded and of surprising import.

There is no mystery as to why such a linkage has been suggested. When Derrida says that *différance* is neither a word nor a concept, that it belongs neither to sensibility nor to intelligibility, neither to existence nor to essence, neither to presence nor to absence, neither to activity nor to passivity, and that it is neither originary nor final, etc., he makes a gesture that inevitably evokes negative theology.[10] Yet, while acknowledging the basis of the allegation, he denies that he is a theologian of any sort.

Two of my friends, whose understanding of Derrida I envy, have quite different views about his relation to religion. One says, "Derrida doesn't have a religious bone in his body." The other finds his thought to be profoundly religious. Derrida himself identifies, while repudiating, one way of coming to the second conclusion. He notes that the study of negative theology could lead us to discover

the becoming-theological of all discourse. From the moment a proposition takes a negative form, the negativity that manifests

---

[9] Paul Tillich, "The Two Types of Philosophy of Religion," in *Theology of Culture* (New York: Oxford University Press, 1964).

[10] Jacques Derrida, "Différance," in *Margins of Philosophy,* trans. Alan Bass (Chicago: University of Chicago Press, 1982), pp. 3–9. Cf. "Denials," p. 74.

itself need only be pushed to the limit, and it at least resembles an apophatic theology. Every time I say: X is neither this nor that . . . I would start to speak of God. God's name would suit everything that may not be broached, approached, or designated, except in an indirect and negative manner. . . . If there is a work of negativity in discourse and predication, it will produce divinity. . . . God would be not merely the end, but the origin of this work of the negative. Not only would atheism not be the truth of negative theology; rather, God would be the truth of all negativity. One would thus arrive at a kind of proof of God—not a proof of the *existence* of God, but a proof of God *by His effects*. . . . 'God' would name *that without which* one would not know how to account for any negativity.

Derrida's comment on this line of thought is brusque to the point of being icy: "This reading will always be possible. Who could prohibit it?"[11]

But if Derrida cannot prohibit this reading, he does not adopt it either; instead he vigorously resists the suggestion that we construe the whence of negativity and alterity as divine. In 1968 he insists that deconstruction should be distinguished from negative theology on at least two grounds. First, it does not affirm the "superessentiality" according to which "God is refused the predicate of existence, only in order to acknowledge his superior, inconceivable, and ineffable mode of being."[12] Second, it does not include that *"nostalgia"* and *"hope"* for presence that he finds, for example, in Heidegger's "quest for the proper word and the unique name," the mystical moment that is always united with the skeptical moment in negative theology.[13]

In 1987 he repeats his insistence that his thinking does not rest on "that ontological wager of hyperessentiality that one finds at work both in Dionysius and in Meister Eckhart."[14] And once again he links this theme with the nostalgia and hope for presence that is the mystical side of their negative theologies, and which he describes as "a silent intuition of God," as "the prom-

---

[11] "Denials," pp. 76–77.

[12] "Différance," p. 6. Cf. p. 26: "This unnameable is not an ineffable Being which no name could approach: God, for example."

[13] Ibid., p. 27. Cf. "The Ends of Man," in *Margins of Philosophy*, pp. 123–34. Cf. "Of an Apocalyptic Tone," pp. 33–34, 53.

[14] "Denials," p. 78. Cf. p. 74.

ise of that presence given to intuition or vision . . . the immediacy of a presence . . . union with God," and as a mystic union "that is not an adequation but an unveiling . . . contact or vision, that pure intuition of the ineffable, that silent union with that which remains inaccessible to speech."[15]

To these themes he adds a new one. Not only does Pseudo-Dionysius, the paradigmatic negative theologian, affirm the reality of a God beyond being with whom he seeks union, but he does so in a prayer addressed to this God.[16] This prayer is "not a preamble, an accessory mode of access. It constitutes an essential moment . . . by addressing itself from the start to the other, to you. But to you as 'hyperessential and more than divine Trinity.' " Derrida's essay becomes a long reminder that prayer (and its partner, praise or encomium) addressed to a hyperessential you are not a part of deconstructive negativity. In Derrida's texts, where skepticism is not in the service of mysticism, the only vocatives are addressed to his readers.[17]

Thus does Derrida protest that he does not have a religious bone in his body. My point is not that his critique of the metaphysics of the sign could not be taken up into a genuinely theological reflection. It may be, for example, that a deconstructive analysis of undecidability can be helpful in developing a theological account of mystery, but that would not justify the identification of indeterminacy and mystery.[18]

It might be argued that religion does not require the structure of I and Thou (the you to whom Derrida does not pray), that the idea of a personal God or gods to whom prayer and encomium can be addressed in the second person belongs to theistic and polytheistic forms of religion but not to other forms that, for the sake of convenience if not precision, we might label pantheistic. Have we not reminded our students at least as often as we have

---

[15] Ibid., pp. 74, 79–80.

[16] For this prayer, see *The Mystical Theology*, in *Pseudo-Dionysius: The Complete Works*, trans. Colm Luibheid (New York: Paulist Press, 1987), p. 135.

[17] The quotation is from "Denials," p. 110. Cf. p. 112, where the necessity is linked to the desired union with God, and pp. 108–111, 117, and 129, where the theme is repeated.

[18] Roger Lundin is so eager to make the second point that he seems afraid to acknowledge the first. See *The Culture of Interpretation* (Grand Rapids, Mich.: Eerdmans, 1993), pp. 204–5.

been reminded ourselves that Buddhism, too, is a religion? But in Derrida's argument prayer does not stand alone; it comes on the scene as a moment in the pursuit of union with the superessential, a pursuit that lies at the heart of Buddhism. There is a promise of salvation, not to be found in Derrida, in the Buddhist assurance "There is, monks, an unborn, not become, not made, uncompounded."[19] In this context we could reformulate his insistence that he is not a negative theologian by saying that he gives a rather Buddhist account of Samsara that is *not* part of a theory of Nirvana. He has a kinship with the skepticism of Buddhist logic, but not with the mysticism of Buddhist hope.[20]

Finally, it might be argued that when Derrida says in another context, "Justice in itself, if such a thing exists, outside or beyond law, is not deconstructible. . . . Deconstruction is justice,"[21] he is at least leaving open a space for the hyperessential; for everything that is not beyond being or essence is deconstructible. If the whence of ethico-political negation can be described as something in itself, outside every text or context that might render it deconstructible,[22] why should we not say, as suggested above, that the whence of meta-predicative negation is also something beyond Being, something hyperessential?

Once again Derrida's response will be, "This reading will always be possible. Who could prohibit it?" But this time the situa-

---

[19] *Udana*, 80–81, in *Buddhist Texts through the Ages*, ed. Edward Conze et al. (New York: Harper & Row, 1964), p. 95.

[20] Derrida may stand closer to the Buddhist than to the Christian tradition that stems from Pseudo-Dionysius. The former represents a challenge to predication and naming as such, while the latter challenges them only in relation to the infinite. Cf. "Denials," p. 77. On the interface between Derrida and Buddhism, see David Loy, "The Deconstruction of Buddhism," in *Derrida and Negative Theology*. But unlike the negative theologians of every religious tradition, he stands with the Sartre who says, "Human reality therefore is by nature an unhappy consciousness with no possibility of surpassing its unhappy state"; *Being and Nothingness*, trans. Hazel Barnes (New York: Philosophical Library, 1956), p. 90.

[21] Jacques Derrida, "Force of Law: The 'Mystical Foundation of Authority,' " in *Deconstruction and the Possibility of Justice*, ed. Drucilla Cornell, Michel Rosenfeld, and David Gray Carlson (New York: Routledge, 1992), pp. 14–15.

[22] Here I am following the suggestion of Simon Critchley that the best reading of "There is nothing outside the text" is "There is nothing outside of context." See section 1.6 of *The Ethics of Deconstruction: Derrida and Levinas* (Oxford: Blackwell, 1992).

tion is different. I don't know whether we should describe the Derrida who speaks of a possible justice in itself as under pressure from or under the spell of Levinas. But in either case, he has opened the door to the hyperessential. Still, it is not clear that we have anything religious enough to be called God, or even the sacred. Derrida surely does not address justice in itself as "you," either in prayer or praise; nor is there either nostalgia or hope for soteriological union with it on some mystical or eschatological journey outside of text or context.[23] Others may have argued that the ethical ultimately unfolds into the religious—who could prohibit them?—but he does not. We do not have to take his interpretation of his own work as final and absolute in order to recognize that he interprets deconstruction as not having a religious bone in its body. Moreover, he has given us strong reasons not to conflate undecidability with sacred mystery or *différance* with the God beyond Being to whom Dionysius and Eckhart pray.

My thesis to this point might seem to be that to find genuine reflection on the otherness of God we must shake free from Derrida and turn directly to Dionysius and Eckhart, who pray to the hyperessential Trinity. But the suggestion I want to make is more nearly the opposite. Although they clearly fit the Derridean definition of the negative theologian, it might be Derrida who brings us closer to a genuine otherness of the divine. For their thought is substantially governed by a Neoplatonism that relegates the divine alterity to the realm of appearance, denying its reality. To the degree that this is the case, they suffer from what I call ontological xenophobia, the fear of meeting a stranger, even if the stranger should be God.

This phrase "meeting a stranger" comes from the already mentioned essay by Tillich. In it he distinguishes two types of encounter with the divine and, correspondingly, two types of philosophy of religion. On the one hand is the "Augustinian"

---

[23] That Derrida is sensitive to the close linkage between the mystical and the eschatological in terms of the nostalgia and hope for pure presence is clear from "Of an Apocalyptic Tone." Their virtual interchangeability is nicely illustrated in Gershom Scholem's *The Messianic Idea in Judaism* (New York: Schocken, 1971).

type whose way of approaching God he describes as "overcoming estrangement," while on the other hand is the Thomistic way, described as "meeting a stranger" (p. 10).[24] "In the first way man discovers *himself* when he discovers God; he discovers something that is identical with himself although it transcends him infinitely, something from which he is estranged, but from which he never has been and never can be separated" (p. 10).

This would be a good description of many Hindu accounts of the relation of the finite self to Brahman or Atman, as in the *Chandogya Upanishad,* with its refrain "That is Reality. That is Atman (Soul). That art thou, Svetaketu."[25] And it would be a good description of the Mahayana Buddhist claim that the Buddha nature is the true nature of everyone and everything:

> The Lord Buddha on his lion-throne
> Dwells in each particle of sand and stone.[26]

It would equally be a good interpretation of Meister Eckhart, to whom I shall turn rather than to Pseudo-Dionysius. In the two sermons quoted by Derrida to illustrate the "ontological wager of hyperessentiality" in negative theology, Eckhart stresses that it is the task of the intellect to apprehend God naked: "The intellect pulls off the coat from God and perceives him bare, as he is stripped of goodness and of being and of all names."[27] "But if all images are detached from the soul, and it contemplates only the Simple One, then the soul's naked being finds the naked, formless being of the divine unity, which is there a being above being . . . how noble is that acceptance, when the soul's being can accept nothing else than the naked unity of

---

[24] Page references to Tillich in the text are from *Theology of Culture.* See n. 9 above.

[25] The Thirteen Principal Upanishads, trans. Robert Ernest Hume (London: Oxford, 1921), 6.8–6.16, pp. 244–50. The same idea, expressed in the formula, "one only, without a second," so central to the thought of Shankara, is found nearby in the same Upanishad at 6.2, p. 241.

[26] Quoted by Edward Conze in *Buddhism: Its Essence and Development* (New York: Harper & Row, 1975), p. 149. Conze adds by way of commentary: "The Mahayana came to the conclusion that it is really the Buddha in us who does the seeking and that it is the Buddha nature in us which seeks Buddha-hood."

[27] Sermon 9, *Quasi stella matutina,* in *Meister Eckhart: Teacher and Preacher,* ed. Bernard McGinn (New York: Paulist Press, 1986), p. 258.

God!"[28] But in order to do this, "You ought to sink down out of all your your-ness, and flow into his his-ness, and your 'yours' and his 'his' ought to become one 'mine'. . . . . But if I am to perceive God without a medium, then I must just become him, and he must become me. I say more: God must just become me, and I must just become God, so completely one that this 'he' and this 'I' become and are one 'is,' and, in this is-ness, eternally perform one work."[29]

If such passages highlight the great gulf fixed between negative theology and Derridean deconstruction, they echo in the passages that signify the deep kinship between Meister Eckhart and Hegel. Drawing on several sermons, the latter quotes the former as saying, "The eye with which God sees me is the eye with which I see him; my eye and his eye are one and the same. . . . If God did not exist nor would I; if I did not exist nor would he. But there is no need to know this, for there are things that are easily misunderstood."[30] In the sermon where Eckhart identifies his eye and the divine eye, he also says, "All this [the eternal Father] reveals to us completely in his only-begotten Son and teaches us that we are this same Son," adding that "there is something in the soul that is so closely related to God that it is one [with him] and not just united. It is one and has nothing in common with anything nor does anything created have anything at all in common with it. . . . If a person were completely like this, he would be completely uncreated and uncreateable. . . . Now all things are alike in God and are God himself."[31]

Similarly, in the sermon where Eckhart makes his own existence a condition of God's, he also says that the soul should be

---

[28] Sermon 83, *Renovamini spiritu*, in *Meister Eckhart: The Essential Sermons*, p. 206. If Plotinus is the father of these last two passages, Plato is the grandfather when he speaks of "the man who pursues the truth by applying his pure and unadulterated thought to the pure and unadulterated object" and makes it his goal to "contemplate things by themselves with the soul by itself"; *Phaedo* 66a–e.

[29] *Renovamini spiritu*, pp. 207–8.

[30] Georg Wilhelm Friedrich Hegel, *Lectures on the Philosophy of Religion*, ed. Peter Hodgson (Berkeley: University of California Press, 1984), vol. I, pp. 347–48 (from the 1824 lectures).

[31] Sermon 12, *Qui audit me*, in *Meister Eckhart: Teacher and Preacher*, pp. 267–70. Cf. Sermon 10, *In diebus suis*, p. 261, "The same knowledge in which God knows himself is the knowledge of every detached spirit and nothing else."

without will, even the will to do God's will, without knowledge, even the knowledge of God's work in the soul, and without possessions, even of a place in which God could work. For all such modes of being involve

> distinction. Therefore I pray to God that he may make me free of 'God,' for my real being is above God if we take 'God' to be the beginning of created things. For in the same being of God where God is above being and above distinction, there I myself was, there I willed myself and committed myself to create this man. Therefore I am the cause of myself in the order of my being, which is eternal, and not in the order of my becoming, which is temporal. And therefore I am unborn.[32]

Derrida finds this kind of talk as troubling as did the church authorities. It denies the finitude we experience in what he calls "the structure of the trace": "Language has started without us, in us and before us. This is what theology calls God." There is a necessity in language that beckons

> toward the event of an order or of a promise that does not belong to what one currently calls history. . . . Order or promise, this injunction commits (me), in a rigorously asymmetrical manner, even before I have been able to say *I*, to sign such a *provocation* in order to reappropriate it for myself and restore the symmetry. That in no way mitigates my responsibility; on the contrary. There would be no responsibility without this *prior coming* (*prévenance*), of the trace, or if autonomy were first or absolute. Autonomy itself would not be possible, nor would respect for the law (sole 'cause' of this respect) in the strictly Kantian meaning of these words.[33]

The Levinasian, even Habermasian character of this notion of an obligation (not merely grammatical) that precedes my

---

[32] Sermon 52, *Beati pauperes spiritu,* in *Meister Eckhart: The Essential Sermons,* pp. 199–202. Cf. the claim of Empedocles, "I go about you as an immortal God, no longer a mortal"; Kathleen Freeman, *Ancilla to the Pre-Socratic Philosophers* (Cambridge, Mass.: Harvard University Press, 1966), p. 64. Eckhart's quotation marks around "God," which Hegel ignores, are the sign of a Neoplatonic distinction between God as the One beyond and before all distinction and "God" as the creator, distinct from the world. When Eckhart says, "When I stood in my first cause, I then had no 'God,' and then I was my own cause. . . . So therefore let us pray to God that we may be free of 'God' " he expresses the nostalgia and hope for pure presence of which Derrida speaks. See n. 13 above.

[33] "Denials," p. 99.

speech, that awaits my entry into any and every language game, is clear enough. What I want to call attention to is that these remarks are directed specifically against Eckhart and Hegel.[34] Derrida's quarrel with negative theology is not just that it begins and ends in prayer, or that it makes a mystical/eschatological wager of hyperessentiality he is unwilling to make, but also that it is allergic to that alterity, "what theology calls God" (who could prohibit it?) though he does not, which makes obligation and responsibility possible.

When Derrida says that "*différance* instigates the subversion of every kingdom. Which makes it obviously threatening and infallibly dreaded by everything within us that desires a kingdom, the past or future presence of a kingdom,"[35] we must ask what he means by this desire for a kingdom. And what if the answer were that to desire a kingdom is to desire that perfect presence to the True or the Real that makes autonomy possible, that turns knowledge into recollection, obligation into self-legislation, and me into my own eternal creator—that this is what he opposes?

It is possible (who could prevent it?) to read this threat to every kingdom as the deconstructive anarchism that revels in destroying every structure in order to be able to play without rules. Derrida would be what Aristophanes took Socrates to be. No doubt there are texts in Derrida and in other postmodernists that could be cited in support of such a reading. But the diagnosis of Eckhart and Hegel as suffering from ontological xenophobia, and it is hardly an isolated text, points in exactly the opposite direction. It is in order to preserve genuine obligation that it is necessary to subvert every kingdom; for every human kingdom, and Derrida knows no other kind, is the attempt to render itself self-sufficient and in this way absolute, to locate itself at that eternal, divine origin that wills creation. Needless to say, as the Alpha, every such kingdom can present itself as the Omega, which is what Levinas means by the violence of his-

---

[34] Among others, including Neoplatonic Christian apophaticism in general, Bruno, Nicholas of Cusa, and, of course, Kant. See "Denials," p. 100.

[35] "Différance," p. 22.

tory and politics.[36] Like Heidegger, and against Nietzsche, it seems that Derrida, without affirming the Wholly Other as Divine, holds open the space for such a possibility.

It might be objected that by linking Eckhart to Hegel Derrida has moved the discussion away from negative theology. A first reply might point out that so far as the Understanding and the *Vorstellungen* of everyday religious discourse are concerned, Hegel is a negative theologian, and that he finds in the rational mysticism and realized eschatology of the *Begriff* or *Idee* that presence that is reserved, in traditional apophaticism, for only occasional or future vision and union.

A second reply, perhaps more to the point, would note that what is at issue here is not negative theology as such but the pantheistic ontology that underlies some of its paradigmatic forms. It is widespread, not only in the apophaticism of much Hindu, Buddhist, and Neoplatonic Christian thought, but also in the cataphatic logocentrism of thinkers like Spinoza and Hegel.[37] Tillich has insisted that the term 'pantheism' "should be defined before it is applied aggressively."[38] This strikes me as a good idea. Since I employ the term "aggressively," that is, as something less than a compliment, I will offer a definition drawn from Tillich himself. Those systems of thought are pantheistic in which "man discovers *himself* when he discovers God; he discovers something that is identical with himself although it transcends him infinitely, something from which he is estranged, but from which he never has been and never can be separated" (p. 10). My point in using this label to side with Derrida in his

---

[36] In the opening paragraphs of the preface to *Totality and Infinity*, trans. Alphonso Lingis (Pittsburgh: Duquesne University Press, 1969). The argument of this paragraph wouldn't be a bad summary of the argument of John C. Caputo's *Against Ethics* (Bloomington: Indiana University Press, 1993).

[37] Hegel says, "to be a follower of Spinoza is the essential commencement of all Philosophy. . . . You are either a Spinozist or not a philosopher at all"; *Hegel's Lectures on the History of Philosophy*, trans. E. S. Haldane and Frances H. Simson (New York: Humanities, 1955), vol. III, pp. 257 and 283. For the same idea in the critically edited lectures of 1825–26, see *Hegel's Lectures on the History of Philosophy: The Lectures of 1825–26*, ed. Robert F. Brown (Berkeley: University of California Press, 1990), vol. III, p. 154.

[38] Paul Tillich, *Systematic Theology* (Chicago: University of Chicago Press, 1951), vol. I, p. 233.

critique of Eckhart and Hegel is not to deny that pantheism can be religious. It is rather to suggest that religion turns to pantheistic modes of thought out of ontological xenophobia, out of fear of meeting a stranger. In both its apophatic and logocentric forms, theology that roots itself in pantheism loses touch with the otherness of God. The divine may infinitely transcend the believing soul in such contexts, but the soul so related to God is illusory or accidental. In my essential being God and I are identical. I can stand at the origin and end of all things and of all knowledge because I am the Alpha and Omega.

The conceptual ground for the pantheistic absorption of alterity is an emanationist or illusionist account of the relation of the One to the Many, the Infinite to the Finite, of Being (or Emptiness) to beings. So it might seem that the otherness of God might be recovered on the path from pantheism to monotheistic creationism. Where God creates the world ex nihilo, the believing soul in its finitude may be an image and likeness of God but not an effulgence or extension of Deity; and yet the finite self is real. It may not be the *ens realissimum*, may not be, in the words of Josiah Royce, so very damn real; but it is not the product of ignorance or misperception. In this context I do not meet God as myself or as identical with myself but as an Other to myself. But perhaps the break with pantheism is not as great as it seems; perhaps it can still be said that God is "something from which [I can be] estranged, but from which [I] never [have] been and never can be separated"(p. 10).

In the Bible of Jewish and Christian monotheism there is a portrait of pure createdness. It is called Eden. There the human self can be neither estranged nor separated from God. Though they are not identical, they dwell together in a peace and harmony that might well evoke, when we think of it, nostalgia and hope for a presence we cannot now enjoy. And yet the possibility of both estrangement and separation is there. It lies in the command that comes to Adam and Eve, not as the voice of their own insight or their own deepest inner self, but as the voice of an Other. Eden is heteronomy from the outset. As Derrida reminds us, if autonomy were first or absolute, there would be no obligation.[39] <u>Innocence here is a double absence. It is the absence of any estrangement or separation from God; and it is the absence of any ontological guarantees that this presence is permanent.</u> In this fairy tale there are as yet no trolls or wicked witches; but neither can we simply say, And they lived happily ever after.

The command is the possibility of distance and disaster, its violation their actuality. With disobedience come both estrangement and separation, which, it turns out, cannot themselves be separated. Presence is now something to be avoided rather than enjoyed. Henceforth even my religion will be impiety, for my pursuit of God will be in the service of my flight from God.

This is the site where Kierkegaard's Climacus meditates on the absolute paradox: "This, then, is the ultimate paradox of thought: to want to discover something that thought itself cannot think. . . . What, then, is the unknown? It is the frontier that is continually arrived at, and therefore when the category of motion [time] is replaced by the category of rest [space] it is the different, the absolutely different."[40]

In answer to the question What might be the absolute paradox, the absolutely different, Climacus explores the hypothesis that it is the god who is teacher and savior, the god who must not only give us the truth but the capacity to recognize it as the truth as well, the assumption being that while we may once have had this capacity, we have now lost it through our own fault. It is this second hypothesis that leads to the crucial point: "But if the god is to be absolutely different from a human being, this can have its basis not in that which man owes to the god (for to that extent they are akin) but in that which he owes to himself or in that which he himself has committed. What, then, is the difference? Indeed, what else but sin. . . . We stated this in the foregoing by saying that the individual is untruth and is this through his own fault." This thought experiment renders the paradox "even more terrible . . . by bringing into prominence the absolute difference of sin."[41]

---

[39] See n. 33 above.

[40] Søren Kierkegaard, *Philosophical Fragments/Johannes Climacus*, trans. Howard V. Hong and Edna H. Hong (Princeton: Princeton University Press, 1985), pp. 37, 44.

[41] Ibid., pp. 46–47.

The claim here is that apart from sin God is not Wholly Other. God becomes Wholly Other only when the self-estrangement of fault renders God a stranger. Henceforth, to Tillich's chagrin, religion can only have the form of meeting a stranger. The corollary is that the creation motif is labile and Janus faced. By itself it does not posit the identity of the human and the divine but rather just the opposite. Still, by itself it has no defenses against being absorbed into a philosophy of identity that provides ontological guarantees against the possibility of our being separated from God, and, apparently, against the possibility of the kind of human fault that would effect such separation. No doubt that is why Kierkegaard's Anti-Climacus describes "as pantheistic any definition of sin that [makes] it out to be something merely negative—weakness, sensuousness, finitude, ignorance, etc."[42] As long as theology has only the categories of cause and effect or infinite and finite to work with, it is vulnerable to the loss of divine alterity that pantheism represents.

On the other hand, when the creation and fall motifs are united, the mild otherness of the former is preserved in the wild otherness of the latter. Such a radical alterity is by no means unproblematic for reflection, but at least theology has been rescued from being the self-congratulations of those who are pleased with their own divinity in spite of their total fear of meeting a stranger.

Climacus does not try to hide the fact that his thought experiment is a plagiarism, that it derives from a particular historical tradition, that it is, in the language of Hegel and the Enlightenment, a paradigm of positivity. In fact, he welcomes the charge of plagiarism and particularity as an indication that this "theory" is not the product of philosophical speculation.[43]

What is philosophy to do in the face of this challenge to its own motifs of autonomy, identity, recollection, etc? Without assuming that the question of what happens to philosophy is the most important question in the world, we can recall two traditional

---

[42] Søren Kierkegaard, *The Sickness unto Death*, trans. Howard V. Hong and Edna H. Hong (Princeton: Princeton University Press, 1980), p. 96. Cf. pp. 82, 117. See n. 59 below.

[43] *Philosophical Fragments*, pp. 35–36, 53–54.

responses. The one has been to identify philosophy, more or less explicitly, with what is here called the pantheistic option, either by replacing creation themes with identity themes or by giving what Anti-Climacus calls pantheistic interpretations of fault, leaving the creation motif to signify continuity over discontinuity by overriding moral distance with ontological kinship. The other has been to see philosophy as faith seeking understanding, to give it an ancillary role in a reflection that, with Climacus, sees sin as the source of God's radical alterity.

It is the either/or between these two alternatives that Climacus tries to set up in *Fragments* with his thought experiment about what it would take to go beyond Socrates.[44] There is something wonderfully honest about these two positions, neither of which is reluctant to admit that it is offended by the other. One has but to think, for example, of Augustine's contrast between Christian confession and Platonist presumption at *Confessions* VII, 20, and of Lessing's "ugly, broad ditch which I cannot get across" because that leap would involve something "against which my reason rebels."[45]

I am not foolish enough to suppose that I can bring to an end the longstanding conflict between faith and reason, so conceived, either by declaring one the victor or by trying to spell out some new type of Hegelian *Aufhebung*, which usually amounts to the same thing, minus candor.[46] I do, however, want to make both an historical and a philosophical observation about the alternative that Augustine describes as "confession," that Climacus describes as "going beyond Socrates," and that Tillich describes as "meeting a stranger."

---

[44] And that Hegel seeks to overcome. See, for example, his treatment of Faith and Enlightenment in chapter 6 of the *Phenomenology*. Neither Socrates nor Lessing, whom Kierkegaard greatly admires, is the primary target of the Climacus writings, but Hegel, just as it is he and not Kant who is the target in *Fear and Trembling*. See my essays "Johannes and Johannes," in *International Kierkegaard Commentary: Philosophical Fragments and Johannes Climacus*, ed. Robert L. Perkins (Macon, Ga.: Mercer University Press, 1994), and "Abraham and Hegel," in *Kierkegaard's Critique of Reason and Society* (University Park, Penn.: Penn State Press, 1991).

[45] *Lessing's Theological Writings*, trans. Henry Chadwick (Stanford: Stanford University Press, 1957), pp. 54–55.

[46] I believe this to be the case with Tillich's concept of theonomy. That it is also the case with Hegel is perhaps best seen by reading his accounts of the Fall in *The Encyclopedia Logic* and in his *Lectures on the Philosophy of Religion*.

I have, in fact, just made the historical observation. It is that Augustine is on the meeting a stranger side of the typology, not on the meeting myself or something identical with myself side. Tillich's identification of Augustinian religion as the act of meeting myself is a howler of the first order. True, he believes that the light of truth was within him, but "I was out of doors," preoccupied with things in space which could not satisfy him. "For I was superior to them, but inferior to you" (VII, 7). With God's help he was able to return inside. "I entered and I saw with my soul's eye (such as it was) an unchangeable light shining above this eye of my soul and above my mind. . . . It was higher than I, because it made me, and I was lower because I was made by it. . . . And when I first knew you, you raised me up so that I could see that there was something to see and that I still lacked the ability to see it. And you beat back the weakness of my sight, blazing upon me with your rays, and I trembled in love and in dread, and I found that I was far distant from you, in a region of total unlikeness" (VII, 10).

Taken by itself this text may seem to ground the relation of "total unlikeness" solely on creation, but taken in context it is clear that creation has been decisively pulled away from Neoplatonic pantheism by its union with an analysis of sin as "a perversity of the will" (VII, 16), and thus of a pride, arrogance, and conceit that had become habit or second nature. That is why the intellectual conversion of book VII, which includes a decisive repudiation of knowledge as recollection, needs to be completed by the conversion of the will in book VIII. When he summarizes that second process with the words "you converted me to you" (VIII, 12), he testifies that overcoming estrangement means meeting the one who, through a separation brought about by himself, had become a stranger. So far is Augustine from being the archetype of meeting God as myself or as something identical with myself—he is in fact the archetype of the type Tillich labels Thomistic. There are real differences between Aquinas and Augustine, but on the issues Tillich raises, Aquinas is an Augustinian. This is why at the outset I said I wanted to recast Tillich's Augustinian/Thomistic typology as a Neoplatonic/Augustinian typology. The faith that overcomes ontological xenophobia recognizes that no original bond of being is strong enough to keep sin from making human being radically other than divine being. It knows that union with God can only have the form of reconciliation, and that reconciliation means the courage to meet one who has become a stranger. If we want to give a name to this faith we could hardly do better than to call it Augustinian.

Tillich sees the thirteenth-century Franciscans, with their emphasis on immediate knowledge of God and their opposition to Thomistic empiricism, as key developers of the Augustinian solution as he defines it (p. 13). But if one consults the locus classicus of this tradition, Bonaventure's *The Soul's Journey into God*, one does not find identity and immediacy, but difference and mediation. Like a good Augustinian, Bonaventure holds that the Uncreated Light shines in the human soul; but, again, like a good Augustinian, he insists on the difference between the unchangeable light and our changeable minds in which it shines. Thus, for example, we judge by a law that is "higher than our mind" and recognize that "nothing is higher than the human mind except him alone who made it."[47] Thus, by virtue of the distinction between the created and uncreated, the immediacy of any resulting knowledge cannot be a sign of identity. Whether we contemplate God by looking outside ourselves, within ourselves, or above ourselves,[48] in every case we know something that is not identical with ourselves.

But Bonaventure does not leave us with a theory of immediate knowledge. The contemplation of God is everywhere mediated by divine grace made necessary by human sinfulness. The journey begins with a prayer for illumination raised by one who is "a sinner and utterly unworthy" and who must follow the path of "burning love for the Crucified. . . . The six wings of the Seraph, therefore, symbolize the six steps of illumination that begin from creatures and lead up to God, whom no one rightly enters except through the Crucified. . . . Therefore John says in the Apocalypse: *Blessed are they who wash their robes in the blood of the Lamb that they may have a right to the tree of life and may enter the*

---

[47] *Bonaventure: The Soul's Journey into God, The Tree of Life, The Life of St. Francis,* trans. Ewert Cousins (New York: Paulist Press, 1978), pp. 81–83.

[48] This classical Augustinian triad shapes the entire *Soul's Journey.* See especially pp. 61 and 94.

city through the gates (Apoc. 22:14)." It would be futile to rely on "endeavor without divine grace," and it would be presumptuous to look for grace without first exercising oneself "in remorse of conscience."[49]

Corresponding to the six stages of the journey are six stages in the powers of the soul: "We have these stages implanted in us by nature, deformed by sin and reformed by grace. . . . In the initial state of creation, man was made fit for the quiet of contemplation. . . . But turning from the true light to changeable good, man was bent over by his own fault. . . . As a result, man, blinded and bent over, sits in darkness and does not see the light of heaven unless grace with justice come to his aid against concupiscence and unless knowledge with wisdom come to his aid against ignorance. All this is done through Jesus Christ."[50] Bonaventure is indeed an Augustinian, but this means that the motifs of creation and the fall are intertwined so as to make it clear that all union with God is mediated by a grace that comes to us from beyond ourselves in order to bridge a gulf we dug but cannot leap over.

The philosophical observation I want to make about the Augustinian tradition, as I have just described it, is that it receives a measure of support from certain phenomenological analyses in the work of Sartre and Levinas. Sartre argues that the reality of other selves cannot be established by arguments that presuppose a Cartesian subjectivity for which everything but the "I think" is an object whose reality and nature is problematic. But this never was how the Other has been given to us. We are aware of the Other, not as a putative object whose reality and subjectivity are hypotheses for which we seek evidence; rather, we are aware of the Other in the Look, when we are the object being looked at by the Other as subject.

But Sartre does not leave his description of the Look at the abstract level of subject and object. He describes three concrete modes of being seen: fear, pride, and shame. Insofar as I am a body, to be seen is to experience fear, for the Other is one who can hurt me. Insofar as I am ego or self, to be seen is to experi-

---

[49] Ibid., pp. 53–56.
[50] Ibid., p. 62.

ence pride or shame, for the Other's look is a value judgment
that can be either an affirming or condemning one. The negativity of this analysis, easily dismissed as part of Sartre's congenital
gloominess, is evident. Two of the three modes of being seen are
painful, and at the physical level, the positive correlate of fear
does not even merit mention. But we need to notice that we are
dealing primarily with a spiritual negativity. The analysis of
shame is more extensive than that of fear and pride combined,
and the most memorable image of the entire analysis, that of
getting caught looking and listening at the keyhole, makes the
shame analysis the most intensive as well.

J. N. Findlay has written, "Sartre may be able to conjure eidetic
meaning into two eyes regarding each other through the same
keyhole, but such confrontations are for the most part best seen
as embarrassing accidents, over which no great eidetic pother
should be made."[51] That is exactly what one would expect a
Neoplatonist to say. But a secular Augustinian, like Sartre, is
willing to make "great eidetic pother" over such an incident for
a very good reason. It plays a key role in the phenomenological
argument that goes beyond the claim that we experience the
Other in being looked at to the stronger claim that we experience
the otherness of the Other most fully in the look of moral con-
demnation.[52]

The look of praise that inspires pride comes from the Other,
but since it simply repeats what I say about myself, or would
like to say, it does not go very far in revealing the otherness of
the Other. What we have here is perhaps the Other as Echo. The
look that inspires fear goes further. Here we have the Other as
Threat. But here the otherness is experienced only as potential
rather than as actual, and it is directed toward my body rather
than my soul, or, to use Kantian language, toward my happiness
rather than my worthiness to be happy. It is in the look that
evokes shame that the otherness of the Other is most fully given.
The Other as Judge, in the judgment before which I stand
ashamed, having been caught in the act of eavesdropping and

---

[51] J. N. Findlay, *Plato: The Written and Unwritten Doctrines* (New York: Humanities, 1974), p. 410.

[52] See *Being and Nothingness*, part 3, ch. 1, especially section IV, "The Look."

peeping at the keyhole, is an actual, not merely potential, negativity; and that negativity is directed toward what, for an Augustinian like Sartre, is the innermost core of my being.

The theological correlate of this phenomenological description is the claim of Climacus that it is sin that makes God Wholly Other. In this context to speak of God as Wholly Other is not to make the ontological claim that there is no continuity whatever (which would be to deny creation) or that there is no basis for recognition whatever (which would be to deny the possibility of conscience). It is to say that in a relation with enough continuity and recognition to make the Other matter to me (would a Martian's disapproval of my behavior bother me?) the deepest possible difference has emerged. We can now see that Tillich's category of the stranger is not really adequate to the Augustinian understanding of the situation. Hosea's notion that God and the sinner are related like a faithful and an adulterous spouse or the Pauline notion that God and the sinner have become enemies (Rom. 5:10) is more to the point. Ontological xenophobia is not just the attempt to use linkages of being to defend myself from the anxiety of meeting a stranger; it is the attempt to avoid meeting the kind of stranger whose moral presence is sufficient to undermine the ultimacy of ontological categories as such, the kind of stranger who might lead me to ask, "Is Ontology Fundamental?" and to answer my own question by exploring the possibility of "Ethics as First Philosophy."[53]

These references to Levinas are meant to suggest that he provides the same kind of phenomenological Augustinianism that we have found in Sartre. It might seem that while Sartre directs us to the look that condemns, Levinas points to the look that commands. But the difference is superficial, for the command is a possible judgment of blame that becomes actual the moment we violate it. Thus Levinas writes

> Freedom is put into question by the Other, and is revealed to be unjustified, only when it knows itself to be unjust . . . guilty.[54]

---

[53] Emmanuel Levinas, "Is Ontology Fundamental?" *Philosophy Today* (summer 1989), pp. 121–29, and "Ethics as First Philosophy," in *The Levinas Reader*, ed. Seán Hand (Oxford: Basil Blackwell, 1989).

[54] Emmanuel Levinas, "Philosophy and the Idea of the Infinite," in Adriaan Peperzak, *To the Other: An Introduction to the Philosophy of Emmanuel Levinas*

But Being . . . is a Neuter . . . which hardens the will instead of making it ashamed. [In ontology the consciousness of finitude] is not revealed as an imperfection, does not refer to the Good, does not know itself to be wicked. . . . Heideggerian ontology subordinates the relation with the other to the relation with the Neuter, Being, and it thus continues to exalt the will to power, whose legitimacy the Other (*Autrui*) alone can unsettle, troubling good conscience. . . . Anonymous, neuter, [Being] directs [existence], ethically indifferent, as a heroic freedom, foreign to all guilt with regard to the Other.[55]

But then the other is not simply another freedom; to give me knowledge of injustice, his gaze must come to me from a dimension of the ideal.[56]

. . . the idea of the infinite means the collapse of the good conscience of the Same. . . . The Other's face is the revelation not of the arbitrariness of the will but its injustice. Consciousness of my injustice is produced when I incline myself not before facts, but before the Other. . . . It is a *shame* freedom has of itself, discovering itself to be murderous and usurpatory in its very exercise. . . . Existence is not condemned to freedom, but judged and invested as a freedom. . . . The life of freedom discovering itself to be unjust, the life of freedom in heteronomy, consists in an infinite movement of freedom putting itself ever more into question. . . . The face-to-face situation in which this freedom is put into question as unjust, in which it finds it has a master and a judge, is realized prior to certainty, but also prior to uncertainty.[57]

It seems that Levinas and Sartre share the phenomenological judgment that it is not in fear but in guilt or shame that we experience the otherness of the Other.[58] It is not in finitude, created or otherwise, but in fault that God becomes Wholly Other.[59]

(West Lafayette, Ind.: Purdue University Press, 1993), p. 99. This essay is also found in Levinas's *Collected Philosophical Papers*, trans. Alphonso Lingis (Dordrecht: Martinus Nijhoff, 1987).

[55] *To the Other*, pp. 102–104.

[56] Ibid., p. 111.

[57] Ibid., pp. 115–18.

[58] In section 4B of *God, Guilt, and Death* (Bloomington: Indiana University Press, 1984), I have argued that at least one standard way of distinguishing guilt and shame is not very convincing. See especially n. 11.

[59] Kierkegaard argues that creation ex nihilo is a sign of the omnipotence necessary to produce a being who is genuinely free: "It is incomprehensible that omnipotence is not only able to create the most impressive of all things—

A world without the possibility of sin would be a kind of cosmic Michael Jordan or Mikhail Baryshnikov, a body of God that always expressed the divine purpose, if God is infinite, or that failed to do so perfectly only through some inertial force such as the Platonic recalcitrance of matter, if God is finite. Such a world would be an organic whole, a Plotinian/Spinozistic/Hegelian totality in which inner differentiation can occur, but in which it is always already *aufgehoben* in an accord beyond alterity. Genuine otherness would be found only in the illusory perception that fails to see the whole story. Gnosticism, with or without myth, becomes the flip side of pantheism.

For the Augustinianism that represents the other path our experience of God might take, the religious and the ethical are inseparable, not in the Kantian sense, in which "morality leads inevitably to religion,"[60] as if religion were the necessary condition of morality, but in the opposite sense that the moral experience of fault is the necessary condition of religion.

This was the experience of Augustine himself, who discovered that he had not come to faith by gaining clarity about such ontological issues as the origin of evil and the possibility of an incorporeal substance (*Confessions*, VII), but only when he became reconciled through repentance to a will conspicuously different from his own (book VIII). In this context, faith involves overcoming ontological xenophobia, or, to speak more precisely, the xenophobia that takes place as ontology.

Tillich is right to note that on this path, which he misleadingly labels Thomistic, the reconciliation that overcomes otherness is contingent (p. 10). Just as there is no ontological necessity to the emergence of real difference, there is no ontological guarantee of its being bridged.[61] This does not mean that reconciliation is

---

the whole visible world—but is able to create the most fragile of all things—a being independent of that very omnipotence." See all of ¶1251 in *Søren Kierkegaard's Papers and Journals*, trans. Howard V. and Edna H. Hong (Bloomington: Indiana University Press, 1970), vol. 2. This is an important commentary on the passage cited above (see n. 42), in which Kierkegaard (as Anti-Climacus) labels "pantheistic" those definitions of fault that reduce it to finitude.

[60] Immanuel Kant, *Religion within the Limits of Reason Alone*, trans. Theodore M. Greene and Hoyt H. Hudson (New York: Harper & Brothers, 1960), p. 7 n.

[61] As Tillich rightly notes, this has epistemological ramifications. That is the whole point of the thought experiment in Kierkegaard's *Philosophical Frag-*

impossible, or that somehow it is second class. But it does mean that it can occur only when the grace and generosity that give forgiveness are met by the humility and contrition that are willing to receive it. For one type of philosophy of religion this language generates a certain anxiety, possibly a phobia, perhaps even a xenophobia. For the other type it leads to the exclamation O felix culpa!

---

ments, to see how it might be possible to go beyond the Socratic assumption that knowledge is recollection, that the truth is within us.

13

Divine Excess: The God Who Comes After

> What, then, is the God I worship? . . . But what do I love, when I love my God?
>
> Augustine, *Confessions*, I, 4 and X, 6

THE TITLE of Calvin Schrag's splendid little book *The Self after Postmodernity*[1] makes explicit his assumption that the postmodern assault on the self as conceived by major strands within the western philosophical tradition is not an abolition, not a annihilation without remainder. Schrag's work is inspired in large part by Paul Ricoeur's attempt, among the shards of the "shattered cogito," to develop a "hermeneutics of the self [that] is placed at an equal distance from the apology of the cogito and from its overthrow . . . at an equal distance from the cogito exalted by Descartes and from the cogito that Nietzsche proclaimed forfeit."[2] The "arduous detours" of this hermeneutics pass through a series of questions: "Who is speaking of what? Who does what? About whom and about what does one construct a narrative? Who is morally responsible for what? These are but so many different ways in which 'who?' is stated."[3] To answer these questions is to answer the question of a selfhood that survives the legitimate deconstruction of its illegitimate pretensions.

The same assumption is at work in another enticing title, *Who Comes after the Subject?*[4] The essays in this volume address "the

---

[1] Calvin O. Schrag, *The Self after Postmodernity* (New Haven: Yale University Press, 1997).

[2] Paul Ricoeur, *Oneself as Another*, trans. Kathleen Blamey (Chicago: University of Chicago Press, 1992), pp. 11, 4, 23.

[3] *Oneself*, p. 19.

[4] *Who Comes after the Subject?*, ed. Eduardo Cadava, Peter Connor, and Jean-Luc Nancy (New York: Routledge, 1991).

critique of the deconstruction of subjectivity." But Jean-l Nancy tells us that with his question he wanted "to suggest a whole range—no doubt vast—in which such a critique or deconstruction has not simply obliterated its object (as those who groan or applaud before a supposed 'liquidation' of the subject would like to believe). That which obliterates is nihilism."[5]

In the same spirit, Jack Caputo has posed the question, Who comes after the God of metaphysics, after the critique of onto-theology? In disseminating this question he doubtless joins Nancy in saying, "I did not send my question . . . to those who would find no validity in it, to those for whom it is on the contrary more important to denounce its presuppositions and to return, as though nothing had happened, to a style of thinking that we might simply call humanist."[6] Or, in the present instance, metaphysical. Or onto-theological. Still, the assumption is that after the deluge we have the need, the desire, and the ability to speak of God. Somehow. But how, and of whom?

I shall reply to this question, but first it is necessary to be as clear as possible about the "after." We are to think and speak of God after . . . After what, precisely? For present purposes the critique that comes before is threefold: the critique of onto-theology in Heidegger, and the closely related critiques of ontology in Levinas and Marion.

If one were to gather an understanding of Heidegger's critique of onto-theology secondhand one might easily think that it is directed primarily at Augustine and Aquinas, Luther and Calvin, Pascal and Kierkegaard—against anyone who affirms a personal creator and redeemer. It is not always sufficiently noticed that his paradigms are Aristotle[7] and Hegel[8] and that the target of his analysis of "the onto-theo-logical constitution of metaphysics" is a tradition that stretches from Anaximander to Nietzsche,[9] which isn't quite the same as the tradition that stretches from Augustine to Kierkegaard.

---

[5] Ibid., p. 4.

[6] Ibid., p. 3.

[7] In the 1949 introduction to *What Is Metaphysics* entitled "The Way Back into the Ground of Metaphysics," in *Pathmarks*, ed. William McNeill (New York: Cambridge University Press, 1998).

[8] In "The Onto-theo-logical Constitution of Metaphysics" in *Identity and Difference*, trans. Joan Stambaugh (New York: Harper & Row, 1969).

[9] *Pathmarks*, p. 280.

Heidegger derives his term from the move by which Aristotle's metaphysics becomes theology. First philosophy starts out as ontology, as the theory of being qua being, but finds that in order to complete itself it needs to posit a highest being, the Unmoved Mover.[10] This ontology that becomes theology Heidegger calls onto-theology. Its fundamental assertion is that there is a Highest Being that is the key to the meaning of the whole of being.

But this affirmation is not obviously incoherent or self-refuting. If there is a critique here, if an overcoming of metaphysics in its onto-theological character is necessary, we shall have to ask what is wrong with this gesture, most overt and unambiguous in its Aristotelian form, but anticipated by Anaximander and reiterated by Hegel and Nietzsche.

Heidegger gives his answer to this question as the answer to another, "How does the deity enter into philosophy . . . ?" to which he replies that for metaphysics "the deity can come into philosophy only insofar as philosophy, of its own accord and by its own nature, requires and determines that and how the deity enters into it."[11]

In order to enter this discourse, God must first get an imprimatur or the Good Housekeeping Seal of Approval from philosophy. This scene in which God makes a (not so) grand entry suggests two others that can help us state why Heidegger thinks this move makes for bad philosophy and bad theology. The first scene occurs in the preface to the second edition of the *Critique of Pure Reason,* where Kant is praising Galileo and others, who "learned that reason has insight only into that which it produces after a plan of its own, and that it must not allow itself to be kept, as it were, in nature's leading-strings, but must itself show the way . . . *constraining nature to give answer to questions of reason's own determining.*"[12]

Heidegger lacks Kant's enthusiasm for this insistence on being

---

[10] Assuming that we can speak here in the singular. In Hegel's version, we begin with a logic that is an ontology and end with an account of Absolute Spirit as the Highest (because, in this case, the all inclusive) Being, which is the key to the whole of being.

[11] *Identity and Difference,* pp. 55–56.

[12] B xiii, emphasis added.

in charge of the questioning. *What Is Metaphysics?* (1929) contains a polemic against science and logic (philosophy's logos) because they are of no help in asking the truly metaphysical question about the nothing (which is the flip side of the question of being). In the postscript to *What Is Metaphysics?* (1943), 'metaphysics' has become a dirty word, and the task is now the overcoming of metaphysics; for posing the question of the nothing (and thus of being) is already to go beyond metaphysics as the truth (foundation?) of objectivising, calculating science. In the introduction to *What Is Metaphysics?* (1949), the metaphysics that needs to be overcome is set forth as onto-theology.

These three essays[13] make it clear why onto-theology is bad philosophy. It converts what might have been the question of being into the question of a being, albeit the Highest Being. In their focus on beings, science and metaphysics together, preoccupied with their own questions, are *Seinsvergessenheit*. When they compel beings to answer questions of their own determining, they desecrate being by depriving it of its mystery and become agents of that will to power that flourishes as modern technology. One needn't be as impressed with the ontological difference as Heidegger is to think there may be something to the charge that in various modes metaphysics has contributed to an arrogant humanism that has helped to create and sustain a very inhuman modern world.

But Heidegger thinks it obvious that when philosophy makes God a theme of discourse on its own terms, theology and not just philosophy is affected.[14] And not for the better. Here a second scene is evoked by Heidegger's analysis, this one from the book of Job. Job refuses to "curse God and die" (2:9–10), but he has a subpoena for God that he would deliver if only he could find him:

> Oh, that I knew where I might find him,
> that I might come even to his dwelling!

---

[13] Along with *Identity and Difference*, of course. All three components of *What Is Metaphysics?* are to be found in *Pathmarks*. They also appear in *Existentialism from Dostoevsky to Sartre*, ed. Walter Kaufmann, rev. ed. (New York: New American Library, 1975).

[14] *Identity and Difference*, p. 56.

> I would lay my case before him,
> and fill my mouth with arguments.
> *I would learn what he would answer me*
> and understand what he would say to me.
> (23:3–5, emphasis added)

Job shouts, Where art Thou? and awaits the divine reply, *me voici*. Here it is not science compelling nature to answer questions of its own determining, but a man seeking to compel God to answer his questions. We know how the story ends. God shows up, but not to answer Job's questions. Rather, it is to insist on being the one who asks the questions:

> Gird up your loins like a man,
> I will question you, and you shall declare to me. (38:3)

The remainder of chapters 38 and 39 is a barrage of questions addressed to Job, after which God says to Job

> Shall a fault finder contend with the Almighty?
> Anyone who argues with God must respond. (40:2)

After Job admits that he does not know how to answer, God repeats the "Gird up your loins. . . . I will question you" admonition (40:7), and we get another divine barrage, including many more questions for Job, who finally acknowledges that he was without understanding and knowledge when he had said to God

> Hear, and I will speak;
> I will question you, and you declare to me. (42:4)

The narrative makes it clear that for all his steadfast piety, Job is on the verge of blasphemy when he insists that God enter his discourse on his terms, that God's job is to answer Job's questions. This is what happens to theology when it allows itself to be seduced by metaphysics. It assumes that the purpose of God-talk is to render the whole of being intelligible to human understanding, in short, to answer our questions.

For Heidegger it is the notion of God as *causa sui* that typifies this notion of God as Ultimate Explainer.[15] The problem is that

---

[15] See the extended analysis in *The Principle of Reason*, trans. Reginald Lilly (Bloomington: Indiana University Press, 1991).

when theology buys into this philosophical project, it renders the God of whom it speaks religiously useless. *Causa sui* is "the right name for the god of philosophy. Man can neither pray nor sacrifice to this god. Before the *causa sui,* man can neither fall to his knees in awe nor can he play music and dance before this god."[16]

Here Heidegger sounds less like Nietzsche celebrating the death of God than like Pascal contrasting the god of the philosophers with the God of Abraham, Isaac, and Jacob. This impression is strengthened when Heidegger challenges Christian theologians to consider whether their appropriation of Greek philosophy was "for better or for worse" with specific reference to the Pauline question, "Has not God let the wisdom of this world become foolishness?" (1 Corinthians 1:20), more specifically, the wisdom that "the Greeks seek" (1:22). "Will Christian theology one day resolve to take seriously the word of the apostle and thus also the conception of philosophy as foolishness?"[17] *We must think God as the mystery that exceeds the wisdom of the Greeks.*

Whereas for Heidegger 'metaphysics' becomes the name of those features of the western philosophical tradition that must be overcome, that role is given to 'ontology' by Levinas, who reserves the name 'metaphysics' for the ethical relation to which he gives priority over ontology.[18] So we have to stay on our terminological toes. Levinas's definition of ontology has an epistemic flavor. It is "theory as comprehension of beings." Thus *Being and Time* continues the western ontological tradition with its "one sole thesis: Being is inseparable from the comprehension of Being."[19]

We should not read this anthropocentrically. It is being that

---

[16] *Identity and Difference,* p. 72.

[17] *Pathmarks,* p. 288. Kierkegaard obviously joins Pascal in the background of Heidegger's critique here.

[18] *Totality and Infinity,* trans. Alphonso Lingis (Pittsburgh: Duquesne University Press, 1969), pp. 42–48. Henceforth cited as TI. Cf. "Is Ontology Fundamental?" in Emmanuel Levinas, *Basic Philosophical Writings,* ed. Adriaan T. Peperzak, Simon Critchley, and Robert Bernasconi (Bloomington: Indiana University Press, 1996). Henceforth cited as IOF.

[19] TI pp. 42, 45.

gives itself to be understood: "Truth can consist only in the exposition of being to itself." In the process by which being comes to consciousness by means of ideality and essence, "being thus carries on its affair of being." That we can think being means

> that the appearing of being belongs to its very movement of being, that its phenomenality is essential, and that being cannot do without consciousness, to which manifestation is made. . . . The thinking subject . . . is then, despite the activity of its searching . . . to be interpreted as a detour that being's essence takes to get arranged and thus to truly appear, to appear in truth. Intelligibility or signifyingness is part of the very exercise of being, of the *ipsum esse*. Everything is then on the same side, on the side of being.[20]

When everything is on the same side we have the totality against which *Totality and Infinity* is a protest. Ontology is that allergic reaction to alterity that is the reduction of the other to the same.[21] A very early (1951), very brief presentation of this critique of ontology is found in the essay "Is Ontology Fundamental?" It states the theme whose many variations are the later writings and gives the exposition of a motif immediately taken up into the massive development section that completes Levinas's authorship. Perhaps we should speak of a first and second subject, of two contrasting themes or motifs. For first there is the presentation of ontology, then, as its critique, the presentation of an alternative, the "relation which is irreducible to comprehension."[22]

The essay begins in praise of Heidegger for his break with the intellectualist tradition of western philosophy. Recognizing the contingency and facticity at work in our thought, he points to the rootedness of thought in a comportment beyond theory and contemplation, to what might be called the priority of existence

---

[20] *Otherwise than Being, or Beyond Essence*, trans. Alphonso Lingis (Boston: Kluwer, 1991), pp. 61, 99, 131, 134. These statements come at the beginning of chapters III, IV, and V. In *Of God Who Comes to Mind*, trans. Bettina Bergo (Stanford: Stanford University Press, 1998), this activity of being is translated being's "gesture." Thus, "The intelligibility of being, which is also its 'gesture of being' [*la geste d'être*]"; p. 36. Cf. pp. 45, 112. In the latter passage, this gesture is the "essance" or the "insistance" of being, terms designed to highlight the verbal character of being, its fundamental self-assertion.

[21] TI pp. 47, 42.

[22] IOF pp. 5, 7–8.

to our conscious intentions. But this radicality is immediately tamed, brought back into the ontological language game, when Heidegger interprets existence as comprehension, openness, understanding, and truth. Thus Heidegger sees the being of beings in their intelligibility.[23]

Since Plato comprehension and intelligibility have meant the subjection of the particular to the universal. For Heidegger, this occurs as the horizonal character of understanding: "The understanding of a being will thus consist in going beyond that being into the *openness* and in perceiving it *upon the horizon of being.* That is to say, comprehension, in Heidegger, rejoins the great tradition of Western philosophy: to comprehend the particular being is already to place oneself beyond the particular. To comprehend is to be related to the particular that only exists through knowledge, which is always knowledge of the universal."[24]

This is not merely a nominalist or an atomist protest. In Levinas's view the purchase of intelligibility through universality or of comprehension through horizonal context is not innocent. Like the universal concept of the intellectualist tradition, the phenomenological horizon allows us to pigeonhole beings into a semantic totality that has a place for everything and correspondingly puts everything in its place. This is the "overcoming" of the object, and not merely in the sense that it is conceptually *mastered and grasped,* revealing as that language may be. Levinas associates this overcoming with possession, consumption, power, property, assimilation, and violence. Possession, in particular, implies that since things belong to me and not to themselves, they are either to be used for or enjoyed by another. We encompass things within our conceptual horizons, thereby enabling us to incorporate them into our practical projects.[25]

Since ontology does this to every being, including other

---

[23] Ibid., 3–5. In TI pp. 28, 65, 67, 71, 75, Levinas will make this latter point in terms of Heidegger's account of disclosure. "The Thinking of Being and the Question of the Other," in *Of God Who Comes to Mind,* has essentially the same dyadic structure as IOF, but there the critique is extended to the Derrida of *Speech and Phenomena.*

[24] IOF p. 5.

[25] Ibid., pp. 7–9. Cf. Heidegger's linkage of metaphysics with modern technology.

human beings, it is not surprising that Levinas associates himself with Kantian ethics as a plea for respect.[26] But how does he make the transition from theory to practice, agreeing in effect with Heidegger that western philosophy culminates in the will to power? Why does he see ontological reason as "a ruse of the hunter who ensnares"?[27] Levinas's answer comes in a single sentence: "If things are only things, this is because the relation with them is established as comprehension."[28] In other words, it is the very nature of comprehension to treat its objects as one of a kind or as part of a whole in such a way as to deprive them of the respect, to speak with Kant, that forbids my reducing them to the ways I can use or enjoy them. Thus, in *Totality and Infinity*, just after he attributes to Heidegger the thesis that "Being is inseparable from the comprehension of Being," Levinas writes, "To affirm the priority of *Being* [as horizon] over *existents* is to already decide the essence of philosophy; it is to subordinate the relation with *someone*, who is an existent, (the ethical relation) to a relation with the *Being of existents*, which, *impersonal* [emphasis added], permits the apprehension, the domination of existents (a relation of knowing), subordinates justice to freedom."[29]

The fly in the ointment is the essentially impersonal character of comprehension, which reduces everything to only a thing. Its form is that of a subject seeing or intending an object. If there is to be room for something like Kantian respect, there will have to be a "relation which is irreducible to comprehension,"[30] one that involves more than subsuming a particular under a universal or apprehending some foreground against a horizonal background. Such a relation is impossible. "Unless it is the other (*Autrui*). Our relation with the other (*autrui*) certainly consists in wanting to comprehend him, but this relation overflows comprehension."[31]

Wherein consists this overflow? Quite simply, in speech, for

---

[26] Ibid., pp. 8, 10. Needless to say, Levinas does not associate himself with Kant's attempt to preserve autonomy in ethics.

[27] Ibid., p. 8.

[28] Ibid., p. 9.

[29] TI p. 45.

[30] See n. 22 above.

[31] IOF p. 6.

the impersonal objects of comprehension are mute. Respect and justice—in short, the ethical relation becomes possible when sight is *aufgehoben* or teleologically suspended in speech.[32] Especially important are those speech acts that go beyond information sharing. If it is as interlocutor that the other overflows comprehension, it is especially by virtue of such speech acts as summoning, invocation, calling, greeting, and imploring, as in prayer.[33] Such acts, and not physiognomy as such, constitute the face of the other, the face that is at once the possibility and impossibility of murder. The voice/face of the other overflows comprehension by refusing to be captured without remainder by any horizon of understanding. It signifies itself, and it does so immediately.[34]

There is a link between Heidegger's critique of onto-theology and Levinas's critique of ontology. Onto-theology, as Heidegger understands it, is the project of rendering the whole of being intelligible to human understanding. Since it has no room for that which overflows comprehension, it distorts our understanding of God (as well as of ourselves and the world of nature). Similarly, ontology, as Levinas presents it, identifies being with its intelligibility to theory, to contemplation, to representation,[35] to intentionality.[36] Thereby it excludes the voice and the face of

---

[32] Thus, in TI pp. 33–35, desire for the transcendent other is desire for the invisible, and "The face speaks. The manifestation of the face is already discourse" (p. 66; cf. pp. 39, 51). The transcendent "cuts across the vision of forms and can be stated neither in terms of contemplation nor in terms of practice. It is the face; its revelation is speech" (p. 193).

[33] IOF pp. 6–8. Here the other is the one to whom I speak. In later writings, in order to emphasize the asymmetry of the relation, the focus is more on the fact that the other speaks to me. There is an important and largely unexplored relation to Habermas in this notion that we are fundamentally related to each other as performers of speech acts.

[34] Ibid., pp. 9–10. In TI pp. 23, 51–52, 65, 67, 74, and 77, Levinas will develop this nonhorizonal immediacy as the claim that the face is *"signification without a context,"* that it expresses itself καθ' αὐτό. I have discussed this theme in "Levinas and the Immediacy of the Face," *Faith and Philosophy* 9, no. 4 (October 1993), pp. 486–502.

[35] See "The Ruin of Representation," in *Discovering Existence with Husserl*, trans. Richard A. Cohen and Michael B. Smith (Evanston: Northwestern University Press, 1998).

[36] See "Intentionality and Metaphysics" and "Intentionality and Sensation," in *Discovering Existence with Husserl*; "Hermeneutics and Beyond" and "Nonintentional Consciousness," in *Entre Nous: On Thinking-of-the-Other*, trans. Mi-

the other who is my neighbor and, a fortiori, the voice of the God who commands us to love our neighbor. *We must think God as the voice that exceeds vision so as to establish a relation irreducible to comprehension.*

Levinas insists that his critique is not an assault on reason but an attempt to go beyond reason as "a ruse of the hunter who ensnares" to an "order of reason . . . where the resistance of beings qua beings is not broken but pacified."[37] Bad reason (ontology) is to be superseded (*aufgehoben*) by good reason (metaphysics). Similarly, Marion insists that his quest for "God without being" and thus a God beyond onto-theology and prior to ontology is the search for a "conceptual thought of God (conceptual, or rational, and not intuitive or 'mystical' in the vulgar sense)."[38]

Marion charges that onto-theology "imposes" its metaphysical names, such as *causa sui*, on God and in doing so hides "the mystery of God as such."[39] And he charges the ontological tradition that makes Being the first name of God with "chaining" God to Being, asking whether God is not better conceived in the first instance as charity, as *agape*, as the good, as gift.[40] When Marion speaks of "the failure of the metaphysical concept of God" and looks for a mode of God-talk that "allows the emergence of a God who is free from onto-theology," it seems that the question concerns the priority of various categories or names in relation to others. But Marion has already just told us, "I am

---

chael B. Smith and Barbara Harshav (New York: Columbia University Press, 1998); and "Beyond Intentionality," in *Philosophy in France Today*, ed. Alan Montefiore (New York: Cambridge University Press, 1983).

[37] IOF pp. 5, 8.

[38] *God without Being*, trans. Thomas A. Carlson (Chicago: Chicago University Press, 1991), p. xxiv. Henceforth cited as GWB.

[39] Ibid., p. xxi. Marion follows Heidegger rather than Levinas in the use of the term 'metaphysics'. In "Metaphysics and Phenomenology: A Relief for Theology," *Critical Inquiry* 20 (Summer 1994), pp. 572–91, he explicitly adopts and provides historical validation for Heidegger's onto-theological concept of metaphysics. For him phenomenology is the philosophical alternative to metaphysics. Hence the importance of *Reduction and Givenness*, trans. Thomas A. Carlson (Evanston: Northwestern University Press, 1998), in which he distinguishes his phenomenology from that of Husserl and Heidegger.

[40] GWB pp. xx–xxiv.

attempting to bring out the absolute freedom of God with regard to *all* determinations."[41] If certain names are privileged
over Being, it will be because they protect this freedom better.

This they accomplish by being icons rather than idols. Although he is interested in conceptual intelligibility, Marion turns
(briefly) to sensible visibility for this analysis, retracing the path
by which the tradition has modeled "seeing" intelligibles with
the mind's eye on seeing sensibles with the body's eye. What
distinguishes an icon from an idol is the how rather than the
what of perception. In other words, a given visible can function
as either idol or icon depending on the nature of the intentional
act directed toward it.

It becomes an idol when the gaze that intends it is satisfied or
(ful)filled with what it sees, when it stops, freezes, settles, or
comes to rest at its visible object.[42] Marion seems to have in mind
Husserl's account of adequation as fulfilled intention, the situation where what is given in experience corresponds exactly to
what would otherwise have been an empty intention.[43] Since one
didn't aim at more than is present, one can be satisfied with
what is given, can be at rest with the results. When "every aim
is exhausted," the gaze "admits no beyond," or, in this case,
"allows no invisible."[44]

Idolatry means that the human gaze has become the measure
of the divine being; God is now equated (hence adequation)
with "what the human gaze has experienced of the divine." In
this way the idol becomes an "invisible mirror," invisible because its role as mirror is not noticed.[45] But of what is it the
mirror, the carbon copy, the exact duplicate? Not of the divine,
unless God should just happen to fit, without remainder, into
the confines of what is humanly visible. Rather, the idol is the
invisible mirror of the gaze, the human capacity by which it is
experienced, and it is this that accounts for the perfect fit (adequation, correspondence, identity) between the aim of the gaze

---

[41] Ibid., pp. xx–xxi, emphasis added.
[42] Ibid., pp. 10–15.
[43] See especially the Fifth and Sixth Investigations of Husserl's *Logical Investigations,* 2 vols., trans. J. N. Findlay (London: Routledge & Keegan Paul, 1970).
[44] GWB p. 13.
[45] Ibid., pp. 13–16.

and the target on which it lands and at which it rests. Idolatry is this preestablished harmony.

The same visible becomes an icon when it is looked at differently, in the spirit, perhaps, of Andrea del Sarto:[46]

> Ah, but a man's reach should exceed his grasp,
> Or what's a heaven for?

The gaze is not satisfied or fulfilled. It does not stop and rest. Instead it never ceases to "transpierce visible things" in an awareness of the essential invisibility of the divine. But this is only possible to a gaze that is always "transpiercing itself."[47] The iconic gaze looks beyond all visible things to the invisible because it refuses to make its own capacity the measure of what it intends. Knowing *itself* to be inadequate to that at which it aims, it does not equate what is given to sight with the God who gives sight.[48]

As the measure of the divine (which in turn becomes the mirror of its human measure), the idolatrous gaze "still remains in possession of the idol, its solitary master."[49] By contrast, the iconic gaze is not the director of the scene in which it plays a supporting role. Its double aim of transpiercing its object and itself to that which is beyond both is triggered by the discovery that it is aimed at. In iconic intention, "the gaze of the invisible, in person, aims at man . . . the icon opens in a face that gazes at our gazes" with the result that "the human gaze is engulfed . . . [and] does not cease, envisaged by the icon, there to watch the tide of the invisible come in. . . . [The icon] offers an abyss that the eyes of men never finish probing."[50]

---

[46] In the poem by Robert Browning that bears his name.

[47] GWB pp. 11, 17.

[48] Like Levinas, Marion alludes to Descartes's discussion of the idea of the infinite as the idea that exceeds our capacity to think it as an instance of iconic thought; ibid., pp. 23, 202.

[49] Ibid., p. 24.

[50] Ibid., pp. 19–21. There are two Levinasian motifs here: the passive "intentionality" of our awareness of the infinite, and the notion "that only the icon gives us a face (in other words, that every face is given as an icon)." In "L'Interloque," in *Who Comes after the Subject,* Marion develops the linguistic thesis, that we are addressed (not as Dasein, which "appeals only to itself," but as *der Angesprochene*), that the one who says I is the one who has already been claimed as me.

The ontological tradition is not embarrassed by the apeironic abyss of sensibility. Armed with the concept, it knows how to introduce some order into chaotic infinity, to dam up the engulfing ocean. Marion's critique of ontology is designed to rescue our God-talk from this move. So he applies the very same idol/icon analysis to the concept that he has developed in relation to vision. When we assume the adequacy of our concepts to the divine reality, we make ourselves the measure and master of that reality and convert it into the invisible mirror of our intellectual capacities. It is not surprising that Marion mentions Feuerbach at this point.[51]

At the level of sense perception, the idolatrous aim is satisfied and thus at rest with the visible, while the iconic gaze transpierces it toward the invisible of which it is a trace. At the conceptual level, the invisible becomes the incomprehensible, that which we aim at by transpiercing not only our images but also our concepts. Now, idolatry is contentment with what the *mind's eye* can see, the assumption (or is it the demand?) that our concepts and the propositions in which we embed them can be equal to (*adequatio*) divine being. As Gregory of Nyssa puts it, "Every concept, as it is produced according to an apprehension of the imagination in a conception that circumscribes and in an aim that pretends to attain the divine nature, models only an idol of God, without at all declaring God himself."[52]

We already know that Marion is interested in fleeing idolatry but not conceptuality, so we are not surprised to find him saying that "the icon also can proceed conceptually, provided at least that the concept renounce comprehending the incomprehensible, to attempt to conceive it, hence also to receive it, in its own excessiveness."[53] In other words, *we must think God as the gift of*

---

[51] GWB p. 16, cf. pp. 29–31. For a phenomenology of that which exceeds adequation, see Marion's "The Saturated Phenomenon," *Philosophy Today* 40, no. 1 (spring 1996), pp. 103–24. Also published in Dominique Janicaud et al., *Phenomenology and the "Theological Turn"* (New York: Fordham University Press, 2000), pp. 176–216.

[52] Quoted in GWB p. 203. See Gregory of Nyssa, *The Life of Moses*, trans. Abraham J. Malherbe and Everett Ferguson (New York: Paulist Press, 1978), pp. 95–96, for context and a different translation.

[53] GWB pp. 22–23.

love who exceeds not merely the images and but also the concepts with which we aim at God.

Like Levinas, Marion points us toward a "relation which is irreducible to comprehension." But this is not just a call for epistemic humility, a kind of *via analogia* following upon a *via negativa* and based on the "absolute freedom of God with regard to *all* determinations."[54] As with Levinas, it is a challenge to theory as the primary mode of God-talk. It isn't simply that we have a goal, adequation, that we cannot achieve. It is that we have a higher goal than making accurate assertions about God. This is why, in the final analysis, "predication must yield to praise—which, itself also, maintains a discourse." There is a silence appropriate to the God relation, not just because our language limps, but because God is love, and love "is not spoken, in the end, it is made. Only then can discourse be reborn, but as an enjoyment, a jubilation, a praise."[55] Marion follows Pseudo-Dionysius in following a "wise silence" with "songs of praise."[56] Praise is the language in which love welcomes the decentering presence of the Divine Other, recognizing the 'of' in 'gift of love' as at once an objective and subjective genitive.[57]

We must think God as the mystery that exceeds the wisdom of the Greeks.

We must think God as the voice that exceeds vision so as to establish a relation irreducible to comprehension.

We must think God as the gift of love who exceeds not merely the images but also the concepts with which we aim at God.

Who comes "after" the critiques that can be summarized in

---

[54] See nn. 22 and 41 above.

[55] GWB pp. 106–7.

[56] *Pseudo-Dionysius: The Complete Works,* trans. Colm Luibheid (New York: Paulist Press, 1987), pp. 50–51. Cf. GWB pp. 76–77, where the theme of praise is linked to the priority of goodness to being as the name of God in Pseudo-Dionysius. I have discussed this theme in Dionysius and Cyril of Jerusalem in "Overcoming Onto-Theology," in *God, the Gift, and Postmodernism,* ed. John D. Caputo (Bloomington: Indiana University Press, 1999). See ch. 1 above.

[57] The absence of a personal other who could be respected, loved, welcomed, even praised is what sets Heidegger off from Levinas and Marion. See John D. Caputo, *Demythologizing Heidegger* (Bloomington: Indiana University Press, 1993), chs. 2–3, and Norman Wirzba, "Love's Reason: From Heideggerian Care to Christian Charity," in *Postmodern Philosophy and Christian Faith,* ed. Merold Westphal (Bloomington: Indiana University Press, 1999).

these three imperatives? What sort of God can withstand the scrutiny they encapsulate? Heidegger, Levinas, and Marion have replied to this question, which does not require only a single answer. I promise once again to give my own response, but only after reflecting briefly on the "must" of these commands. Whence this obligation? With what right (*quid juris*) does philosophy, or, more precisely, these philosophies (for these critiques make it clear that "philosophy" does not speak with a single voice, even when seeking to overcome onto-theological metaphysics) dictate how we shall think and speak of God? Is not the arrogance of onto-theology reenacted when the critique thereof assumes the same hegemony? Are we not exchanging a tsar for a Stalin, a shah for an Ayatollah?

Under the heading of "Double Idolatry" Marion has raised this very question in relation to Heidegger.[58] It is a legitimate question, and, given the substantial overlapping consensus among our three critiques and the sternness with which we are told how we "must" think about God, we cannot restrict the question to Heidegger.

One or more of these commandments can come to have normative force for us in one of two ways. They can be philosophically persuasive without any (apparent) theological assumptions, in other words, independently (it would seem) of how we think, affirmatively or negatively, about God. Or they can be philosophically persuasive in significant part precisely because they highlight, or reinforce, or make explicit what we already think about God.

In either case we are dealing with cognitive dissonance and reflective equilibrium. Even if with our trio we deny primacy to theory in the God relation, we want our philosophical theorizing about God-talk to be at peace with our pre- and post-reflective, everyday thinking about God. So we seek reflective equilibrium.

If we do not achieve it at first, we experience cognitive dissonance. One side or the other (or perhaps both) needs revision. We have learned in other contexts that there is no single, self-evident solution to the problem. Faced with an anomaly, we can revise our theory or question either our data or our intuitions.

---

[58] GWB ch. 2. I have tried to sort out the issues raised by his critique in "Overcoming Onto-Theology" (ch. 1 above).

I suggest two principles, or better, warnings, for dealing with situations of cognitive dissonance between our philosophical and theological persuasions (meaning by the latter our God-talk habits, whether academically formed or not and whether they are affirmative or negative). I believe, though I shall not try to show, that one can find support for them in all three of our thinkers.

The first of these I shall call the Warning against Philosophical Arrogance. This warning is implicit in the *quid juris* questions just posed and in Marion's "Double Idolatry" charge. It is the reminder that the days of Absolute Monarchy are over in philosophy, that no philosophy is Absolute Knowledge or possesses Absolute Authority, that no theology should be expected automatically and a priori to bow the knee before philosophy's correction.[59] If cognitive dissonance arises, it may be my philosophical theory that needs to be revised to accommodate my theology.

The second is like unto the first and is called the Warning against Theological Arrogance. It is the reminder that my theology does not cease to be human, all too human, just because it purports to be about God. In a variety of ways, both formal and substantive, it can be more idolatrous than iconic.[60] The days of Absolute Monarchy, Absolute Knowledge, and Absolute Authority are over in theology too, and in the search for reflective equilibrium, it may be my theology that needs revision in the light of a philosophical critique. All the more so if that critique has it roots, consciously or unconsciously, in a theological horizon in which I also stand. The suspicion of idolatry originates in prophetic belief (e.g., Kierkegaard) as well as in skeptical unbelief (e.g., Nietzsche).[61]

*   *   *

---

[59] Marion takes offense especially at Heidegger's essay "Phenomenology and Theology," in *The Piety of Thinking,* trans. James G. Hart and John C. Maraldo (Bloomington: Indiana University Press, 1976), in which phenomenology is repeatedly assigned the task of "correcting" theology.

[60] Substantive idolatry would occur when my God is the invisible mirror, not of my cognitive capacities, but of my (our) unholy interests.

[61] In *Suspicion and Faith: The Religious Uses of Modern Atheism* (New York: Fordham University Press, 1998), I have accused Marx, Nietzsche, and Freud of plagiarizing the Bible, suggesting that their hermeneutics of suspicion has its true origin in prophetic biblical faith.

So, then, who comes "after" the overcoming of onto-theologically constituted metaphysics? I shall not try to say how we "must" think, for while I take the triple Thou Shalt developed above very seriously, I also think there are many ways to think and talk about God that remain within the parameters they specify. So I shall speak of how we "may" think and talk about God. Who am I to say how we "must" think about God?

I began this essay by posing its question in words taken from Augustine's *Confessions*. Now I want to answer that question quite simply and directly. The God who comes after onto-theology, who would be overcome by metaphysics (in Heidegger's sense) and whose flourishing is thus the overcoming of metaphysics, can be the God of Augustine. I believe the reader can confirm at each stage of its development that nothing in the triple critique presented above precludes the affirmation of a personal creator and redeemer who speaks to us as gift and as command and who evokes from us the sacrifices of prayer, praise, song, and even, perhaps dance (though each critique precludes certain ways of understanding such God-talk, in particular certain epistemic metaclaims about it). Without trying to defend everything Augustine says about God, I will try to show how his God, especially as presented in the *Confessions*, not only can withstand the scrutiny encapsulated in the threefold "must" we have been exploring, but even can be seen as part of its prehistory, an origin (by no means absolute) from which these critiques might emerge. Heidegger has affirmed what Levinas and Marion have enacted, namely, that faith requires and thus can motivate the critique of onto-theology. That critique is not the monopoly of atheistic postmodernism, and, a fortiori, not of cynical nihilism.

This triple critique, sometimes called postmodern, just might help us to recover premodern resources that an arrogant modernism taught us we had outgrown.[62] But only if postmodern

---

[62] I find it of no small interest that at the second Villanova conference on postmodernism and religion, held in October 1999, papers by Jean Greisch and Graham Ward focused sympathetic attention on Augustine. Recent scholarship has reminded us of the Christian texts that belong to the prehistory of Heidegger's thinking. See especially John van Buren, *The Young Heidegger: Rumor of the Hidden King* (Bloomington: Indiana University Press, 1994), and Theodore Kisiel, *The Genesis of Heidegger's* Being and Time (Berkeley: University of Califor-

thinking does not simply continue what is in effect the Enlightenment myth of progress by excluding from discussion a priori ("we're past that") all concepts of a transcendent, personal Creator and Savior. I am not suggesting that we try to go back sixteen centuries. Apart from the fact that we couldn't if we wanted to, I, for one, wouldn't want to. Augustine doesn't, indeed couldn't, address many of the issues that a contemporary theology needs to bring into contact with our God-talk. Even when he does address issues that we are still facing, his solutions are sometimes plainly unacceptable. (Need I mention the Donatists?)

But Augustine's God transcends Augustine and Augustine's time. With the help of an essentially Augustinian God, Luther and Kierkegaard raised powerful protest against the totalizing thinking of their times (and the social systems attached thereto, in both cases "Christendom"). On close examination, postmodern critiques so far from making the world safe from intrusion by this God look more like an invitation to reconsideration and possibly reacquaintance. Those whose God-talk is Augustinian, in the ways spelled out below, need not be allergic to postmodern critique nor intimated by postmodern atheism and/or minimalism (ethics without ontology presented as religion). Nor should those who are allergic to Augustinian God-talk assume that theistic discourse can responsibly be ignored. We all have our "in-house" discussions and debates, but only ghetto thinking is willing to restrict itself to preaching to the choir.

Augustine begins his *Confessions* with two citations from the Psalms: *"Can any praise be worthy of the Lord's majesty? How magnificent his strength! How inscrutable his wisdom"* (I:1).[63] Already he is "lost in wonder, love, and praise"[64]—especially praise.

---

nia Press, 1993). Levinas is not the least bashful about the "more ancient volcano" of Hebraic "prophetic speech" and "messianic eschatology" from which his thought emerges (as described by Derrida in "Violence and Metaphysics," in *Writing and Difference,* trans. Alan Bass (Chicago: University of Chicago Press, 1978), pp. 82–83.

[63] Quotations from the *Confessions* will be from the Pine-Coffin translation (Baltimore: Penguin Books, 1961) by book and chapter number. I follow his practice of placing biblical phrases in italics.

[64] The phrase comes from Charles Wesley's hymn "Love Divine, All Loves Excelling."

Having read his Marion, he remembers that "predication must yield to praise"—so he immediately reminds himself that any predications implicit in the psalmist's questions have their telos in praise: "Man is one of your creatures, Lord, and his instinct is to praise you . . . he is part of your creation, he wishes to praise you. The thought of you stirs him so deeply that he cannot be content unless he praises you, because you made us for yourself and our hearts find no peace until they rest in you" (I:1). For the time being, at least, the best antidote to restless anxiety is praise.

Three times in this brief passage Augustine affirms God as creator, and this will be a constantly recurring theme in what is to follow. It would not be difficult to show that his creator is an uncaused cause, a *causa sui*, if you please. But this is conspicuously not the *causa sui* Heidegger has in mind, before whom there is no prayer or sacrifice, no awe, music, or dance. The *Confessions* are indeed one long prayer, addressed continuously to God. We see how ontology is teleologically suspended in prayer when Augustine writes, "In you are the first causes of all things not eternal, the unchangeable origins of all things that suffer change, the everlasting reason of all things that are subject to the passage of time and have no reason in themselves. Have pity, then, on me, O God, for it is pity that I need" (I:6).

Augustine opens book VIII with the words of the psalmist, *"You have broken the chains that bound me; I will sacrifice in your honour,"* and he opens book IX by linking sacrifice to praise as appropriate responses to God's grace. Nor are prayer and sacrifice unaccompanied by awe, as we see, for example, when he describes his encounter with the Uncreated Light that "was above me because it was itself that Light that made me, and I was below because I was made by it." (*N.B.* Here again we have the affirmation of God as creator, as *causa sui*.) "I gazed on you with eyes too weak to resist the dazzle of your splendour. Your light shone upon me in its brilliance, and I thrilled with love and dread alike. I realized that I was far away from you. It was as though I were in a land where all is different from your own" (VII:10).

A few pages later we find Augustine looking for the immutable source (an unoriginated origin) of his own changeable reason, which somehow knows "the immutable itself. For unless, by some means, it had known the immutable, it could not possibly have been certain that it was preferable to the mutable. And so, in an instant of awe, my mind attained to the sight of the God who is. Then, at last, *I caught sight of your invisible nature, as it is known through your creatures"* (VII:17).

Unlike the *causa sui* of onto-theology, "who" is religiously otiose, Augustine's Creator evokes prayer, sacrifice, and awe. What about singing and dance? I must confess (a good thing to do when writing on the *Confessions*) that I have not found Augustine dancing. But he sings, and thereby hangs a tale. As he recounts in book X how far he has come and how far he still has to go in the life of faith, he writes, "Let my brothers draw their breath in joy for the one and sigh with grief for the other. Let hymns of thanksgiving and cries of sorrow rise together from their hearts, as though they were vessels burning with incense before you" (X:4).[65] This does not come as easily to Augustine as it might to others: "Without committing myself to an irrevocable opinion, I am inclined to approve of the custom of singing in church, in order that by indulging the ears weaker spirits may be inspired with feelings of devotion." His hesitancy stems from the fear of finding "the singing itself more moving than the truth which it conveys" (X:33).[66] Yet in the very next chapter we find him saying, "But O my God, my Glory, for these things too I offer you a hymn of thanksgiving. I make a sacrifice of praise to him who sanctifies me" (X:34). And he complains that the books of the Platonists "make no mention of tears of confession or of *the sacrifice that you will never disdain.* . . . In them no one sings" (VII:21).

Although he affirms a Highest Being who is the clue to the meaning of the whole of being, it is clear (and will become clearer) that Augustine is not an onto-theologian in Heidegger's sense. Yet he, and the whole theistic tradition of which he is a

---

[65] Like the psalms of Israel, Christian liturgies regularly include both hymns of praise and prayers of confession. Incense is a psalmic image of the offering of these to God.

[66] One can appreciate the nature of Augustine's concern by comparing meditative, devotional settings of the *Stabat Mater* by Palestrina, Vivaldi, or Pärt with the operatic versions by Verdi and Rossini. No doubt Augustine would classify the Pergolesi with the latter, though I would place it with the former.

major representative, are widely thought to be paradigms of that heresy. One reason for that, no doubt, is an incomplete reading of Heidegger. But that is not the whole story. Insofar as there is a great deal of Platonism in Augustine, there surely are onto-theological themes and possibilities. His preoccupation with immutable truth and the role of the vision metaphor in his account of knowledge are but two conspicuous examples. Are not these the seeds from which the metaphysics of presence grows? It is regularly acknowledged that there is a continuous *Aufhebung* or recontextualizing of Augustine's Platonism in his Christianity. He is both "the greatest disciple and the profoundest critic of Plotinus."[67] We need to see the teleological suspension of Neo-platonism in Christianity as his continuous resistance to the temptations of onto-theology.

When we hear Augustine panting, "Truth! Truth! How the very marrow of my soul within me yearned for it" (III:6), we might think him engaged in the "metaphysical" project of rendering the whole of reality intelligible to human understanding. But a closer look reveals something quite different. In the first place, inspired by Cicero's *Hortensius,* his heart "began to throb with a bewildering passion for the *wisdom* of eternal truth" (III:4, emphasis added), and he never forgets the essential linkage, already present in Cicero and the Platonists, between wisdom and truth.

In the second place, he subordinates propositional truth to its ultimate object, the source of all wisdom and knowledge. He complains of the Manichees, "Much of what they say about the created world is true, but they do not search with piety for the Truth, its Creator" (V:3). This is why Augustine can say to God, "you are Truth itself" (III:61), and can speak of the "Word made flesh" as "Truth in person" (VII:19).

Finally, just because truth is not ultimately our mastery of the world's form but the personal God on whom we are dependent for the whole of our life, including its knowledge, it is God's agenda that has priority; and God's highest priority is love. When we encounter Truth itself in person, we find, not the an-

---

[67] John Burnaby, *Amor Dei: A Study of the Religion of St. Augustine* (London: Hodder & Stoughton, 1938), p. vi.

swer to all our questions or a possession that gives us power, but the command to transcend ourselves in love for the Other (I:5). Thus, "Blessed are those who love you, O God, and love their friends in you and their enemies for your sake" (IV:9). In the final analysis, knowledge is *aufgehoben* in its proper telos, love of God (of which praise is a part) and neighbor (both friend and enemy). Although there is a good deal of Platonic eros in this—the 'blessed' above signifies a eudaemonism Augustine shares with Plato—Augustine insists that charity is not one of the things to be learned from the Platonist books (VII:20).[68] Christian *caritas* is more than Platonic *eros*. No doubt part of the reason lies in the personal character of that for whom the heavenly eros longs and in an ethic that goes beyond justice and friendship within the polis to love of enemy, commanded by "Truth itself" and modeled for us by "Truth in person."

The vision metaphor is central to Platonism and to the metaphysics of presence that constitutes so many of the footnotes to Plato. It suggests an immediate, intuitive presence to the world's essential intelligibility. Augustine is anything but skittish about the vision metaphor, and his illumination theory of knowledge mirrors Plato's account of the subject, the object, and the light that enables the subject to "see" the object, whether it be a sensible or intelligible object. Of course, the light is a personal God and not an impersonal Good or One. But what is to keep this God from being reduced to the means by which philosophy carries out its onto-theological project of bringing everything to the presence of direct insight in which the totality of being becomes the transcendental signified for a mind that is its perfect mirror, a resting place that idolatrously calls forth no transpiercing?

The first thing to notice is that vision is not the only sense to play a metaphorical role in Augustine. For example, just after telling us in a passage already cited how he caught sight of the God who *is*, he describes his inability to maintain that moment by saying he "had sensed the fragrance of the fare but was not yet able to eat it" (VII:17). Thus he prays, "Let us scent your

---

[68] This is also why Augustine speaks of "the Light that charity knows" (VII:10) rather than the Light that the soul detached from the body knows. Cf. the contrast between the biblical *kardia* and the Heideggerian *Kampf* in Caputo, *Demythologizing Heidegger*.

fragrance and taste your sweetness" (VIII:4). In the famous passage in which he describes the mystical ascent he shared with his mother, Monica, he tells us that "for one fleeting instant we reached out and touched it" (IX:10). And in an astonishing passage, he includes all five senses: "You called me; you cried aloud to me; you broke my barrier of deafness. You shone upon me; your radiance enveloped me; you put my blindness to flight. You shed your fragrance about me; I drew breath and now I gasp for your sweet odour. I tasted you, and now I hunger and thirst for you. You touched me, and I am inflamed with love of your peace" (X:27).

It might be argued that all the senses signify immediate presence. But while there was already for Augustine a long tradition of interpreting conceptual knowledge as a kind of seeing, neither for him nor for us is there that kind of linkage between intelligibility and smell, taste, or touch. To this it might be argued that these are the senses of mystical, trans-conceptual immediacy and that mysticism is just another version of the metaphysics of presence.[69]

Two responses seem to me in order. First, mysticism, of which there is plenty in Augustine, may well be a version of the metaphysics of presence, but it is not the onto-theological version. Mysticism, so far from being the demand that the whole of reality be intelligible to representational, calculative thinking is the conscious, even insistent, realization that it cannot be.[70]

Second, and more important, in the all-five-senses passage just cited, hearing relates not merely to sound but to speech: "You called me." The continuous *aufhebung* of vision in the voice is

---

[69] Derrida speaks of "a certain complicity" between rationalism and mysticism. See *Of Grammatology,* trans. Gayatri Chakravorty Spivak (Baltimore: Johns Hopkins University Press, 1976), p. 80. Hegel's philosophy is often called a rationalized mysticism.

[70] This is why Derrida is right to recognize the affinity as well as well as the discontinuity between negative theology and deconstruction. See "Différance," in Jacques Derrida, *Margins of Philosophy,* trans. Alan Bass (Chicago: University of Chicago Press, 1982); *Derrida and Negative Theology,* ed. Harold Coward and Toby Foshay (Albany: SUNY Press, 1992); "Sauf le nom (Post-Scriptum)," in Jacques Derrida, *On the Name,* ed. Thomas Dutoit (Stanford: Stanford University Press, 1995); and the very helpful discussion by John D. Caputo in *The Prayers and Tears of Jacques Derrida* (Bloomington: Indiana University Press, 1997).

utterly central to Augustine's understanding of God. It is made
possible by the personal character of his Highest Being and First
Cause such that he constantly addresses God as "you." But this
you is not just someone to whom Augustine speaks, but someone who speaks to Augustine. The God of Augustine is the
Highest Voice and the First Interlocutor.

Let me list a few examples. In the midst of confessing his hunger for "Truth! Truth!" upon reading the *Hortensius*, Augustine
not only says to God "you are Truth itself," but also "you have
spoken to me" (III:6). If and as we find truth, we find that it has
already found us and has addressed us. In a striking description
of the incarnation, Augustine writes, "Our Life himself came
down into this world and took away our death. He slew it with
his own abounding life, and with thunder in his voice he called
us from this world to return to him in heaven. . . . He did not
linger on his way but ran, calling us to return to him, calling us
by his words and deeds, by his life and death, by his descent
into hell and his ascension into heaven" (IV:12). The passage
cited above where Augustine thrills "with love and dread alike"
and realizes how far he is from God continues, "and I heard
your voice calling from on high, saying 'I am the food of full-
grown men. Grow and you shall feed on me' " (VII:10). Then,
after Augustine and Monica had completed their joint ascent to
"the Selfsame,"[71] they suppose "that this state were to continue,
that all other visions of things inferior were to be removed, so
that this single vision entranced and absorbed the one who be-
held it and enveloped him in inward joys." But their account of
the condition whose permanence would be the "beatific vision"
would be quite shocking to any respectable, card-carrying Neoplatonist. What if, they ask, we and all created beings were to
transcend ourselves and direct our attention to the one who
made us, falling silent, "and he alone should speak to us, not
through them but in his own voice, so that we should hear him
speaking, not by any tongue of the flesh or by an angel's voice,

---

[71] Pine-Coffin loses his nerve at this point, saying, simply, "the eternal God."
For an illuminating account of Augustine on the Selfsame, see the paper mentioned in n. 62 by Jean Greisch, forthcoming from Indiana University Press
with the papers of the second Villanova conference, edited by John D. Caputo
and Michael Scanlon.

not in the sound of thunder or in some veiled parable, but in his own voice, the voice of the one whom we love in all these created things; suppose that we heard him himself . . . [and] suppose this state were to continue . . . would not this be what we are to understand by the words, *Come and share the joy of your Lord?*" (IX:10).

It is clear from these examples that the voice of God is not just the claim of a propositional content upon our capacity for assent. It is a voice of law and of grace, a voice that decenters the would-be autonomous self both by demanding our love and by giving itself in and as love. That which is visible but mute cannot do this. In my encounter with God I am never the spectator but always the one addressed.[72] No doubt that is why, having spoken of sacrificing and singing before God, Augustine says with reference to the Platonists' books, "In them no one listens to the voice which says, *Come to me all you that labour*" (VII:21). It is also why, in spite of Augustine's desire to gain understanding for what he has believed, faith is never the opinion (*pistis, doxa*) of Plato's divided line, a purely cognitive act of an inferior sort.

We see this in the dramatic culmination of his conversion. In book VII his intellectual problems have been resolved to his satisfaction. He believes, but he has not come to faith. It is in book VIII that "I heard the sing-song voice of a child in a nearby house. Whether it was the voice of a boy or a girl I cannot say, but again and again it repeated the refrain 'Take it and read, take it and read'. . . . I stemmed my flood of tears and stood up, telling myself that this could only be a divine command to open my book of Scripture and read." Only then, when he had heard God speaking to him through the voice of a child and through Scripture and had obeyed, was he able to say, "You converted me to yourself" (VIII:12).[73]

---

[72] A similar *Aufhebung* takes place in Levinas. I encounter the Other as a visible, as a face, but never merely as a visible. "The face speaks," even if empirically it is mute. See n. 32 above. Cf. Sylviane Agacinski, "Another Experience of the Question, or Experiencing the Question Other-Wise," in *Who Comes after the Subject.*

[73] In his book *Divine Discourse: Philosophical Reflections on the Claim That God Speaks* (New York: Cambridge University Press, 1995), Nicholas Wolterstorff brilliantly illuminates the significance of this phenomenon of indirect or double discourse, where one speaker speaks through the utterances or inscriptions

We have seen that for Augustine predication yields to praise, truth is in the service of love, and vision is *aufgehoben* in the voice that precedes and supersedes all our intentional acts (in both senses of intentional, cognitive and volitional). It would appear that Augustine has flunked Metaphysics 101. For metaphysics, in its onto-theological constitution, "the deity can come into philosophy only insofar as philosophy, of its own accord and by its own nature, requires and determines that and how the deity enters into it."[74] But the tradition of which Aristotle and Hegel are paradigms is not about praise, or commanded love, or the decentering voice. It has other work for God to do, namely, to make the whole of reality intelligible to human understanding. Augustine relates to this tradition, not by providing sacred texts for its canon but by being a howitzer aimed at its central assumptions.

We can see this in one final way by noting that God remains for Augustine an ultimately ineffable mystery. He is not shy about predication when it comes to God. He regularly affirms that God is creator, unchangeable, and omnipresent. In response to the question "What, then, is the God I worship?" he writes, "You, my God, are supreme, utmost in goodness, mightiest and all-powerful, most merciful and most just." But this is not a catechetical Q&A on the attributes of God. For he immediately continues, "You are the most hidden from us and yet the most present amongst us, the most beautiful and yet the most strong, ever enduring and yet we cannot comprehend you. . . . For even those who are most gifted with speech cannot find words to describe you" (I:4).

This question, the epigraph for this essay, is repeated twice, in slightly altered form, in book X: "What do I love when I love God?" (X:6–7). Given the intensely personal character of Augustine's God, it may seem strange that three times, once at the beginning and twice at the end of his story, he acknowledges

---

of another. I have suggested that because he assumes that God speaks and analyzes some of the ways in which this might be understood, Wolterstorff is "engaged in the very Heideggerian task of overcoming metaphysics in its ontotheological sense." See my "Theology as Talking about a God Who Talks," *Modern Theology* 13, no. 4 (October 1997), p. 526.

[74] See n. 11 above.

the divine mystery with a What question. To be sure, the third time he follows it up with a Who question: "Who is this Being who is so far above my soul?" (X:7), but he seems to prefer the What form. Perhaps the reason is simply this. Through intense conversation over a long period of years, Augustine has a fairly good idea Who God is, although that question has not been satisfied and silenced. But in terms of the essence of this Interlocutor, he remains more deeply puzzled. The *Wesensschau* that philosophy requires is, for Augustine (as for Aquinas), precisely what he does not have.[75]

Be that as it may, Augustine points to two reasons why none of the many answers he can give to the What? or the Who? question is adequate to the question. First, there is the temporary limitation of his earthly condition: "This much I know, although *at present I am looking at a confused reflection in a mirror, not yet face to face,* and therefore, as long as I am away from you, during my pilgrimage, I am more aware of myself than of you." This will continue "until I see you face to face and *my dusk is noonday*" (X:5). The illumination of which Augustine is currently capable, compared to what it will be in the life to come, is as dusk to noonday. Augustine, bishop and theologian nonpareil, is still in the cave.

Perhaps, however, this limitation is permanent, as we learn from a passage that at first sounds like a Platonic reflection on God as *ipsum esse* and *causa sui*:

"We exist," [heaven and earth] tell us, "because we were made." . . . It was you, then, O Lord, who made them, you who are beautiful, for they too are beautiful, you who are good, for they too are good; you who are, for they too are. But they are not beautiful and good as you are beautiful and good, nor do they have their being as you, their Creator, have your being. In comparison with you they have neither beauty nor goodness nor being at all. This we know, and thanks be to you for this knowledge.

Up to this point we have classic onto-theology. God earns a living by gathering all things into an intelligible whole and by making it possible for us to understand this totality.

---

[75] For Aquinas's consistent denial that we can grasp the essence of God, see John F. Wippel, "Quidditative Knowledge of God," in *Metaphysical* [sic] *Themes in Thomas Aquinas* (Washington, D.C.: Catholic University of America Press, 1984).

Everything is turned topsy-turvy, however, by the brief sentence with which the chapter ends: "But our knowledge, compared with yours, is ignorance" (XI:4). The deficiency of our knowledge, vis-à-vis God's, is not quantitative but qualitative. Like everything about us, it is participatory, not originary, dependent on a Light that we ourselves are not and therefore cannot supply.[76] It is far from evident that this deficiency will be eradicated even when, according to Augustine's confident hope, we see God face to face in the life to come. Because the soul is created, it is not divine. Even when it is lifted out of the cave into the immediate presence of the Uncreated Light, its knowledge will remain human and not divine.[77]

But if the Highest Being, who is the clue to the meaning of the whole of being, remains a mystery that continues to elude our cognitive grasp, the whole of being, no matter how many facts we can learn about it, remains mysterious. If philosophy begins in wonder for the Greeks, it ends in wonder for Augustine. And love. And praise.

We might say that Augustine has carefully read his Heidegger, his Levinas, and his Marion and has learned that we *must think God as the mystery that exceeds the wisdom of the Greeks*, that *we must think God as the voice that exceeds vision so as to establish a relation irreducible to comprehension*, and that *we must think God as the gift of love who exceeds not merely the images but also the concepts with which we aim at God*.

---

[76] It is in an Augustinian tone of voice that Gabriel Marcel says "that the more I actually participate in being, the less I am capable of knowing or saying in what it is that I participate"; *Creative Fidelity*, trans. Robert Rosthal (New York: Farrar, Straus and Giroux, 1964), p. 56.

[77] Speaking of mystical union with God, *The Cloud of Unknowing* promises "a real knowledge and experience of God as he is. Not as he is in himself, of course, for that is impossible to any save God" (New York: Penguin Books, 1978, ch. 14). Following the same logic, Gregory Palamas teaches that our knowledge does not transcend its finitude even in heaven. See *The Triads*, trans. Nicholas Gendle (New York: Paulist Press, 1983), pp. 32–39 and p. 123 n. 45. And Aquinas holds that when in rapture or in the beatific vision we are supernaturally enabled to see the very essence of God, we still do not comprehend God. See *Summa Theologiae* I.12.1.3 and *De Veritate* VIII.2 and XVIII.1.

14

Nietzsche As a Theological Resource

NOT EVERY CONSTRUAL of the theological enterprise will be able to entertain the possibility of Nietzsche as a resource, if not exactly an ally. For example, if theology interprets itself onto-theologically, it will be unable to see any ambiguity or irony in his self-designations as immoralist and anti-Christ. They will simply be the literal confessions of a loathed enemy. The possibility of Nietzsche as *ancilla theologiae* presupposes at least an interruption of the interpretation of theology in onto-theo-logical terms.

Heidegger himself suggests that there might be theological motives for such an interruption. Speaking in a Pascalian tone of voice about the god of philosophy, he writes, "Man can neither pray nor sacrifice to this god. Before the *causa sui*, man can neither fall to his knees in awe nor can he play music and dance before this god."[1] Metaphysics, when constituted onto-theo-logically, is a totalizing thinking that like its successor, technological, calculative thinking, "reduce[s] everything down to man" (ID p. 34). The "god-less thinking" that abandons the god of the philosophers "is thus perhaps closer to the divine God" (ID p. 72). This way of looking at things obviously opens the door at least a crack to Nietzsche and his death of God announcements. But how do we get to this point of view?

Heidegger's account of the onto-theo-logical project takes its point of departure from Aristotle's attempt to unite ontology, the study of being as such, with theology, the study of the highest being. The particular object of theology, according to Aris-

---

[1] Martin Heidegger, *Identity and Difference*, trans. Joan Stambaugh (New York: Harper & Row, 1969), p. 72. Henceforth cited as ID.

totle, belongs to the general concerns of ontology because the unmovable substance he takes to be the highest being would not be merely one being among others. In relation to all other beings it would be at once the *prima causa* and *ultima ratio*. Consequently this science would be first philosophy "and universal in this way, because it is first" (*Metaphysics* 1026a30).

This notion that all being is to be understood from the highest being has a natural attractiveness to monotheists who hold that every being (as substance or as essence) is either God or created by God. So it is not surprising to find historical examples of theologies that interpret the God of Abraham in onto-theo-logi-cal modes, with or without help from Aristotle.

But Heidegger's account of this metaphysical marriage of ontology and theology raises a red warning flag. It is obvious that in the onto-theo-logical project "the deity enters into philosophy." But Heidegger asks how this happens and on whose terms; he answers that in this project "the deity can come into philosophy only insofar as philosophy, of its own accord and by its own nature, requires and determines that and how the deity enters into it" (ID pp. 55–56). And what is the task that philosophy assigns to the deity? It is the ontological task of gathering the whole of being into an intelligible totality. God has become a means to a human end. Philosophy's demand that the world should be entirely intelligible to human thought becomes the demand that God be philosophy's phactotum in carrying out this project. This total intelligibility requires that "Being manifests itself as thought," the central theme of the Logos tradition in western metaphysics, if not in the Gospel of John. It is along this trajectory that we move, ever so quickly, from the book of Genesis to Hegel's *Science of Logic* (ID pp. 57–60).

It may be worth our while to descend from these global descriptions to see onto-theo-logy at work in its everydayness. At a colloquium not long ago I heard a speaker defending a certain Thomism. Along the way she made two interesting moves that were picked up by a questioner during the discussion time. First, she presented Alasdair MacIntyre's critique of the secularization and impoverishment of theology from within in the attempt to address Christianity to the secular mind. She quoted Mac-Intyre's claim "Nothing has been more startling than to note how much contemporary Christian theology is concerned with trying to perform Feuerbach's work all over again" with the result that Christianity becomes "a way of life in accordance with the liberal values and illiberal realities of the established order."[2] With specific reference to Tillich's theology, MacIntyre was quoted as saying, "When Feuerbach explained that he did not believe in the God of orthodoxy because God could at best only be a name for man's ultimate concerns, he was not regarded by theologians as being a particularly subtle defender of the Christian religion."[3]

The second move was the portrayal of Protestant and Jansenist (and eventually nominalist) theologies as "a deviated Christian tradition" because of their ethical views, especially in relation to the corruption of human nature by sin. Once again MacIntyre was quoted as finding the consequence of such views to be "that from any human standpoint the divine commandments do become arbitrary fiats imposed on us externally; our nature does not summon us to obey them, because we cannot recognize them as being for our good."[4]

The questioner asked whether the brand of Thomism being defended was not an instance of the Feuerbachianism whose denunciation prefaced the defense. According to the "deviated" views in question, divine commands do not make sense to us humans; at least sometimes we find them to be "arbitrary fiats imposed on us externally." Our nature does not welcome them because at least sometimes "we cannot recognize them as being for our good." But how could this be an objection against the views in question unless there were already operative an a priori requirement of total intelligibility, the demand that God should always make sense to our human intellects in their present (finite and fallen) condition? Would not any God who accepted these ground rules be one created in our image rather than the other way around? Would not such a God be but a projection of what

---

[2] Alasdair MacIntyre, *Marxism and Christianity* (Notre Dame, Ind.: University of Notre Dame Press, 1968), p. 2.

[3] Alasdair MacIntyre, *Secularism and Moral Change* (London: Oxford University Press, 1967), p. 69.

[4] Alasdair MacIntyre, "Atheism and Morals," in *The Religious Significance of Atheism* (New York: Columbia University Press, 1967), p. 39.

makes sense to our current fashion of thinking? Wouldn't we have here a historicized (Marxian) version of Feuerbach? Would the fact that the current fashions of thinking, however traditional or revolutionary, to which God would have to conform are those of religious rather than secular people make the project any less Feuerbachian?

It seems to me that the onto-theo-logical project has a shadow, a flip side, a cousin, a (fraternal) twin. If, in its presence, one looks for signs of a socio-theo-logical project, one is seldom disappointed. In this instance God enters into social theory rather than ontology, but on the same terms, as a means to human ends. In the first case the demand is to render the world (including God as its Alpha and Omega) fully intelligible. In this second case the demand is to render the world fully ours, to legitimate the political, economic, and technological hegemonies from which the faithful in any given case benefit, including compassionate, paternalistic hegemonies (which used to be called benevolent despotisms), from which the faithful benefit psychologically without having to pay too high a price in terms of power or wealth.

In both cases the will to power, carefully hidden from itself, puts God to work as its man Friday (or perhaps in these liberated days, as its girl Friday—for a female God is no less likely to be co-opted by human will to power). In either of these modes, theology has everything to fear and nothing to gain from Nietzsche. But if theology has another vocation, one that includes vigilance against its own onto-theo-logical and socio-theo-logical tendencies, the story might be different.

We can put it this way. If Nietzsche is right in his interpretation of Spinoza's *conatus* as the will to power, then everything tends to absolutize itself, to treat the world as its oyster, as the collective means to its own flourishing. In its content, monotheistic religion provides a powerful challenge to this tendency among human selves and societies. Thus Kierkegaard (as Anti-Climacus) can write, "Every human being is to live in fear and trembling, and likewise no established order is to be exempted from fear and trembling . . . fear and trembling signify that there is a God—something every human being and every established order ought not to forget for a moment."[5]

A FALLACY AND A PROPHYLAXIS

But monotheism also represents an all but irresistible temptation to slide (without noticing the non sequitur involved) from the confession that the object of the believer's thinking is absolute to the confusion that takes that thinking itself to be ipso facto absolute. If philosophical theology were to need a name for this sliding, we might call it cognitive transubstantiation; for what happens is that the intentional act, which remains to all appearances human, takes on the ontological perfections of its divine intentional object.

Of course, this has all the cogency of assuming that to think of the Grand Canyon is to think deeply. But onto-theo-logians and socio-theo-logians who have more or less lost their footing on this slippery slope do not like to be reminded of this. It takes a certain perversity to want to be reminded of the fallacy of misplaced transubstantiation. It takes thinkers more committed to the truth, whatever it may be, than to the truth as we think we have discovered it so far. It takes thinkers caught up in what is for Nietzsche the last of the ascetic ideals. Ironically, it is just such theologians for whom Nietzsche can be a resource.

A prophylactic resource. A protection, not against the theological equivalent of unwanted pregnancy, but against the theological equivalent of syphilis or AIDS, a deadly virus that kills theology by transforming what would be discourse about God into discourse about ourselves and by transforming altruistic virtues into egoistic vices.

In other words, I am not suggesting that Nietzsche is a theological resource in the way in which scripture and tradition are. Still, there is something quasi-scriptural and quasi-traditional about his relation to the theologian. For he performs, if we will

---

[5] Søren Kierkegaard, *Practice in Christianity*, trans. Howard V. and Edna H. Hong (Princeton: Princeton University Press, 1991), p. 88.

let him, the task of prophetic protest, the ad hominem critique of theology by its own professed standards. And for Jewish and Christian monotheism, if I am not mistaken, both scripture and tradition include important strands of prophetic protest. Amos and Jesus are quite different from Nietzsche, but all three managed to get very religious people angry at them in strikingly similar ways.

The first Nietzschean prophylaxis is his perspectivism. This is his version of the hermeneutics of finitude, and as such it should be of interest to theologians. For finitude is a theological theme that stands in intimate connection with the doctrine of creation. Just to the degree that Nietzsche's account of human finitude is compelling, it can illumine the theologian's understanding of creation, even if it comes wrapped in the assurance that there is no Creator after all (or should we say "before all"?).

Nietzsche's perspectivism is one of the negative footnotes to Plato in the history of philosophy. Both the Platonism of antiquity and the Cartesianism of modernity, along with all their legitimate children, have been the flight from perspective, the attempt to reflect oneself out of one's situation so as to see reality *sub specie aeternitatis.* Theology has often been a fellow traveler on these flights, tempted, in part, by the fallacious assumption mentioned above, that since it speaks of the Absolute it must speak absolutely. This is part of the reason, incidentally, that Nietzsche doesn't see much difference between Christianity and Platonism and describes the former as Platonism for the masses.

Against both the philosophical and the theological forms of this flight, Nietzsche is a constant reminder that we see the world from a particular historical, sociological, and even physiological perspective. In the presence of the metaphysics of presence that thinks it possible to reflect oneself out of perspective altogether and obtain "the view from nowhere," Nietzsche keeps quoting, as it were, from St. Paul. No matter how badly we want to see reality face to face, we can only see "in a mirror, dimly," even "in a riddle" (1 Cor. 13:12). So he speaks of truth as "linguistic legislation," as "customary metaphors, and as "illusions about which one has forgotten that this is what they are."[6]

---

[6] Friedrich Nietzsche, *The Portable Nietzsche,* trans. Walter Kaufmann (New York: Viking Press, 1954), pp. 44–47.

Perhaps there is an element of rhetorical overkill here. But perhaps very strong language is needed to remind us that our truth is human, all too human, and for that reason it is always meaningful to ask, Whose truth? There is a lot of sense in the claim that if God is real, in something like the traditional theistic sense, then reality is intelligible. But it does not follow that it is intelligible to us, since we are not God. As Kierkegaard's Climacus reminds us, "Existence itself is a system—for God, but it cannot be a system for any existing spirit."[7]

Objection: "This is your second reference to Kierkegaard. Perhaps by reminding us of the important affinities between these two, once the fathers of existentialism but now seen more often as proto-pomos, you hope to render more plausible your claim that Nietzsche might be useful to the theologian. But why not just turn to Kierkegaard, who, after all, is something of a theologian himself?"

Reply: (a) By all means, turn to Kierkegaard. I am the last one to discourage you. I myself spend more time reading and writing about Kierkegaard than Nietzsche. (b) Nietzsche is also something of a theologian—of which more hereafter.

(c) I am making no claim for Nietzsche's indispensability. There are many thinkers from whom there is much to learn about the finitude of human knowledge. Hume and Sextus Empiricus, Kant and Kierkegaard, Marx and Freud, Peirce and Dewey, Heidegger and Wittgenstein, Rorty and Derrida—the list can be extended with ease. But Nietzsche (along with several others just mentioned) has this advantage. By virtue of his atheism he has built in a special protection against the fallacy of misplaced transubstantiation. Of course, he and his descendants need to be reminded that from the fact that we are not the absolute point of view it does not follow that there is no absolute point of view; and Kierkegaard's "Existence is a system for God" is important as such a reminder. But I believe there is real value in looking at human finitude in a landscape from which God has been entirely removed. Uncreated finitude is doubtless different from created finitude, so such a mise-en-scène cannot

---

[7] Søren Kierkegaard, *Concluding Unscientific Postscript*, trans. Howard V. and Edna H. Hong (Princeton: Princeton University Press, 1992), vol. I, p. 118.

be ultimate from a theological standpoint. But it can be part of a much needed system of checks and balances for the theologian who seeks to claim divine origin but not divine nature for human thought, to remember that we are made, not begotten.

Objection: "But there's a problem of self-referential consistency here. Is it not a performative contradiction to present as an absolute truth the claim that all human insight is relative to its perspective?"

Reply: No doubt. But that is to read Nietzsche in the worst possible light and to invite the suspicion that one is desperate to discredit him. There are at least two other possibilities. One more charitable reading would have him saying something like this: "All human truth is relative to the believer's perspective, except the truth that this is so; this latter truth is the one insight we have that transcends perspective." So far as I can see, there is nothing self-contradictory about this claim. But while it has the virtue of being charitable, it does not strike me as plausible, either in itself or as a reading of Nietzsche.

An interpretation that is both charitable and plausible, at least as a reading of Nietzsche, would go like this: "All human truth is relative to the believer's perspective, including the truth of perspectivism. While we may find perspectivism compelling, no formulation of it can claim to be final, certain, and beyond revision." Perspectivism need not be presented as an absolute truth; it can be presented as an account of how reality looks from where one is situated. It does not thereby cease to be of value. The account of the game given by the winning coach cannot claim to be *the* truth about the game; other accounts must be taken into account, including those from the losing coach, the players, the referees, the radio and TV announcers, the fans, and the people selling hot dogs. But that does not mean that we do not listen with attention to what the winning coach has to say about the game.

Objection: "That may all be OK for games and even for philosophical theories. But for the theologian to talk that way would be to abandon the kerygmatic mission of theology, to cut the gospel out of the gospel. Within the American Academy of Religion it may be OK for the theologian to be no more than a purveyor of opinion (so long as that opinion is politically correct);

but real theology needs to sustain a relation to the faithful and not just the curious, to church, synagogue, mosque, etc. We cannot ask the clergy to say, 'This is how it looks from where I stand.' "

Reply: But St. Paul talks that way, and he was not, to the best of my knowledge, a member of the AAR. He sought to relate to both synagogue and church. Yet he insists that our knowledge is partial, that we see as in a riddle. Speaking precisely of "the light of the gospel of the glory of Christ, who is the image of God," he insists that "we have this treasure in clay jars, so that it may be made clear that this extraordinary power belongs to God and does not come from us" (2 Cor. 4:4 and 7). It was in reference to the epistemological dimension of the clay jar metaphor, I believe, that an evangelical Protestant theologian once described the Bible as "the divinely revealed misinformation about God." Coming from a staunch defender of biblical inerrancy, that is a profound, almost Nietzschean appreciation of our cognitive finitude. Not even in giving us a divinely inspired and inerrant biblical self-revelation could God transcend our finitude and enable us to see reality as it truly is, that is, as God sees it.

Objection: "Let me try again. Doesn't Nietzsche's perspectivism lead to theological silence, to a negative theology cut off from all positive theology? And isn't Feuerbach right in warning us against theologians of this sort? They affirm the existence of God: 'But this existence does not affect or incommode [them]; it is a merely negative existence, an existence without existence, a self-contradictory existence,—a state of being which, as to its effects, is not distinguishable from non-being. . . . The alleged religious horror of limiting God by positive predicates is only the irreligious wish to know nothing more of God, to banish God from the mind.' "[8]

Reply: It was a deep appreciation of human finitude that generated negative theology in the first place. So it would not be surprising if one path out of Nietzschean meditations on human finitude leads in the direction of negative theology. I think it is on this path that Derrida has found himself discussing the rela-

---

[8] Ludwig Feuerbach, *The Essence of Christianity*, trans. George Eliot (New York: Harper and Brothers, 1957), p. 15.

tion of deconstruction to negative theology.[9] But it does not follow that the negative theology for which one gains a new respect
by the serious reading of Nietzsche needs to be cut off from
positive theology. Nietzsche himself was something of a positive
theologian and prophet. He is quite kerygmatic about his Dionysian faith and about the metaphysics of eternal recurrence that
undergirds it.

Is he inconsequent in this regard? I think not. What Nietzsche's positive theology suggests to me is that his perspectivism
places no constraints on *what* we can say about the sacred, but
only on *how* we say it. I want to suggest two things about that
how. First, if we cannot have the absolute knowledge that philosophy has often demanded and professed, our theological discourse will have to embody the appropriate humility. But it is
important that we not confuse humility with timidity (especially
in the presence of Nietzsche, who sees through that fraud
quicker than anyone else). Should we be tentative in our beliefs
about God? Not if that means we should hold them without
conviction, but only if it means we should hold them without
arrogance, the arrogance that is willing to impose them on others but unwilling to learn from others.

The second adverbial constraint placed on theological discourse by perspectivism is a bit more complicated. It relates to
the onto-theo-logical project. That project, it will be recalled, was
to call upon God as the highest being to bring intelligibility to
the totality of being. To this end God was presented as *prima
causa* and as *ultima ratio*. I believe perspectivism requires us to
abandon this project because it challenges the slide from claiming that reality is a system for God to claiming that it can be a
system in and for our knowledge. If reality cannot be a system
for us, then whether or not there is a God for whom it can be, it
cannot be a system for us. (P • (Q v ~ Q)) ⊃ P

Does this mean we must give up speaking of God as creator?
Not if I am right about the *what* and the *how*. What it requires us
to give up is the assumption that when we speak of God as cre-

---

[9] The key texts are "Différance" in *Margins of Philosophy*, trans. Alan Bass
(Chicago: University of Chicago Press, 1982), and the entire volume *Derrida
and Negative Theology*, ed. Harold Coward and Toby Foshay (Albany: SUNY
Press, 1992), but especially "How to Avoid Speaking: Denials."

ator we have explained the world. A colleague of mine who is a very creative philosophical theologian once put it this way: "The only thing you can get out of a cosmological argument is the conclusion that there is an explanation of the world. You haven't thereby given that explanation." My suggestion is that this applies to creation talk, whether its origin is in revealed or natural theology.

It is in the doctrine of analogy that Aquinas qualifies his positive theology with the radical finitism of his negative theology. Although Nietzsche does not thematize his doctrine in this way, my suggestion is that its truth and his practice come down to the same thing, that negative theology places no constraints on *what* we can say about God but only on the *how*. When he insists, as he regularly does, that we do not know God through the divine essence, he says, in effect,

> Philosophical theology gives us the rationally revealed misinformation about God, and *sacra doctrina* gives us the scripturally revealed misinformation about God. We can say whatever reason or scripture lead us to say about God, and we can hold the resultant beliefs with deep conviction. What we cannot say is that in them we know either God or the world as they truly are. Thus we cannot say that our beliefs are final or that they embody the intelligibility of reality. That finality and that intelligibility are only to be found in the mind of God.

Final objection (for now—a nicely Nietzschean caveat—No?):

You're preaching to the wrong congregation. To beat up on onto-theo-logy at the AAR is truly an exercise in carrying coals to Newcastle. We are not the Christian Coalition, dogmatically confident in a metaphysics and corresponding ethics to the point of being willing to impose it on everybody else. Our problem is, if anything, just the opposite. We are so sensitive to the situated character of thought that we have no gospel at all, unless it is the gospel of finitude. There is next to nothing we are willing to say about God with conviction, and we are the last place on earth to refer anyone with spiritual hunger. The only topic about which we are confident is the situated relativity of whatever we say.

Final reply (for as long as you cease launching objections):
(a) There are fundamentalisms of the left as well as of the

right, theologically, politically, and culturally speaking. Nor is the AAR free from the kind of dogmatisms of which Nietzschean perspectivism is a critique. Its dominant culture has an orthodoxy, or perhaps several orthodoxies, that are quite as intolerant of dissent as the orthodoxies they have replaced. One of these orthodoxies is a dogmatic Nietzscheanism that needs to be subjected to Nietzschean critique.

(b) An important aspect of this latter point concerns the *what* and the *how*. Theologians within the dominant culture of the AAR are frequently perspectivists, whether they get this from Nietzsche or elsewhere. But they construe finitism to be a constraint on *what* may be said. Fully aware of the difficulty, if not impossibility, of providing unsituated warrant for this or that theological notion, they sometimes continue to assume that since they are in the university rather than the church, only what is capable of universal warrant, untied to any particular community of belief and practice, is permitted. The result is the thinnest of theological soups. Or, perhaps, one of the new orthodoxies, whose universal warrant consists in being unchallenged by any but fringe groups in the AAR. To take seriously that universal warrant may be both impossible *and* unnecessary might be liberating in more places than one suspects on a superficial view.

In short, my sense is that when Nietzsche's ox goes a-goring, there are more than enough oxen to go around.

A Second Prophylaxis

In addition to his hermeneutics of finitude, Nietzsche has an hermeneutics of suspicion. He believes that the philosopher "has a *duty* to suspicion today, to squint maliciously out of every abyss of suspicion."[10] The reason is that "the decisive value of an action lies precisely in what is *unintentional* in it, while everything about it that is intentional, everything about it that can be seen, known, 'conscious,' still belongs to its surface and skin— which, like every skin, betrays something but *conceals* even more.

---

[10] Friedrich Nietzsche, *Beyond Good and Evil*, trans. Walter Kaufmann (New York: Random House, 1966), ¶34.

In short, we believe that the intention is merely a sign and symptom that still requires interpretation."[11] Needless to say, the actions spoken of here include, but are not restricted to, cognitive acts: believings, presupposings, questionings, not questionings, and so forth.

Although Nietzschean suspicion operates in the epistemological as well as in the ethical realm (and belongs, in fact, to what we might today call the vice squad of virtue epistemology), he is careful to distinguish it from skepticism. "In former times," he writes, "one sought to prove that there is no God—today one indicates how the belief that there is a God could *arise* and how this belief acquired its weight and importance: a counter-proof that there is no God thereby becomes superfluous."[12]

Strong skepticism says, "The evidence shows that God does not exist."[13] Weak skepticism (agnosticism) says, "The evidence for God's existence is insufficient to warrant belief. We do not know that God does not exist, but it would be irrational to believe so." Suspicion does not ask about the evidence at all. The question is not whether the belief in question is true but how it has arisen and what gives it its survival value as a belief. In other words, it asks both what motives give rise to this belief and what functions it performs to pay, so to speak, for its upkeep. These two questions, of motive and of function, we can subsume under the concept of interest. Whereas skepticism asks about the evidence that supports a belief, suspicion asks about the interests that support a belief. *N.B.* In this shift the concept of support has changed. Evidence supports a belief epistemically; interests support a belief psychologically. One concerns the truth of a belief, the other its usefulness.

Here, as is often the case, skepticism gives rise to suspicion. If I am convinced that a belief is false or insufficiently warranted, I may become curious about how people come to hold and to

---

[11] Ibid., ¶32. For a fuller account, see my "Nietzsche and the Phenomenological Ideal," *The Monist* 60, no. 2 (April 1977), pp. 278–88.

[12] Friedrich Nietzsche, *Daybreak: Thoughts on the Prejudices of Morality*, trans. R. J. Hollingdale (New York: Cambridge University Press, 1982), book I, ¶95.

[13] The immediate issue here is the existence of God, but the distinctions are quite general and can be applied to beliefs of all sorts. For nonreligious examples, see "Help from Gilbert and Sullivan," chapter 3 of my *Suspicion and Faith: The Religious Uses of Modern Atheism* (Grand Rapids, Mich.: Eerdmans, 1993).

sustain such a belief. But while the question of interest may presuppose a negative judgment about evidence psychologically, it
does not do so logically; and Nietzsche is clear about this. He
tells us explicitly that the discourse of suspicion is an alternative
to the discourse of skepticism. It represents a different way of
discrediting beliefs. Or, to speak more precisely, of discrediting
believings. For, as Nietzsche clearly sees, suspicion as such is
neutral with respect to *objective* questions about the truth of beliefs or the evidence supporting them. It is directed, *subjectively*,
toward the believer's interests. It addresses the *what* only indirectly, the *how* directly.

Like the hermeneutics of suspicion to be found in Kierkegaard, Marx, and Freud (once again, no claim for utter unique-
ness is made here), Nietzsche's rests on two important premises.
The first is a distinction between latent and manifest content, a
theory of the unconscious. Because consciousness conceals, beliefs are signs and symptoms in need of interpretation.

Second, the theory of the unconscious is a theory of repression, bad faith, and self-deception. The fundamental project that
gives rise to the interests in question is the will to power, and
while Nietzsche wants to restore innocence rather than blame to
this core of our being, he recognizes that it is at odds with currently prevailing moralities, with our operative superegos. Self-
deception occurs, not simply because there are interests at work
in our believings, but because these interests so often are those
we cannot acknowledge without shame.

Elsewhere I have compared Nietzsche to Marx and Freud in
this way. What is religion most essentially according to these
theories of bad faith?

> For Freud—ontological weakness seeking consolation.
> For Marx—sociological power seeking legitimation.
> For Nietzsche—sociological weakness seeking revenge.[14]

For Freud what is shameful is not our weakness before the cruelty of nature (death) and society (guilt), but the dishonesty involved in allowing wish fulfillment to provide consolation not
supported by reason. Although Nietzsche does not share

---

[14] Ibid., p. 229.

Freud's confidence in reason, the dishonesty theme is central to his critique as well. In other words, for Nietzsche religious belief involves lapses from both moral and intellectual virtue.

It is now possible to see three ways in which the door is open to a religious appropriation of the hermeneutics of suspicion. They take us from seeing how it is a possible tool in the theologian's tool kit to seeing how it is a necessary tool.

First, because it is neutral with regard to the truth of the beliefs in question, the theologian's commitment to those beliefs is not a barrier. Asking questions about what motives lead to various beliefs and what role they play in the lives of the believing soul and the believing community (and Nietzsche moves easily back and forth between the I and the We, between psychology and sociology) does not presuppose either that the beliefs are false or that the one asking the questions takes them to be.

There is an important consequence to this. There is no a priori reason why the interests supporting a true belief should not be disreputable. Just as it is possible, as Aristotle and Kant have insisted so vigorously, to do the right thing for the wrong reason, so it is possible to believe the truth in ways that are shameful. It may be true that God will judge the wicked, but if I hold this belief in a spirit of hateful vengeance and use it to establish my (or our) moral superiority in ways that blind me to my (or our) own faults, my believing is discredited by what suspicion reveals.

There are two corollaries to this consequence: (a) It would be to commit the genetic fallacy to assume that a belief is shown to be false by showing that believers (sometimes, often, always) employ shameful interests in the support of that belief. (b) It would be to commit something like the same fallacy in reverse to defend oneself or one's community against a suspicion-generated critique by trying to show that the beliefs in question are in fact true, or that they haven't been shown to be false. Since truth is not the point, truth is not an adequate defense. Both sides need to be reminded, frequently and forcefully, what the logic of the situation is.

The second opening to a theological appropriation of the hermeneutics of suspicion derives from its parallel with the hermeneutics of finitude. Just as finitude is a theological theme in relation to the doctrine of Creation, suspicion is a theological theme in relation to the doctrine of the Fall. In the theologian's language, it traces the noetic effects of human sinfulness. Nietzsche didn't intend his doctrine of the will to power to be a secular, phenomenological account of original sin or his practice of suspicion to be an extension of the Pauline, Augustinian, and Lutheran employment of sin as an epistemological category; but he can be fruitfully read in that way. When he is, it begins to look as if suspicion is not simply an optional tool for the theologian but an indispensable one for any theologian who takes sin seriously.

We might note the following irony involved in the case of the theologian who does not take sin seriously. This usually happens out of the desire to take modern secular thought seriously, to avoid keeping theology in an ecclesiastical ghetto; but in the aftermath of secular suspicion, as developed by Marx, Freud, and Nietzsche, any theologian who does not take sin seriously loses touch thereby with some of the most powerful secular thinkers of the modern (and postmodern) world.

The third theological opening to suspicion is perhaps nothing but the flip side of the second. The theologian's work is in the service of the truth about the true God. For this reason the theologian shares, if in a somewhat more reflective mode, the prophet's abhorrence of idolatry. But just to the degree that human interests play a controlling role in the way we think and speak about God, that God becomes an idol, a God made with human hands. Conceptual and linguistic hands, to be sure; but since they are not less human than those that make graven images, the gods that result are no less idols. Of course, idols need not be new constructions out of whole cloth; they can be produced by editing, revising, taming.

A theology that wishes to be sensitive to such tendencies, not only in the work of its adversaries, but most importantly in its own work, will find the hermeneutics of suspicion an indispensable part of its methodology. Perhaps 'methodology' is not the right name for this practice, for we are not dealing here with the proper relation of a subject to its epistemic object. It is rather a question of the relation of the epistemic subject to itself, to its own shameful interests, which it does not always manage to keep unemployed. Seen in this light, suspicion is more nearly a spirituality than a methodology. So perhaps we should call it a practice and a posture rather than a tool. But it remains an obligatory and not an optional part of the theologian's art.

A final observation about Nietzschean suspicion: To this point I have spoken of it in relation to theology proper, beliefs about God. But we need to know very little about Nietzsche to realize that he is concerned with ethics at least as much as with metaphysics. He reverses the charge of Lactantius, that the virtues of the pagans are splendid vices, and argues that this is true of the altruistic virtues that the Jewish and Christian traditions sum up in the notion of neighbor love.

Now is not the time for a detailed tour of Nietzsche's moral inventory: (a) of his discovery of the spirit of revenge behind ideals of justice; (b) of his discovery of the desire for moral superiority behind ideals of pity or compassion; or (c) of his discovery of laziness, timidity, cowardice—what Zarathustra calls the "wretched contentment" of those "weaklings who thought themselves good because they had no claws"[15]—behind all kinds of goodness. But such a tour, and it does take time, is an integral part of the spirituality mentioned above. Among its potential benefits to the theologian I mention but two. First, it counters the idealistic and existentialist withdrawals from metaphysics to ethics by suggesting that the latter is as problematic as the former. Second, it reminds the theologian that in ethics as well as in metaphysics, the *how* must never be rendered peripheral by the *what*. The heart of the matter is the heart.

Nietzsche wouldn't put it quite this way, but he shows us that whether it is a matter of metaphysics or of ethics, the theological project betrays itself when it abstracts the project of getting it right from the task of becoming righteous. Nor have we avoided this problem simply by abandoning dogmatic, objectivistic, foundationalist, totalizing conceptions of getting it right in favor of pluralistic and perspectival understandings of understanding. However necessary the hermeneutics of finitude may be, it remains in bad faith without an equally serious hermeneutics of suspicion.

---

[15] *The Portable Nietzsche,* p. 230.

INDEX